Intergroup Relations

MW00800651

Intergroup Relations
The role of motivation and emotion

**Edited by Sabine Otten, Kai Sassenberg,
and Thomas Kessler**

 **Psychology Press**
Taylor & Francis Group

HOVE AND NEW YORK

First published 2009
by Psychology Press
27 Church Road, Hove, East Sussex BN3 2FA

Simultaneously published in the USA and Canada
by Psychology Press
711 Third Avenue, New York, NY 10017

*Psychology Press is an imprint of the Taylor & Francis Group,
an Informa business*

First issued in paperback 2012

Copyright © 2009 Psychology Press

Typeset in Times by RefineCatch Limited, Bungay, Suffolk

Cover design by Andy Ward
Cover image: Sebastian Groteloh

All rights reserved. No part of this book may be reprinted or
reproduced or utilised in any form or by any electronic,
mechanical, or other means, now known or hereafter
invented, including photocopying and recording, or in any
information storage or retrieval system, without permission in
writing from the publishers.

This publication has been produced with paper manufactured to strict
environmental standards and with pulp derived from sustainable
forests.

British Library Cataloguing in Publication Data
A catalogue record for this book is available from the British Library

Library of Congress Cataloging-in-Publication Data
Intergroup relations : the role of motivation and emotion / edited by
Sabine Otten, Kai Sassenberg and Thomas Kessler.
    p. cm.
Includes bibliographical references and index.
ISBN 978–1–84169–705–5 (hb : alk. paper) 1. Intergroup relations.
2. Motivation (Psychology) 3. Emotions. I. Otten, Sabine.
II. Sassenberg, Kai, 1971– III. Kessler, Thomas, 1965–
HM716.I583 2009
302.3–dc22

                                                          2008049336

ISBN: 978–1–84169–705–5 (hbk)
ISBN: 978–0–415–64867–7 (pbk)

Contents

List of contributors

Marilynn B. Brewer is at the Department of Psychology, Ohio State University, USA.

Rupert Brown is at the Department of Psychology, University of Sussex, UK.

Sezgin Cihangir is at the Department of Social and Organizational Psychology, Leiden University, The Netherlands.

Stéphanie Demoulin is at the Department of Psychology, Catholic University of Louvain-la-Neuve, Belgium.

Immo Fritsche is at the Department of Social Psychology, Friedrich-Schiller-University of Jena, Germany.

Nicole S. Harth is at the International Graduate College, Friedrich-Schiller-University of Jena, Germany.

Jolanda Jetten is at the School of Psychology, University of Queensland, Australia and the School of Psychology, University of Exeter, UK.

Kai J. Jonas is at the Department of Social Psychology, University of Amsterdam, The Netherlands.

Thomas Kessler is at the School of Psychology, University of Exeter, UK.

Toon Kuppens is at the Department of Psychology, Catholic University of Louvain-la-Neuve, Belgium.

Jacques-Philippe Leyens is at the Department of Psychology, Catholic University of Louvain-la-Neuve, Belgium.

Maya Machunsky is at the Department of Psychology, Mannheim University, Germany.

Thorsten Meiser is at the Department of Psychology, Mannheim University, Germany.

Sabine Otten is at the Department of Social and Organizational Psychology, University of Groningen, The Netherlands.

Kai Sassenberg is at the Knowledge Media Research Center, Tübingen, Germany.

Daan Scheepers is at the Department of Social and Organizational Psychology, University of Leiden, The Netherlands.

Thomas W. Schubert is at the Department of Social and Organizational Psychology, ISCTE, Lisbon, Portugal.

Bernd Simon is at the Institute for Psychology, Christian-Albrechts-University, Kiel, Germany.

Russell Spears is at the School of Psychology, Cardiff University, UK and the Department of Social Psychology, University of Amsterdam, The Netherlands.

Sven Waldzus is at the Department of Social and Organizational Psychology, ISCTE, Lisbon, Portugal.

Michael Wenzel is at the School of Psychology, Flinders University, Adelaide, Australia.

Karl-Andrew Woltin is at the Department of Psychology, Catholic University of Louvain-la-Neuve, Belgium.

Stephen C. Wright is at the Psychology Department, Simon Fraser University, Canada.

Vincent Yzerbyt is at the Department of Psychology, Catholic University of Louvain-la-Neuve, Belgium.

Foreword

This book is a timely tribute to Amélie Mummendey's many achievements in social psychology. While its content reflects Amélie's longstanding interest in the social psychology of intergroup relations, the book obviously has its origin in an impressive web of interpersonal relations. This international web of colleagues and friends, many of whom are former students of hers, is itself probably one of the best indicators of Amélie's successful academic activities. Similarly, the subtitle of the book – *The Role of Motivation and Emotion* – contains a wisdom that goes beyond its mere descriptive function. It hints at the secret of her success. But more of that later.

Amélie Dorothea Mummendey was born in the German city of Bonn in June 1944. It was summer time, but times were far from sunny and easy. Germany was staggering toward the overdue collapse of an inhumane regime that had poisoned all sorts of intergroup relations and thus paved the way to war and genocide. It is difficult to imagine how this catastrophe and its aftermath could *not* have left a trace in the intellectual development of a perceptive person like Amélie. Even more than six decades later this trace becomes apparent when she vividly and succinctly reminds the newest generation of social psychology students in an insightful textbook chapter (written together with Thomas Kessler) that "The dimensions of these crimes in terms of numbers of victims and perpetrators involved, administrative and organizational sophistication, cruelty and brutality clearly exceed anything ever experienced or imagined thus far in history." Henri Tajfel once commented that intuition could profitably serve as the first, but not as the last refuge for a social scientist. With similar wisdom Amélie succeeded in admitting personal experiences as inspirational resources, but then productively transcended these in her (re)search for a deeper, more general understanding of the social psychological dynamics of intergroup relations. How fortunate for social science when sincere concern for social issues combines with open-minded curiosity and intellectual power!

But first things first. Amélie Mummendey studied psychology in Bonn and earned her PhD from the University of Mainz and her "Habilitation" from the University of Münster. Before Amélie's scientific interest in intergroup relations became manifest in the 1980s, she had already become well known for her contribution to research on aggressive behavior together with Hans-Dieter Schmidt (later Mummendey), Gaby Löschper, Volker Linneweber, and Manfred Bornewasser. This foreword is not the right place, nor would there be sufficient space, to appropriately acknowledge all aspects of that contribution. Mention of only one highlight must therefore suffice. I was and still am most impressed by her social interactional approach to aggressive behavior. In particular, the empirical demonstration that people's judgments of behavior as aggressive critically depend on their interactional position or perspective as either "actor or victim" was simply ingenious. In addition to its social and practical relevance, it was also of high theoretical import because it illustrates the fundamental relativity, not relativism, in the construction of social reality. Sabine Otten was also involved in that research, but her collaboration with Amélie also fell in the period of transit from research on aggressive behavior to research on intergroup relations (including the combination of both lines of research).

In the early 1980s Amélie's interest in intergroup relations materialized in the form of a series of highly influential publications with Hans-Joachim Schreiber on judgments about ingroups as "Better or different" than outgroups and on related pathways to ingroup favoritism. At about the same time I became Amélie Mummendey's student. Ironically, my first personal contact with Amélie was during her office hour which I attended to inquire about the possibility to transfer to another university. Having discovered my interest in social psychology I approached her with the question "where in Germany is the best place to study social psychology." Amélie modestly suggested a few other universities. Fortunately, shortly before I left her office, she casually added another piece of information. Had she not done so, this foreword would probably have been written by somebody else. She simply added that "Münster isn't such a bad place for social psychology either." I looked her in the eye, understood, and stayed. This was the beginning of a wonderful mentorship!

Amélie Mummendey was a professor of social psychology at the University of Münster for 25 years. During that period she was offered chairs of social psychology at the University of Hamburg and the University of Bonn. After careful deliberation she declined both offers. Both her careful deliberation and the resulting decisions are telling examples of her admirable ability to give reason precedence over distracting sentiment. This ability reliably guided her to focus on what really mattered and soberly to evaluate the various options as to whether they would afford her the opportunity to accomplish that or not. In the succinct words of the late Jim Tedeschi, Amélie demonstrated that she was not an honor seeker, but a truth seeker. So she stayed in Münster a bit longer until the real thing came along in 1997. Meanwhile she initiated and carried out together with Sabine Otten, Mathias Blanz, Rosemarie Mielke, and others two very influential lines of research, one on the "positive–negative-asymmetry" in social discrimination and one on strategies to cope with threatened or negative social identities. At the same time she initiated and led the interdisciplinary graduate program on "Cognitive and Social Representation of Problems and Conflicts: Genesis, Prediction and Coping." However, with hindsight, it seems that all that was just a warm-up – for the best was yet to come.

In 1997 Amélie Mummendey accepted an offer of the University of Jena and changed places, but not character. In Jena the productivity of Amélie and her team virtually exploded. Within a very short time she built up one of the most productive and influential social psychology departments in Germany, Europe, and beyond. Most notably, Amélie became head of the International Graduate College (IGC) "Conflict and Cooperation between Social Groups: Dynamics of Change in Intergroup Relations" – a cooperation with the Universities of Kent and Sussex (both UK) and the Catholic University of Louvain-la-Neuve (Belgium). She also initiated and became head of the research group ("Forschergruppe") "Discrimination and Tolerance in Intergroup Relations" funded by the German Research Foundation DFG. Together with an ever-expanding group of young researchers Amélie continued to investigate social psychological issues of high social relevance. These include, inter alia, social discrimination, but also tolerance between social groups and constructive versus destructive coping with social change and threats to social identity. The empirical findings of the Jena group as well as a number of new theoretical models developed by them have been published in the most prestigious international social psychology journals. Their contributions have also found interested audiences at all major social psychology conferences around the globe. In fact, the annual Jena Workshop on Intergroup Processes initiated by Amélie and her team more than a decade ago has itself developed into a major academic event regularly attended by the most influential experts in our field. While Amélie was and still is undoubtedly the *spiritus rector* of social psychology in Jena, she also acted as a mentor for an impressive number of young(er) researchers trained in Jena, many of whom are meanwhile successfully leading their own research teams at various universities across Europe and beyond. I won't even try to provide a complete list of names and whereabouts in this foreword. The representative list of contributors to this book bears sufficient witness to this achievement of Amélie's as well as to her remarkable ability to build and maintain amicable networks of international cooperation with peers of her caliber.

As the world is sometimes just, Amélie Mummendey received several awards for her scientific achievements as well as for her service to the academic community. To name just a few, she was awarded the Henri-Tajfel Lecture 1993, the German Psychology Prize 2001, and numerous honorary memberships in prestigious national and international science councils and academies. Most recently, Amélie assumed the position of Vice-Rector for the Jena Graduate Academy founded in 2006. This new position is the logical continuation and successful culmination of her consistent interest in and persistent engagement with creating stimulating environments and plentiful opportunities for a better education and training of the new generation of social scientists in Germany.

As promised at the outset, I want to return to the secret of her success. Drawing on my own long-lasting academic "love affair" with Amélie as well as on an informal survey I recently conducted on this question among the contributors to this book, I am convinced the secret lies in her genuine enthusiasm for social psychology. Contact with her enthusiasm is highly contagious, emotionally engaging, and motivating. Amélie's productive power to move and mobilize people is further strengthened by her anti-ideological openness to new ideas and her radical willingness to reconsider what may have seemed decided or even self-evident before – to others as well as to herself.

I trust that the other contributors to this book will agree with me that all the good things I have said here about Amélie are evidently true. If anybody, only Amélie, with her unique combination of critical mind and humbleness, may ask me to reconsider my enthusiastic praise – a request that I, a gratefully stubborn admirer of hers, would happily refuse!

Bernd Simon
Kiel, February 2008

Introduction

This book brings together a selection of recent work on the role of motivation and emotion in intergroup behavior. However, it is also a tribute to Amélie Mummendey who inspired many of the chapter authors to join her in her endeavor to understand the determinants of both negative and positive intergroup relations. Some of the authors in this volume had Amélie as advisor during their early career. Others are colleagues involved in the same fields of research, who experienced her both as a good friend and as an inspiring and intellectually challenging colleague in scientific debates. To most if not all of us, Amélie has been an excellent role model when it comes to combining sound theoretical and empirical analysis with the aim to contribute to addressing current societal challenges; we hope and think that the chapters in this book provide fine examples of what such good blend can look like.

The chapters in this book represent the state-of-the-art knowledge on various topics within the field of intergroup relations. They are written in a comprehensible and non-technical fashion. Thus, the book addresses researchers in the field emphasizing the role of motivation and emotions in intergroup relations. However, the book addresses also students at a graduate level (i.e., Master and PhD students) as well as advanced undergraduate students delving into intergroup relations, prejudice, and social discrimination. Undergraduate students in particular may enjoy and profit more from the present volume if they first consult some introductory textbook chapters on intergroup relations. The present book builds on and extends this knowledge and provides additional material and perspectives that will guide fruitful discussion in seminars and lectures.

Obviously, in times of increasing mobility and diversity, understanding what determines the relation between social groups is not just an intriguing intellectual puzzle, but highly relevant in national and international politics, and in each and everyone's daily life. The empirical and theoretical study of intergroup relations has advanced dramatically since Sherif and colleagues (Sherif, Harvey, White, Hood, & Sherif, 1961) demonstrated in their summer camp studies that the nature of interdependence between groups can determine intergroup harmony and tension, and since Henri Tajfel and his collaborators (Tajfel, Billig, Bundy, & Flament, 1971) showed that even an arbitrary, ad hoc categorization into two groups can elicit preference and favoritism towards ingroup as compared with outgroup members. Over the years, the study of intergroup relations has become increasingly popular, and it looks like the peak has still not been reached. Our knowledge of intergroup phenomena has strongly advanced. In addition, there is also increasing knowledge on how intergroup relations can be improved.

At the same time, the study of intergroup relations has been facilitated by societal developments and by advancing knowledge in other fields of social psychology. Because of the increasing degree of migration and diversity in modern societies, questions about multiple identities, about the representation of superordinate, inclusive identities, and about how to balance social identities at different levels of inclusiveness, have gained a lot of importance. The request for solutions to the resulting problems of modern societies has provided research questions and motivated a great deal of intergroup research. At the same time, the social-psychological study of intergroup relations has greatly profited from developments in other areas in social psychology. Very relevant was social cognition research, which has offered paradigms and evidence helping to understand the intra-personal processes underlying intergroup behavior much better, such as the automatic aspects of both ingroup favoritism and outgroup derogation. Another highly influential trend stems from emotion research, and herein especially from appraisal theories of emotions. Since intergroup emotion theory was proposed in 1993 (Smith, 1993), there has been a lot of evidence revealing that people can experience emotions on behalf of their groups, and that such group-based emotions follow the same regularities in terms of underlying appraisals and resulting action tendencies as individual level emotions. Finally, motivational and, in particular, self-regulation approaches have become more and more influential in social psychology over the last two decades. These process approaches to motivation have meanwhile also inspired intergroup research and sharpened the understanding of what guides positive and negative intergroup behavior.

The present book captures these recent trends in intergroup research. Its first part, "Classical approaches to motivation in intergroup relations," comprises four chapters that demonstrate how classical theories in the field have been further developed, enriched, and more sophisticatedly tested over the years. In chapter 1, starting with basic assumptions from optimal distinctiveness theory, Marilynn Brewer discusses the complexities of dual and multiple, cross-cutting identities and nested ingroups, and their implications for phenomena such as ingroup and outgroup trust. Chapter 2 by Russell Spears, Jolanda Jetten, Daan Scheepers, and Sezgin Cihangir puts forward an alternative account for a very classic research finding in the domain of intergroup relations. Taking the positive distinctiveness principle from social identity theory as a starting point, they explain ingroup bias in the minimal group paradigm as driven by a striving for distinctiveness rather than for a more positive group image: People discriminate because the resulting differentiation creates a meaningful sense of group identity that distinguishes the ingroup from other groups. The third chapter, by Sven Waldzus, introduces theory and research about the ingroup projection model. This model is strongly based on self-categorization theory and social identity theory. In a nutshell, it reveals that groups that are combined within a higher-order, more inclusive identity tend to claim positive ingroup distinctiveness for their subgroup by claiming the prototype of the inclusive group that serves as a frame of comparison for the included groups. By combining the issue of dual identity with the issue of distinctiveness striving, entitlement, and discrimination, this chapter is strongly linked to all other chapters in this first part of the book. Chapter 4, finally, written by Michael Wenzel, builds a bridge between classical research on social justice and intergroup research. For the three domains of justice (distributive justice, procedural justice, and retributive justice) he provides both theoretical and empirical evidence suggesting that the analysis of justice processes can profit a lot from taking into account social identity concerns.

The second part comprises three chapters dealing with "Recent approaches to motivation and intergroup relations." The first chapter in this part, by Maya Machunsky and Thorsten Meiser, applies insights about the impact of mood on memory and (social) cognition in the field of intergroup relations. The detrimental effects of both positive and negative affect for ingroup bias are discussed. In chapter 6, Kai Sassenberg and Karl-Andrew Woltin introduce a self-regulation approach to intergroup behavior. The existing findings from research on the impact of several self-regulation motives on intergroup behavior are integrated into a group-based self-regulation approach, thereby providing a more detailed understanding of group motivation. Chapter 7 by Immo Fritsche and Thomas Schubert, addresses a phenomenon that has only recently received more extensive attention in social psychology, namely social exclusion. The chapter summarizes numerous findings and models on the motivational determinants and consequences of social exclusion.

The third part of the book focuses on "Emotions and intergroup relations." Vincent Yzerbyt and Toon Kuppens open this section by presenting intergroup emotions theory and their own research program on group-based emotions in chapter 8. Special attention is paid to the fact that action tendencies resulting from emotions can often explain behavior towards an outgroup much better than (longstanding) attitudes towards this group. In the following chapter, Sabine Otten summarizes theory and research on the role of social identities in aggressive interactions, and the specific role of intergroup emotions herein. Chapter 10, by Rupert Brown, concentrates on two emotions in particular: collective shame and collective guilt. Specifically, he focuses on post-conflict intergroup situations, and on determinants of forgiveness in perpetrator–victim relations. In chapter 11, Jacques-Philippe Leyens and Stéphanie Demoulin deal with the relation of dominant and dominated groups. They show that dominated groups tend to infra-humanize the dominated ones: Members of dominating groups consider typically human emotions (such as shame, or guilt) to be more typical for their group than for the dominated group. The authors show that this type of bias is distinct from racism.

The fourth and final part of the book deals with "Motivated change in intergroup relations." Chapter 12, by Bernd Simon, deals with the link between collective identification and collective action in politicized social contexts. He argues there is an identity-action-identity cycle such that collective identity shapes collective action, which, in turn, reflects back on collective identity. In Chapter 13, Thomas Kessler and Nicole Harth describe relevant theory and research on social change, thereby focusing specifically on ways people cope with status inequalities. In this context, they propose and show that a model of social change including assumptions from both social identity theory and relative deprivation theory is best suited to predict intergroup behavior in times of social change. Stephen Wright presents in chapter 14 an analysis on how cross-group friendships help to improve intergroup relations. The focus of this chapter is on how changes in the relational and group-based self motivate changes in intergroup behavior. Finally, in chapter 15, Kai Jonas provides an overview of the few scientifically based intervention and prevention methods for the improvement of intergroup relations. Moreover, theoretical and methodological guidelines for the development and evaluation of such methods based on the insights about intergroup relations are outlined.

Let us conclude this introduction with a few more personal words: We, the three editors of this book, have all been taught by and collaborated with Amélie Mummendey for many years, and, certainly, we have been infected by her passion to strive for understanding intergroup relations. Like her, and like the other authors in this book, we will probably never get rid of this virus. It is deeply ingrained in our work, and actually we do not want to be cured, but rather hope to succeed in convincing others that the study of intergroup relations is worthwhile, timely, and strongly needed. Therefore, this book aims at making its readers aware of current relevant topics and developments within the field of intergroup relations. A good researcher should be driven by a question, much more than by a need for status and reputation; that has always been Amélie's philosophy. Luckily, her own career shows that being driven by research questions can well go together with finally gaining high status and an excellent reputation. Hence, we seriously hope that this book will provide its readers with challenging questions and thoughts that might provide good grounds for their own research and professional development.

Finally, we would like to thank those who contributed to a large extent to the quality of this book. We are grateful that the following colleagues volunteered as reviewers and gave insightful and thorough feedback to the authors: Marilynn Brewer, Rupert Brown, Peter Fischer, Immo Fritsche, Ilka Gleibs, Ernestine Gordijn, Nina Hansen, Eric Igou, Johann Jacoby, Craig McGarty,

Jessica Salvatore, Thomas Schubert, Jeroen Vaes, Alberto Voci. Last but not least, we especially wish to thank Karin Kaldewey for editing the chapters and doing everything that was necessary so that a collection of manuscripts actually became a book.

Sabine Otten, Kai Sassenberg, and Thomas Kessler

References

Sherif, M., Harvey, O. J., White, B. J., Hood, W. R., & Sherif, C. W. (1961). *The Robbers Cave experiment: Intergroup conflict and cooperation.* Norman: University of Oklahoma.

Smith, E. R. (1993). Social identity and social emotions: Toward new conceptualizations of prejudice. In D. M. Mackie & D. L. Hamilton (Eds.), *Affect, cognition, and stereotyping: Interactive processes in group perception* (pp. 297–315). San Diego, CA: Academic Press.

Tajfel, H., Billig, M. G., Bundy, R. P., & Flament, C. (1971). Social categorization and intergroup behaviour. *European Journal of Social Psychology, 1,* 149–178.

Part I

Classical approaches to motivation in intergroup relations

1 Motivations underlying ingroup identification

Optimal distinctiveness and beyond

Marilynn B. Brewer
Ohio State University

Since classic social identity theory had its origins in the minimal group paradigm and the study of ingroup bias, the focus of most of the initial research on social identity was on the *consequences* of salient social identities for intergroup relations (Tajfel, 1981; Tajfel & Turner, 1979; Turner, 1975) and intragroup behavior (Hogg, 1992). It wasn't until some time later that attention turned toward understanding the *antecedents* of social identity and the psychological processes underlying identification with ingroups in the first place. Self-categorization theory (Turner, Hogg, Oakes, Reicher, & Wetherell, 1987) provided one answer to the question of origins of social identity, implicating basic social categorization processes (Oakes, 1987). But for many social psychologists, the idea that social identification – with all its significant emotional and behavioral concomitants – is based solely on "cold cognition" was intuitively incomplete. Because group identity sometimes entails self-sacrifice in the interests of group welfare and solidarity, understanding why and when individuals are willing to relegate their sense of self to significant group identities requires motivational as well as cognitive analysis. Motivational explanations are also needed to account for why group membership does not always lead to identification and why individuals are more chronically identified with some ingroups rather than others.

The present chapter reviews some of the motivational theories of social identification, with a focus on Brewer's (1991) optimal distinctiveness theory. Implications of optimal distinctiveness for intragroup versus intergroup attitudes and behavior are then discussed, particularly how the need for clear ingroup boundaries constrains our capacity for group-based trust and cooperation. Finally, we consider how these constraints might be lifted if we shift our attention from social identity as identification with a single group or social category to social identity as a complex representation of multiple group memberships.

Motivational approaches to social identity

Self-esteem

The motivational concept most associated with social identity theory is that of self-esteem enhancement. And it is true that initial development of social identity theory (e.g., Tajfel & Turner, 1979; Turner, 1975) implicated self-esteem in postulating a need for "positive distinctiveness" in ingroup–outgroup comparisons (see also Spears et al., chapter 2 in this volume). However, it is not clear from these writings whether positive self-esteem was being invoked as a motive for social identity itself, or as a motive for ingroup favoritism *given that* social identity had been engaged. Whatever the original intent, subsequent research on the role of self-esteem in ingroup bias has generally supported the idea that enhanced self-esteem may be a *consequence* of achieving a positively distinct social identity, but there is little evidence that the need to increase self-esteem motivates social identification in the first place (Rubin & Hewstone, 1998). On the contrary, there is considerable evidence that individuals often identify strongly with groups that are disadvantaged, stigmatized, or otherwise suffer from negative intergroup comparison (e.g., Branscombe, Schmitt, & Harvey, 1999; Crocker, Luhtanen, Blaine, & Broadnax, 1994; Jetten, Branscombe, Schmitt, & Spears, 2001; Turner, Hogg, Turner, & Smith, 1984).

Cognitive motives: Uncertainty reduction

Given the inadequacy of self-esteem as an explanation for why social identity is engaged, other motives have been proposed that do not require positive ingroup status as a basis for attachment to groups and self-definition as a group member. One proposal is that group identity meets fundamental needs for reducing uncertainty and achieving meaning and clarity in social contexts (Hogg & Abrams, 1993; Hogg & Mullin, 1999). In support of this hypothesis, Hogg and his colleagues (Grieve & Hogg, 1999; Mullin & Hogg, 1998) have generated compelling evidence that identification and ingroup bias are increased under conditions of high cognitive uncertainty and reduced or eliminated when uncertainty is low. And it is undoubtedly true that one function that group memberships and identities serve for individuals is that of providing self-definition and guidance for behavior in otherwise ambiguous social situations (Deaux, Reid, Mizrahi, & Cotting, 1999; Vignoles, Chryssochoou, & Breakwell, 2000). However, group identity is only one of many possible modes of reducing social uncertainty. Roles, values, laws, and so forth serve a similar function without necessitating social identification processes. Thus uncertainty reduction alone cannot account for the pervasiveness of group identification as a fundamental aspect of human life.

Uncertainty reduction as a theory of social identity places the explanation for group identification in a system of cognitive motives that includes needs for meaning, certainty, and structure. An alternative perspective is that the motivation for social identification arises from even more fundamental needs for security and safety. Consistent with this idea, Baumeister and Leary (1995) postulate a universal need for *belonging* as an aspect of human nature derived from our vulnerability as lone individuals who require connection with others in order to survive. But belonging alone cannot account for the selectivity of social identification, since any and all group memberships should satisfy the belonging motive. My own theory (Brewer, 1991) postulates that the need for belonging and inclusion is paired with an opposing motive – the need for differentiation – that together regulate the individual's social identity and attachment to social groups.

Optimal distinctiveness theory: Basic premises

Optimal distinctiveness theory is an extension of social identity theory, developed to account for why individuals seek identification with social groups and to explain the role of social identities in achieving and maintaining a stable self-concept. Briefly, the theory is based on the thesis that distinctiveness per se is a factor underlying the selection and strength of social identities because distinct social groups satisfy basic psychological needs derived from our evolutionary history as a social species.

The theory has its origins in the premise that group living represents the fundamental survival strategy that characterizes the human species. In the course of our evolutionary history, humans have lost most of the physical characteristics and instincts that make possible survival and reproduction as isolated individuals or pairs of individuals, in favor of other advantages that require cooperative interdependence with others in order to survive in a broad range of physical environments. In other words, as a species we have evolved to rely on cooperation rather than strength, and on social learning rather than instinct as basic adaptations. The result is that, as a species, human beings are characterized by *obligatory interdependence* (Brewer, 1997; Caporael, 1997). For long-term survival, we must be willing to rely on others for information, aid, and shared resources, and we must be willing to give information and aid and to share resources with others.

For individual humans, the potential benefits (receiving resources from others) and costs (giving resources to others) of mutual cooperation go hand in hand and set natural limits on cooperative interdependence. The decision to cooperate (to expend resources to another's benefit) is a dilemma of trust since the ultimate benefits depend on everyone else's willingness to do the same. Social differentiation and clear group boundaries provide one mechanism for achieving the benefits of cooperative interdependence without the risk of excessive costs (Brewer, 1981). By limiting aid to mutually acknowledged ingroup members, total costs and risks of nonreciprocation can be contained. Psychologically, expectations of cooperation and security promote positive attraction toward other ingroup members and motivate adherence to ingroup norms of appearance and behavior that assure that one will be recognized as a good or legitimate ingroup member. Symbols and behaviors that differentiate the ingroup from local outgroups become particularly important here, to reduce the risk that ingroup benefits will be inadvertently extended to outgroup members, and to ensure that ingroup members will recognize one's own entitlement to receive benefits. Assimilation within and differentiation between groups is thus mutually reinforcing, along with ethnocentric preference for ingroup interactions and institutions (Brewer, 1999, 2007).

If social differentiation and intergroup boundaries are functional for social cooperation, and social cooperation is essential for human survival, then there should be psychological mechanisms at the individual level that motivate and sustain ingroup identification and differentiation. The optimal distinctiveness model postulates just such motivational mechanisms. According to the model, social identities derive "from a fundamental tension between human needs for validation and similarity to others (on the one hand) and a countervailing need for uniqueness and individuation (on the other)" (Brewer, 1991, p. 477). More specifically, it is proposed that social identities are selected and activated to the extent that they help to achieve a balance between needs for inclusion and needs for differentiation in a given social context.

The basic premise of the optimal distinctiveness model is that the two identity needs (inclusion/assimilation and differentiation/distinctiveness) are independent and work in opposition to motivate group identification. Optimal identities are those that satisfy the need for inclusion *within* the ingroup and simultaneously serve the need for differentiation through distinctions *between* the ingroup and outgroups. In effect, optimal social identities involve *shared distinctiveness* (Stapel & Marx, 2007). Individuals will resist being identified with social categorizations that are either too inclusive or too differentiating but will define themselves in terms of social identities that are optimally distinctive. Equilibrium is maintained by correcting for deviations from optimality. A situation in which a person is overly individuated will excite the need for assimilation, motivating the person to adopt a more inclusive social identity. Conversely, situations that arouse feelings of deindividuation will activate the need for differentiation, resulting in a search for more exclusive or distinct identities.

Evidence for competing social motives comes from empirical demonstrations of efforts to achieve or restore group identification when these needs are deprived. Results of experimental studies have shown that activation of the need for assimilation or the need for differentiation increases the importance of distinctive group memberships (Pickett, Silver, & Brewer, 2002), that threat to inclusion enhances self-stereotyping on group-characteristic traits (Brewer & Pickett, 1999; Pickett, Bonner, & Coleman, 2002; Spears, Doosje, & Ellemers, 1997), and that threat to group distinctiveness motivates overexclusion (Brewer & Pickett, 2002) and intergroup differentiation (Hornsey & Hogg, 1999; Jetten, Spears, & Manstead, 1998; Jetten, Spears, & Postmes,

2004; Roccas & Schwartz, 1993). Further, assignment to distinctive minority group categories engages greater group identification and self-stereotyping than does membership in large, inclusive majority groups (Brewer & Weber, 1994; Leonardelli & Brewer, 2001; Simon & Hamilton, 1994). Thus there is converging evidence that group attachment is regulated by motives for inclusion and distinctiveness.

Optimal distinctiveness: Some qualifications and clarifications

Although hypotheses derived from optimal distinctiveness theory have been tested by different researchers in many different contexts, some aspects of the theory are frequently misunderstood. Importantly, the model does *not* postulate that optimal distinctiveness is a property of some groups rather than others and that individuals directly seek identification with such optimal groups. Rather, optimality is an interactive product of current levels of activation of the opposing motives for inclusion and differentiation and group properties that determine its level of inclusiveness and distinctiveness. This leads to three important principles that are essential to understanding optimal distinctiveness.

First, *optimal distinctiveness is context specific.* Context affects both the activation of motives or needs and the relative distinctiveness of specific social categories. Consider, for example, my professional group memberships. In the context of an international psychology conference, categorization as a "psychologist" is far too inclusive, and a subcategory such as "social psychologist" is more likely to be optimally distinctive. On the other hand, in the context of my local community, my identity as a social psychologist is too highly differentiated and, instead, categorizing my occupation as an "academic" is optimal. Identifying myself as an academic or a university professor places me in a social group with a significant number of other members of my community who share that occupational status and yet distinguishes *us* from neighbors who belong to other professions or occupational categories. "Shared distinctiveness" is contextually defined.

Second, *optimal distinctiveness is a dynamic equilibrium.* Even within a given context, optimality is not necessarily fixed because inclusion and differentiation motives are also subject to temporal influences and change over time. When one enters a new group, for example, the awareness of one's marginal status as a newcomer may enhance the need for inclusion relative to the need for differentiation, but as time goes on and inclusion is more secure, differentiation needs become more salient and maintaining group distinctiveness assumes a higher priority. Groups also exhibit dynamic shifts across time in their relative focus on enhancing inclusiveness or reestablishing distinctiveness and exclusiveness.

Finally, *identity motives vary across situation, culture, and individuals.* Asking how "strong" an individual's inclusion motive is like asking how strong is the individual's hunger motivation. Like any need or drive, inclusion and differentiation motives vary as a function of current levels of satiation or deprivation. However, individuals may differ in how sensitive they are to changes in levels of inclusiveness. Just as some individuals start feeling ravenously hungry after an hour or two since they last ate while other individuals don't even notice they haven't eaten all day, so some people will react strongly to a slight loss of inclusiveness (or slight expansion of group boundaries), whereas others will be more tolerant of a range of ingroup inclusiveness. Thus, although the principles incorporated in the optimal distinctiveness model are presumed to be universal, the model can also accommodate individual, situational, and cultural differences in the relative activation of inclusion and differentiation needs and the nature of optimal identities.

Put more formally, the model (as depicted in Figure 1.1, taken from Brewer, 1991) has four important parameters – the height (intercept) of the need for differentiation, the height (intercept) of the need for inclusion, the negative slope of the need for inclusion, and the positive slope of the need for differentiation. Of these four, one is presumed to be fixed. The intercept (zero activation) of the need for differentiation is assumed to be at the point of complete individuation (the endpoint of the inclusiveness dimension). All of the other parameters are free to vary; any changes in the intercept or slope of the inclusion drive or the slope of the differentiation drive will alter the point of equilibrium that represents an optimal identity. Thus, the model depicted in Figure 1.1 is just one member of a class of models containing all possible variations in these parameters, and differences across situations, cultures, and individuals can be represented in terms of variation in the slopes of the two drives (which can vary independently). (See Brewer & Roccas, 2001, for a discussion of how cultural differences can be reflected in model parameters and the point of equilibrium.)

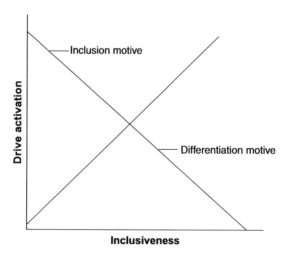

Figure 1.1 The optimal distinctiveness model of group identification (from Brewer, 1991).

Again, the overall point is to emphasize that optimal distinctiveness is not a fixed property of groups or of individuals but a consequence of motivational dynamics at both levels.

Optimal identity: The upside and downside

If social identity motives derive, ultimately, from needs for security and cooperative interdependence, this has important implications for the functions and limits of social identification as a motivator of prosocial behavior. More specifically, the theory predicts that the dynamics of trust and cooperation will be shaped by the need for distinct boundaries between ingroup and outgroups and associated differences between intragroup and intergroup behaviors.

Ingroup trust

On the positive side, optimal group identities can be thought of as bounded communities of mutual trust and generalized reciprocal cooperation (Yamagishi, Jin, & Kiyonari, 1999). Mere knowledge that another individual shares a salient group identity is sufficient to engage depersonalized trust (Yuki, Maddux, Brewer, & Takemura, 2005) and willingness to sacrifice immediate self-interest for collective welfare (Brewer & Kramer, 1986; Wit & Kerr, 2002). Ingroup behavior is governed by norms and sanctions that reinforce expectations of mutual cooperation and trustworthiness. Trust is supported by implicit understandings that ingroup members will monitor the behavior and interactions of other group members, sanctioning deviations from group expectations about appropriate ingroup attitudes and behavior. Thus, shared ingroup membership may be taken as prima facie evidence that other members of the group will live by the codes of conduct that bind them together as a group (Kramer, Brewer, & Hanna, 1996).

If, as I argue here, the basis for universal ingroup preference is derived from the security and trust associated with ingroup exchanges, then it is reasonable that the most reliable dimensions of ingroup positivity are those related to trustworthiness, cooperativeness, and honesty. Consistent with this perspective, a set of studies conducted by Leach, Ellemers, and Barreto (2007) implicate morality traits (e.g., honesty, sincerity) as the characteristics most important to positive ingroup evaluation. Factor analysis results showed morality to account for more ingroup favorability than either competence or sociality, and when asked directly, participants also reported that morality was more important. Further, experimental manipulations of morality versus competence and sociality information showed that only morality affected levels of ingroup attachment. Thus, it appears that it is perceptions of trust and reliability that underlie ingroup favoritism rather than positivity per se, as would be expected from the self-enhancement explanation.

Implications for intergroup relations

The dilemma in all this is that the conditions for ingroup cooperation and trust require group boundaries and clear differentiation between intragroup and intergroup social exchange. The social motives postulated by optimal distinctiveness theory at the individual level create a propensity for adhering to social groups that are both bounded and distinctive. Secure inclusion implies exclusion. The adaptive value of groups lies in interactional norms that facilitate reciprocal exchanges within the group (Gil-White, 2001; Henrich et al., 2001), but are not extended to outsiders. A consequence of ingroup identification and intergroup boundaries is that individuals modify their social behavior depending on whether they are interacting with ingroup or outgroup members.

None of this implies that strong identification with ingroups necessitates conflict with outgroups. Contrary to the notion that ingroup positivity and outgroup derogation are reciprocally related, ingroup love does not imply outgroup hate (Brewer, 1999, 2007). Indeed, results from both laboratory experiments and field studies indicate that variations in ingroup positivity and social identification do not systematically correlate with degree of bias or negativity towards outgroups (Brewer, 1979; Hinkle & Brown, 1990; Kosterman & Feshbach, 1989). Further, the positive ingroup biases exhibited in the allocation of positive resources in the minimal intergroup situation are essentially eliminated when allocation decisions involve the distribution of negative outcomes or costs (e.g., Mummendey & Otten, 1998; Mummendey et al., 1992), suggesting that individuals are willing to differentially benefit the ingroup compared to outgroups but are reluctant to harm outgroups more directly.

What ingroup favoritism does imply is that positivity and trust extend only to the boundary of the ingroup and not across groups. Thus, intergroup relations are characterized by *lack* of trust, though not necessarily active *dis*trust. For example, in our own experiments on group-based trust, we find that knowing that a stranger belongs to one's own ingroup elevates trusting choices to near 90% (Yuki et al., 2005). With an outgroup stranger, on the other hand, trusting choices drop significantly – but only to around 50%, not to 0 as would be expected if outgroups were assumed to be hostile and malevolent. Instead, exchanges with outgroup members appear to be characterized by uncertainty and lack of trust, rather than by automatic distrust or negativity.

Nonetheless, ingroup positivity and bounded trust are not completely benign. Just as there is a realistic basis for ethnocentric trust of ingroups, differences in norms and sanctions applied to ingroup behavior compared to behavior in interactions with outgroup members provide a realistic basis for outgroup distrust and negative stereotypes. At the same time that groups promote trust and cooperation within, they caution wariness and constraint in intergroup interactions. Thus, even in the absence of overt conflict between groups, the differentiation between ingroup and outgroup behavior creates a kind of self-fulfilling prophecy in the realm of intergroup perceptions. As LeVine and Campbell (1972) put it, "if most or all groups are, in fact, ethnocentric, then it becomes an 'accurate' stereotype to accuse an outgroup of some aspect of ethnocentrism" (p. 173).

Combined with the accentuation principle that exaggerates perceived differences between social categories, this leads to a set of "universal stereotypes" to characterize ingroup–outgroup differences. Whereas "we" are trustworthy, peaceful, moral, loyal, and reliable, "they" are clannish, exclusive, and potentially untrustworthy. What is particularly interesting about this pattern of stereotypes is that the same behaviors that are interpreted as reasonable caution on the part of the ingroup in dealings with outgroup members become interpreted as "clannishness" and indicators of mistrust when exhibited by outgroupers toward the ingroup.

Optimal distinctiveness theory also has implications for when individuals will feel that their ingroup identity and the functions it serves are being threatened. If ingroups provide for both secure inclusion and intergroup differentiation, then anything that undermines either of these needs will activate attempts to restore optimality and enhance intergroup distinctions. The effects of threats to ingroup distinctiveness on hostility toward the threatening outgroup have been well documented (Jetten et al., 2004). But similar effects can be obtained when the individual's sense of inclusion within the ingroup has been threatened (Pickett & Brewer, 2005). When a member of a group is led to believe that he or she is not a typical group member or is not fully accepted as part of the group, that individual should experience distress to the extent that he or she relies on that particular group for the satisfaction of belongingness, security, or assimilation needs. Peripheral group members not only need to be concerned with being similar to other ingroup members, but also concerned that they are not confused with the outgroup. This leads to the prediction that marginal ingroup members will be most concerned with maintaining intergroup distance and endorsing negativity toward outgroups. Thus, the motivational dynamics underlying strong ingroup attachment can lay the groundwork for intergroup hostility and conflict.

Limits on inclusiveness: Can they be overcome?

The dilemma that optimal distinctiveness theory poses for the modern world is this: How do we accommodate the need for distinctive ingroup identities that is rooted in our evolutionary past under conditions where interdependence transcends group boundaries at a global level? The need for social identity and preservation of ingroup distinctiveness has long been recognized as a constraint on the "common ingroup identity" prescription for reducing intergroup discrimination (Brewer & Gaertner, 2001; Hornsey & Hogg, 1999). It was this recognition that led Mummendey and Wenzel (1999; see also Waldzus, chapter 3 in this volume) to argue that the question we should be asking is not how we can eliminate intergroup differences but rather under what conditions can intergroup differences be accepted, or even celebrated?

Dual identities: Nested subgroups

One answer that has been endorsed by many social identity researchers is the idea that individuals can hold more than one group identity at a time, maintaining a distinct social identity at the subgroup level while also identifying with a superordinate category that subsumes their own subgroup and parallel outgroups (Gaertner & Dovidio, 2000; Hewstone, 1996; Hewstone & Brown, 1986; Hornsey & Hogg, 2000). The argument is that embracing a more inclusive superordinate identity does not necessarily require each group to forsake its original group identity completely (Gaertner, Rust, Dovidio, Bachman, & Anastasio, 1994). In some intergroup contexts, when members simultaneously perceive themselves as members of different groups but also as part of the same team or superordinate entity, intergroup relations between these subgroups are more positive than if members only consider themselves as separate groups. For example, minority students in a multi-ethnic high school who identified themselves using both a minority subgroup and an American superordinate identity had lower intergroup bias than those students who identified themselves using only their minority group identity (Gaertner et al., 1994). Also, the greater the extent to which majority and minority students perceived the student body as "different groups . . . all playing on the same team" (the dual identity item), the lower their degree of intergroup bias. By contrast, the more they conceived of the student body as "belonging to different groups" the higher the intergroup bias. In terms of promoting more harmonious intergroup interactions, a dual identity capitalizes on the benefits of common ingroup membership as well those accrued from mutual differentiation between the groups (see Hornsey & Jetten, 2004).

However, the effectiveness of dual identities for increasing harmony between groups may vary across intergroup domains. For example, maintaining strong identification with the earlier subgroup identities following a corporate merger may threaten the primary goal of the merger (Bachman, 1993). Similarly, in step-families, the salience of the former family identities, even with the simultaneous recognition of a more inclusive family identity, may violate members' expectations about what their ideal family should be like (Banker & Gaertner, 1998). Further, optimal distinctiveness theory would predict that identification with superordinate and subgroups would not be equivalent. When need for distinctiveness is activated and subgroup differences are salient, identification and loyalty to subgroups are likely to take priority over loyalty to the superordinate when interests conflict.

Thus, the dual identity strategy is a vulnerable one. As Mummendey and Wenzel (1999) argue, nesting groups within a common superordinate category may actually *increase* intergroup rejection, compared to conditions without a salient superordinate identity. The superordinate context invites social comparison between ingroup and outgroups at the subgroups level. This introduces new motivational dynamics that may turn indifference toward the outgroup into distrust and hostility. When groups have a shared superordinate identity, the norms and values by which intergroup differences are evaluated are derived from the representation (prototype) of the inclusive category. If members of a subgroup project their own ingroup attributes onto the superordinate category, ingroup norms then become general standards against which other subgroups can be judged. Any differences between the ingroup and other subgroups are seen as nonnormative, devalued, and justifiably discriminated against. (See Waldzus, chapter 3 in this volume for further discussion of ingroup projection and discrimination.) Based on these processes, dual identities may exacerbate the moral superiority bias that characterizes ingroup–outgroup perceptions in general.

Cross-cutting categories and multiple identities

Even though nested social identities recognize that individuals may have more than one social identity salient at any one time, the problem is that this form of dual identity leaves ingroup–outgroup distinctions intact within the context of a superordinate category. Embedded categories at different levels of inclusiveness, however, represent only one form of multiple ingroup identities. Individuals may also be members of social categories that overlap only partially, if at all. Many bases of social category differentiation – gender, age, religion, ethnicity, occupation – represent cross-cutting cleavages. From the standpoint of a particular person, other individuals may be fellow ingroup members on one dimension of category differentiation but outgroup members on another. (For instance, for a woman business executive, a male colleague is an ingroup member with respect to occupation but an outgrouper with respect to her gender identification.) It is possible that such orthogonal social identities are kept isolated from each other so that only one ingroup–outgroup distinction is activated in a particular social context. But there are reasons to expect that simultaneous activation of multiple ingroup identities is both possible and has potential for reducing prejudice and discrimination based on any one category distinction (Crisp & Hewstone, 2007).

Evidence from both anthropology (e.g., Gluckman, 1955) and political sociology (e.g., Coser, 1956) has long suggested that societies characterized by cross-cutting loyalty structures are less prone to schism and internal intergroup conflict than societies characterized by a single hierarchical loyalty structure. More recently, social psychologists have also begun to consider the implications of such multiple cross-cutting social identities for reduction of ingroup bias at the individual level (e.g., Brown & Turner, 1979; Deschamps & Doise, 1978; Marcus-Newhall, Miller, Holtz, & Brewer, 1993; Vanbeselaere, 1991). A number of mechanisms have been proposed for why cross-cutting group memberships would decrease ingroup bias and intergroup discrimination. For one thing, the increased complexity of a multiple social categorization reduces the salience or degree of differentiation associated with any one ingroup–outgroup distinction. Beyond the cognitive effects of category complexity, motivational factors also enter to reduce the likelihood of intense ingroup–outgroup discrimination. First, the presence of multiple group loyalties potentially reduces the importance or significance of any one social identity for self-definition or belonging. Further, cross-category connections and consistency (balance) motives mitigate against negative attitudes toward outgroups that contain members who are fellow ingroupers on some other category dimension. Finally, cross-cutting category memberships increase the degree of interpersonal interaction and contact across any particular category boundaries (Brewer, 2000).

Experimental studies with both natural and artificial categories have demonstrated that adding a cross-cutting category distinction reduces ingroup bias and increases positive attitudes toward crossed category members compared to simple ingroup–outgroup differentiation (Vanbeselaere, 1991) or compared to situations in which category distinctions are convergent or superimposed (Bettencourt & Dorr, 1998; Crisp, Hewstone, & Rubin, 2001; Marcus-Newhall et al., 1993; Rust, 1996). In these studies, cooperative interaction in the context of cross-cutting social identities and roles increases intracategory differentiation and reduces perceived intercategory differences, resulting in fewer category-based evaluations of individual group members. Further, the benefits of cross-categorization may be enhanced when both category distinctions are embedded in a common superordinate group identity (Crisp & Hewstone, 2000; Crisp, Walsh, & Hewstone, 2006; Rust, 1996). Thus, crossed categorization and common ingroup identities may work together to produce enhanced inclusiveness and reduced intergroup discrimination.

In the right circumstances, cross-cutting identities within a shared superordinate context may solve the problem of ethnocentric ingroup projection that undermines the potential positive effects of dual identities (Mummendey & Wenzel, 1999). Intolerance and social discrimination against other subgroups arise from cognitive representation of the superordinate category in terms of a single, simple prototype that is generalized from the ingroup's own attributes, norms, and values. Research based on this model has confirmed that ingroup projection is a precursor to social discrimination (Wenzel, Mummendey, Weber, & Waldzus, 2003). In their original formulation of this model, Mummendey and Wenzel (1999) suggested that more vague, complex, or differentiated representations of the superordinate identity would be associated with greater tolerance and acceptance of plurality. If the prototype of the inclusive category is complex and multimodal, then there is no single evaluative standard against which all subgroups are judged and differences can be perceived as normative rather than deviant. In a set of follow-up experiments, Waldzus, Mummendey, Wendei, and Weber (2003) demonstrated that manipulating the complexity of the superordinate category leads to a decrease in ingroup projection (perceived prototypicality of the ingroup relative to the outgroup) and associated attitudes toward the outgroup.

Social identity complexity and superordinate ingroups

Given the critical role of cognitive representation of the shared superordinate identity for tolerance and intergroup acceptance in a pluralistic society, it is important to understand what factors give rise to more or less complex representations. A superordinate that is structurally differentiated by criss-crossing subcategory distinctions (rather than differentiation along a single dimension) is more likely to be seen as a complex entity. Within a system of cross-categorization, individuals have multiple social identities that do not fully converge. Who shares ingroup membership and what norms and values are activated may vary across one's own multiple ingroups, reducing the tendency to project a single ingroup image onto the superordinate. Thus, how individuals represent their own subgroup identities may influence how they represent more inclusive category memberships.

Roccas and Brewer (2002) introduced the construct of *social identity complexity* to refer to the extent to which individuals think about their multiple group memberships such that different identities are both differentiated and integrated in the individual's subjective cognitive representation of those group memberships. Ingroups defined by different dimensions of categorization (e.g., religion, gender, ethnicity) are typically only partially overlapping when assessed objectively, but subjective perceptions of the extent of group membership overlap may vary widely among individuals. An individual may perceive his or her ingroups as having highly overlapping sets of members, such that a set of group memberships may even form a single, exclusive compound category (e.g., white Catholic Republican doctors). This would be described as a *simple* identity structure. The opposite end of the continuum would be characterized by an individual who recognizes that his or her ingroup memberships are composed of distinct but overlapping member sets. This would be described as a *complex* identity structure (e.g., whites *and* Catholics *and* Republicans *and* doctors.). Social identity complexity depends on the recognition of both the existence of multiple group memberships and the lack of convergence among those memberships.

In the research on social identity complexity conducted up to this point (Brewer & Pierce, 2005; Roccas & Brewer, 2002), an individual's social identity complexity has been operationalized using a self-report measure that directly asks individuals about the extent to which they perceive the memberships and characteristics of their social groups to be overlapping. According to Roccas and Brewer (2002), individuals who perceive a greater overlap among their identities (i.e., high scorers) have simpler identities, while those who perceive less overlap (i.e., low scorers) have more complex identities. Therefore, an individual's score on such an overlap measure is inversely related to his or her social identity complexity.

Roccas and Brewer (2002) hypothesized that both cognitive and motivational factors indicate that social identity complexity should be associated with tolerance toward outgroups. They note that individuals with high levels of social identity complexity are more likely to be cognitively aware that individuals who are outgroup members on some group dimension are also likely to be an ingroup member when considered on some different dimension. Also, the motivation to favor one's ingroup may be diminished when one recognizes the cross-cutting nature of ingroup memberships, which reduces both the importance of the ingroup in intergroup comparisons as well as the significance of any particular social identification for an individual's self-definition and collective self-esteem. In support of these ideas, Roccas and Brewer (2002) presented initial data suggesting that higher social identity complexity was associated with higher endorsement of openness, lower power orientation, and higher universalism values on the Schwartz Value Inventory (Schwartz, 1992). Initial research also demonstrated that greater social identity complexity was associated with less social distance to an outgroup (Russian immigrants) among Israeli participants.

More recently, Brewer and Pierce (2005) assessed the relationship between social identity complexity and tolerance in a large-sample survey of adults from Ohio. A mail survey was used to identify potential participants for a telephone interview and to obtain a listing of group memberships from each respondent. These group memberships were then used to construct a personalized phone interview for each respondent contacted. Specifically, three of the participant's own identified memberships were used when asking each respondent about the extent of the overlap between each of these groups. The phone survey also collected responses on items measuring attitudes toward affirmative action and multiculturalism, as well as emotional distance from outgroups as measured by "feeling thermometer" questions. These variables were then tested for a relationship to the overlap measure of social identity complexity.

The results confirmed previous expectations and findings; social identity complexity was associated with both tolerance-related policy preferences and affect toward outgroups. The measure of perceived overlap among three ingroups was significantly correlated with attitudes toward affirmative action, multiculturalism, and affect toward outgroups after controlling for age, education, and ideology. Respondents with lower overlap scores (higher social identity complexity) showed more positive outgroup attitudes on each of these measures. The finding seems particularly compelling when it is noted that the overlap scores computed in this study did not include the participants' racial and ethnic group memberships, but were based on categories such as church membership and sports fandom groups. The subjective representation of these non-ethnic groups was nonetheless related to tolerance of ethnic outgroups in the manner predicted by Roccas and Brewer (2002).

The data collected in the Ohio survey also provided an opportunity to test the relationship between social identity complexity (as measured by the perceived overlap among multiple ingroups) and ethnocentric projection to a shared superordinate identity – America. In addition to rating the overlap among pairs of ingroups, each respondent also rated the degree of similarity among their various ingroups, including similarity of each ingroup to "the typical American." Thus, for each respondent we had a measure of projected similarity of each of three ingroups to the prototype of America as a superordinate identity. The mean of the three similarity ratings constituted our measure of ethnocentric projection. We then correlated this similarity measure with the overlap measure of social identity complexity (which did *not* include America as one of the ingroups) and found that they were significantly related: $r = .52$ ($p < .01$). Thus, the more complex individuals perceived their own ingroup memberships to be, the less they projected attributes of their ingroups to a shared superordinate identity. This is only an indirect test of the idea that multiple cross-cutting ingroups give rise to more complex representations of the superordinate, but the results are consistent with Mummendey's analysis of the relationship between ethnocentric projection and intergroup tolerance.

Conclusion

Optimal distinctiveness theory was originally developed to explain and predict identification with a single ingroup in a given social context. However, the postulated motives for inclusion and differentiation can also be applied to the representation of multiple ingroup memberships considered simultaneously. Specific ingroups may be salient and optimal within a particular context, but there may also be an optimal level of perceived overlap among all of one's ingroups that satisfies both needs. A high degree of overlap (convergence) creates a highly exclusive ingroup (e.g., Catholic social psychologist soccer fans) that may be too extremely differentiated to meet needs for inclusion. On the other hand, ingroups with very little overlap may be difficult to represent as a complex but integrated social identity. Multiple partially overlapping ingroups may be both complex and optimal.

The motives underlying group identification did not evolve under the conditions of global interdependence that characterize our modern world. As a consequence of our evolutionary history, our sense of personal security and certainty are maximized in the context of shared ingroup membership and clear ingroup–outgroup distinctions. Attempts to merge groups or erase social category distinctions threaten optimal identities and limit our capacity for identification with larger, more inclusive categories. But the complexity of the modern world does provide us with multiple ways to meet identity needs, with multiple group identities that are optimal within different contexts. To the extent that we recognize the cross-cutting nature of our own group identities, we enhance the capacity for acceptance of intergroup differences and life in a pluralistic social system.

References

Bachman, B. A. (1993). *An intergroup model of organizational mergers.* Unpublished PhD dissertation, University of Delaware.

Banker, B. S., & Gaertner, S. L. (1998). Achieving stepfamily harmony: An intergroup relations approach. *Journal of Family Psyholgy, 12,* 310–325.

Baumeister, R. F., & Leary, M. R. (1995). The need to belong: Desire for interpersonal attachments as a fundamental human motivation. *Psychological Bulletin, 117,* 497–529.

Bettencourt, B. A., & Dorr, N. (1998). Cooperative interaction and intergroup bias: Effects of numerical representation and cross-cut role assignment. *Personality and Social Psychology Bulletin, 24,* 1276–1293.

Branscombe, N. R., Schmitt, M. T., & Harvey, R. D. (1999). Perceiving pervasive discrimination among African-Americans: Implications for group identification and well-being. *Journal of Personality and Social Psychology, 77,* 135–149.

Brewer, M. B. (1979). In-group bias in the minimal intergroup situation: A cognitive-motivational analysis. *Psychological Bulletin, 86,* 307–324.

Brewer, M. B. (1981). Ethnocentrism and its role in intergroup trust. In M. Brewer & B. Collins (Eds.), *Scientific inquiry in the social sciences* (pp. 214–231). San Francisco: Jossey-Bass.

Brewer, M. B. (1991). The social self: On being the same and different at the same time. *Personality and Social Psychology Bulletin, 17,* 475–482.

Brewer, M. B. (1997). On the social origins of human nature. In C. McGarty & S. A. Haslam (Eds.), *The message of social psychology* (pp. 54–62). Oxford: Blackwell.

Brewer, M. B. (1999). The psychology of prejudice: Ingroup love or outgroup hate? *Journal of Social Issues, 55,* 429–444.

Brewer, M. B. (2000). Reducing prejudice through cross-categorization: Effects of multiple social identities. In S. Oskamp (Ed.), *Reducing prejudice and discrimination. The Claremont Symposium on Applied Social Psychology* (pp. 165–183). Mahwah, NJ: Lawrence Erlbaum Associates, Inc.

Brewer, M. B. (2007). The importance of being *we*: Human nature and intergroup relations. *American Psychologist, 62,* 728–738.

Brewer, M. B., & Gaertner, S. L. (2001). Toward reduction of prejudice: Intergroup contact and social categorization. In R. Brown & S. Gaertner (Eds.), *Blackwell handbook of social psychology: Intergroup processes* (pp. 451–472). Oxford: Blackwell.

Brewer, M. B., & Kramer, R. M. (1986). Choice behavior in social dilemmas: Effects of social identity, group size, and decision framing. *Journal of Personality and Social Psychology, 50,* 543–549.

Brewer, M. B., & Pickett, C. L. (1999). Distinctiveness motives as a source of the social self. In T. Tyler, R. Kramer, & O. John (Eds.), *The psychology of the social self* (pp. 71–87). Mahwah, NJ: Lawrence Erlbaum Associates, Inc.

Brewer, M. B., & Pickett, C. L. (2002). The social self and group identification: Inclusion and distinctiveness motives in interpersonal and collective identities. In J. Forgas & K. Williams (Eds.), *The social self: Cognitive, interpersonal, and intergroup perspectives* (pp. 255–271). Philadelphia: Psychology Press.

Brewer, M. B., & Pierce, K. P. (2005). Social identity complexity and outgroup tolerance. *Personality and Social Psychology Bulletin, 31,* 428–437.

Brewer, M. B., & Roccas, S. (2001). Individual values, social identity, and optimal distinctiveness. In C. Sedikides & M. Brewer (Eds.), *Individual self, relational self, collective self* (pp. 219–237). Philadelphia: Psychology Press.

Brewer, M. B., & Weber, J. G. (1994). Self-evaluation effects of interpersonal versus intergroup social comparison. *Journal of Personality and Social Psychology, 66,* 268–275.

Brown, R. J., & Turner, J. C. (1979). The criss-cross categorization effect in intergroup discrimination. *British Journal of Social and Clinical Psychology, 18,* 371–383.

Caporael, L. R. (1997). The evolution of truly social cognition: The core configurations model. *Personality and Social Psychology Review, 1,* 276–298.

Coser, L. A. (1956). *The functions of social conflict.* New York: Free Press.

Crisp, R. J., & Hewstone, M. (2000). Multiple categorization and social identity. In D. Capozza & R. Brown (Eds.), *Social identity processes: Trends in theory and research* (pp. 149–166). Beverly Hills, CA: Sage.

Crisp, R. J., & Hewstone, M. (2007). Multiple social categorization. In M. Zanna (Ed.), *Advances in experimental social psychology* (Vol. 39, pp. 163–254). Orlando, FL: Academic Press.

Crisp, R. J., Hewstone, M., & Rubin, M. (2001). Does multiple categorization reduce intergroup bias? *Personality and Social Psychology Bulletin, 27,* 76–89.

Crisp, R. J., Walsh, J., & Hewstone, M. (2006). Crossed categorization in common ingroup contexts. *Personality and Social Psychology Bulletin, 32,* 1204–1218.

Crocker, J., Luhtanen, R., Blaine, B., & Broadnax, S. (1994). Collective self-esteem and psychological well-being among White, Black, and Asian college students. *Personality and Social Psychology Bulletin, 20,* 503–513.

Deaux, K., Reid, A., Mizrahi, K., & Cotting, D. (1999). Connecting the person to the social: The functions of social identification. In T. Tyler, R. Kramer, & O. John (Eds.), *The psychology of the social self* (pp. 91–113). Mahwah, NJ: Lawrence Erlbaum Associates, Inc.

Deschamps, J.-C., & Doise, W. (1978). Crossed category memberships in intergroup relations. In H. Tajfel (Ed.), *Differentiation between social groups* (pp. 141–158). Cambridge: Cambridge University Press.

Gaertner, S. L., & Dovidio, J. F. (2000). *Reducing intergroup bias: The common ingroup identity model.* Philadelphia: Psychology Press.

Gaertner, S. L., Rust, M. C., Dovidio, J. F., Bachman, B. A., & Anastasio, A. (1994). The contact hypothesis: The role of a common ingroup identity on reducing intergroup bias. *Small Groups Research, 25,* 224–290.

Gil-White, F. (2001) Are ethnic groups biological "species" to the human brain? *Current Anthropology, 42,* 515–554.

Gluckman, M. (1955). *Customs and conflict in Africa.* London: Blackwell.

Grieve, P. G., & Hogg, M. A. (1999). Subjective uncertainty and intergroup discrimination in the minimal group situation. *Personality and Social Psychology Bulletin, 25,* 926–940.

Henrich, J., Boyd, R., Bowles, S., Camerer, C., Fehr, E., Gintis, H., et al. (2001). In search of Homo economicus: Experiments in 15 small-scale societies. *American Economic Review, 91*(2), 73–79.

Hewstone, M. (1996). Contact and categorization: Social psychology interventions to change intergroup relations. In C. N. Macrae, C. Stangor, & M. Hewstone (Eds.), *Stereotypes and stereotyping* (pp. 323–368). New York: Guilford.

Hewstone, M., & Brown, R. J. (1986). Contact is not enough: An intergroup perspective on the "contact hypothesis." In M. Hewstone & R. Brown (Eds.), *Contact and conflict in intergroup encounters* (pp. 1–44). Oxford: Basil Blackwell.

Hinkle, S., & Brown, R. (1990). Intergroup comparisons and social identity: Some links and lacunae. In D. Abrams & M. Hogg (Eds.), *Social identity theory: Constructive and critical advances* (pp. 48–70). Hemel Hempstead, UK: Harvester Wheatsheaf.

Hogg, M. A. (1992). *The social psychology of group cohesiveness. From attraction to social identity*. Hemel Hempstead, UK: Harvester Wheatsheaf.

Hogg, M. A., & Abrams, D. (1993). Towards a single-process uncertainty-reduction model of social motivation in groups. In M. Hogg & D. Abrams (Eds.), *Group motivation: Social psychological perspectives* (pp. 173–190). Hemel Hempstead, UK: Harvester Wheatsheaf.

Hogg, M. A., & Mullin, B.-A. (1999). Joining groups to reduce uncertainty: Subjective uncertainty reduction and group identification. In D. Abrams & M. A. Hogg (Eds.), *Social identity and social cognition* (pp. 249–279). Oxford: Blackwell.

Hornsey, M. J., & Hogg, M. A. (1999). Subgroup differentiation as a response to an overly-inclusive group: A test of optimal distinctiveness theory. *European Journal of Social Psychology, 29*, 543–550.

Hornsey, M. J., & Hogg, M. A. (2000). Subgroup relations: A comparison of the mutual intergroup differentiation and common ingroup identity models of prejudice reduction. *Personality and Social Psychology Bulletin, 26*, 242–256.

Hornsey, M. J., & Jetten, J. (2004). The individual within the group: Balancing the need to belong with the need to be different. *Personality and Social Psychology Review, 8*, 241–264.

Jetten, J., Branscombe, N. R., Schmitt, M. T., & Spears, R. (2001). Rebels with a cause: Group identification as a response to perceived discrimination from the mainstream. *Personality and Social Psychology Bulletin, 27*, 1204–1213.

Jetten, J., Spears, R., & Manstead, A. S. R. (1998). Intergroup similarity and group variability: The effects of group distinctiveness on the expression of in-group bias. *Journal of Personality and Social Psychology, 74*, 1481–1492.

Jetten, J., Spears, R., & Postmes, T. (2004). Intergroup distinctiveness and differentiation: A meta-analytic integration. *Journal of Personality and Social Psychology, 86*, 862–879.

Kosterman, R., & Feshbach, S. (1989). Toward a measure of patriotic and nationalistic attitudes. *Political Psychology, 10*, 257–274.

Kramer, R. M., Brewer, M. B., & Hanna, B. A. (1996). Collective trust and collective action: The decision to trust as a social dilemma. In R. Kramer & T. Tyler (Eds.), *Trust in organizations* (pp. 357–389). Thousand Oaks, CA: Sage.

Leach, C. W., Ellemers, N., & Barreto, M. (2007). Group virtue: The importance of morality (vs. competence and sociability) in the positive evaluation of in-groups. *Journal of Personality and Social Psychology, 93*, 234–249.

Leonardelli, G., & Brewer, M. B. (2001). Minority and majority discrimination: When and why. *Journal of Experimental Social Psychology, 37*, 468–485.

LeVine, R. A., & Campbell, D. T. (1972). *Ethnocentrism: Theories of conflict, ethnic attitudes and group behavior*. New York: Wiley.

Marcus-Newhall, A., Miller, N., Holtz, R., & Brewer, M. B. (1993). Cross-cutting category membership with role assignment: A means of reducing intergroup bias. *British Journal of Social Psychology, 32*, 125–146.

Mullin, B.-A., & Hogg, M. A. (1998). Dimensions of subjective uncertainty in social identification and minimal intergroup discrimination. *British Journal of Social Psychology, 37,* 345–365.

Mummendey, A., & Otten, S. (1998). Positive–negative asymmetry in social discrimination. In W. Stroebe & M. Hewstone (Eds.), *European review of social psychology* (Vol. 9, pp. 107–143). Chichester, UK: Wiley.

Mummendey, A., Simon, B., Dietze, C., Grunert., M., Haeger, G., Kessler, S., et al. (1992). Categorization is not enough: Intergroup discrimination in negative outcome allocations. *Journal of Experimental Social Psychology, 28,* 125–144.

Mummendey, A., & Wenzel, M. (1999). Social discrimination and tolerance in intergroup relations: Reactions to intergroup difference. *Personality and Social Psychology Review, 3,* 158–174.

Oakes, P. J. (1987). The salience of social categories. In J. Turner, M. Hogg, P. Oakes, S. Reicher, & M. Wetherell (Eds.), *Rediscovering the social group: A self-categorization theory* (Chapter 6, pp. 117–141). Oxford: Blackwell.

Pickett, C. L., Bonner, B. L., & Coleman, J. M. (2002). Motivated self-stereotyping: Heightened assimilation and differentiation needs result in increased levels of positive and negative self-stereotyping. *Journal of Personality and Social Psychology, 82,* 543–562.

Pickett, C. L., & Brewer, M. B. (2005). The role of exclusion in maintaining in-group inclusion. In D. Abrams, M. Hogg, & J. Marques (Eds.), *Social psychology of inclusion and exclusion* (pp. 89–112). New York: Psychology Press.

Pickett, C. L., Silver, M. D., & Brewer, M. B. (2002). The impact of assimilation and differentiation needs on perceived group importance and judgments of group size. *Personality and Social Psychology Bulletin, 28,* 546–558.

Roccas, S., & Brewer, M. B. (2002). Social identity complexity. *Personality and Social Psychology Review, 6,* 88–106.

Roccas, S., & Schwartz, S. (1993). Effects of intergroup similarity on intergroup relations. *European Journal of Social Psychology, 23,* 581–595.

Rubin, M., & Hewstone, M. (1998). Social identity theory's self-esteem hypothesis: A review and some suggestions for clarification. *Personality and Social Psychology Review, 2,* 40–62.

Rust, M. C. (1996). *Social identity and social categorization.* Unpublished doctoral dissertation, University of Delaware.

Schwartz, S. H. (1992). Universals in the content and structure of values: Theoretical advances and empirical tests in 20 countries. In M. Zanna (Ed.), *Advances in experimental social psychology* (Vol. 25, pp. 1–65). San Diego, CA: Academic Press.

Simon, B., & Hamilton, D. L. (1994). Social identity and self-stereotyping: The effects of relative group size and group status. *Journal of Personality and Social Psychology, 66,* 699–711.

Spears, R., Doosje, B., & Ellemers, N. (1997). Self-stereotyping in the face of threats to group status and distinctiveness: The role of group identification. *Personality and Social Psychology Bulletin, 23,* 538–553.

Stapel, D. A., & Marx, D. M. (2007). Distinctiveness is key: How different types of self–other similarity moderate social comparison effects. *Personality and Social Psychology Bulletin, 33,* 437–448.

Tajfel, H. (1981). *Human groups and social categories.* Cambridge: Cambridge University Press.

Tajfel, H., & Turner, J. C. (1979). An integrative theory of intergroup conflict. In

W. G. Austin & S. Worchel (Eds.), *The social psychology of intergroup relations* (pp. 33–47). Monterey, CA: Brooks/Cole.

Turner, J. C. (1975). Social comparison and social identity: Some prospects for intergroup behaviour. *European Journal of Social Psychology, 5*, 5–34.

Turner, J. C., Hogg, M., Oakes, P., Reicher, S., & Wetherell, M. (1987). *Rediscovering the social group: A self-categorization theory*. Oxford: Blackwell.

Turner, J. C., Hogg, M., Turner, P., & Smith, P. (1984). Failure and defeat as determinants of group cohesiveness. *British Journal of Social Psychology, 23*, 97–111.

Vanbeselaere, N. (1991). The different effects of simple and crossed categorizations: A result of the category differentiation process or of differential category salience? In W. Stroebe & M. Hewstone (Eds.), *European review of social psychology* (Vol. 2, pp. 247–278). Chichester, UK: Wiley.

Vignoles, V. L., Chryssochoou, Z., & Breakwell, G. M. (2000). The distinctiveness principle: Identity, meaning, and the bounds of cultural relativity. *Personality and Social Psychology Review, 4*, 337–354.

Waldzus, S., Mummendey, A., Wenzel, M., & Weber, U. (2003). Towards tolerance: Representations of superordinate categories and perceived ingroup prototypicality. *Journal of Experimental Social Psychology, 39*, 31–47.

Wenzel, M., Mummendey, A., Weber, U., & Waldzus, S. (2003). The ingroup as *pars pro toto*: Projection from the ingroup onto the inclusive category as a precursor to social discrimination. *Personality and Social Psychology Bulletin, 29*, 461–473.

Wit, A. P., & Kerr, N. L. (2002). Me versus just us versus us all: Categorization and cooperation in nested social dilemmas. *Journal of Personality and Social Psychology, 83*, 616–637.

Yamagishi, T., Jin, N., & Kiyonari, T. (1999). Bounded generalized reciprocity: Ingroup boasting and ingroup favoritism. *Advances in Group Processes, 16*, 161–197.

Yuki, M., Maddux, W. W., Brewer, M. B., & Takemura, K. (2005). Cross-cultural differences in relationship- and group-based trust. *Personality and Social Psychology Bulletin, 31*, 48–62.

2 Creative distinctiveness

Explaining in-group bias in minimal groups

Russell Spears
Cardiff University/University of Amsterdam

Jolanda Jetten
University of Queensland/University of Exeter

Daan Scheepers and Sezgin Cihangir
University of Leiden

Creative distinctiveness: Explaining in-group bias in minimal groups

Do we really need another explanation for the minimal in-group bias effect? You might think that we would not pose this question (using this device) unless our answer was in the affirmative, but the short answer presented in this chapter is actually "No!" (bluff is another useful device). So how, you might ask, do you get a chapter of that? Our answer is that the *original* explanation for the effect will do perfectly well, thank you. The problem is that, in our view at least, nobody has properly tested the original explanation. Our cunning plan was to make this original explanation explicit, and to test it. An overview of the results of this quest forms a fitting tribute to Amélie Mummendey who herself has contributed so much to the understanding of intergroup relations generally, and this paradigm in particular. We return to the links between her contribution to the field and the work presented here at the end of the chapter.

So let us start by reminding ourselves of the minimal in-group bias effect, and the original explanation. As most readers of this volume will know, the minimal group paradigm was developed by Tajfel and colleagues (Tajfel, Flament, Billig, & Bundy, 1971) to demonstrate that people could discriminate in favour of their own group without there being any material resources at stake for the members themselves. They showed that people categorized simply on the basis of their preference for painters (Klee vs. Kandinsky) discriminated in favour of other unknown people who shared their preference, in terms of real or symbolic reward allocations. This was an important theoretical point because the dominant and most credible group-level explanation of intergroup discrimination available at the time focused on realistic conflicts over material resources (LeVine & Campbell, 1972; Sherif, 1966).

Tajfel and colleagues plausibly thought that they had found a motive for intergroup discrimination that did not reduce to self-interest or personal motives. After rejecting a "generic norm" explanation (that we discriminate because of a norm of competitiveness) as circular, Tajfel settled on the explanation that groups discriminate in order to achieve a "positive group distinctiveness" – a principle that became one of the building blocks and explanatory principles of social identity theory, and intergroup discrimination in particular (Tajfel & Turner, 1979; see also Mummendey, 1995).

However, further experimental attempts to evaluate the original explanation took a slightly strange path. Because attention focused on the "positive" element in the differentiation explanation, research was side-tracked into what has become known as the "self-esteem hypothesis" (Abrams & Hogg, 1988). The self-esteem hypothesis is the principle that intergroup discrimination (or positive differentiation) can enhance group standing and self-esteem (Abrams & Hogg, 1988, also added a second corollary that low self-esteem could motivate discrimination). The focus on self-esteem meant that the importance of distinctiveness was largely neglected. This was unfortunate because group distinctiveness is an important component of positive group distinctiveness and, as we have argued before, one that is actually closer to the group-level spirit of social identity theory than esteem and enhancement motives (Spears, Jetten, & Scheepers, 2002).

This is not to say that self-esteem is unimportant, and when conceptualized and measured at the group level this can form an important explanation of differentiation between groups, minimal and otherwise. More generally, we do not rule out other explanations of in-group bias in the minimal group paradigm. For example, explanations in terms of interdependence and self-interest have made a comeback in recent years (e.g., Gaertner & Insko, 2000; Stroebe, Lodewijkx, & Spears, 2005). The minimal group effect is probably multiply determined ("over-determined"). For example Diehl (1990) provides a nice overview of some of these competing explanations and a programme of research to test between them. The purpose here is not to disavow other explanations but rather to (re)appraise the role of distinctiveness processes that have somewhat disappeared from view.

As we implied at the very start, this *idea* is not new. We have articulated these theoretical ideas, grounded in social identity theory, and also the earlier work of Tajfel on the meaning of group identity, in earlier theoretical statements (Spears et al., 2002; Spears, Scheepers, Jetten, Doosje, Ellemers, & Postmes, 2004). However in this chapter we aim to provide more evidence for our case than we have hitherto. The gist of our argument is that in minimal groups one reason why people discriminate is because the resulting differentiation creates a meaningful sense of group identity that distinguishes in-group from out-group. We refer to this process as "creative distinctiveness", the process of generating or establishing group distinctiveness where none previously existed.

This process serves an identity function because it helps to define who we are. Importantly, we think that this creative distinctiveness process, though occurring in individual minds, is a group-level process. Thus, in the spirit of social identity theory, group-level phenomena are best explained by group-level processes; reductions to individual-level explanation (personality explanations such as authoritarianism, for example) are not well placed to capture the group forms that discrimination and prejudice often take (Billig, 1976; Reynolds, Turner, & Haslam, 2001; Tajfel, 1979). This is important because one problem with the self-esteem hypothesis is that it too was (in early conceptualizations at least) perhaps too easily reduced to an individualistic enhancement motive. Similarly, more recent attempts to explain the minimal group bias are open to the charge of reducing this group phenomenon to individual motives. For example, Hogg's (2000) subjective uncertainty reduction approach to group differentiation is not immune to this charge. In our research, we attempt to distinguish the group-level meaning associated with creative distinctiveness from the uncertainty reduction model.

Another recent explanation that operates quite explicitly at the individual level is the argument that favouritism reflects the operation of a self-anchoring process or "self-heuristic" in which people project from the individual self to the group as a whole (Cadinu & Rothbart, 1996; Otten, 2002). Given the meaningless nature of minimal groups, relying on knowledge of the self to determine group allegiance (quite literally) makes much sense, and provides an individual-level solution to the lack of meaning. Once again we are not disputing this explanation but argue that creative distinctiveness provides a group-level solution to the provision of meaning.

It is claimed that the laws of physics (Einsteinian as well as Newtonian) break down when applied to the creation of the universe (the "Big Bang"). So it may be with the creation of groups (and creative distinctiveness): "normal" social identity principles may break down when group identities are in the process of being created. Thus, whereas some social identity researchers have argued that group identification can stimulate in-group bias (e.g., Hinkle & Brown, 1990; but see Turner, 1999; Spears, Doosje, & Ellemers, 1999), we propose that the process of creative distinctiveness operates the other way round – group members differentiate *in order* to generate group identification and thus a meaningful group identity. In other words we suggest that we should not look for mediators of in-group bias and differentiation that emerge in minimal groups, but rather we should see such differentiation *as* the mediator (the reason, motive) for group meaning, itself generating group identification and group-esteem. The motor–dynamo metaphor may be useful here to understand this process. In the days before cars and motorbikes had starter motors we had to crank or kick-start these vehicles. Creative distinctiveness can be seen as the "dynamo" that gets group identity and identification kick-started, so to speak.

The early stages of group creation are likely to turn other processes on their head also. For example, a recurring theme in self-categorization theory is that – strategic factors aside – group members who are more prototypical are more likely to display group-level responses like conformity and in-group bias (e.g., Jetten, Spears, & Manstead, 1997). However, from the perspective of the creative distinctiveness process in minimal groups, we might expect exactly the reverse: Those people feeling themselves to be low in prototypicality may lack the sense that they are part of a meaningful group and may need to generate this through in-group bias. We therefore consider the impact of prototypicality and other factors that might affect group meaning in the studies below.

To support our line of argument for the creative distinctiveness process we first present some already published work (Scheepers, Spears, Doosje, & Manstead, 2002). We then report on some work in the pipeline that is even more directly concerned with this theme (Spears, Jetten, & Cihangir, 2008), designed to test creative distinctiveness more directly.

Making sense of minimal groups: Preliminary evidence

In some published research we have found evidence that differentiation in minimal groups seems to serve a different function to that in established groups with group goals and interests (Scheepers et al., 2002). Specifically we argued that in-group bias in more minimal groups serves an *identity* function in so far as differentiation can create meaningful group differences in otherwise meaningless groups. This argument is essentially the creative distinctiveness principle (Spears et al., 2002).

We compared the identity function associated with creative distinctiveness in minimal groups with the "contrast case" of groups that have a clear goal (e.g., of furthering group interests through intergroup competition). We argued that in such cases a more instrumental function comes to the fore; to further group interests in line with realistic group conflict and interdependence approaches (Gaertner & Insko, 2000; LeVine & Campbell, 1972; Sherif, 1966). This does not necessarily mean the identity function becomes unimportant, however, because group identity forms an important basis for group action once it is formed.

In an initial experiment designed to differentiate these functions we created quasi-minimal groups by means of the classic procedure (preference for paintings of Klee or Kandinsky, which we further related to perceptual style). All participants were assigned to the same group of "synthetic perceivers". Participants, working individually at computers, then rated a series of pictures that had been collectively created by members of their own group, or members of the out-group (analytic perceivers) and then rated their collective esteem. After this, participants engaged in a group task where they were asked to choose colours to complete an abstract picture (similar to those they had rated) alternately with three other in-group members. The key manipulation in this study was the feedback accompanying this group task: Half of the participants were told that the task was part of a group competition with other groups, in which the best would win a reward (goal condition). The other participants were not given information that intergroup relations were competitive (no goal condition). Participants then rated in-group and out-group products, and also collective self-esteem again (see Scheepers et al., 2002, for further details of the cover story).

We predicted that groups in both conditions would evaluate products made by their own in-group category more favourably than out-group products at time 1 – serving the identity function and creative distinctiveness – and that this would predict collective self-esteem (enhancing group identity). However, we predicted a two-way interaction such that subsequent in-group bias on the product rating task at time 2 would be higher in the goal than the no-goal condition, as this served the group goal (i.e., competing with the out-group). For the no-goal condition, because group identity had already been formed through positive differentiation (creative distinctiveness, the identity function) we predicted lower levels of in-group bias. This is what we found.

In a second experiment, we extended the design. Participants were given an opportunity to differentiate between group products at time 1 or were not. We also included a group goal manipulation relating to intergroup competition, resulting in a 2×2 design. The rationale here was that the absence of a prior opportunity to differentiate between the groups would exacerbate the need to differentiate in order to create group distinctiveness and a meaningful group identity, especially in the condition where there was no subsequent group goal. However, in the opposite corner of the 2×2 design we predicted that it would be those participants who had created a meaningful identity by means of the differentiation opportunity, and were also given the group goal of competition, who would subsequently positively differentiate the groups on product ratings, albeit for more instrumental reasons.

Results confirmed these predictions. On in-group bias measures of product ratings and a range of other measures (e.g., self-esteem, cohesion, group identification, and group effort on the task) we consistently found a two-way interaction between the differentiation opportunity and group goal factors, with scores highest in the conditions where both factors were absent (consistent with creative distinctiveness, eliciting the identity function) and both were present (eliciting the instrumental function of furthering competition).

This research provides important preliminary evidence for the creative distinctiveness process. However, we should acknowledge that the methods used to manipulate group meaning were somewhat indirect (via group goals). The outcome measure (intergroup differentiation) is also only one indicator of in-group bias and diverges from the classic reward allocations used in classic minimal group studies (see Jetten, Spears, & Postmes, 2004). The groups in these studies were also not as minimal as they could be because painter preference was linked to perceptual styles. These issues raise questions of generalizability to the classic minimal group paradigm. In the line of research discussed below, we therefore model our methods and measures more closely on the classical minimal group paradigm and procedures.

Minimal vs. meaningful groups and creative distinctiveness

Establishing the effect: Study 1

In these studies we used the classic minimal group paradigm in which participants are categorized by painter preference (although assignment to group was actually random). We manipulated the meaningfulness of group identity by providing additional feedback in the meaningful conditions, stating that previous research had shown that painter preference was also associated with personality differences, namely greater extraversion versus a more introverted personality (or vice versa). We chose this personality dimension because most people should be able to construe themselves as having both extraverted and introverted aspects and experiences (most people read books and go to parties), to assure credibility. Pre-testing also showed this to be a relatively neutral distinction. Although there might be some concern about using a personality distinction to define group identity, any personal attribute can in principle become group-defining when shared and displaying "fit" (Oakes, 1987; Simmel, 1955). In the studies we collapsed across extraverted and introverted categorizations and we refer to them as meaningful groups below, as there were few systematic differences between them. The main dependent measure in our design was the degree of in-group bias, which we measured in two standard ways: 1) by means of the Tajfel reward matrices in which group members could award points to anonymous members of the two groups, and 2) by evaluative in-group bias measured in terms of evaluative trait ratings applied to in-group and out-group.

The other key measure in our design was a measure of group identification. As explained earlier, a key indicator of group meaning should be the degree to which people identify with their group. Identification provides a more independent (and arguably less circular) indicator of group meaning than differentiation or distinctiveness measures. We measured group identification twice, once before the in-group bias opportunity and again afterwards, in order to get a more sensitive measure of the effect of differentiation on identification (i.e., controlling for variation at time 1). This relates to our rationale that differentiation should serve to boost post-differentiation identification with the group as a way of enhancing group meaning elicited by the creative distinctiveness process.

The order in which our two measures on in-group bias were presented formed the second factor in this first study. This order could be considered a straightforward counterbalancing procedure but there was also a theoretical consideration behind it. We reasoned that the need to differentiate (positively) in-group from out-group to create group distinctiveness should be strongest on the first measure encountered. This is in line with motivational theories that pose that motivations once satiated or fulfilled will recede (e.g., Kuhl, 1986). We were noncommittal about the strength of any such order effect (or interaction) because in the relatively meaningless minimal situation it is unclear how much participants might differentiate in order to create the group distinctiveness that gives them a sense of group identity.

To analyse the matrices we computed the various pulls associated with in-group bias (see Bourhis, Sachdev, & Gagnon, 1994). The most relevant measures of in-group bias were in-group favouritism (the pull of maximum in-group profit and maximum differentiation on maximum joint profit, averaged over two pull scores, and a similar pull on fairness) and maximum differentiation (the pull of maximum differentiation on maximum in-group profit and maximum joint profit). The evaluative in-group bias measure was derived from scales rating the in-group and the out-group on three positive traits and computing a positive evaluative difference between the two.

Analyses revealed the predicted main effect of in-group bias for both the matrices and the evaluative in-group bias measure. There was no effect of order but there was marginally significant interaction between factors for the evaluative in-group bias measure. Inspection of the means revealed that this followed the predicted pattern: Evaluative in-group bias was highest (and reliable) in the minimal condition where this measure was presented first, whereas it was low (and indeed close to parity for both groups; bias was non-significant) in the three other cells.

So far so good. It seems that our proposal that groups would show more in-group bias when they are minimal than when meaningful was clearly confirmed. This is consistent with our reasoning that discrimination in the minimal group paradigm provides the differentiation and group distinctiveness that give meaning to the group identity. The next step was to gain some insights into the process responsible for the differential pattern of differentiation.

Given our rationale that in-group bias in the minimal groups reflects creative distinctiveness, in order to create a more meaningful group identity, we treated in-group bias as the mediator of group meaning (the latter measured by identification). As a first step we checked for an increase in group identification as a function of the experimental manipulation of group meaning. Because we would expect the meaningful conditions to evoke or imply group identification (albeit not necessarily through intergroup differentiation), we also controlled for identification measured after the manipulation but before the in-group bias measures in these analyses. This analysis indeed revealed a reliable main effect on group identification after the in-group bias measures such that identification was higher in the minimal condition. There was also an interaction between meaning and measure order in this analyses such that identification was highest in the minimal groups when the evaluative bias measure was first, with a reversal of this pattern in the meaningful condition. This pattern is similar to the trend for the evaluative in-group bias measure, and seems to suggest that the creative distinctiveness process is particularly strong for minimal groups when the evaluative bias measure comes first, being associated with increased group identification.

In a final step we entered the various in-group bias measures as predictors to assess whether these could act as mediators of the identification main effect. The maximum differentiation pull measure of in-group bias was the only reliable predictor of identification but this reliably reduced the meaning main effect to non-significance, indicating that this differentiation measure mediated this main effect (Baron & Kenny, 1986). This supports our argument that in-group bias (in this case maximum differentiation) creates group distinctiveness, and boosts identification (and group meaning) as result.

However, we found no evidence that the other in-group bias measures mediated the interaction on post-bias identification. Interestingly though, a measure of prototypicality exhibited the same pattern as the identification and evaluative in-group bias measures. This points to a fairly consistent pattern of indicators of group meaning rating high in the minimal groups when the evaluative bias measure is taken first. It seems that the greater evaluative differentiation found in this condition (prompted by the attempt make the minimal groups meaningful) is not necessary when the reward allocations are first used as the basis for differentiation, providing the creative distinctiveness.

When (positive) evaluative differentiation comes first and is used to create distinctiveness this may make the groups particularly important to group members. We know that the evaluative dimension is one of the most important dimensions of meaning (Osgood, Suci, & Tannenbaum, 1957), and a dimension that is particularly relevant to intergroup relations (Berndsen, Spears, McGarty & van der Pligt, 1998; Schopler & Insko, 1992; Spears, 2002; Tajfel & Turner, 1979). Having been encouraged to perceive one's group as more positive than the other, it may then be more satisfying or even justified to affirm the group in various ways. Self-perception processes may add to this "dynamo" effect (if we first see our group as more positive, it is then easy to identify as a member of a positive group).

How do we interpret the fact that identification and prototypicality are also relatively high in the meaningful groups, but when the matrices are present first? One way to interpret this is in line with the studies of Scheepers et al. (2002), presented earlier, in which we argued that groups that already have an established and meaningful group identity, have a firm foundation for instrumental motives and intergroup competition. Although there was no evidence of an interaction on the reward measures themselves, the very fact of making these reward allocations first may have made salient instrumental motives associated with group membership, namely gaining rewards and benefits for one's own group. This mind-set may have enhanced the meaning of the group (identification, prototypicality) for group members in this condition.

We gain further evidence for these interpretations when we examined the within cell correlations between the various measures of in-group bias and our key indicator of group meaning, group identification. For the minimal group conditions only the evaluative in-group bias and the maximum differentiation measures reliably predicted identification. These are the purest measures of differentiation, and could arguably contribute most to establishing clear group meaning (accentuating differences). However in the meaningful conditions two different measures, the measures of in-group bias (the pull of maximum in-group profit and maximum differentiation on maximum joint profit and on fairness, respectively), reliably predicted identification. These measures of in-group bias are those more typically associated with maximizing in-group rewards (rather than differentiation per se) and are thus closer to instrumental motives of enhancing material outcomes (Scheepers Spears, Doosje, & Manstead, 2006). So group identification is best predicted by those measures of in-group bias that map on to the identity and instrumental group functions in the contexts that make these functions more relevant and salient.

We were also able to rule out the possibility that in-group bias served to enhance (and mediate) certainty at the group and individual levels. The experimental manipulations had no effects on either of these measures, despite the fact that group certainty was quite strongly correlated with group identification. In short, even though there was some evidence that some of the in-group bias measures did correlate with group certainty, there was no evidence that the function of in-group bias here was to reduce subjective uncertainty.

Ruling out some alternative explanations: Study 2

A second study was designed to address a number of possible alternative explanations for the differences in in-group bias found in our first study. One possible problem with the design of the first study is that, because it manipulates the meaning associated with both groups (i.e., introverted versus extraverted, or neither in the minimal case), we cannot determine whether the effects are a result of the meaning associated with the in-group or the out-group (or indeed both). Moreover, because we used a personality dimension to characterize the out-group it is possible that one reason people did not discriminate in the meaningful conditions is that the personality feedback results in greater individuation of out-group members. Individuating the out-group has been shown to reduce discrimination (Wilder, 1978) so this could provide an alternative explanation for the reduced in-group bias in the meaningful conditions.

To address these concerns we attempted to manipulate the meaning of the in-group and out-group independently in this second study. So for example in the in-group meaningful/out-group minimal conditions we informed participants that research had shown that their preference for Painter A was diagnostic of extraversion (or introversion). However, preference for the other painter turned out *not* to be diagnostic of personality. In a third manipulated factor we varied the order of in-group bias measures as before.

We also employed measures of both individuation and group entitativity. We found that members of meaningful groups were not individuated more and meaningful groups were actually seen as more entitative than minimal out-groups, so differential individuation was ruled out as an alternative explanation of the in-group bias effects in Study 1.

Unfortunately, we found no reliable effects on the matrices or the evaluative in-group bias measures. Part of the reason why we did not replicate the minimal versus meaningful group difference may be a result of the increased complexity of the design because of the attempt to disentangle in-group and out-group meaning. However we conducted some further exploratory analyses to examine evidence of some similar process to those found in our first study. Correlational analyses confirmed that all measures of in-group bias (both matrices and evaluative in-group bias) positively predicted group identification. Moreover, neither group certainty nor individual certainty was reliably associated with the in-group bias measures. Although of course we cannot determine the direction of causality from such data, the fact that identification was measured after all in-group bias measures is at least consistent with the relation between in-group bias and identification found in the previous study, and with the argument that differentiation can create distinctiveness and group meaning.

Further analyses were conducted to examine whether prototypicality moderated the effect of the manipulations on in-group bias. To recap, the reasoning here is that (low) prototypicality can itself be taken as an individual difference indicator of a lack of group meaning. A reliable four-way interaction on evaluative differentiation was found between the three manipulated variables (in-group meaning, out-group meaning and order) and measured prototypicality. Although these effects are complex, the pattern of means and slopes make sense in terms of the creative distinctiveness rationale. The highest evaluative in-group bias was found when both groups were defined in minimal terms, especially for people low in prototypicality and when the evaluative in-group bias measure came first. In other words when all the factors predicted to reduce meaning were in place, and when the measure on which the effect occurred was in primary position, evaluative in-group bias was at its highest.

However, as part of this pattern, in-group bias was also high when the in-group was meaningful, when the out-group was minimal, when the matrices were presented first, and among people defined as high in prototypicality. This latter effect could be interpreted as an example of the more instrumentally motivated in-group bias that accompanied groups for whom identity is already established, and where there is a goal to maximize in-group outcomes (arguably made salient by the presentation of the matrices first). Recall in the previous study, that the interactions between meaning and order on identification and prototypicality, in which the matrices were presented first for meaningful groups, boosted these measures and we interpreted this in relation to more instrumental group-serving motives. This finding is in line with evidence that highly prototypical in-group members are the most likely to show group-serving tendencies such as in-group bias (e.g., Jetten et al., 1997). That we find contrasting effects when the in-group is meaningful rather than minimal provides some, albeit tentative, evidence that different process are at play here (see Scheepers et al., 2002).

Replication and extension: Study 3

These ideas remain speculative and so it was necessary to follow up Study 2 with a further study in which we attempted to find further evidence for the effects of the group meaning manipulation. In this next study we also manipulated prototypicality within the group in order to assess its contribution to the sense of group meaning as proposed in our interpretation.

In this experiment we reverted to the same basic paradigm used for our first study in which in-group and out-group members were either differentially defined in terms of the extraversion–introversion distinction (meaningful groups) or not (minimal groups). In order to manipulate prototypicality, at the beginning of the experiment we presented participants with some personality and visual problem solving tasks, and after the group categorization procedure participants were given feedback about whether they were prototypical for their group, ostensibly on the basis of their score on the personality and problem solving measures. Using graphical feedback their position in the group was indicated at the centre of the (bell curve) distribution (i.e., prototypical) or towards a tail of the distribution (see Jetten et al., 1997).

To recap the rationale, we predicted that in-group bias would be stronger in the minimal than in the meaningful conditions, and also that in-group bias would be stronger for people low in prototypicality. Results revealed main effects of the meaning manipulation on the two in-group bias pull scores (maximum differentiation and maximum in-group profit on maximum joint profit, and maximum differentiation and maximum in-group profit on fairness, respectively) and the evaluative in-group bias measure. The means were in the predicted direction: all in-group bias scores were significantly higher in the minimal condition than in the meaningful condition.

The maximum differentiation pull score did not vary as a function of the meaning manipulation, although the means were again in the predicted direction. However, a significant effect of prototypicality was found on this indicator of in-group bias. As predicted, *low* prototypicality was associated with increased in-group bias. Although all means were also in this same predicted direction for the prototypicality manipulation, only the maximum differentiation and maximum in-group profit on maximum joint profit in-group bias pull also approached conventional significance levels. There were no reliable interactions between the two manipulated factors.

In this study we found no difference on group identification as a function of the manipulated variables (in contrast to Study 1). This may be partly attributable to a failure to employ a pre-measure of group identification that would allow us to control for any variations in identification prior to differentiation. However, as before we examined the within-cell correlations to gain further insight into how the various measures of in-group bias might relate to indictors of group meaning, such as group identification.

In the minimal group condition, three out of four in-group bias measures significantly correlated with in-group identification, including all pull scores. Only the correlation between identification and the evaluative differentiation measure was not significant. None of the in-group bias measures was reliably associated with either measure of certainty. In the meaningful conditions, by contrast, none of the in-group bias measures reliably predicted group identification (and neither did the certainty scales).

Overall then, the within-cell correlation patterns provide further support for the creative distinctiveness prediction that in-group bias should predict identification particularly under more minimal conditions. Once again, there was very little evidence for group certainty as a motive or reason explaining in-group bias.

To summarize, this study was important because it replicated the basic minimal versus meaningful effect established in our first study. This supports our suspicion that some of the complexities of the "disentangling" manipulation in the second study may have been the reason why we did not observe the effect there. Moreover, in the latest study we were able to follow up some of the exploratory internal analyses based on the role of group prototypicality and confirm that *low* prototypicality can drive in-group bias in line with the creative distinctiveness prediction.

Summary

To summarize, in this research programme we have generated cumulative evidence supporting our rationale that minimal groups will produce more in-group bias on both reward allocation measures and evaluative ratings. Although not all studies produced reliable results on all measures, where differences were found the meaningful groups produced less discrimination than the minimal groups. We also gained some insights into the creative distinctiveness and differentiated meaning making process that we propose underlies this by showing that intergroup differentiation mediated effects of the meaning manipulation on identification (Study 1) and by showing that in-group bias measures predicted group identification primarily under more minimal (meaningless) conditions in all studies.

As well as manipulating meaning directly by associating group membership with a personality dimension (introversion/extraversion) we found conceptually similar effects when meaning was manipulated in terms of one's relation to the group (prototypicality). Because prototypicality is a group-level property this provides some reassurance that group-level meaning is the crucial factor in these studies. This point is important because by using the personality dimension of introversion–extraversion as our manipulated source of meaning, a critic could argue that it is meaning more generally (or personally), rather than in relation to the intergroup context, that is the crucial factor here.

In some further research we have addressed this issue more explicitly by manipulating feedback about the nature of the group, and specifically whether the group was formed by interpersonal bonds of mutual liking between group members, or by identification with the group as an entity in itself (see Postmes, Spears, Lee, & Novak, 2005; Prentice, Miller, & Lightdale, 1994). This research revealed evidence that when the group was not defined as a distinctive entity but as the sum of the interpersonal bonds within it, in-group bias increased in a similar fashion to the minimal group control condition (Spears et al., 2008). This suggests once again that it is group-level meaning (attributes that define the group as distinct at the intergroup level) that provides the distinctiveness that abrogates the need for differentiation or discrimination.

Final thoughts, implications, and Amélie-orations

We have presented evidence here for the creative distinctiveness process as a new take on the old group distinctiveness principle, originally evoked by Tajfel and Turner in social identity theory, as an explanation of ingroup bias in the minimal group paradigm. This provides a group-level analysis and explanation of in-group bias in minimal groups that is faithful to the group-level analysis of the social identity approach. Rather than "old wine in a new bottle", we have simply opened a nice bottle of vintage wine. In social psychology just as in viticulture, sometimes old is also best (or wiser).

But what do these processes tell us about discrimination and intergroup relations in real life? Although we rarely encounter minimal groups in real life, and the groups to which we belong to rarely if ever start life as such, we think there are nevertheless some important lessons that can translate to the outside world. There are many occasions where we take on new group identities and are unclear about the meaning of these group identities. Established group memberships may sometimes have little group meaning on certain dimensions or in new situations that are not (yet) diagnostic of group membership. Moreover, as we have shown, concepts such as group prototypicality, that are eminently applicable to naturally occurring groups, have implications for group meaning and creative distinctiveness processes more generally. Creative distinctiveness may be particularly relevant in such cases – operating as a "dynamo" to kick-start our own group induction, and commitment towards novel and newly acquired groups.

Indeed research confirms that new and peripheral group members (i.e., those typically low in prototypicality) can be among the most partisan towards out-groups (e.g., Noel, Wann, & Branscombe, 1995). This finding has previously been interpreted as reflecting a strategic ingratiation processes, but intergroup differentiation motivated by creative distinctiveness may also genuinely increase identification and a sense of belonging to the group. This may be functional if it helps us to fit in and enhances our feeling that we belong. However, it can also be dysfunctional when this generates conflict between groups, where there is no apparent a priori basis for it. Such findings help to explain how easy it is to generate differences between groups and loyalties within them.

Finally, it is important to reflect on how these findings relate to the impressive body of work of the person to whom this festschrift is dedicated. The key themes of group distinctiveness and group meaning are important ones that recur in many aspects of Amélie Mummendey's work, throughout her career. For example, a series of studies and papers grouped under the (sub)title "different just means better" gets to the crux of the elements that comprise positive distinctiveness, which lies at the heart of social identity theory, and our story here. Although we argue that (group) distinctiveness is not reducible to positive evaluation and enhancement, clearly evaluative and distinctiveness processes are both important parts of the story (two main effects and an interaction, so to speak). Indeed, we found that when evaluative differentiation preceded reward allocations this seemed to give the evaluative side of positive distinctiveness a boost on subsequent measures.

As with our focus here, Amélie has also paid close attention to the minimal group paradigm, and like us persevered with this paradigm where others had perhaps lost interest or moved on. In fact she quite literally saw positive as well as negative value in an analysis of this paradigm. Her analysis of the positive–negative asymmetry of reward allocations provided proof that participants meaningfully differentiate between the different forms of differentiation that reward and punishment imply (e.g., Mummendey, 1995; Mummendey & Otten, 1998). The fact that people were sensitive to the dimension of differentiation shows that they were not always ready to differentiate at any cost, especially if it meant that this might undermine a positive group image (see also Reynolds, Turner, & Haslam, 2000). In short, this also depends on the meaning of differentiation in context.

More recently the influential work on the in-group projection model (e.g., Mummendey & Wenzel, 1999; Waldzus & Mummendey, 2004), once again shows the value of group-level meaning that has been a recurring theme here. We have been pushing the argument that our analysis requires a group-level understanding that does not reduce meaning to an individual-level property, an abstraction of generic coherence or uncertainty reduction, for example, but is irreducibly "groupy". The in-group projection model extends and develops the self-categorization principles underlying this argument, by showing that group-level meaning itself only has full content and meaning when we consider the higher order frame of reference in which groups are compared (the superordinate group that provides the comparative context). The model makes clear that when addressing the issue of group meaning we often need to move up to higher floors in the building to get a better perspective on what our group means, looking down on the broader context, rather than moving down to the basement of reductionism, so to speak.

In short, although always open to alternative perspectives I would claim that Amélie has been a stalwart proponent of the group level of analysis throughout her research. In a brief moment of levity I once proposed in a Jena presentation, where I was invited by Amélie to defend the group level against the primacy of the individual self, that Amélie's interest in the group level of analysis was perhaps inevitable. Not only was she the leader of one of the foremost centres of intergroup research in the world, but she formed a three-person group all by herself ("Amélie, mum and I").

And of course, in much of her research and writing, Amélie tackled the issue of group distinctiveness explicitly and head on. Indeed the subtitle of one of her papers refers to two of the key players in our story here, group distinctiveness and intergroup differentiation, as "an old couple living in divorce" (Mummendey, 1995). Well, it may seem too late, some 13 or so years on, to call off the divorce (maybe 13 is a lucky number), but we hope to have shown in this chapter that maybe the marriage was not so bad after all, and Amélie has been a good marriage guidance counsellor along the way. "Amelioration" after all means relieving ills and changing things for the better, and although it is beyond our ability to solve all the intergroup problems of the world, Amélie, as one of our foremost ambassadors has certainly given us important tools to better understand if not improve relations between groups.

Acknowledgements

Our thanks go to Kai Sassenberg and Sabine Otten for their feedback and support in the production of this chapter and also to an anonymous reviewer for their insightful feedback.

References

Abrams, D., & Hogg, M. (1988). Comments on the motivational status of self-esteem in social identity and intergroup discrimination. *European Journal of Social Psychology*, *18*, 317–334.

Baron, R. M., & Kenny, D. A. (1986). The moderator–mediator variable distinction in social psychological research: Conceptual, strategic and statistical considerations. *Journal of Personality and Social Psychology*, *51*, 1173–1182.

Berndsen, M., Spears, R., McGarty, C., & van der Pligt, J. (1998). Dynamics of differentiation: Similarity as a precursor and product of stereotype formation. *Journal of Personality and Social Psychology*, *74*, 1451–1463.

Billig, M. (1976). *Social psychology and intergroup relations*. London: Academic Press.

Bourhis, R. Y., Sachdev, I., & Gagnon, A. (1994). Intergroup research with the Tajfel matrices: Methodological notes. In M. P. Zanna & J. M. Olson (Eds.), *The social psychology of prejudice: The Ontario symposium* (Vol. 7, pp. 209–232). Hillsdale, NJ: Lawrence Erlbaum Associates, Inc.

Cadinu, M. R., & Rothbart, M. (1996). Self-anchoring and differentiation processes in the minimal group setting. *Journal of Personality and Social Psychology*, *70*, 661–677.

Diehl, M. (1990). The minimal group paradigm: Theoretical explanations and empirical findings. *European Review of Social Psychology, 1*, 263–292.

Gaertner, L., & Insko C. A. (2000). Intergroup discrimination in the minimal group paradigm: Categorization, reciprocation or fear? *Journal of Personality and Social Psychology, 79*, 77–94.

Hinkle, S., & Brown, R. (1990). Intergroup comparisons and social identity: Some links and lacunae. In D. Abrams & M. A. Hogg (Eds.), *Social identity theory: Constructive and critical advances* (pp. 48–70). New York: Springer-Verlag.

Hogg, M. A. (2000). Subjective uncertainty reduction through self-categorization: A motivational theory of social identity processes and group phenomena. *European Review of Social Psychology, 11*, 223–255.

Jetten, J., Spears, R., & Manstead, A. S. R. (1997). Identity threat and prototypicality: Combined effects on intergroup discrimination and collective self-esteem. *European Journal of Social Psychology, 27*, 635–657.

Jetten, J., Spears, R., & Postmes, T. (2004). Intergroup distinctiveness and differentiation: A meta-analytic integration. *Journal of Personality and Social Psychology, 86*, 862–879.

Kuhl, J. (1986). Motivation and information processing: A new look at decision making, dynamic change and action control. In R. M. Sorrentino & E. T. Higgins (Eds.), *Handbook of motivation and cognition* (Vol. 1, pp. 404–434). New York: Guilford.

LeVine, R. A., & Campbell, D. T. (1972). *Ethnocentrism: Theories of conflict, ethnic attitudes and group behavior.* New York: Wiley.

Mummendey, A. (1995). Positive distinctiveness and intergroup discrimination: An old couple living in divorce. *European Journal of Social Psychology, 25*, 657–670.

Mummendey, A., & Otten, S. (1998). Positive–negative asymmetry in social discrimination. *European Review of Social Psychology, 9*, 107–143.

Mummendey, A., & Wenzel, M. (1999). Social discrimination and tolerance in intergroup relations: Reactions to intergroup difference. *Personality and Social Psychology Review, 3*, 158–174.

Noel, J. G., Wann, D., & Branscombe, N. (1995). Peripheral in-group membership status and public negativity toward out-groups. *Journal of Personality and Social Psychology, 68*, 127–137.

Oakes, P. J. (1987). The salience of social categories. In J. C. Turner, M. A. Hogg, P. J. Oakes, S. D. Reicher, & M. S. Wetherell (Eds.), *Rediscovering the social group: A self-categorization theory* (pp. 117–141). Oxford: Blackwell.

Osgood, C. E., Suci, H. J., & Tannenbaum, P. H. (1957). *The measurement of meaning.* Urbana, IL: University of Illinois Press.

Otten, S. (2002). "Me and us" or "us and them"? The self as a heuristic for defining novel in-groups. *European Review of Social Psychology, 13*, 1–34.

Postmes, T., Spears, R., Lee, A. T., & Novak, R. J. (2005). Individuality and social influence in groups: Inductive and deductive routes to group identity. *Journal of Personality and Social Psychology, 89*, 747–763.

Prentice, D. A., Miller, D. T., & Lightdale, J. R. (1994). Asymmetries in attachments to groups and to their members: Distinguishing between common-identity and common-bond groups. *Personality and Social Psychology Bulletin, 20* (Special Issue: The self and the collective), 484–493.

Reynolds, K. J., Turner, J. C., & Haslam. S. A. (2000). When are we better than them and they worse than us? A closer look at social discrimination in positive and negative domains. *Journal of Personality and Social Psychology, 78,* 64–80.

Reynolds, K. J., Turner, J. C., & Haslam, S. A. (2001). The role of personality and group factors in explaining prejudice. *Journal of Experimental Social Psychology, 37,* 427–434.

Scheepers, D., Spears, R., Doosje, B., & Manstead, A. S. R. (2002). Integrating identity and instrumental approaches to intergroup differentiation: Different contexts, different motives. *Personality and Social Psychology Bulletin, 28,* 1455–1467.

Scheepers, D., Spears, R., Doosje, B., & Manstead, A. S. R. (2006). Diversity in in-group bias: Structural factors, situational features, and social functions. *Journal of Personality and Social Psychology, 90,* 944–960.

Schopler, J., & Insko, A. (1992). The discontinuity effect in interpersonal and intergroup relations: Generality and mediation. *European Review of Social Psychology, 2,* 121–151.

Sherif, M. (1966). *Group conflict and co-operation: Their social psychology.* London: Routledge & Kegan Paul.

Simmel, G. (1955). *The web of group-affiliations.* New York: The Free Press. (Translation of "Die Kreuzung sozialer Kreise", Soziologie (München: Duncker & Humblot) by Reinhard Bendix).

Spears, R. (2002). Four degrees of stereotype formation: Differentiation by any means necessary. In C. McGarty, V. Yzerbyt, & R. Spears (Eds.), *Stereotypes as explanations: The formation of meaningful beliefs about social groups* (pp. 127–156). Cambridge: Cambridge University Press.

Spears, R., Doosje, B., & Ellemers, N. (1999). Commitment and the context of social perception. In N. Ellemers, R. Spears, & B. Doosje (Eds.), *Social identity: Context, commitment, content* (pp. 59–83). Oxford: Blackwell.

Spears, R., Jetten, J., & Cihangir, S. (2008). *Creative distinctiveness and minimal in-group bias.* Unpublished manuscript, Cardiff University, UK.

Spears, R., Jetten, J., & Scheepers, D. (2002). Distinctiveness and the definition of collective self: A tripartite model. In A. Tesser, J. V. Wood, & D. A. Stapel (Eds.). *Self and motivation: Emerging psychological perspectives* (pp. 147–171). Lexington, MA: APA.

Spears, R, Scheepers, D., Jetten, J., Doosje, B., Ellemers, N., & Postmes, T. (2004). Entitativity, group distinctiveness and social identity: Getting and using social structure. In V. Yzerbyt, C. M. Judd, & O. Corneille (Eds.), *The psychology of group perception: Contributions to the study of homogeneity, entitativity and essentialism* (pp. 293–316). Philadelphia: Psychology Press.

Stroebe, K. E., Lodewijkx, H. F. M., & Spears, R. (2005). Do unto others as they do unto you: Reciprocity and social identification as determinants of in-group favoritism. *Personality and Social Psychology Bulletin, 31,* 831–846.

Tajfel, H. (1979). Individuals and groups in social psychology. *British Journal of Social and Clinical Psychology, 18,* 183–190.

Tajfel, H., Flament, C., Billig, M. G., & Bundy, R. F. (1971). Social categorization and intergroup behaviour. *European Journal of Social Psychology, 1,* 149–177.

Tajfel, H., & Turner, J. C. (1979). An integrative theory of intergroup conflict. In W. G. Austin & S. Worchel (Eds.), *The social psychology of intergroup relations* (pp. 33–48). Monterey, CA: Brooks/Cole.

Turner, J. C. (1999). Some current issues in research on social identity and self-categorization theories. In N. Ellemers, R. Spears, & B. Doosje (Eds.), *Social identity: Context, commitment, content* (pp. 6–34). Oxford: Blackwell.

Waldzus, S., & Mummendey, A. (2004). Inclusion in a superordinate category, ingroup prototypicality, and attitudes towards outgroups. *Journal of Experimental Social Psychology, 40,* 466–477.

Wilder, D. A. (1978). Reduction of intergroup discrimination through individuation of the outgroup. *Journal of Personality and Social Psychology, 36,* 1361–1374.

3   The ingroup projection model

Sven Waldzus

*Instituto Superior de Ciências do Trabalho e da Empresa
(ISCTE)*

Sometimes we do not like a certain group of people. We simply cannot stand them. They did not do anything particular to us. The problem is rather that they are what they are: Different. In 1999, Mummendey and Wenzel (1999) presented an approach that tries to explain intergroup conflict by means of an analysis of our evaluative response towards outgroups that are different from us. Their theoretical framework, which has become known as the "Ingroup Projection Model", integrates three old themes in social psychology: Self-relevance of social categorization and psychological group formation (Allport, 1954; Tajfel & Forgas, 1981; Turner, 1987), the notion of proto-typicality in intra-category differentiation (Rosch, 1978), and social projec-tion (Allport, 1924; Krueger, 2007). Based on this analysis, they developed ideas on how to overcome intergroup conflict without abandoning intergroup differences by creating a context in which different groups may be able to respect or at least tolerate each other. Since then, much empirical research has been done that supports their ideas, and which has also inspired several theoretical advancements and elaborations of the original approach.

The others' difference

How do we usually evaluate others, particularly other groups? One popular answer to this question is the idea of ethnocentrism. When Sumner (1906) described traditional customs and conventions ("mores") of people all over the world, including pre-industrial societies, he defined ethnocentrism straightforwardly as follows (Sumner, 1906, p. 13):

> the technical name of this view of things in which one's own group is the centre of everything, and all others are scaled and rated with reference to it. . . Each group nourishes its own pride and vanity, boasts itself superior, exalts its own divinities, and looks with contempt on outsiders.

In established cultures, customs are usually taken for granted, rarely ques-tioned within a group, except in times of socio-economic or geopolitical change. He listed an overwhelming number of examples, including the ancient

Greeks considering everybody else as barbarians. Probably everybody can name one or several examples of such an ethnocentric perspective from their own experience or from hearsay. However, in our complex societies things are not always that easy.

The ethnocentric response is neither the only possible one, nor is it trivial. Sometimes we like others, not *although*, but rather *because* they are different. Northern Europeans sometimes sympathize with the Southern Europeans because they associate with the Mediterranean lifestyle certain aspects of quality of life that they miss. Since World War II, US pop-symbols have been adopted by adolescents all over the world, because they are "cool", and in German universities students of physics are sometimes admired by students of biology and chemistry, because the subjects they study appear to be more difficult or scientifically more fundamental than their own. In other cases, we can easily accept a group's difference, since it has no relevance for us. Our response is neutral, indifferent or interested at most. Hardly anyone in western societies cares if people living deep in the Amazon jungle appear naked on a TV screen in a documentary, something that would be considered most of the time unacceptable when done by any one of "us".

If we do look at others in an ethnocentric way, this is not trivial, since it requires a psychological explanation: Why does it happen that we often take our own group's values and norms as a standard not only for our own group, but also for others that by definition do not belong to us? If others are not like us, why do we measure them with the same standard? A fish is a fish and a bird is a bird. Who would blame a fish for not having feathers and being unable to fly?

Thus, in order to understand when and why we sometimes devalue an outgroup because of its difference, a psychological model is needed that specifies the predictors and processes responsible for these kinds of evaluations.

Self-categorization and relative prototypicality as a basis for the evaluation of outgroups

Social categorization is not neutral, since it potentially involves us as group members. When thinking of a group, the question whether we are in it or not matters (Tajfel & Forgas, 1981). In decades of research on intergroup bias an impressive amount of knowledge has been accumulated that links categorization into ingroup and outgroup with ingroup favoritism (e.g., Hewstone, Rubin, & Willis, 2002). One prominent explanation of this link is our desire to feel good about ourselves. It is a general social psychological principle that people normally tend to value "me and mine" (Smith & Mackie, 2007). People compare their ingroups with relevant outgroups and under certain conditions they may engage in social competition in order to achieve or maintain a positive social identity, something that can be acquired through positive distinctiveness from relevant comparison outgroups (Tajfel & Turner, 1986). However, a closer look at the research inspired by this social identity approach reveals that it speaks more to our ways of evaluating our own group positively than to our hardly deniable tendency to evaluate outgroups negatively. While "ingroup love" can well explain a striving for positive ingroup distinctiveness, it hardly can explain "outgroup hate" (Brewer, 2001). Moreover, what does it actually mean to be "positively distinct"?

Self-categorization theory (Turner, 1987), which is the theoretical basis of the ingroup projection model, answers the latter question by incorporating the notion of categorization and prototypicality into the explanation of psychological group formation. It assumes that part of our self-concept is categorical knowledge, representing social groups as self-categories that we are in (ingroups), or not (outgroups). These self-categories differ from each other not only in their domain, but also in their level of inclusiveness, so that less inclusive categories (e.g., biologists) are included in more inclusive ones (e.g., natural scientists), which themselves can be included in even more inclusive categories (e.g., scientists, human beings). Within such a hierarchy, less inclusive ingroups and outgroups are comparable with each other, because (and only if) they are sub-categories of the same superordinate category. Social scientists are comparable with natural scientists because they are all scientists.

Within categories, members, as well as sub-categories, differ in terms of their prototypicality, that is, in the degree to which they are representative exemplars of that category (Rosch, 1978; see also Spears, Jetten, Scheepers, & Cihangir, chapter 2 in this volume). Note that although research on category representation has meanwhile shown that categories are not necessarily stored in memory as abstract prototypes, it is beyond doubt that exemplars differ in terms of prototypicality (Smith, 1998). Penguins or chickens are less prototypical birds than robins. In the same way, natural and social scientists may differ in the degree to which they are prototypical scientists.

At this point it is important to remember that a superordinate category that includes ingroup and outgroup is also an ingroup, but on a higher level of inclusiveness, and that, if it is self-relevant, people tend to evaluate it positively. Scientists usually think that being a scientist is a good thing. The interesting implication of this is that the more prototypical a subgroup is for that category, the more similar it is to something positive. That makes prototypes of superordinate self-categories standards of value-laden comparisons between ingroups and outgroups. Accordingly, one of the hypotheses of self-categorization theory is that (Turner, 1987, p. 61):

> ethnocentrism, attraction to one's own group as a whole, depends upon the perceived prototypicality of the ingroup in comparison with relevant outgroups (relative prototypicality) in terms of the valued superordinate self-category that provides the basis for the intergroup comparison.

Hence, positive distinctiveness of an ingroup means that the ingroup is more prototypical than the outgroup for a positively valued superordinate self-category.

As a logical consequence, Mummendey and Wenzel (1999) conclude that the relative prototypicality of the ingroup is not only positively related to attraction to the ingroup, but also negatively related to attraction to the outgroup. The higher the relative prototypicality of the ingroup, the lower is by definition the relative prototypicality of the outgroup, and, thus, the more negative (or less positive) is the evaluation of the outgroup. A natural scientist who thinks that natural scientists are more prototypical (i.e., more scientific) than social scientists will not really appreciate what social scientists do, in particular, what they do in their scientific work differently than natural scientists.

The hypothesis, that prototypicality matters for the evaluation of a group (Turner, 1987) had not been tested empirically until Mummendey and Wenzel (1999) moved the question of outgroup evaluations to the top of the agenda. Since then, however, several studies have been conducted in which the relative prototypicality of an ingroup is measured together with attitudes towards the outgroup. In a series of studies, German participants had less positive attitudes towards Poles, Italians or the British, the more they considered Germans – in comparison with the respective outgroup – to be prototypical Europeans (Waldzus, Mummendey, Wenzel, & Weber, 2003; Waldzus, Mummendey, & Wenzel, 2005). In the same vein, the more psychology students considered themselves to be prototypical students compared to business students, the less positive were their attitudes towards them (Wenzel, Mummendey, Weber, & Waldzus, 2003). In a meta-analysis summarizing over 26 studies within various intergroup contexts, Wenzel, Mummendey, and Waldzus (2007) found a moderate but substantial negative average correlation between relative ingroup prototypicality and positive attitudes towards the outgroup (Figure 3.1).

When thinking of prototypicality as a criterion for group evaluation, it is important to keep in mind that inclusion in the superordinate category is a necessary condition for such a criterion to be applied. A chicken is a non-prototypical bird, but a fish is no bird at all. Waldzus and Mummendey (2004) found that attitudes of Germans towards Poles only depended on their relative prototypicality when Europe was made salient as a superordinate category, since Poles and Germans are both subgroups of Europeans. In contrast, when Western Europe was made salient as a more inclusive category that includes Germans but not Poles, attitudes towards Poles were independent of their (dis)similarity to Western Europeans. These findings were replicated in a second study, showing that attitudes of single parenting mothers towards single parenting fathers were correlated with their relative prototypicality for the superordinate category of single parents, but not with their similarity to the prototype of mothers, which is also a more inclusive category but does not include single parenting fathers.

Thus, the borders of superordinate categories actually mark the scope of applicability of category-related standards. This can explain why sometimes the fact that a group is different from us does not contribute to our evaluation

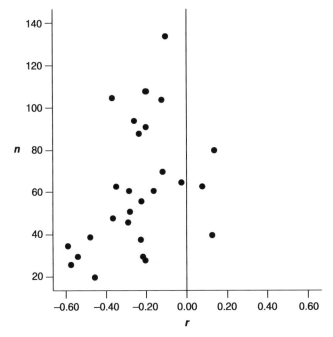

Figure 3.1 Correlations between attitudes towards the outgroup and relative prototypicality of the ingroup compared to the outgroup (*r*), in 27 studies with
29 hypothesis tests and a total *N* of 1842 participants (*n* = sample size for
each test; data from Wenzel, Mummendey, & Waldzus, 2007).

of that group. Natural scientists would criticize social scientists, but not
musicians, for not being scientific enough.

One interesting consequence of using category prototypes as standards for
comparison is that evaluations of groups depend on the salient contexts and
differ from domain to domain. Categories like Europeans and Students are
quite general and thus may have an influence on rather global attitudes.
However, more specific superordinate categories allow for more differentiated
evaluations. For instance, in the study with single parenting mothers evaluating single parenting fathers, relative prototypicality in terms of being a
single parent was only related to evaluations of single fathers' ability to raise
and educate children, but not to their general attractiveness (Waldzus &
Mummendey, 2004).

Projection and disagreement as a source of intergroup conflict

With prototypicality as a common and adaptive – as it is context- sensitive –
basis for group evaluation, everything could end up in harmony. All groups
could agree on their relative standing within valued superordinate categories.
The more prototypical a group is, the more it would be respected by its own

members and by other groups in terms of what is relevant in a particular superordinate category. Surely, such harmonious intergroup relations exist, in which groups accept justified differences in reputation based on shared perceptions of differences in prototypicality. However, as mentioned above, our self-involvement has an impact on how we see our own groups and others. Moreover, compared to non-social categories, social categories are less clearly defined by observable facts, and their definition is very much a matter of social construction. This invites debate, and groups may disagree on the definition of what it means to be a good representative of the superordinate category, that is, of what is prototypical. Social scientists may have a different idea of what real science is than natural scientists.

Mummendey and Wenzel (1999) assume that group members are inclined to frame the standard of comparison in a way that makes their own group appear to be prototypical. According to them, outgroups are negatively evaluated because of their difference if two conditions come together: (a) if they are included together with the ingroup in a more inclusive, superordinate self-category rendering both groups comparable on relevant dimensions (*inclusion*), and (b) if ingroup members project distinct characteristics, attributes, values, norms, etc. of their own group to the superordinate category (*ingroup projection*). Thus, ethnocentrism is the outcome of a combination of inclusion and ingroup projection. The superordinate category, which is a reference standard for all subgroup comparisons, is seen in an ethnocentric way as being more similar to the ingroup than to the outgroup. The ingroup is taken as a *pars pro toto* and appears to be in line with expectations derived from the superordinate prototype. Conversely, the outgroup is not only different from the ingroup, but also appears to deviate from this superordinate prototype.

Ingroup projection can be considered as a particular case of social projection. While projection has played a prominent role in psychopathology (e.g., Freud, 1917/1999; Holmes & Houston, 1971), social psychologists have studied social projection as a principle that is relevant when we think of and evaluate others (Holyoak & Gordon, 1983). It is defined as the tendency to believe that one's own thoughts, feelings and behaviors are shared by others (Allport, 1924; Krueger 2007). Just like social projection in general, ingroup projection is not a directly observable process. That is why in empirical research it is usually defined by the outcome of such a generalization process, namely as an increased overlap between the definition of the ingroup and the definition of the superordinate category.

Evidence for such an overlap has been found in a study by Waldzus, Mummendey and Wenzel (2005), which made use of the flexibility of stereotyping in varying frames of reference. German participants were asked to compare themselves with different outgroups, namely either with Italians or with the British. As expected, Germans did not see themselves the same way in the two conditions. Compared to the Italians they characterized themselves for instance as more reserved and stiff, while compared to the British they thought they had tastier meals and were more companionable. Evidence for ingroup projection would be obtained if these variations in the German self-stereotype were mirrored by parallel variations in the European stereotype. This was indeed what was found. When, because of the manipulation of the comparison outgroup, the Germans' self-stereotype changed slightly from being reserved and stiff in the direction of having tastier meals and being more companionable, the same happened for the stereotype of Europeans.

Overall, the German participants saw Europeans as more similar to the Italians than to the British, but this was less the case when they compared themselves with Italians than when they compared themselves with the British. What is exciting about this result is that from a simple information integration point of view (Anderson, 1981), one would assume the opposite: If Italians are among the two groups to which participants have to pay attention, Europeans should appear to be more Italian than in a condition in which Italians are not mentioned at all. However, the opposite was the case. Those German participants who had to compare themselves with Italians, and, thus, saw themselves as very different from them, also saw Europeans to be less "Italian" compared to those German participants who compared themselves with the British.

Recently, Bianchi, Mummendey, Steffens, and Yzerbyt (2007) conducted research with response time data revealing that ingroup projection can occur automatically, outside people's conscious awareness. In a study with both Italian and German participants they used a subliminal semantic priming paradigm in which words comprising three group labels (i.e., "Italian", "German" and "European") were presented as primes for only a few milliseconds on a computer-screen. After each prime, participants had to recognize words as target stimuli, which were attributes that varied in their valence as well as in their relevance to the groups under consideration. As predicted, Italian participants were faster in recognizing typical Italian rather than typical German characteristics following the prime "European". In contrast, German participants showed a spontaneous association between the prime "European" and typical German characteristics. Valence had no impact on the results. Moreover, in a further study Bianchi et al. found that these associations between the ingroup stereotype and the stereotype of Europeans were sensitive to the comparison context, just as in the results of Waldzus et al. (2005) mentioned above.

Further evidence for ingroup projection was found in studies comparing the perspectives of different groups within the same intergroup context. If all groups project, so goes the idea, two groups within the same superordinate category should disagree about their relative prototypicality. Social scientists should consider themselves to be comparatively more scientific than they are seen by natural scientists and vice versa. Such a disagreement has been found in various studies and different intergroup contexts. Students of different subjects disagree about their prototypicality for the category students (e.g., psychology vs. business administration, Wenzel et al., 2003). Different subgroups of bikers (chopper bikers vs. sport bikers), teachers (primary-school teachers vs. secondary-school teachers) and Germans (East Germans vs. West Germans) see themselves as relatively more prototypical of the larger category than they are seen by members of the respective outgroup (Waldzus, Mummendey, Wenzel, & Boettcher, 2004). In the same vein, Black Americans associate America-related words more strongly with the group of Black Americans than do White and Asian Americans (Devos & Banaji, 2005).

The fact that groups disagree on their relative prototypicality is extremely important for the study of intergroup conflicts. Projection leads to conflicting world views not only in terms of preferences for one or the other group, but also in terms of what is considered an adequate treatment of members of certain groups: importantly, being prototypical relates to social justice. Self-categories are not only sources of group-based attraction (Hogg & Hains, 1996), but also of social status, which includes specific privileges that are associated with group membership. Scientists have a certain reputation as experts and a right to receive funding for their research. Differences in relative prototypicality between groups legitimize differences in social status and entitlements (Wenzel, 2004; see also Wenzel, chapter 4 in this volume). Weber, Mummendey, and Waldzus (2002, Study 1), found that business administration (BA) students, who consider BA students from a university to be more prototypical than BA students from a polytechnic school, also consider status differences between these two groups legitimate. The same was found for Germans considering themselves more prototypical European than Poles (Study 2) and for members of artificial groups created in the laboratory (Study 3).

Thus, when groups disagree about their relative prototypicality, this can lead to intergroup conflicts about the legitimacy of status differences and the equal or unequal distribution of resources. The more groups disagree about their prototypicality, the more illegitimacy is perceived by one or the other group, and the stronger should be the intergroup conflict. While groups may or may not see intergroup difference in itself to be a problem, they very likely feel threatened and questioned in their world view and in their beliefs about themselves when confronted with an outgroup that disagrees with their values and sometimes allegedly legitimate superiority.

Intergroup discrimination as disagreement on relative prototypicality

The explanation of how disagreement on relative prototypicality triggers intergroup conflict has consequences for our understanding of intergroup discrimination. In the studies above, the diverging perspective of the respective outgroup has been taken as a criterion to detect ingroup projection, since in most cases it is impossible to say objectively what is the "true" level of prototypicality and how far a group exaggerates this prototypicality as a result of projection. Although we know that if there is disagreement on relative prototypicality "someone" does project, we can hardly say which of the groups does it more than the other. If natural scientists were to claim that they are more prototypical scientists than social scientists, and social scientists were to disagree with that, who would be right? Whose perspective is based on projection, and whose perspective simply reflects accurate estimations of existing or non-existing differences in prototypicality?

Indeed, some studies on perspective differences revealed that the two involved groups often agree on which of them is more prototypical. Asian Americans, for instance, showed stronger implicit associations between America and White Americans than between America and Asian Americans (Devos & Banaji, 2005). Nevertheless, even in cases of agreement on which of the two groups is more prototypical, there might still be potential for intergroup conflict when groups disagree on the *degree* to which they differ in prototypicality. For instance, although East Germans in the study of Waldzus et al. (2004) agreed that West Germans are more typical Germans than East Germans, they saw a smaller difference in prototypicality than West Germans did.

The conflict does not come from the fact that one group claims to be more prototypical, but rather from the disagreement on this matter. In a long tradition of intergroup research, intergroup discrimination has often been operationalized as simple ingroup favoritism, or as an unequal, mostly negative treatment of members of certain groups. In contrast, Mummendey and Wenzel (1999) consider the disagreement between the two groups involved as the essence of intergroup discrimination, potentially resulting from the reciprocal process of projecting ingroup attributes onto the more inclusive category. They define social discrimination as "an ingroup's subjectively justified unequal, usually disadvantageous, evaluation or treatment of an outgroup, that the latter (or an outside observer) would deem unjustified" (p. 159).

The emphasis on disagreement in this definition is in line with an older definition by Allport (1954), who stated that "Discrimination comes about . . . when we deny to individuals or groups of people equality of treatment which they may wish" (p. 51). Interestingly, Allport refers to a United Nations memorandum of the Secretary-General[1] that does not include disagreement in the definition. Like many subsequent documents in international law, it does, however, include the notion of illegitimacy, which means that differentiation between groups is not always discrimination, but only if it is unjustified. As psychologists we know that there can be a great deal of disagreement about what is "justified", and by including the "which they may wish" in the definition of discrimination, Allport gives some authority on this issue to the groups involved.

Thus, following up on earlier work by Amélie Mummendey and her co-workers on perspective-specific divergence in aggressive interactions (e.g., Mummendey, Linneweber, & Löschper, 1984; Mummendey, Bornewasser, Löschper, & Linneweber, 1982, Mummendey & Otten, 1989; Otten & Mummendey, 2002; Otten, Mummendey, & Wenzel, 1995), the ingroup projection model clearly emphasizes that social discrimination is a concept that is specific to certain contexts and to the perspectives of the groups involved.

Evaluations and decisions about the allocation of resources are done with reference to expectations and standards, and those standards are often open for debate. Thus, what is justified from the point of view of one group might be seen as unjustified from the point of view of another (see also Leyens & Demoulin, chapter 11 in this volume).

It is important to note that such an understanding has nothing to do with political indifference or moral relativism. There is no doubt that we are dealing with an unacceptable case of intergroup discrimination when people are disadvantaged in job applications because of their being female or being black. However, our evaluation of such behavior as discrimination has to do with our own group memberships, political values, and interests rather than with the psychology behind the behavior itself. What we gain by taking into account perspective dependency is that we can explain how it happens that people often engage in discriminative behavior without any consciousness of doing something wrong, which makes it difficult to change. For any intervention in intergroup relations, this has to be taken into account (see also Jonas, chapter 15 in this volume).

Determinants of ingroup projection and new approaches to reduce intergroup conflict

The ingroup projection model was developed not only to understand the evaluation of outgroups, but also to analyze conditions of intergroup tolerance. For a long time intergroup researchers assumed that prejudice comes out of social categorization combined with a desire for positive distinctiveness. Not surprisingly, most previous approaches to prejudice reduction tried in one or the other way to reduce the importance of intergroup differences (Park & Judd, 2005). Inspired by Allport's contact hypothesis (1954; see also Wright, chapter 11 in this volume) and social identity theory, they often relied on alternative ways to represent the categorical structure of the intergroup situation, such as de-categorization as individuals (Brewer & Miller, 1984), or re-categorization of ingroup and outgroup into a more inclusive common ingroup (Gaertner, Dovidio, Anastasio, Bachman, & Rust, 1993). Only a few researchers suggested changing the context of intergroup difference rather than the difference itself, for instance by making intergroup difference normative and desirable by involving groups in complementary tasks necessary for shared success (Brown & Hewstone, 2005; Hewstone & Brown, 1986).

The ingroup projection model offers a similar, but more general approach to the reduction of prejudice. The key for this new approach is the assumption that outgroups are negatively evaluated because of their deviance from superordinate prototypes rather than because of their being different from the ingroup. If it was possible to hinder ingroup projection from turning a perception of difference into a perception of deviance, intergroup conflict could be reduced even if intergroup differences were maintained (Park & Judd, 2005). However, how can one reduce or block ingroup projection?

To answer this question one has to understand the determinants of ingroup projection. Mummendey and Wenzel (1999) propose two important predictors. First, they assume that ingroup projection is stronger for those group members who are strongly identified with both their ingroup on the subgroup level and the inclusive category on the superordinate level (*dual identification*). Second, they assume that ingroup projection will be reduced if the prototype of the superordinate category, for one or the other reason, is not definable as a simple ethnocentric standard.

Dual identification

Group members who identify strongly with their group should be particularly motivated to see it in a positive light and to see their group scoring high on dimensions they consider relevant. At the same time, the standards for group evaluation, which are derived from the prototype of a superordinate category, should be considered more important if people identify with the group that this superordinate category represents. Social scientists who identify strongly with their group of social scientists should have a particular interest in seeing social scientists as being scientific, but only if being a scientist is important for their own personal self-definition. Moreover, people who are used to thinking of themselves as members of a certain group and also as members of the superordinate category should, after a while, develop a cognitive association between the two in their mind, since both are often activated when people think about themselves.

Indeed, Wenzel et al. (2003, Study 1) found that those students who highly identified with both their study major (psychology, business administration) and with being a student had a stronger tendency for ingroup projection than the others. The same pattern has been found for Germans identifying strongly with both Germany and with Europe: When comparing themselves with Poles, these dual identifiers saw themselves more relatively prototypical for Europeans than the other participants did (Study 2; Waldzus et al., 2003). Moreover, in a study with more than 1500 participants from five different regions in Spain, Strotmann (2007) found that participants identifying strongly with both their region and Spain saw their regional group as more prototypical than did other participants.

The definition of the superordinate prototype

Changing – at least within a decent time-span – identification with groups is an almost impossible ambition. Thus, for interventions the fact that dual identification is a precondition for ingroup projection seems to be of limited relevance. It is probably more effective to focus on another determinant of ingroup projection suggested by Mummendey and Wenzel (1999), namely the *representation of the superordinate category*. They hypothesize that ingroup projection should be contingent on the possibility of representing the superordinate category as a definable prototype; if what characterizes the superordinate category is not easily definable, such characteristics can hardly be used as a standard from which the outgroup deviates. This hypothesis is of considerable relevance, since interventions that reduce prejudice by changing the representation of the superordinate category can leave the identification with the subgroup and perception of intergroup differences untouched, two things people often resist changing (see also Brewer, chapter 1 in this volume).

In a first attempt, and using somewhat different vocabulary, Mummendey and Wenzel (1999) suggested several ways in which the definability of the superordinate prototype can be diminished. Three of them have been studied empirically: vagueness, complexity, and limitation of scope.

Vagueness

If the definition of the superordinate category implies that it is vague or unclear, it cannot be assumed that the prototype of this category carries the ingroup's characteristics more than those of the outgroup. If it would be clear that, given the long history of science, nobody is really able or in the position to tell what a real scientist is, natural scientists should be less able to project their model of science to the superordinate category of scientists. This hypothesis has been tested in a study by Waldzus et al. (2003, Study 1). After rating Europe on several characteristics, half of the German participants (vagueness condition) received feedback that other Germans' ratings of Europe on the same characteristics differed completely from their own ratings and from each other, suggesting that there was no agreement within the ingroup on what Europeans are like. The other half of the participants (control condition) received feedback that the ratings of other Germans closely resembled their own ratings. As expected, the relative prototypicality of Germans in comparison with Poles was higher in the control than in the vagueness condition.

One intuitive argument that could be made here is that a vague or unclear superordinate category might facilitate rather than inhibit projection. Indeed, in the vagueness condition, projection was as high as in the control condition for those participants who were dually identified, and, thus, had probably a stronger interest in projection. However, what the notion of "being unclear" actually means according to Mummendey and Wenzel (1999) is that the prototype is unclear *by definition* rather than just left open for any motivated interpretation. A typical vague category like this is artists. Hardly anyone can claim what it means to be an artist without taking the risk of disqualifying him/herself from the discourse. There is a prescriptive component involved, similar to the one in negative theology, which defines the nature of God by what he/she is *not* rather than by applying concrete attributes.

Complexity

Mummendey and Wenzel (1999) define a complex prototype as a case in which "the distribution of representative members on the prototypical dimension is . . . multimodal" (p. 167). Although this statement is not very accessible, one can get the idea if one thinks of an example, such as a robin and an eagle. Most people would agree that both are prototypical birds, although quite different at the same time. The world of birds would be much poorer if one of them did not exist. A superordinate category that allows for different ways to be prototypical is called complex. Since complexity makes it difficult to identify "the one and only" prototype, some researchers prefer to talk of a complex representation of the superordinate category (represented by multiple prototypes) instead of a complex prototype. In any case, inducing or emphasizing the complexity of the superordinate category should reduce ingroup projection.

In a first approach to this hypothesis, Waldzus et al. (2003, Study 3) operationalized complexity by making participants focus on diversity. Half of their German participants were asked to imagine that they would have to explain to another person what the "diversity" of Europe is (complexity condition). The other half of participants received the same instruction except that the word "diversity" was replaced by the word "unity" (control condition). Participants had to write down their ideas into an open text field. Participants in the control condition showed the usual pattern of ingroup projection: They saw Germans to be more prototypical than Poles for the superordinate category of Europe, and this difference was even more pronounced for participants who identified with Germans and Europeans simultaneously. For participants in the complexity condition, as expected, ingroup projection was reduced. They considered Germans and Poles as equally prototypical, irrespective of identification.

With the same manipulation, a reduction of ingroup projection was achieved in the study of Waldzus et al. (2005), again with Germans as the ingroup and Europeans as the superordinate category, but with the British and Italians as outgroups. Moreover, in this study, complexity also led to more positive attitudes towards the outgroup, mediated by a reduction of perceived relative prototypicality of the ingroup.

One cognitive explanation for the effect of complex superordinate categories is that they might facilitate the use of orthogonal, that is independent, dimensions when relating subgroups to the superordinate category (high-complexity mindset). In line with this reasoning, a recent study by Meireles (2007) showed that business administration students who had to compare themselves with accountancy students showed less ingroup projection to the superordinate category of management science students when they were primed in advance with such a high-complexity mindset.

Note that the intergroup context in which ingroup projection was measured (business administration students vs. accountancy students) was not mentioned in the mindset priming task. Thus, the reduction of relative ingroup prototypicality by the high complexity priming cannot be explained by the activation of ideological or normative concepts, which eventually had been the case in the previous studies when participants were asked to focus on diversity. This is not to say that normative concerns could not contribute to the reduction of ingroup projection through complexity. The important conclusion is rather that one way to reduce ingroup projection of high prototypical groups is the induction of a high-complexity mindset.

Narrow scope

The prototype of a superordinate category has a narrow scope if it is defined only by a few dimensions and, thus, only applies to a few aspects of life. For instance, if everybody who has German citizenship is considered a German, the German prototype has a narrower scope than if only those are considered German who also speak German, follow German customs and identify themselves as Germans. A prototype with narrow scope should make ingroup projection more difficult since it abstains from prescriptions in all those domains in which a prototype with broader scope would define normative positions.

   This hypotheses was tested in the study of Meireles (2007) mentioned above. Apart from the manipulation of low-complexity vs. high-complexity mindsets, it also manipulated scope by priming the use of either many (broader scope) or few dimensions (narrow scope). Indeed, ingroup projection was not only reduced in the high-complexity condition, but also in the narrow scope condition.

Moderators of the meaning of relative prototypicality

Group status and size

Even though overall results of numerous studies are consistent with the originally hypothesized relations in the ingroup projection model, there is nonetheless a considerable amount of heterogeneity in the findings (see Figure 3.1). One important moderator for ingroup projection has already been identified: The available evidence suggests that all manipulations that render the prototype of the superordinate category less definable (i.e., unclear, complex or being of narrow scope) only reduce relative prototypicality for higher status majorities, which indeed consider themselves as more prototypical than the outgroup. For lower status minority groups, who see themselves often as less prototypical for one or another reason, they had no effect. One explanation would be that such groups represent the superordinate category already by default in a more complex way, since they acknowledge the outgroup's prototypicality anyway. However, this speculation needs further testing.

Evaluation of the superordinate category

Another important moderator is the evaluation of the superordinate category. Although people tend to evaluate their ingroup generally positively, they can sometimes be members of negative reference groups (Turner, 1987). If the superordinate category is such a negative reference group, it is of course more desirable if the ingroup is less prototypical than the outgroup. Thus, all relations of relative prototypicality with ingroup identification, outgroup evaluation, and legitimacy of status differences should be reversed. This hypothesis was tested in a study with German participants as the ingroup and Poles as the outgroup. The evaluation of Europe as the superordinate category was manipulated by asking participants to write down either what they think is positive about Europe or what is negative about Europe. As predicted, in the positive Europe condition, identification with Germans was positively related to relative prototypicality of Germans, which in turn was negatively related to attitudes towards Poles and positively related to perceived legitimacy of Germans' higher status. All these relations reversed in the negative Europe condition (Weber et al., 2002; Wenzel et al., 2003).

Group-based motivation

A final group of moderators is related to the motivational dynamic of ingroup projection. In their original approach, Mummendey and Wenzel (1999) put much emphasis on the function of ingroup projection as a way to achieve positive distinctiveness within a relevant intergroup context, which can contribute to one's social identity. Indeed, some studies support this idea. For instance, Ullrich, Christ, and Schlüter (2006) found that dual-identified Germans were more resistant to the entry of Turkey into the European Union when they felt threatened, and Finley (2006) found in studies on group mergers that ingroup projection is related to threats to distinctiveness. However, there is early experimental evidence that ingroup projection can also occur as a cognitive bias, which need not necessarily be motivated by the particular intergroup relation (Machunsky, Meiser, & Mummendey, in press).[2] Indeed it seems that both social identity concerns and cognitive principles play a role, and that which of them triggers ingroup projection in a particular situation depends on variables at both the individual (e.g., mood, need for closure) and the societal level (security of intergroup context) (see also Machunsky & Meiser, chapter 5 in this volume; Waldzus, Rosa, & Meireles, 2007). One issue for future research will be to disentangle these two motivational processes.

Challenges and outlook to future research

Measurement issues

As mentioned above, ingroup projection as a process is not directly observable, which makes measurement a challenge for anyone who wants to study this phenomenon. Often, measures of ingroup projection are based on ratings of the typicality of certain attributes for the ingroup, the outgroup, and the superordinate group, respectively. The more ingroup-typical rather than outgroup-typical traits are associated with the superordinate group, the stronger is the ingroup projection. Other explicit measures work with graphical presentations allowing for global prototypicality ratings or just use blatant unipolar items asking for the ingroup's and the outgroup's prototypicality.

One problem of all these measures is that they are very different in their response format. As a result, they are often not as highly correlated as one would expect from different measures of the same construct. Moreover, attribute-based prototypicality measures work with aggregated data, whereas global graphical or item-based ratings of the groups' overall prototypicality assess a potentially quite different aspect. Future research with larger sample sizes is required to clarify these issues.

A further problem with measures of relative prototypicality results from their relational character. Since prototypicality is theoretically a relative construct, it has two components, namely prototypicality of the ingroup and of the outgroup. Combining both in a difference score is consistent with the theoretical construct, but produces statistical problems, such as reduced reliability. This problem is not specific to prototypicality, but is typical for all relational constructs, such as ingroup favoritism. Moreover, it also applies to the implicit measures that have been used, such as semantic priming (Bianchi et al., 2007) and the implicit association test (Devos and Banaji, 2005). These problems are a challenge for research on ingroup projection and it seems that there is no fast and universal solution. Sometimes it can be very informative to analyze ingroup prototypicality and outgroup prototypicality separately (Edwards, 1994; Ullrich, in press; Wenzel, Mummendey, & Waldzus, 2007). In general, these measurement issues have to be addressed differently in each case, weighing construct validity, consistency demands, and practicality in a reasonable way.

Common ingroup or superordinate category: Contradictory implications of dual identity

Dual identity has been found to increase ingroup projection and to potentially trigger intergroup conflict. Although logically convincing and empirically supported, this result is at odds with another prominent approach to prejudice reduction, the common ingroup identity model (CIIM; Gaertner et al., 1993). This model started from encouraging findings that prejudice could be reduced by representing the intergroup situation rather as a one-group situation in which the ingroup and the outgroup are included in a more inclusive common ingroup, so that previous outgroup members turn into members of the more inclusive common ingroup.

Confronted with the fact that group members often stick to their subgroup identity, the model was modified insofar as a dual identity condition was suggested to solve the problem: Groups may maintain their subgroup identity but at the same time identify with the common ingroup (Gaertner & Dovidio, 2000; Gaertner, Dovidio, Nier, Ward, & Banker, 1999). Thus, whereas the CIIM predicts positive effects of dual identity on intergroup relations, the ingroup projection model predicts the opposite, since dual identity increases ingroup projection and, in turn, disagreement and conflict.

Interestingly, the effects of dual identity are rather mixed. Sometimes dual identity improves attitudes towards the outgroup, sometimes it does not, or makes things even worse. Researchers working on both models are currently collaborating with each other in order to identify under which conditions one can expect processes predicted by the CIIM or those predicted by the ingroup projection model. Several moderators such as the relevance of the super-ordinate category/common ingroup for subgroup comparisons or the acti-vation of the superordinate category as figure vs. its activation as ground have been suggested, but conclusive results are still pending. Thus, the role of dual and other complex identities in the improvement of intergroup relations is still open for debate and a hot issue in current intergroup research (see also Brewer, chapter 1 in this volume).

Final conclusions

Overall, the ingroup projection model offers an inspiring new approach to the study of intergroup relations and the role of prototypicality. It is, to a certain degree, a sophisticated application of self-categorization theory, which, com-bined with the idea of social projection, can explain evaluative judgments in intergroup relations. Results are supportive for most of the model's hypothe-ses. At the same time they show how important it is to take into account perspectivity and context-specific interpretations of social reality whenever the evaluation of outgroups and its implications for intergroup relations are studied.

Notes

1 It states that "discrimination might be defined as a detrimental distinction based on grounds which may not be attributed to the individual and which have no justified consequences in social, political or legal relations (color, race, sex, etc.), or on grounds of membership in social categories (cultural, language, religious, political or other opinion, national circle, social origin, social class, property, birth or other Status)" (The Main Types and Causes of Discrimination, Memorandum submitted by the Secretary-General, E/CN.4/Sub.2/40/Rev.1, 7 June 1949, paras. 87–88, cited

in Expulsion of aliens, Memorandum by the Secretariat, International Law Commission, Geneva, 1 May–9 June and 3 July–11 August 2006, p. 180).
2 Some years ago a West German friend of mine started a sentence with "Do you remember that time, when East Germany came to Germany". Looking at me he stopped in the middle of the sentence, and we both couldn't help laughing.

References

Allport, F. H. (1924). *Social psychology*. Boston: Houghton-Mifflin.

Allport, G. W. (1954). *The nature of prejudice*. Reading, MA: Addison-Wesley.

Anderson, N. H. (1981). *Foundation of information integration theory*. New York: Academic Press.

Bianchi, M., Mummendey, A., Steffens, M., & Yzerbyt, V. (2007). *What do you mean by European? Evidence for spontaneous ingroup projection*. Unpublished manuscript.

Brewer, M. B. (2001). Ingroup identification and intergroup conflict: When does ingroup love become outgroup hate? In R. D. Ashmore & L. Jussim (Eds.), *Social identity, intergroup conflict, and conflict reduction* (pp. 17–41). Oxford: Oxford University Press.

Brewer, M. B., & Miller, N. (1984). Beyond the contact hypothesis: Theoretical perspectives on desegregation. In N. Miller & M. B. Brewer (Eds.), *Groups in contact: The psychology of desegregation* (pp. 281–302). New York: Academic Press.

Brown, R., & Hewstone, M. (2005). An integrative theory of intergroup contact. In M. P. Zanna (Ed.), *Advances in experimental social psychology* (Vol. 37, pp. 255–343). San Diego, CA: Elsevier Academic Press.

Devos, T., & Banaji, M. R. (2005). American = White? *Journal of Personality and Social Psychology, 88*, 447–466.

Edwards, J. R. (1994). The study of congruence in organizational behavior research: Critique and a proposed alternative. *Organizational Behavior and Human Decision Processes, 58*, 51–100.

Finley, S. (2006). *Social groups in times of change: The impact of a threatened identity*. Unpublished doctoral thesis, Australian National University, Canberra, Australia.

Freud, S. (1999). Vorlesungen zur Einführung in die Psychoanalyse [Introductory lectures on psychoanalysis]. In A. Freud (Ed.), *Gesammelte Werke/Sigmund Freud* (Vol. 11). London: Imago Publishing. (Original work published 1917)

Gaertner, S. L., & Dovidio, J. F. (2000). *Reducing intergroup bias: The common ingroup identity model*. Philadelphia: Psychology Press/Taylor & Francis.

Gaertner, S. L., Dovidio, J. F., Anastasio, P. A., Bachman, B. A., & Rust, M. C. (1993). The common ingroup identity model: Recategorization and the reduction of intergroup bias. In W. Stroebe & M. Hewstone (Eds.), *European review of social psychology* (Vol. 4, pp. 1–26). Chichester, UK: Wiley.

Gaertner, S. L., Dovidio, J. F., Nier, J. A., Ward, C. M., & Banker, B. S. (1999). Across cultural divides: The value of a superordinate identity. In D. A. Prentice & D. T. Miller (Eds.), *Cultural divides. Understanding and overcoming group conflict* (pp. 173–212). New York: Sage.

Hewstone, M., & Brown, R. (1986): Contact is not enough: An intergroup perspective on the "contact hypothesis". In M. Hewstone & R. Brown (Eds.), *Contact and conflict in intergroup encounters* (pp. 1–44) Oxford: Blackwell.

Hewstone, M., Rubin, M., & Willis, H. (2002). Intergroup bias. *Annual Review of Psychology, 53*, 575–604.

Hogg, M. A., & Hains, S. C. (1996). Intergroup relations and group solidarity: Effects of group identification and social beliefs on depersonalized attraction. *Journal of Personality and Social Psychology, 70,* 295–309.

Holmes, D. S., & Houston, B. K. (1971). The defensive function of projection. *Journal of Personality and Social Psychology, 20,* 208–213.

Holyoak, K. J., & Gordon, P. C. (1983). Social reference points. *Journal of Personality and Social Psychology, 44,* 881–887.

Krueger, J. (2007). From social projection to social behaviour. In W. Stroebe & M. Hewstone (Eds.), *European review of social psychology* (Vol. 18, pp. 1–35). Hove, UK: Psychology Press.

Machunsky, M., Meiser, T., & Mummendey, A. (in press). Subtyping parts of the ingroup: On the moderating role of subtyping for the ingroup prototypicality–ingroup bias link. *Experimental Psychology.*

Meireles, C. S. (2007). *Tolerance in intergroup relations: Cognitive representations reducing ingroup projection.* Unpublished masters thesis, Lisbon University Institute (ISCTE), Portugal.

Mummendey, A., Bornewasser, M., Löschper, G., & Linneweber, V. (1982). Defining interactions as aggressive in specific social contexts. *Aggressive Behavior, 8,* 224–228.

Mummendey, A., Linneweber, V., & Löschper, G. (1984). Actor or victim of agression: Divergent perspectives – divergent evaluations. *European Journal of Social Psychology, 14,* 297–311.

Mummendey, A., & Otten, S. (1989). Perspective specific differences in the segmentation and evaluation of aggressive interaction sequences. *European Journal of Social Psychology, 19,* 23–40.

Mummendey, A., & Wenzel, M. (1999). Social discrimination and tolerance in intergroup relations: Reactions to intergroup difference. *Personality and Social Psychology Review, 3,* 158–174.

Otten, S., & Mummendey, A. (2002) Social discrimination and aggression: A matter of perspective-specific divergence? In W. Kallmeyer & C. F. Graumann (Eds.), *Perspectivity and perspectivation in discourse* (pp. 233–250). Wilrijk: John Benjamins Publishers.

Otten, S., Mummendey, A., & Wenzel, M. (1995). The evaluation of aggressive interactions in interpersonal and intergroup contexts. *Aggressive Behavior, 21,* 205–224.

Park, B., & Judd, C. M. (2005). Rethinking the link between categorization and prejudice within the social cognition perspective. *Personality and Social Psychology Review, 9,* 108–130.

Rosch, E. (1978) Principles of categorization. In E. Rosch & B. B. Lloyd (Eds.), *Cognition and categorization* (pp. 27–48). Hillsdale, NJ: Lawrence Erlbaum Associates, Inc.

Smith, E. R., & Mackie, D. M. (2007). *Social psychology* (3rd ed.). Philadelphia: Psychology Press.

Smith, R. E. (1998). Mental representation and memory. In D. Gilbert & S. Fiske (Eds.), *Handbook of social psychology* (4th ed., Vol. 1, pp. 391–445). Boston: McGraw-Hill.

Strotmann, B. (2007). *Regional and national identity in Spain: The role of relative prototypicality.* Unpublished masters thesis, University of Marburg, Germany.

Sumner, W. G. (1906). *Folkways.* Boston: Ginn & Company.

Tajfel, H., & Forgas, J. P. (1981) Social categorization: Cognitions, values and groups. In J. P. Forgas (Ed.), *Social cognition: Perspectives on everyday understanding* (pp. 113–140). London: Academic Press.

Tajfel, H., & Turner, J. C. (1986). The social identity theory of intergroup behavior. In S. Worchel & G. Austin (Eds.), *Psychology of intergroup relations* (pp. 7–24). Chicago: Nelson-Hall.

Turner, J. C. (1987). A self-categorization theory. In J. C. Turner, M. A. Hogg, P. J. Oakes, S. D. Reicher, & M. S. Wetherell (Eds.), *Rediscovering the social group: A self-categorization theory* (pp. 42–67). Oxford: Blackwell.

Ullrich, J. (in press). Reconsidering the "relative" in relative ingroup prototypicality. *European Journal of Social Psychology.*

Ullrich, J., Christ, O., & Schlüter, E. (2006). Merging on Mayday: Subgroup and superordinate identification as joint moderators of threat effects in the context of European Union's expansion. *European Journal of Social Psychology, 36,* 857–875.

Waldzus, S., & Mummendey, A. (2004). Inclusion in a superordinate category, ingroup prototypicality, and attitudes towards out-groups. *Journal of Experimental Social Psychology, 40,* 466–477.

Waldzus, S., Mummendey, A., & Wenzel, M. (2005). When "different" means "worse": In-group prototypicality in changing intergroup contexts. *Journal of Experimental Social Psychology, 41,* 76–83.

Waldzus, S., Mummendey, A., Wenzel, M., & Boettcher, F. (2004). Of bikers, teachers and Germans: Groups' diverging views about their prototypicality. *British Journal of Social Psychology, 43,* 385–400.

Waldzus, S., Mummendey, A., Wenzel, M., & Weber, U. (2003). Towards tolerance: Representations of superordinate categories and perceived in-group prototypicality. *Journal of Experimental Social Psychology, 39,* 31–47.

Waldzus, S., Rosa, M., & Meireles, C. (2007) *News from the freezer: Cognitive aspects of ingroup projection.* Oral presentation at the 10th Jena Workshop on Intergroup Processes, 15–19 June 2007 at Schloß Oppurg, Germany.

Weber, U., Mummendey, A., & Waldzus, S. (2002). Perceived legitimacy of intergroup status differences: Its prediction by relative ingroup protypicality. *European Journal of Social Psychology, 32,* 449–470.

Wenzel, M. (2004). A social categorisation approach to distributive justice. In W. Stroebe & M. Hewstone (Eds.), *European review of social psychology* (Vol. 15, pp. 219–257). Hove, UK: Psychology Press.

Wenzel, M., Mummendey, A., & Waldzus, S. (2007). Superordinate identities and intergroup conflict: The ingroup projection model. In W. Stroebe & M. Hewstone (Eds.), *European review of social psychology* (Vol. 18, pp. 331–372). Hove, UK: Psychology Press.

Wenzel, M., Mummendey, A., Weber, U., & Waldzus, S. (2003). The ingroup as pars pro toto: Projection from the ingroup onto the inclusive category as a precursor to social discrimination. *Personality and Social Psychology Bulletin, 29,* 461–473.

4 Social identity and justice

Implications for intergroup relations

Michael Wenzel
Flinders University, Adelaide

Perhaps the greatest shift in the psychology of justice in the last two decades has been the acknowledgement and theorizing of the link between justice and identity; specifically social identity, which derives from one's membership in a social group, together with its emotional and evaluative connotations (Tajfel, 1978). This link can be understood to be bidirectional, with identity determining notions of justice, deservingness and entitlements; and justice or injustice affecting those subjected to it in terms of their sense of identity, inclusion/exclusion, status, and group values. Such theoretical notions found their impact first in the area of *procedural justice*, that is, the fairness of decision-making processes (Lind & Tyler, 1988), coinciding with the discovery that people's perceptions of justice are affected by the quality of their interpersonal treatment such as politeness and respect (Bies & Moag, 1986). These findings did not fit the theoretical mould of then prevalent instrumental models which regarded concerns about fair procedures as driven by the interest in achieving favourable and fair outcomes (e.g., Thibaut & Walker, 1975). While the identity-relevance of procedural justice has been contrasted with a self-interested concern about *distributive justice* (e.g., Tyler, 1994), that is, the fairness of outcomes and resource distributions, more recent theoretical and empirical work argues that distributive justice is also based in identity processes (Skitka, 2003; Tyler & Blader, 2003; Wenzel, 2004). Furthermore, *retributive justice*, that is, the fairness of sanctioning responses to rule-breaking and acts of injustice, has also seen the application of identity-based models (Tyler, Boeckmann, Smith, & Huo, 1997; Vidmar, 2000), but such theoretical perspectives are still emerging (e.g., Wenzel, Okimoto, Feather, & Platow, 2008). In this chapter, I briefly retrace a selection of theoretical notions with regard to the justice–identity link in the areas of distributive and procedural justice, before then outlining for the area of retributive justice a more recent identity-based model of victim responses to rule-breaking. The aim is, first, to advance a more integrative understanding of the multi-faceted justice concept and its interconnections with identity. Second, given that social identity is at the heart of intergroup relations, the theme of this book, I discuss implications of identity-based conceptualizations of justice for intergroup behaviour.

Identity and distributive justice

Distributive justice refers to the concern that people, who are considered potential recipients in a given situation, receive the share of resources they are due or entitled to. Thus, at the core of distributive justice perceptions is a notion of entitlement: what someone should get based on who they are or what they have done (Lerner, 1991). The main theoretical traditions in social psychology address the question of what a person is entitled to either with reference to his or her relevant inputs in an exchange relationship relative to the inputs and outcomes of a relevant other (e.g., Adams, 1965), or based on distinct allocation principles including equality (disregarding any differentiating characteristics), need (considering the recipients' neediness), and merit (considering inputs situationally defined) (e.g., Mikula, 1980). Both traditions face the challenge of specifying which inputs and/or principles are considered relevant and appropriate in a given context; and in both traditions authors have resorted to a notion of instrumentality where inputs and principles are egocentrically defined to advance one's immediate or long-term self-interest (Deutsch, 1985; Walster, Walster, & Berscheid, 1978). Yet, evidence suggests that people pursue justice even at their own cost, for example increasing their inputs after being inequitably advantaged (Greenberg, 1988), or offering a powerless other an equal share in dictator games (van Dijk & Vermunt, 2000). Thus, theoretical predictions of how people will perceive entitlements in a given situation remain difficult, and our theoretical understanding of a commitment to justice as independent from (and sometimes counter to) self-interest seems insufficient.

A categorization approach to distributive justice

To address these issues, I developed an approach to distributive justice that understands perceptions of entitlement in terms of social categorization processes and thus ties them to one's social self-definition in a given context (for a review see Wenzel, 2004). Specifically, based on an Aristotelian notion that distributive justice means that equals should be treated equally, and unequals differently, perceptions of categorical equivalence and differentiation should be central to entitlement beliefs. Fundamental to both is the perception of what the category of potential recipients is in a given allocation situation. Resource allocations have boundaries; we consider who is, in principle, eligible for a share in the resources and who is not. For example, company profits are distributed within the company and are unlikely to be shared with contracted suppliers. However, the categorical definition of boundaries is a social construction. For example, human rights may be considered a defining prerogative of humans but could in some form be extended to animals as well, depending on the perceiver's more or less inclusive self-definition as distinctively human or as one of many living beings (Clayton & Opotow, 2003). Generally, the definition of justice boundaries, as with the salience of any social categorization, should depend on an interactive function of a category's contextual fit and the perceiver's readiness to use (and define themselves in terms of) a certain categorization (Oakes, 1987).

The definition of the category of potential recipients can imply two different processes. First, categorizing people as belonging to the same category implies a psychological equivalence of its members; they are expected to be similar, act similarly, hold the same beliefs (Turner, 1987) and, I argue, be treated the same. Hence, to the extent that their shared category is strongly salient and, in the process, inhibits differentiations within the category, all potential recipients should be regarded as entitled to the same outcome. This non-differentiating entitlement may take the form of direct equality (e.g., receiving an equal share of resources) or equalization that compensates for initial outcome differences (e.g., considering the recipients' neediness towards establishing the same outcomes). In general terms, potential recipients will be regarded as entitled to an outcome that is prototypical of their shared category (where the prototype of a category is again not fixed but rather a function of the same interactive processes of fit and readiness that determine categorization processes as a whole; Oakes, Haslam, & Turner, 1998).

Second, the social category defining the potential recipients in a given situation implies relevant, identity-defining value dimensions on which its members may be differentiated. The more members are perceived to represent values and goals that define the group's distinct social identity (i.e., the more prototypical they are), the greater the attraction and the leadership qualities attributed to them (Turner, 1987, 1991) and, I argue, the more deserving they will be found. Thus, to the extent that the situation demands or allows for intracategory differentiation, more prototypical recipients (persons or subgroups) will be considered as deserving a greater share of the resources. In other words, the values seen as representing the social identity of potential recipients are relevant inputs in the given situation and determine perceptions of entitlement.

This conceptualization implies that perceptions of entitlements (whether differentiating or non-differentiating) reside in the perceived common identity of the potential recipients, which means that a commitment to justice (relatively independent from mere self-interest) can be understood as deriving from one's psychological investment in that shared identity. When people identify with the shared category, their choices are more likely to be affected by their notions of justice rather than by self-interest. Consistent with this, I found that members of a team that succeeded in achieving a certain benefit were more likely to attribute a greater benefit entitlement to the team member who best represented the team's distinctive strength, rather than to themselves, but only so when an experimental manipulation established a high level of identification with their team (Wenzel, 2002, Study 2).

Conversely, people who feel their entitlements have been violated should be concerned about this not merely because they did not get the desired outcomes but rather because of the identity implications. First, if they felt entitled to the outcomes because of their perceived shared identity and psychological equivalence to other potential recipients, then being denied those outcomes would instead communicate their non-equivalence, their second-rate status or even psychological exclusion from the group. For example, after the German unification, East Germans felt like second-class citizens because of their considerably lower economic situation compared to West Germans (see Mummendey, Kessler, Klink, & Mielke, 1999). Second, if people felt entitled to a certain outcome share based on the view that they represented values that defined the identity of the relevant common group, then being denied that share would dispute their relative prototypicality and/or challenge their view of what are relevant identity-defining values. For example, an outstanding intellectual snubbed for a national Citizen of the Year award in favour of a sports star may feel this reflects an anti-intellectualism that is counter to national values. Hence, the experience of distributive injustice may be so stinging because it implicates threats to a valued identity; a threat to one's *status* (psychological exclusion or second-class membership) and/or a threat to the *values* one associates with that identity (which may define oneself as a valuable member; Wenzel, 2001).

Implications for intergroup relations

If the recipients in a given distribution context are groups rather than individuals, perceptions of entitlement and their violation have implications for the relevant groups' identity and relative status, which may also affect relations between them. Interestingly, these implications derive from the groups sharing a common identity as potential recipients in the given context. Referring again to the situation after German re-unification, research findings indicated that East Germans felt particularly entitled to a better economic situation when they strongly self-categorized as Germans, which constituted the relevant category of potential recipients they shared with the better-off West Germans. Further, East German respondents indicated a stronger willingness to engage in social protest as a consequence of the entitlement violation when they strongly identified as Germans (Wenzel, 2000). Thus, contrary to the influential view that a common ingroup identity elicits more harmonious relations between groups (e.g., Gaertner & Dovidio, 2000), such a common identity can be the basis for feelings of injustice and intergroup conflict. When shared inclusion is seen to imply an entitlement to similar outcomes or status, frustration of such an entitlement is likely to lead to resentment. Social protest or hostility against the other group is based on a self-definition in terms of that shared category and the presumed *equivalence* of the groups at this more abstract level.

Likewise, perceptions of a group's entitlements can also derive from the *differentiation* between the groups on values that are considered defining for the more abstract, common identity. For example, when Turkey was denied membership in the European Union (EU), German respondents found such a denial justified (and Turkey undeserving of EU membership), the more untypical for the relevant overarching European identity they regarded Turkey, relative to Germany, across a number of value dimensions (Wenzel, 2001). While referring to a common identity, the representation of that identity in terms of defining values may *not* be common to the groups. Rather, the groups may represent the shared category in a way that portrays their own group as relatively more deserving, from which they gain a relatively higher status and a more positive social identity (Tajfel & Turner, 1986). For example, in that same EU study (Wenzel, 2001), respondents who strongly identified with Germany perceived Turkey to be relatively un-European, and Germany as typifying more strongly the values that define Europe. In other words, the common identity can become the source for intergroup conflict because the included subgroups tend to represent it from their particular vantage points in a way that advances their own group's goals, status and identity (an idea developed in more detail in the ingroup projection model; Mummendey & Wenzel, 1999; Wenzel, Mummendey, & Waldzus, 2007; see also Waldzus, chapter 3 in this volume). From this perspective, a group should tend to regard its inferior status or outcomes, relative to a comparison outgroup, as unfair and illegitimate, to the extent that it regards its own distinctive attributes as embodying the identity of the common group (Weber, Mummendey, & Waldzus, 2002). Perceptions of illegitimacy, in certain circumstances, then trigger the group's resentment, intergroup hostility, and collective action (Mummendey et al., 1999; Tajfel & Turner, 1986).

However, it is also possible that members of advantaged and disadvantaged groups agree on the prototype and values of their common group. Specifically, low-status group members may accept that dimensions on which they occupy relatively lower positions are defining values of their common identity, and that their subgroup is thus less prototypical for the common group (Devos & Banaji, 2005; Waldzus, Mummendey, Wenzel, & Boettcher, 2004). To the extent that this is true, they should find their own group as less deserving and their group's relative disadvantage as justified and legitimate. Hence, what system-justification theory (Jost & Hunyady, 2002) describes as a disadvantaged group's false consciousness, that is, the acceptance of its lower status position as legitimate, may be understood in terms of its commitment to a higher-order common group. Low-status group members might accept a given prototype representation of that common group, even if it justifies their disadvantage, partly because this representation might provide them with a positive social identity in terms of their common group membership and its positive distinctiveness to other comparison groups. Disadvantaged groups in the US, for example, might accept that they have lower ambition and entrepreneurship compared to advantaged groups, thus legitimizing the inequality, because by doing so they reaffirm these dimensions as important American values that positively differentiate Americans from other nations.

To sum up, a categorization approach to distributive justice helps us to understand how perceptions of both legitimacy and illegitimacy of status relations and inequality are based in identity processes. Specifically, it contributes to a more differentiated analysis of the role of common groups in intergroup relations, where a common group identity is not only a basis for mutual attraction, but also for a sense of entitlement deriving either from one's group's perceived equivalence or its relative prototypicality.

Identity and procedural justice

Procedural justice refers to the perception that procedures and interactions employed in decision-making (e.g., about the allocation of certain outcomes) are fair and consistent with certain principles (e.g., Leventhal, 1980). In early theorizing, it was argued or implied that people are concerned about procedural justice because fair procedures would allow them some level of control over the decision outcomes and thus enable their pursuit of self-interests and goals (Leventhal, 1980; Thibaut & Walker, 1975). However, Thibaut and Walker's (1975) research showed that procedural qualities, such as being given a voice in the decision-making process, affected perceptions of fairness and the acceptance of decisions independent of the decision outcome. Later research showed that being given a voice to express one's views had favourable effects and led to greater perceptions of justice, even when, by design, it could not affect the decision outcome (e.g., because voice was only granted after the decision was already made; Lind, Kanfer, & Earley, 1990). Moreover, while earlier research focused on voice and other features of the formal decision-making process, subsequent research also showed that informal aspects of interactions between decision-making authorities and subordinates affected perceptions of procedural fairness, such as providing explanations for the decisions, showing consideration for those affected by the decision, politeness and respect (Tyler & Bies, 1990). Thus, a proper theoretical understanding of procedural justice effects needs to account for their relative independence from outcome concerns and explain why people are concerned about the quality of their interactions with authorities and decision-makers.

Relational models of procedural justice

As a theoretical answer to these issues, Lind and Tyler (1988) formulated the group value model of procedural justice, which was subsequently expanded to theorize more specifically the attribution of legitimacy to authorities (Tyler & Lind, 1992) and cooperation in groups and organizations (Tyler & Blader, 2003). The common thread of these "relational models" is the notion that qualities of procedures and authority interactions have symbolic meaning and communicate something about the identity of the person in relation to the authority and the group it represents. Specifically, it is argued that the authority's politeness and respect, lack of bias, and trustworthiness and benevolence communicate that one is a valued member of the group who enjoys high standing or respect within the group. On the other hand, such formal and informal qualities of decision-making also signal that the authority and the group it represents uphold ethical values, which allows one to take pride in the group (Tyler, Degoey, & Smith, 1996). Both intragroup respect and pride in the group feed into a positive social identity that people should seek more strongly when they identify with the group and refer to it to define their social self (Smith, Tyler, Huo, Ortiz, & Lind, 1998). In other words, concern for one's social identity as a member of the group represented by the authority (i.e., a kind of common group) underlies one's motivation to seek or demand procedural fairness. In turn, being treated procedurally fairly elicits a sense of respect and pride that bolsters one's identification with and commitment to the group and, thus, increases one's willingness to comply with its authority and contribute voluntarily to the group beyond what is requested (Tyler & Blader, 2003).

Implications for intergroup relations

Procedural justice is not only relevant to interpersonal and intragroup processes, but can also have implications for groups and their relations to each other. Specifically, when people feel their whole group is subjected to unfair treatment, or when they believe they are unfairly treated because of their membership in a certain social group, the experience of procedural unfairness amounts to a form of group relative deprivation, which can lead to questioning the legitimacy of the authority (Tyler & Lind, 2001). Similar to outcome deprivation, such group-level procedural unfairness can lead to social protest, resistance and hostility to the group seen as responsible for the unfairness (Wenzel, 2000).

Conversely, fair treatment of those affected by a decision can increase the legitimacy of the decision and the decision-maker, particularly when the decision is unfavourable in terms of material self- or group interests. Procedural fairness thus appears to be an avenue for maintaining the legitimacy of authorities and intergroup harmony, even where the interests of the affected groups conflict and no decision could possibly please them all (Tyler et al., 1997). In this sense, a common identity shared by the different groups involved can have beneficial effects on intergroup relations. This is because, when sufficiently identified with the common group, subgroup members will be mainly concerned about the application of procedural fairness, which, if realized, will have positive effects, strengthen their commitment to the common group and acceptance of the decision, irrespective of the groups' conflict of interest (even where subgroup identification remains high; Huo, 2003; Huo, Smith, Tyler, & Lind, 1996).

Similar to the individual level, it is assumed that one important mechanism for such group-level procedural justice effects is the *respect* it expresses for the group as a whole. Correspondingly, Huo and Molina (2006) found that subgroup respect, that is, the recognition, acceptance and positive evaluation of a subgroup by members of a common group, led minority groups to evaluate the common group more positively and display more positive intergroup attitudes. Such subgroup respect might imply that the authorities do not solely appeal to the common identity but also recognize relevant subgroup identities. Indeed, Huo, Molina, Sawahata, and Deang (2005) found under conditions of dual identity salience, that is, the simultaneous recognition of subgroup and common group identities, the strongest effect of fair treatment in maintaining positive reactions to authorities whose decisions affected them adversely. Part of the reason for this benefit of fair processes on intergroup relations and the commitment to superordinate authorities may be that subgroup respect is largely an autonomous, non-comparative source of positive social identity that does not depend on being treated better or more respectfully than other groups (Tyler & Smith, 1999).

However, there may be limits to the benefits of procedural justice in maintaining positive intergroup relations. First, a recent study by Leung, Tong, and Lind (2007) found in contexts where decisions affected the outcomes and interests of the common group as a whole (rather than individuals or subgroups), that identification with the common group increased concerns about the favourability of the decision for the group, with procedural fairness becoming less predictive of decision acceptance. Of course, it can be argued, what is favourable to a common group, what are its goals and interests, is susceptible to the particular perspectives of diverse subgroups, and this question may thus ignite again intergroup conflict. Importantly, Leung et al. (2007) argue that it is not always inherent in a decision whether it has outcome implications for individuals/subgroups or the common group as a whole; rather, this is a question of decision framing. Hence, subgroups or individuals who see an impending decision as threatening their interests might attempt to frame the decision as negatively affecting the good of the common group. Appealing to a shared identity, they could suspend procedural fairness concerns and push for a decision that advances the common good (as they define it). For example, a newly elected government may break with their election platform of easing the tax burden of low-income earners at the cost of high-income earners, because such measures might threaten the economy (as high-income earners claim). While procedurally unfair (breach of promise), collectively identifying voters might accept the decision because of its presumed benefits for the common good.

Second, the importance of procedural justice as a basis of decision acceptance (and, conversely, procedural unfairness as a driver of social protest) may not only depend on the level of identification with the common group but also its representation and, thus, the treatment or outcomes typically associated with it. For example, in the study referred to earlier (Wenzel, 2000), East Germans who felt they were not given procedural justice showed stronger tendencies to engage in social protest, but this was not dependent on (or moderated by) their level of identification with the relevant common group, Germany. In contrast, the effect of perceived distributive injustice *was* moderated by self-categorization as Germans, as discussed above. The reason for this could have been that, for East Germans, being German was associated with high material status and wealth, which were thus considered entitlements of East Germans qua being German. Fair process and voice in decision-making was, in this context, perhaps less seen as a defining characteristic of being German and thus less strongly considered as an entitlement by which East Germans measured their situation as Germans. Extrapolating from this, fairness in decision-making and interactions with authorities may not always be people's highest concern, specifically if it is not considered an entitlement implied in the common group identity. Such a perspective would conceptualize the fairness of distributions and procedures more integratively, with either depending on perceptions of entitlements, but merely entitlements of a different kind. Which entitlements come to the fore might be a matter of how the inclusive category is construed, depending on the vantage point of the perceiver.

To sum up, relational models of procedural justice help us to understand how the procedural fairness in decision-making can maintain intergroup harmony, even when the decision advantages some groups over others. Specifically, the benefits of procedural justice are based on group members' commitment to a relevant common group, and the inclusion and respect procedural fairness communicates to the subgroup. However, its benefits may be somewhat limited when the decision is portrayed as affecting the common good (potentially partially defined), or when outcome entitlements derive more clearly from the salient representation of the common group than procedural entitlements do.

Identity and retributive justice

If we understand both distributive and procedural justice as involving a notion of entitlement (to certain outcomes or procedures, respectively), the violation of those entitlements is the precondition for the experience of injustice. If this were the whole story, the restoration of justice should be possible by (re-)creating a situation where the entitlements are met. However, when we blame another person or group for an entitlement violation, regarding it as a deliberate transgression, the restoration of entitlement does commonly not suffice to restore a sense of justice. The fact of a wilful norm violation remains and cannot be simply undone. The transgression itself, beyond the injustice it created, requires a response. The question of what restores justice after a transgression is a matter of retributive justice (Vidmar, 2000).

A common response to transgressions is to impose a punishment on the offender; and while goals of punishment may be diverse, research suggests that the goal of restoring a sense of justice, by meeting a notion of just deserts, is primary (Carlsmith, Darley, & Robinson, 2002). However, how exactly punishment of an offender can restore a sense of justice is not immediately clear. In fact, based on anecdotal observations, punishment is not always necessary to restore a sense of justice in victims; sometimes victims may prefer an expression of remorse from the offender, and/or they would like to be able to forgive the offender. In criminal justice, we have indeed witnessed in recent decades the emergence of restorative justice as an alternative paradigm to traditional court-based justice. In its most proto-typical form, victim and offender (and representatives of their wider group) work through the transgression together in order to achieve an understanding of the harm done to the victim and community, the values violated and the actions required to deal with the injustice (e.g., Braithwaite, 1998).

To sum up, for a proper theoretical understanding of justice responses to transgressions, we need to specify what exactly punishment can achieve for a sense of justice, what exactly the nature of the hurt is, and how punishment can deal with it. Similarly, we need to account for the limits of punishment and the promise of restorative alternatives. Finally, if either punishment or restorative processes can restore a sense of justice in victims, when is each of them sought or considered appropriate in restoring justice?

A retributive/restorative model of responses to injustice

To answer these and related questions, we have recently embarked on a research programme that distinguishes between two notions of justice after transgressions: retributive and restorative justice (Wenzel et al., 2008). Retributive justice is the notion of just deserts: because of having violated rules or norms offenders deserve to be punished; and the punishment is necessary and sufficient to restore a moral balance (see Carlsmith et al., 2002). Importantly, it is the punishment per se that restores justice; it is not required that the offender agrees to the punishment or is somehow reformed by the punishment. The process is rather one of assertion against the offender, through unilaterally imposing punishment, suffering or humiliation on the offender. In contrast, based on, but essentially abstracting from, the practices that recently emerged in the criminal justice arena, restorative just-ice is the notion that justice is fully restored when the affected parties, victim and offender, come to a consensus about the harm done and the values violated and, through this consensus, reaffirm the validity of the shared values. The process is one of dialogue in which all affected parties are given a voice and seek to come to a shared understanding (Okimoto & Wenzel, 2008; Wenzel et al., 2008). While punishment need not be part of the process, the parties may bilaterally decide that punishment is required, for example, as an action that affirms their consensus, repairs some of the harm done to the victim or community, and/or encourages the offender to re-commit to the community and its values (see Okimoto & Wenzel, in press).

In order to understand when each of these two justice notions is likely to be adopted, we need to consider the symbolic meaning that is communi-cated when an offender deliberately (or negligently) violates rules and the entitlements of others (Wenzel et al., 2008). Specifically, two such symbolic implications of transgressions can be distinguished. First, when violating a rule and harming another the offender may be seen as putting him or herself above the rule, above the victim and above the community. In effect, the offender humiliates and disempowers the victim, expresses contempt for the community and, thus, illegitimately appropriates status and power vis-à-vis victim and community. In order to undo this and restore a moral balance, the offender in turn needs to be disempowered and degraded. The imposition of punishment, with its implied humiliation and disempowerment of the offender, would seem the most effective response to this. Second, the offender's transgression can also primarily be seen as the violation of values that were supposed to be shared between victim, offender, and the wider community, questioning the validity of values that define their common identity. The reaffirmation of the values would thus be paramount for the restoration of justice. A renewal of consensus about the values, and specifically an acknowledgement of that consensus by the offender, would seem the most effective response.

Summing up, when a transgression is primarily understood as an illegitimate appropriation of status and power, victims (and affected onlookers) should more likely adopt a retributive justice notion; but when the transgression is primarily understood as a questioning of values presumed to be shared, victims (and affected onlookers) should more likely adopt a restorative justice notion. It should be emphasized, however, that these are probabilistic predictions, because status/power and value concerns are not necessarily independent of each other, and certain elements of retributive and restorative justice responses might address both concerns (Okimoto & Wenzel, 2008; Wenzel et al., 2008).

This conceptualization also has consequences for the role of identity. First, status and power are inherently relative: the offender's status or power gain is at the cost of the victim's (or community's). Status/power concerns imply that, as a victim, one defines oneself in comparison to the offender and as distinct from the offender; as self versus non-self and, thus, as having different identities in the given situation. Hence, in situations where victims define their identity as different from the offender's, they are more likely to be concerned about the status/power implications of the transgression and therefore more likely to adopt a retributive notion of justice that deals with these concerns. Second, the perception of a transgression as questioning the validity of values implies the expectation that the offender shares the same values as the victim (or community). Such an expectation is based on the categorization of the offender as similar to the victim and, thus, as sharing a relevant identity in the given context (Turner, 1987). Hence, in situations where victims believe they share a relevant common identity with the offender, they are more likely to be concerned about the value implications of the transgression, and therefore more likely to adopt a restorative notion of justice that deals with these concerns. Wenzel, Okimoto, Feather, and Platow (in press) provide evidence for these predictions. For example, in a scenario of company theft, a common identity (i.e., the offender belonging to the same company rather than being temporarily hired from a different company) decreased the adoption of a retributive justice notion and increased the endorsement of restorative justice.

Implications for intergroup relations

When the offender and the victim are groups, or they are individuals who are perceived to act as members of their different groups, the transgression, its symbolic meaning, and the quality of responses, can obviously have implications for the relations between the groups. In fact, many groups who have problematic relations seem to have a history of perpetration and victimization (although often with both groups assuming both roles at different points of the conflict): African Americans and European Americans, Israelis and Palestinians, Protestants and Catholics in Northern Ireland, or Indigenous and Non-Indigenous Australians. It is therefore surprising that relatively little theory and research has focused on intergroup transgressions as a factor in intergroup relations (e.g., DeRidder & Tripathi, 1992; Lickel, Miller, Stenstrom, Denson, & Schmader, 2006), although recent research on collective guilt and collective forgiveness has been an important addition in this respect (e.g., Branscombe & Doosje, 2004).

Research on intergroup aggression suggests that groups are likely to be more group-serving or rigid in their interpretation of an act committed by an outgroup, attributing greater severity, intentionality, and non-normativeness to the transgression compared to individual victims vis-à-vis individual offenders (Mummendey & Otten, 1993). Correspondingly, groups are likely to respond with greater levels of retaliation, leading to an accelerated escalation of the conflict (Meier & Hinsz, 2004). From the perspective of the Retributive/Restorative Model, however, it can be argued that not only could the appraisal of the severity or intensity of the transgression differ in intergroup compared to interpersonal contexts, but also the qualitative symbolic meaning attributed to the transgression.

Specifically, because in intergroup transgressions offender and victim are (or belong to) different groups, they are less likely to perceive a common identity. Instead, they should be more likely to see and evaluate their group in comparison and competition with the outgroup (Turner, 1981). Hence, the status and power implications of the transgression may be a greater concern in intergroup contexts. Groups may react more strongly to a transgression that seems aimed at lowering the ingroup's status and power. In contrast, in intragroup situations where offender and victim are members of the same social group and share a common identity, the value implications of the transgression may be a greater concern and responded to more strongly (Vidmar, 2002).

A recent study provided some evidence for these predictions (Okimoto & Wenzel, 2007). Students at an Australian university were presented with a (fictitious) newspaper report about an attempted terrorist attack in Australia. The suspects were said to be either Australian born or foreign nationals illegally in Australia, depending on the experimental condition. Further, a communication from the terrorists indicated that they committed the act in order to either thwart Australia's presumed regional power aspirations, or question its values and way of life. Identification with Australia was measured. The results showed that suspect group membership and motive did not have any effects on the punitivity of the response when respondents identified only weakly with Australians. However, when respondents identified strongly with Australians, suspect group membership and motive interacted significantly. The retribution sought for ingroup offenders was stronger when their motive was to question Australia's values rather than to undermine its status/power, but the retribution sought for outgroup offenders was stronger when their motive was to disempower the ingroup rather than to challenge its values. These findings are consistent with the prediction that status/power concerns over a transgression are more important in intergroup contexts, and value concerns more important in intragroup contexts.

However, further research will need to investigate whether these different primary concerns in intra- and intergroup contexts also lead to the adoption of different notions of justice and different concrete responses to a transgression (e.g., retaliation versus reconciliation). Moreover, the unfolding story is likely to be more complicated. First, even members of two groups in a relevant intergroup context might, in certain circumstances, refer to a common identity – even if it might just be the very abstract common identity of humanity. To the extent that this is true, value concerns could be just as relevant as concerns about status and power. Likewise, restorative justice might then be a more salient justice notion, and restorative alternatives to retaliation and revenge, such as seeking an apology and offering forgiveness, might be more likely to be endorsed (see also Wohl & Branscombe, 2005).

Second, concerns about status, power, and values might be even more interdependent in intergroup contexts than in interpersonal contexts. For example, a group might derive a positive social identity and sense of status from the distinct values it holds (and that it might think any group should hold). A transgression that questions those values might thus also challenge the group's status. So, a western nation like Australia may feel some pride about its liberal values such as tolerance and individualism. A terrorist act might be considered a challenge to its status *because* it questions those values. Under these conditions, a value challenge might lead to the endorsement of a retributive justice notion and punitive responses.

Third, even where groups refer to a common identity and presumably shared values, the kind of justice notion and the punitive or restorative quality of the response chosen could also depend on the nature of the values as they are understood by the victim group. For example, Mummendey (2007) argues that group values can take the form of minimum or maximum goals, and the quality of the response to a violation of the goals might differ.

Minimum goals are absolute, and any deviation from them is *negative* and disqualifies the transgressor; maximum goals are gradual and desirable, and failure to contribute to the goals is *less positive* (see Brendl & Higgins, 1996). Hence, Mummendey argues, with a transgression that violates minimum goals the response should be more punitive and exclusionary, whereas a violation of maximum goals could allow for more restorative and re-integrative responses (Fritsche, Kessler, Mummendey, & Neumann, in press).

To sum up, the retributive/restorative model helps us to understand how perceptions of injustice can affect intergroup relations, specifically by theorizing the symbolic meaning of such transgressions in terms of status/power and value concerns. It is argued that these symbolic meanings attributed to the transgression affect whether either a more retributive or a restorative justice notion is adopted, where the former is more likely to invite conflict escalation and the latter conciliation.

Conclusions

The present chapter clearly shows that the concept of justice is important for an understanding of the relations between social groups. This is true not only for distributive justice, the facet that intergroup research has traditionally focused on, for example, through the concept of group relative deprivation (e.g., Vanneman & Pettigrew, 1972) or the concept of (il)legitimacy of status relations in social identity theory (Tajfel & Turner, 1986). Rather, procedural and retributive/restorative justice are also highly relevant; for example, towards bridging interethnic differences and realizing multiculturalism (e.g., Huo, 2003; Tyler et al., 1997), and dealing constructively with the groups' history and past wrongs (e.g., Branscombe & Doosje, 2004). Particularly, an analysis of justice in its interrelations with identity is very useful in this context.

Indeed, the present discussion shows that our understanding of all three facets of justice – distributive, procedural and retributive/restorative justice – benefits from an analysis in terms of identity processes; and such an analysis allows a more integrative view of justice as a tripartite concept (see also Tyler et al., 1997). Specifically, there are two identity-relevant dimensions that permeate all three forms of justice; that is, a sense of justice based on inclusion and a sense of justice based on differentiation. We may be reminded here of Brewer's (1991) theory of optimal distinctiveness that also argues for two such identity motives (which are assumed to be competing forces demanding a kind of balance). In the present analysis this means parallel arguments can be made for distributive, procedural and retributive/restorative justice.

On the one hand, people derive a sense of identity, meaning, and esteem from their *inclusion* in a valued social group. In distributive justice, a realization of one's entitlements as an equal member or subgroup of a relevant group reflects and confirms one's inclusion in that group and one's social identity as part of that group. Outcomes that fall short of such entitlement signal that a person or subgroup is not fully considered part of the group, and such an identity threat (given a sufficient level of identification) might partly underlie concern for distributive justice in this situation. In procedural justice, the experience that group representatives treat its members or subgroups fairly, grant them voice, and meet them with respect, confirms one's positive evaluation of the group and fosters one's pride in the group. Unfair procedures signal that the group is not maintaining moral values, and is not a positive source of collective self-esteem, and such a threat (given a sufficient level of identification) might partly underlie concern for procedural justice. In response to a transgression, one's victimization by an offender who is believed to share the same relevant identity questions values that were expected to be shared. Concerns about the values of the common group (given a sufficient level of identification) should primarily motivate a restorative justice notion, to renew the consensus with the offender and revalidate the values that define the common identity.

On the other hand, people derive a sense of identity, meaning, and esteem from their *differentiation* from other groups or members. In distributive justice, a realization of one's entitlements as a relatively prototypical member or subgroup of a relevant group reflects and confirms one's high status in that group (and/or the values that one considers as making up the group's identity and defining prototypicality for the group). Outcomes that fall short of such entitlements signal that a person or subgroup is not considered prototypical of the group, and such a threat to their status and/or values might partly underlie concern for distributive justice in this situation. In procedural justice, the experience that one is treated fairly by group representatives, granted voice, and shown respect, confirms one's sense of positive appreciation as a member of the group and fosters one's sense of relative standing in the group. Procedurally unfair treatment signals that the group is not holding the person or subgroup in high esteem, as not particularly worthy or central to the common group; and such a threat might partly underlie concern for procedural justice. In response to a transgression, one's victimization by an offender, in opposition to whom one defines one's self or group, is seen as assuming power and status over the self or ingroup. Concerns about status and power vis-à-vis the offender (and within the community) should primarily motivate a retributive justice notion and punitive response, to degrade and disempower the offender.

The present chapter has not only shown how these identity processes of equivalence and differentiation are implicated in distributive, procedural and retributive/restorative justice, but also that they may apply to justice issues in intergroup as well as interpersonal/intragroup situations. An analysis of justice in terms of identity processes adds an important perspective on the understanding of intergroup relations, not least so because perceptions of justice and injustice are a primary cause of intergroup conflict and determinant of the quality of intergroup relations (see also Brown, Chapter 10 in this volume).

Acknowledgements

Thanks to Tyler Okimoto for his comments on an earlier version of this chapter, and to Julie Peard for her help with manuscript preparation.

References

Adams, J. S. (1965). Inequity in social exchange. In L. Berkowitz (Ed.), *Advances in experimental social psychology* (Vol. 2, pp. 267–299). New York: Academic Press.

Bies, R. J., & Moag, J. (1986). Interactional justice: Communication criteria of fairness. In R. Lewicki, M. Bazerman, & B. Sheppard (Eds.), *Research on negotiation in organizations* (pp. 43–55). Greenwich, CT: JAI Press.

Braithwaite, J. (1998). Restorative justice. In M. Tonry (Ed.), *The handbook of crime and punishment* (pp. 323–344). Oxford: Oxford University Press.

Branscombe, N. R., & Doosje, B. (Eds.) (2004). *Collective guilt: International perspectives*. Cambridge: Cambridge University Press.

Brendl, C. M., & Higgins, E. T. (1996). Principles of judging valence: What makes events positive or negative? In M. P. Zanna (Ed.), *Advances in experimental social psychology* (Vol. 28, pp. 95–160). San Diego, CA: Academic Press.

Brewer, M. B. (1991). The social self: On being the same and different at the same time. *Personality and Social Psychology Bulletin, 17*, 475–482.

Carlsmith, K. M., Darley, J. M., & Robinson, P. H. (2002). Why do we punish? Deterrence and just deserts as motives for punishment. *Journal of Personality and Social Psychology, 83*, 284–299.

Clayton, S., & Opotow, S. (2003). Justice and identity: Changing perspectives on what is fair. *Personality and Social Psychology Review, 7*, 298–310.

DeRidder, R., & Tripathi, R. C. (Eds.) (1992). *Norm violation and intergroup relations*. New York: Clarendon Press/Oxford University Press.

Deutsch, M. (1985). *Distributive justice: A social-psychological perspective*. New Haven, CT: Yale University Press.

Devos, T., & Banaji, M. R. (2005). American = white? *Journal of Personality and Social Psychology, 88*, 447–466.

Fritsche, I., Kessler, T., Mummendey, A., & Neumann, J. (in press). Minimal and maximal goal orientation and reactions to norm violations. *European Journal of Social Psychology*.

Gaertner, S. L., & Dovidio, J. F. (2000). *Reducing intergroup bias: The common ingroup identitiy model*. Philadelphia: Psychology Press.

Greenberg, J. (1988). Equity and workplace status: A field experiment. *Journal of Applied Psychology, 73*, 606–613.

Huo, Y. J. (2003). Procedural justice and social regulation across group boundaries: Does subgroup identity undermine relationship-based governance? *Personality and Social Psychology Bulletin, 29*, 336–348.

Huo, Y. J., & Molina, L. E. (2006). Is pluralism a viable model of diversity? The benefits and limits of subgroup respect. *Group Processes and Intergroup Relations, 9*, 359–376.

Huo, Y. J., Molina, L. E., Sawahata, R., & Deang, J. M. (2005). Leadership and the management of conflicts in diverse groups: Why acknowledging versus neglecting subgroup identity matters. *European Journal of Social Psychology, 35*, 237–254.

Huo, Y. J., Smith, H. J., Tyler, T. R., & Lind, E. A. (1996). Superordinate identification, subgroup identification, and justice concerns: Is separatism the problem, is assimilation the answer? *Psychological Science, 7,* 40–45.

Jost, J. T., & Hunyady, O. (2002). The psychology of system justification and the palliative function of ideology. *European Review of Social Psychology, 13,* 111–153.

Lerner, M. J. (1991). Integrating societal and psychological rules of entitlement. In R. Vermunt & H. Steensma (Eds.), *Social justice in human relations* (Vol. 1, pp. 13–32). New York: Plenum Press.

Leung, K., Tong, K.-K., & Lind, E. (2007). Realpolitik versus fair process: Moderating effects of group identification on acceptance of political decisions. *Journal of Personality and Social Psychology, 92,* 476–489.

Leventhal, G. S. (1980). What should be done with equity theory? New approaches to the study of fairness in social relationships. In K. J. Gergen, M. S. Greenberg, & R. H. Willis (Eds.), *Social exchange: Advances in theory and research* (pp. 27–55). New York: Plenum Press.

Lickel, B., Miller, N., Stenstrom, D. M., Denson, T. F., & Schmader, T. (2006). Vicarious retribution: The role of collective blame in intergroup aggression. *Personality and Social Psychology Review, 10,* 372–390.

Lind, E. A., Kanfer, R., & Earley, P. C. (1990). Voice, control, and procedural justice: Instrumental and noninstrumental concerns in fairness judgments. *Journal of Personality and Social Psychology, 59,* 952–959.

Lind, E. A., & Tyler, T. R. (1988). *The social psychology of procedural justice.* New York: Plenum Press.

Meier, B. P., & Hinsz, V. B. (2004). A comparison of human aggression committed by groups and individuals: An interindividual–intergroup discontinuity. *Journal of Experimental Social Psychology, 40,* 551–559.

Mikula, G. (1980). On the role of justice in allocation decisions. In G. Mikula (Ed.), *Justice and social interaction* (pp. 127–166). New York: Springer-Verlag.

Mummendey, A. (2007, June). *Tolerance and rejection in intergroup relations.* Paper presented at the 10th Jena Meeting on Intergroup Processes, Castle Oppurg, Germany.

Mummendey, A., Kessler, T., Klink, A., & Mielke, R. (1999). Strategies to cope with negative social identity: Predictions by social identity theory and relative deprivation theory. *Journal of Personality and Social Psychology, 76,* 229–245.

Mummendey, A., & Otten, S. (1993). Aggression: Interaction between individuals and social groups. In R. B. Felson & J. T. Tedeschi (Eds.), *Aggression and violence: Social interactionist perspectives* (pp. 145–167). Washington, DC: American Psychological Association.

Mummendey, A., & Wenzel, M. (1999). Social discrimination and tolerance in intergroup relations: Reactions to intergroup difference. *Personality and Social Psychology Review, 3,* 158–174.

Oakes, P. J. (1987). The salience of social categories. In J. C. Turner, M. A. Hogg, P. J. Oakes, S. D. Reicher, & M. S. Wetherell (Eds.), *Rediscovering the social group: A self-categorization theory* (pp. 117–141). Oxford: Basil Blackwell.

Oakes, P. J., Haslam, S. A., & Turner, J. C. (1998). The role of prototypicality in group influence and cohesion: Contextual variation in the graded structure of social categories. In S. Worchel, J. F. Morales, D. Paez, & J.-C. Deschamps (Eds.), *Social identity: International perspectives* (pp. 75–92). London: Sage.

Okimoto, T., G., & Wenzel, M. (2007). *National identity and retributive responses to terrorism: Symbolic identity implications in inter and intra-group conflict.* Unpublished manuscript.

Okimoto, T. G., & Wenzel, M. (2008). The symbolic meaning of transgressions: Towards a unifying framework of justice restoration. In K. A. Hegtvedt & J. Clay-Warner (Eds.), *Advances in group processes: Justice* (Vol. 25, pp. 291–326). Bingley, UK: Emerald.

Okimoto, T. G., & Wenzel, M. (in press). Punishment as restoration of group and offender values following a transgression: Value consensus through symbolic labelling and offender reform. *European Journal of Social Psychology.*

Skitka, L. J. (2003). Of different minds: An accessible identity model of justice reasoning. *Personality and Social Psychology Review, 7,* 286–297.

Smith, H. J., Tyler, T. R., Huo, Y. J., Ortiz, D. J., & Lind, E. (1998). The self-relevant implications of the group-value model: Group membership, self-worth, and treatment quality. *Journal of Experimental Social Psychology, 34,* 470–493.

Tajfel, H. (Ed.). (1978). *Differentiation between social groups: Studies in the psychology of intergroup relations.* London: Academic Press.

Tajfel, H., & Turner, J. C. (1986). The social identity theory of intergroup behavior. In S. Worchel & G. Austin (Eds.), *Psychology of intergroup relations* (pp. 7–24). Chicago: Nelson-Hall.

Thibaut, J., & Walker, L. (1975). *Procedural justice: A psychological analysis.* Hillsdale, NJ: Lawrence Erlbaum Associates, Inc.

Turner, J. C. (1981). The experimental social psychology of intergroup behaviour. In J. C. Turner & H. Giles (Eds.), *Intergroup behaviour* (pp. 66–101). Oxford: Basil Blackwell.

Turner, J. C. (1987). A self-categorization theory. In J. C. Turner, M. A. Hogg, P. J. Oakes, S. D. Reicher, & M. S. Wetherell (Eds.), *Rediscovering the social group: A self-categorization theory* (pp. 42–67). Oxford: Blackwell.

Turner, J. C. (1991). *Social influence.* Buckingham, UK: Open University Press.

Tyler, T. R. (1994). Psychological models of the justice motive. *Journal of Personality of Social Psychology, 67,* 850–863.

Tyler, T. R., & Bies, R. J. (1990). Beyond formal procedures: The interpersonal context of procedural justice. In J. Carroll (Ed.), *Applied social psychology and organizational settings* (pp. 77–98). Hillsdale, NJ: Lawrence Erlbaum Associates, Inc.

Tyler, T. R., & Blader, S. L. (2003). The group engagement model: Procedural justice, social identity, and cooperative behavior. *Personality and Social Psychology Review, 7,* 349–361.

Tyler, T. R., Boeckmann, R. J., Smith, H. J., & Huo, Y. J. (1997). *Social justice in a diverse society.* Boulder, CO: Westview.

Tyler, T. R., Degoey, P., & Smith, H. (1996). Understanding why the justice of group procedures matters: A test of the psychological dynamics of the group-value model. *Journal of Personality and Social Psychology, 70,* 913–930.

Tyler, T. R., & Lind, E. A. (1992). A relational model of authority in groups. In M. Zanna (Ed.), *Advances in experimental social psychology* (Vol. 25, pp. 115–191). New York: Academic Press.

Tyler, T. R., & Lind, E. A. (2001). Understanding the nature of fraternalistic deprivation: Does group-based deprivation involve fair outcomes or fair treatment? In I. Walker & H. J. Smith (Eds.), *Relative deprivation: Specification, development, and integration* (pp. 44–68). New York: Cambridge University Press.

Tyler, T. R., & Smith, H. J. (1999). Justice, social identity, and group processes. In

T. R. Tyler, R. M. Kramer, & O. P. John (Eds.), *The psychology of the social self* (pp. 223–264). Mahwah, NJ: Lawrence Erlbaum Associates, Inc.

van Dijk, E., & Vermunt, R. (2000). Strategy and fairness in social decision making: Sometimes it pays to be powerless. *Journal of Experimental Social Psychology, 36*, 1–25.

Vanneman, R. D., & Pettigrew, T. F. (1972). Race and relative deprivation in the urban United States. *Race, 13*, 461–486.

Vidmar, N. (2000). Retribution and revenge. In J. Sanders & V. L. Hamilton (Eds.), *Handbook of justice research in law* (pp. 31–63). New York: Kluwer/Plenum.

Vidmar, N. (2002). Retributive justice: Its social context. In M. Ross & D. T. Miller (Eds.), *The justice motive in everyday life* (pp. 291–313). New York: Cambridge University Press.

Waldzus, S., Mummendey, A., Wenzel, M., & Boettcher, F. (2004). Of bikers, teachers and Germans: Groups' diverging views about their prototypicality. *British Journal of Social Psychology, 43*, 385–400.

Walster, E., Walster, G. W., & Berscheid, E. (1978). *Equity: Theory and research.* Boston: Allyn & Bacon.

Weber, U., Mummendey, A., & Waldzus, S. (2002). Perceived legitimacy of intergroup status differences: Its prediction by relative ingroup prototypicality. *European Journal of Social Psychology, 32*, 449–470.

Wenzel, M. (2000). Justice and identity: The significance of inclusion for perceptions of entitlement and the justice motive. *Personality and Social Psychology Bulletin, 26*, 157–176.

Wenzel, M. (2001). A social categorization approach to distributive justice: Social identity as the link between relevance of inputs and need for justice. *British Journal of Social Psychology, 40*, 315–335.

Wenzel, M. (2002). What is social about justice? Inclusive identity and group values as the basis of the justice motive. *Journal of Experimental Social Psychology, 38*, 205–218.

Wenzel, M. (2004). A social categorisation approach to distributive justice. In W. Stroebe & M. Hewstone (Eds.), *European review of social psychology* (Vol. 15, pp. 219–257). Hove, UK: Psychology Press.

Wenzel, M., Mummendey, A., & Waldzus, S. (2007). Superordinate identities and intergroup conflict: The ingroup projection model. In W. Stroebe & M. Hewstone (Eds.), *European review of social psychology* (Vol. 18, pp. 331–372). Hove, UK: Psychology Press.

Wenzel, M., Okimoto, T. G., Feather, N. T., & Platow, M. J. (in press). *Justice through consensus: Shared identity and the preference for a restorative notion of justice.* European Journal of Social Psychology

Wenzel, M., Okimoto, T. G., Feather, N. T., & Platow, M. J. (2008). Retributive and restorative justice. *Law and Human Behavior, 32*, 375–389.

Wohl, M. J. A., & Branscombe, N. R. (2005). Forgiveness and collective guilt assignment to historical perpetrator groups depend on level of social category inclusiveness. *Journal of Personality and Social Psychology, 88*, 288–303.

Part II

Recent approaches to motivation and intergroup relations

5　Mood and cognition in intergroup judgment

Maya Machunsky and Thorsten Meiser
Mannheim University

Positive or negative mood forms an affective background state that does not necessarily originate from the appraisal of a specific situation or event and, thus, has to be distinguished from concrete emotions like love, joy, fear or anger (Schwarz & Clore, 1996). Positive and negative mood states can exert effects on information processing and social judgment in different ways (see Fiedler, 2001; Forgas, 1992, 1995, 2001). On the one hand, mood facilitates the accessibility of information that was encoded in a similar affective state or whose valence is congruent to the mood state at the time of retrieval. As a consequence, mood can affect social judgments that rely on the retrieval and integration of information from memory. On the other hand, mood states influence the kind of cognitive processing that is engaged to form a social judgment in the first place. That is, mood determines whether a social judgment is derived by a substantive search for relevant information in memory, by the use of heuristic cues like stereotype labels, or by a motivated search for positive or negative information that serves self-enhancement or mood-repair purposes. The different ways in which mood states affect memory, information processing and social judgment in general are elaborated in the first section of this chapter.

The information-processing strategies that are induced by mood states have immediate implications for judgments and social behavior in intergroup contexts. Since positive mood states encourage heuristic processing and the perception of remote associations, they increase the likelihood of "mindless discrimination" of outgroup members (Forgas & Fiedler, 1996) as well as the likelihood of recategorizing the ingroup and outgroup to a joint social category (Dovidio, Gaertner, Isen, & Lowrance, 1995). Negative mood states, in contrast, give rise to substantial information processing and to a motivational need for mood repair, which reduces the likelihood of mindless discrimination but increases the likelihood of motivated ingroup favoritism and outgroup derogation in the service of self-enhancement (Forgas & Fiedler, 1996). Based on the general discussion of mood effects on memory and social cognition in the first section, the second section of this chapter therefore provides an overview of the theoretical approaches and empirical findings concerning the effects of positive and negative mood states on intergroup judgments and intergroup behavior.

Mood effects on memory, information processing and social judgment

Mood and memory

Inasmuch as social judgments rely on the integration of information that is retrieved from memory, the analysis of affective influences on learning and memory is essential for the understanding of the cognitive processes that determine – and possibly bias – judgments and decisions, including the amount, accuracy, and potential selectivity of information retrieval. A large body of evidence has demonstrated that the affective content of information has noticeable effects on attention and memory. Stimuli with negative valence were shown to attract more attention than stimuli with positive valence (Pratto & John, 1991), and stimuli that are relevant for the perceiver's approach or avoidance reaction were shown to attract more attention than stimuli whose valence is not relevant for the perceiver's reaction (Wentura, Rothermund, & Bak, 2000). In a similar vein, stimuli with positive or negative valence lead to better recognition and episodic memory than neutral stimuli, and memory for stimuli with negative valence exceeds memory for stimuli with positive valence (e.g., Dewhurst & Parry, 2000; Ochsner, 2000).

Apart from the impact of an event's affective content on learning and memory, the affective state of the perceiver also modulates memory performance. Negative and depressive mood states have often been found to be associated with memory deficits (see Hertel & Meiser, 2000), which are presumably the result of an inefficient use of spontaneous processing strategies (Hertel & Hardin, 1990) and impaired inhibition of task-irrelevant information processing at encoding (von Hecker & Meiser, 2005). Positive mood, in contrast, enhances recognition for events that actually occurred, but also increases the rate of false alarms for events that can be reconstructed as part of an activated schema (Bless, Clore, Schwarz, Golisano, Rabe, & Wölk, 1996; Levine & Bluck, 2004). Taken together, these results reveal that mood states moderate memory processes during encoding and retrieval, including a stronger reliance on schematic knowledge in the case of positive mood.

Importantly, over and above the effects of stimulus valence and the perceiver's mood state per se, there is an interaction between the affective content of events and the perceiver's mood on learning and memory. This interaction is reflected by the phenomenon of *mood congruence* (Blaney, 1986; Bower, 1981; Forgas & Bower, 1987), which denotes an advantage of learning and retrieval for those stimuli whose valence match the perceiver's current mood state as opposed to stimuli that do not match the mood state. For example, in a classical study participants recalled more pleasant than unpleasant incidents from their childhood in a happy mood state, whereas the difference was reversed in a sad mood state (Bower, 1981).

An extension of the principle of mood congruence was demonstrated by Förster and Strack (1996). In an incidental learning task, the authors showed that recognition accuracy for positive and negative words was higher if participants performed movements expressing a positive reaction (i.e., nodding) during the encoding of positive words, and movements expressing a negative reaction (i.e., shaking one's head) during the encoding of negative words, as compared to a condition in which the motor expression did not match word valence. Because the approach and avoidance related meaning of the head movements was concealed by a cover story, these findings support the notion that memory performance depends on the compatibility between an event's valence on the one hand and the perceiver's affective state and behavior on the other, even if the affective implication is outside of awareness.

Concerning the perceiver's mood as a determinant of memory perform- ance, there is also an interaction between mood during encoding and mood during retrieval. This interaction is a special case of the general principle of state-dependent memory, which means a memory advantage if the internal condition (e.g., one's pharmacological state, physiological state, mood, etc.) at retrieval matches the internal condition at encoding. The specific phenom- enon of *mood-state dependent memory* was demonstrated in experiments by Bower (1981; see also Blaney, 1986), which revealed better recall of word lists if mood at encoding and mood at retrieval were either both positive or both negative as compared to conditions where mood was positive at one occasion (i.e., encoding or retrieval) but negative at the other. Further research showed that the detrimental effect of mood changes between encoding and retrieval depends on the kind of information processing during encoding, such that memory for internally generated information is more susceptible to mood changes than memory for externally presented information (Eich & Metcalfe, 1989). This result fits the general assumption that mood effects on memory are stronger in *productive tasks*, in which the to-be-remembered material is actively processed and associated with knowledge and contextual informa- tion, than in merely *reproductive tasks*, in which the to-be-remembered material is stored without being associated with internal or external context information (Fiedler, 1990).

Taken together, affective influences on human learning and memory have been demonstrated in terms of:

- effects of stimulus valence on attention and memory performance,
- effects of the perceiver's mood state on memory performance and reconstructive memory processes (e.g., intrusions from schemata),
- mood congruency in learning and recall, and
- mood state-dependent memory.

These various effects can be expected to have an impact on social judgments to the extent to which these judgments are based on information that is retrieved from memory. However, mood also modulates the cognitive processes of thinking and judgment formation, including the use of memory retrieval as a basis for judgments and decisions, as will be considered next.

Mood and information processing

In the literature on social cognition, it has early been realized that people in happy mood states are more likely to use intuition and heuristics as a basis for judgments and decisions than are people in neutral or sad mood states (e.g., Isen, 1987; see Forgas, 2001, for an overview). The notion that positive affect leads to a more heuristic processing style and to a more creative way of thinking has been corroborated in many studies that employed a variety of cognitive tasks in combination with different methods of mood manipulation. To name but a few examples, positive mood was shown to increase performance in a creative problem-solving task (i.e., Duncker's candle problem; Isen, Daubman, & Nowicki, 1987) and to improve efficiency in a complex decision scenario, such that decisions were reached faster and by considering fewer details under positive mood without sacrificing accuracy (Isen & Means, 1983).

Moreover, positive mood states facilitate the detection of commonalities among loosely related concepts as part of an intuitive and creative processing style, as has been shown in categorization tasks and remote associates tests. In categorization tasks, atypical elements of a set are judged as more typical under positive mood than under neutral or negative mood (Isen & Daubman, 1984), and participants in positive mood are more likely to find a concept that is common to three remotely associated words (Isen et al., 1987). Importantly, participants show better discrimination in coherence judgments between remotely associated word triads and semantically unrelated triads under positive mood than under neutral or negative mood even if the common concept for associated triads cannot be named (Bolte, Goschke, & Kuhl, 2003). These results indicate that positive affect enhances the use and efficiency of intuitive processes in situations in which strategically controlled retrieval processes may fail.

The picture of a more heuristic and less analytically focused processing style under positive mood has recently been complemented by the finding that positive mood states enhance cognitive flexibility in task settings that require shifts of attention (Dreisbach & Goschke, 2004). More specifically, this study demonstrated that positive affect reduces perseveration, so that previously relevant information which is irrelevant in a new task set can successfully be ignored. However, this flexibility comes at the cost of increased susceptibility to distraction by novel information that is in fact irrelevant and should be ignored.

To summarize, mood states affect the way of thinking and information processing, such that positive mood reduces the use of an analytically focused processing style and thus enhances:

- creative problem solving,
- heuristic processing,
- the formation of broader categories,
- the detection of commonalities among loosely related concepts, and
- the flexibility of cognitive processes,

relative to negative mood.

Mood and social judgment

As we have seen so far, mood states can influence judgments by enhancing the accessibility of events that have mood-congruent valence or that were encoded in a similar affective state in the past, and mood can also influence judgment formation via the use of a more heuristic and flexible processing style as opposed to a more analytically focused processing style. It is therefore not surprising that mood is considered a central moderating variable of judgments and decisions in various domains of social psychological research.

For instance, mood was shown to push forward rather general judgments, in that momentary and transient affective states are heuristically taken as informational bases to come to a judgment of overall well-being and life satisfaction (Schwarz & Clore, 1983). The use of this *mood-as-information heuristic* was further shown to depend on the possibility to attribute the current affective state to external sources, rather than to life satisfaction and general well being. More precisely, the possibility to attribute one's state to an external source counteracted the use of current mood as an informational basis in the case of negative mood, but not in the case of positive mood (Schwarz & Clore, 1983). These findings indicate that the mood-as-information heuristic reflects a misattribution of the prevailing affective state to the target of judgment, and they suggest as well that directive influences of mood are also at work, such as a search for the origin of negative mood with a potential for mood repair.

A similar combination of cognitive and motivational mood effects was observed in the field of person perception. According to the cognitive principle of mood congruence, positive details of person descriptions are attended to more carefully than negative details under positive mood, whereas the reverse holds true under negative mood (Forgas & Bower, 1987). The resulting person judgments are also biased towards the prevailing mood state, with more positive person judgments formed by happy than by sad participants. However, the initial mood congruence was shown to turn to mood incongruence after a series of judgments (Forgas & Ciarrochi, 2002): Over a series of person or self descriptions, the generated descriptions become more negative in the case of happy mood, and more positive in the case of sad mood, reversing the initial effect of mood congruence. This reversal can be interpreted as support for a model of effective mood management, which implies that mood states are initially maintained or even enhanced by mood-congruent processing, but are controlled and regulated in the later course of the task by accessing mood-incongruent information (see also Josephson, Singer, & Salovey, 1996; Parrott & Sabini, 1990; Sedikides, 1994).

Besides the informational value of affective states for judgments and mood-management strategies, mood modulates the way cognitive processing takes place, and thus influences judgmental biases that crucially depend on the choice of a heuristic versus analytical processing style. One case in point is the so-called fundamental attribution error, which reflects the tendency to attribute overt behavior to dispositional person characteristics and to use observed behavior in person judgments even if the behavior was obviously coerced by external or situational factors. In line with the assumption that the fundamental attribution error is a consequence of heuristic processing that overlooks the impact of situational and external forces on behavior, and building on the aforementioned evidence that positive mood increases the use of heuristic strategies whereas negative mood strengthens the use of more analytical processing, the fundamental attribution error was shown to be exacerbated under positive mood and to diminish under negative mood (Forgas, 1998).

In a similar vein, the effectiveness of persuasive communication for attitude change essentially depends on characteristics of the message and on the cognitive processing style of the perceiver (Chaiken, 1980; Petty, Cacioppo, & Goldman, 1981). As a consequence, persuasive effects should be moderated by mood states via their effects on processing style. Studies that investigated attitude change as a function of argument quality and mood state revealed that argument quality determines the extent of attitude change when the message is received under negative mood (Bless, Bohner, Schwarz, & Strack, 1990; Bless, Mackie, & Schwarz, 1992), which underlines the assumption that negative mood leads to an analytical way of processing. When a persuasive message is received in positive mood, in contrast, attitude change is not affected by argument quality, unless attention is explicitly directed to the quality of argument by instruction (Bless et al., 1990). This evidence supports the view that positive mood reduces the spontaneous use of elaborative, argument-based processing. Similarly, when mood is induced after the persuasive message was received but before the attitude judgment has to be formed, judgment formation relies on rather global impressions of the message in the case of positive mood, but on more detailed information in the case of negative mood (Bless et al., 1992). This line of research on mood and the effectiveness of persuasive communication, which nicely fits the view that affective states exert their impact on social judgment via effects on cognitive processing style, was recently extended from the reception of persuasive messages to the production of such messages, showing that people produce arguments of better quality under negative mood than under positive mood (Forgas, 2007).

Last but not least, mood effects have been analyzed in the domain of social stereotyping, with demonstrations of mood effects on the use of prevailing stereotypes as well as on the formation of novel stereotypes. More specifically, research on the use of existing stereotypes showed that judgments of a target person were more strongly biased towards an activated stereotype if a happy mood was induced as compared with a neutral mood (Bodenhausen, Kramer, & Süsser, 1994). However, this effect was eliminated if participants were made to believe that they would have to justify their judgments. These results corroborate the view that stereotypes provide heuristic mental devices that are utilized under positive mood and avoided under negative mood, but the results also reflect the cognitive flexibility under positive mood to employ heuristic shortcuts when appropriate, and to engage more elaborate cognitive procedures in situations of accountability.

Further evidence that mood moderates the use of simplifying processing strategies of social stereotyping stems from research on stereotype formation about novel groups in settings with a confounding context factor. Confounding context factors can give rise to biases in the perception of a correlation between social group membership and relevant attributes such as likeability or performance. These biases can arise in terms of spurious correlations, in which the role of a confounding factor is overlooked (Schaller & O'Brien, 1992), or in terms of pseudo-contingencies, in which erroneous inferences are drawn from skewed base rates or from pairwise correlations with a confounding factor (Fiedler & Freytag, 2004; Meiser & Hewstone, 2004). In line with the assumption that negative mood states reduce the use of heuristic processes that contribute to the perception of biased correlations, a recent study on stereotype formation and personality revealed that chronically negative mood states are inversely related to the strength of the erroneous stereotype emerging from a scenario with a confounding context factor (Meiser & Hewstone, 2008). Naturally occurring negative mood therefore seems to counteract the use of simplifying reasoning schemes in inductive stereotype formation.

The reviewed research has thus brought convincing evidence that mood affects social judgments:

- by taking mood as information about the target of judgment,
- by influencing susceptibility to heuristic cues and biases, for example in attribution and persuasion, and
- by affecting the use of social stereotypes as heuristic devices in impression formation.

Furthermore, there is evidence that:

- mood elicits motivated processing with the goal of mood management and repair.

Conclusions

Our brief overview of research on mood and cognition demonstrated that mood is an essential moderator of memory and information processing that may determine the contents and the processes of social judgments in various domains. As such, mood can be expected to play a pivotal role for judgmental biases also in the specific domain of intergroup attitudes and intergroup behavior, as is discussed in the remainder of this chapter.

The role of mood in intergroup judgment

The whole range of mood effects that have been discussed in the preceding section can also be observed in the specific field of intergroup evaluations and judgments. However, because intergroup research focuses on the differential evaluation of ingroup and outgroup (i.e., ingroup bias), mood effects are particularly interesting if they lead to more positive ingroup evaluations relative to outgroup evaluations and, thus, to a possible deterioration of intergroup relations, or to more positive outgroup evaluations relative to ingroup evaluations and, thus, to a possible amelioration of intergroup relations. In other words, mood effects are especially interesting if they lead to an increase or decrease of ingroup bias (i.e., to a better evaluation of the ingroup relative to the outgroup). To explain why mood affects ingroup and outgroup evaluations differentially, additional assumptions need to be specified.

In the following, we elaborate to which extent *mood congruency effects*, *mood management effects*, and *information processing effects of mood* play an important role in an intergroup context. More insight into the complex interplay between mood and ingroup and outgroup evaluations is provided particularly by experiments by Forgas and Fiedler (1996) and by Dovidio, Gaertner, Isen, Rust, and Guerra (1998) who demonstrated that mood has no simple effect on intergroup judgments, but that the relation between mood and intergroup evaluations is moderated by contextual or personal factors. Based on the notion that mood determines the extent to which information is processed heuristically and holistically (e.g., Isen, 1987; Isen & Means, 1983), we also present an experiment that showed that mood does not necessarily alter the amount of ingroup bias but can modify the judgmental basis of ingroup bias (Machunsky & Meiser, 2008). Finally, we attempt to integrate the diverse mood effects on ingroup bias.

Mood congruence in intergroup judgments

Building on the cognitive principle of *mood congruence* (e.g., Bower, 1981), Kenworthy, Canales, Weaver, and Miller (2003) hypothesized that ingroup bias will increase under sadness. In particular, the authors' model assumes that mood has a guiding function, such that attention is selectively directed to mood-congruent cues of the target stimulus. Only if the a priori valence of the stimulus is congruent with the momentary mood state, mood will bias judgments resulting in an exaggerated response to targets with mood-congruent a priori valence (see also Miller, Urban, & Vanman, 1998). Assuming that outgroups hold more negative cues than ingroups, negative mood should exaggerate ingroup-favoring tendencies by derogating the outgroup because of its negative cues while leaving ingroup evaluations more constant.

Kenworthy and colleagues (2003) investigated this hypothesis in a crossed categorization paradigm. In such a paradigm, participants are categorized according to two dimensions simultaneously, resulting in a 2 × 2 table with one double ingroup (i.e., ii), two crossed groups (i.e., io and oi) and a double outgroup (i.e., oo). Kenworthy et al. (2003) created for each participant ideographical ii, io, oi and oo targets according to the information provided by participants at the beginning of the experiment, so that the experiment dealt with meaningful and important crossed categories. For instance, if a participant had indicated being a smoker and a fraternity member, the ii target was a smoking fraternity member, the io target a non-smoking fraternity member, the oi target a smoking non-fraternity person, and the oo target a non-smoking non-fraternity person.

It has typically been found that people evaluate the four targets according to a so-called additivity pattern (ii > crossed > oo, see Crisp & Hewstone, 2006). Under negative mood, however, a weak pattern of social exclusion was expected such that the difference between ingroup and crossed groups evaluation is much more pronounced than the difference between crossed groups and double outgroup evaluation (i.e., ii >> crossed > oo), because negative mood will affect the judgments of targets that hold negative cues (i.e., outgroup membership). In a series of experiments, Kenworthy et al. (2003) found evidence for these assumptions: Under neutral mood, judgments followed an additivity pattern, whereas a weak social exclusion pattern was observed after sadness had been induced. Thus, *mood congruency* was found to play a role also in intergroup situations.

Mood management in intergroup judgments

Mood management refers to regulation of both positive and negative moods whereas *mood repair* refers especially to the up-regulation of negative mood (Forgas, 1995). Concerning the intergroup context, Esses and Zanna (1995) hypothesized that the ingroup in particular can serve as a means to repair one's negative mood. The authors also followed the *cognitive principle of mood congruence* and argued that negative stereotypes are especially likely to come to mind when people are in a negative mood. Due to motivational influences, however, the ingroup is expected to be judged differently. Because being a member of a favorable ingroup is considered as hedonic, *mood repair* should increase ingroup attitudes. Thus, the authors expected more positive ingroup judgments under negative mood. As a consequence of both *mood repair* strategies concerning the ingroup and *mood congruence* concerning the outgroup, ingroup bias is expected to increase under negative mood. An experiment in which several national groups served as ingroups and outgroups provided support for this reasoning.

However, this result was not replicated in the following studies, so that some doubts remain. Esses and Zanna (1995) reasoned that the effect might be a result of the specific induction of negative mood. In particular, participants were requested to recollect negative life events. The self-relevant nature of this induction procedure might have triggered downward comparison or stereotype activation, which are both strategies to enhance one's threatened (social) self-esteem (Fein & Spencer, 1997; Spencer, Fein, Wolfe, Fong, & Dunn, 1998).

Information processing effects of mood and intergroup judgments

In the first section of this chapter we outlined the various effects mood can have on information processing. To reiterate a few effects that are important for the following paragraphs: Positive mood states lead to a more *heuristic processing style* with less focus on the details of information, to the *perception of more commonalities* between remotely associated stimuli, and to the *formation of broader categories*.

Extending the findings of Bodenhausen et al. (1994) who showed that positive mood increased the heuristic use of category labels and associated stereotypes, it could be argued that ingroup and outgroup labels can also be used heuristically. More specifically, using ingroup and outgroup labels heuristically should lead to more ingroup bias, as ingroups are in general associated with more positive valence than outgroups. In other words, judgments should be influenced less by the specific target information and more by group labels if heuristic processing is triggered by positive mood.

Such an effect of positive mood was reported by Abele, Gendolla, and Petzold (1998). In two experiments, participants received positive or negative individuating information about target persons. For half of the targets category information was also provided, so that targets belonged either to the minimal ingroup or the minimal outgroup. The results showed that individuating information was weighted similarly under neutral and positive mood when group labels were not available, so that the difference in likeability judgments between positive and negative targets was of the same size in both mood conditions. However, when group labels were introduced, the difference in likeability between positive and negative targets decreased and category information received more weight, such that ingroup bias increased under positive mood. In line with the assumption that positive mood states lead to stronger reliance on heuristic cues, target judgments were more guided by the target's group membership than by specific positive or negative target information if participants were in an elated mood state. Moreover, positive mood seems to particularly increase ingroup likeability, whereas outgroup likeability remains more or less at the same level.

The boundary condition of this specific mood effect was investigated by Forgas and Fiedler (1996). Like Abele et al. (1998), the authors predicted that positive mood would lead to a *heuristic use* of category labels and, hence, to more ingroup bias. For negative mood they expected a more strategic use of category labels in the sense of *mood repair* strategies, resulting also in more ingroup bias. However, the expected effects of positive and negative mood were hypothesized to be further qualified by category relevance such that positive mood would trigger heuristic processing especially under low category relevance, whereas negative mood would trigger strategic processing especially under high category relevance. In other words, participants were expected to engage in fast and simplified processing under positive mood and low relevance of ingroup–outgroup membership, whereas they were expected to engage in deliberate processing with the goal to repair their mood state under negative mood and high personal relevance of group membership. Both the latter and the former process should lead to more ingroup bias compared to a control condition. Long response latencies were expected to reflect the deliberate, motivated processing style; short response latencies should reflect the heuristic processing style.

The authors tested their hypotheses in a series of experiments in which participants were members of minimal groups. Category relevance was manipulated by informing people that group membership was highly meaningful and related to many personal and social characteristics. The analyses revealed that participants were more discriminatory under positive mood than under negative mood if group membership was of low relevance. In contrast, if group membership was of high relevance, participants were more discriminatory under negative mood than under positive mood. Moreover, the findings supported the hypothesized process using latencies as indicators of processing modus. In both the high and the low relevance condition, positive mood reduced processing latency. But whereas short latencies led to more discriminatory behavior in the low relevance condition, long latencies led to more discriminatory behavior in the high relevance condition, indicating that under low relevance the heuristic processing of the judgmental task increased ingroup bias, whereas under high relevance the deliberate and motivated mood repair strategy increased ingroup bias. In sum, these experiments supported that the interaction of personal features such as category relevance and affective state determine the processing strategy and thereby the outcome of (intergroup) evaluations.

In contrast to the detrimental effects of positive mood based on a *heuristic processing style*, there are also approaches that emphasize the positive effects of elated mood for intergroup relations. These approaches mainly rest on the finding that elated mood leads to the *formation of broader categories* (Isen & Daubman, 1984; Isen, Niedenthal, & Cantor, 1992). Dovidio et al. (1995) for instance found that the likelihood of recategorization, which is characterized as the representation of an ingroup and an outgroup within a common superordinate category, increased under positive mood. More precisely, the authors found that positive mood broadened categorization so that less typical targets (i.e., outgroup members) were also perceived as ingroup members. Because the perception of ingroup and outgroup members as belonging to one superordinate category is negatively related to ingroup bias, the authors found that positive affect is helpful in intergroup contact.

Based on the findings of Dovidio et al. (1995), Urada and Miller (2000) investigated the effects of elated mood in a crossed categorization paradigm and hypothesized that a broadened ingroup category has especially positive effects for the evaluation of crossed targets (i.e., io and oi), such that crossed targets are perceived more ingroup like and are, thus, evaluated better. However, the results showed a moderating effect, in that the positive effect of elated mood only occurred for crossed targets with a dominant ingroup membership. In other words, crossed targets that were ingroup members on a dominant (i.e., important) categorization dimension but not crossed targets that were outgroup members on a dominant dimension (i.e., io targets but not oi targets) were evaluated better under positive mood. For instance, if a participant considered US citizenship (as opposed to other nationalities) as an important category and being politically liberal (as opposed to conservative) as a not so important category, conservative Americans but not liberal non-Americans were evaluated better as a consequence of positive mood.

The moderation of the relation between mood effects and intergroup evaluation by category dominance was explained in previous research by Isen et al. (1992), who found an asymmetrical broadening effect of positive mood: Positive and neutral but not negative stimuli are more likely to be categorized as members of a positive category. Accordingly, Urada and Miller (2000) reasoned that broader categorization would not affect stimuli with strong negative cues like members of dominant outgroups.

Also Crisp and Hewstone (2000) obtained positive effects of elated mood in a crossed categorization paradigm using minimal groups. But in contrast to Urada and Miller (2000), the authors found that all four groups (i.e., ii, io, oi, and oo) were evaluated equally positively under elated mood. Apparently, one major difference in the two studies is the nature of the intergroup situation, which was minimal in the one case and highly meaningful in the other case. Such variations in personal relevance can significantly affect the choice of processing strategy, such that motivated processing becomes more likely with an increase in personal relevance (Forgas & Fiedler, 1996).

So far we have seen that positive mood can affect information processing in two ways: On the one hand, it triggers *heuristic processing*, which has detrimental effects for intergroup evaluations; on the other hand, it triggers the *formation of broader categories*, which has ameliorating effects for intergroup evaluations. A nice integration of these, at first glance, contradicting results was suggested by Dovidio et al. (1998). Building on the Common Ingroup Identity Model (CIIM), Dovidio and colleagues (1998) suggested that positive affect would improve intergroup judgments (by the formation of broader categories) only if a common ingroup is salient. In an experiment with real groups that have a history of antagonism (e.g., liberals versus conservatives) participants were either made aware of a common superordinate category or of the simple ingroup–outgroup distinction, and they were set in a positive or negative mood state. This study yielded more ingroup bias under positive mood if the intergroup distinction was made salient. If, however, a common ingroup was salient, positive mood led to less ingroup bias. Hence, effects of *heuristic use* of category labels on the one hand and the *formation of broader categories* on the other hand were observed within one experiment, which nicely demonstrates how the context can moderate mood effects in intergroup evaluations.

Mood processes in the context of intergroup evaluations were also investigated in an as yet unpublished study (Machunsky & Meiser, 2008). The major interest of this study was to investigate whether mood changes the basis of ingroup bias in the framework of the ingroup projection model (IPM; Mummendey & Wenzel, 1999; Wenzel, Mummendey, & Waldzus, 2008; see also Waldzus, chapter 3 in this volume). The IPM postulates that relative ingroup prototypicality is related to ingroup bias. However, in recent studies we found that the relation between relative ingroup prototypicality and ingroup bias is not a stable phenomenon but is moderated by the mental ingroup representation, such that the assumed link only occurs if the ingroup is represented in a simple (as opposed to complex) manner (Machunsky, Meiser, & Mummendey, in press).

In the new experiment, we investigated how mood affects the link between ingroup prototypicality and ingroup bias. Building on the notion that mood affects processing style, we assumed that relative ingroup prototypicality might be taken as a *heuristic cue* for intergroup evaluations if people are in a positive mood state, but less so if they are in a neutral or negative mood state. More specifically, recent research suggests that relative ingroup prototypicality can also be assessed at an implicit level, which indicates that prototypicality information is automatically available (Bianchi, Mummendey, Steffens, & Yzerbyt, 2009). However, whether this highly accessible information is used as a basis for intergroup evaluations (as suggested by the IPM) or whether people start elaborating the intergroup situation in a more piecemeal manner before making intergroup evaluations might depend on the processing mode that is currently prevailing.

Supporting our hypothesis, the analyses revealed that participants in a positive mood state relied on relative ingroup prototypicality to make intergroup judgments, as indicated by a significant positive relation between relative ingroup prototypicality and ingroup bias. In contrast, intergroup judgments were not predicted by perceived relative ingroup prototypicality for participants in a neutral or negative mood state. The results suggest that relative ingroup prototypicality guides intergroup judgments under positive mood, whereas different kinds of cognitive processes guide intergroup judgments under neutral and negative mood.

Conclusions

Although incidental mood effects in intergroup relations have long been recognized, it is for no more than 15 years that they have been investigated more systematically. And although there is now evidence for various different effects of mood on intergroup judgments, we still know little about the exact conditions under which certain processes are likely to occur.

Considering the cited studies, we may conclude that the categorization-broadening effect of positive mood is a stable phenomenon. However, it might be restricted to targets that are not too different from or atypical of the ingroup, as demonstrated by Urada and Miller (2000) who found that crossed category targets only profited from positive mood when they were members of a dominant ingroup (and a non-dominant outgroup), but not if they were members of a dominant outgroup (and a non-dominant ingroup). Similarly, in the Dovidio et al. studies (1995, 1998) positive effects of positive mood were only obtained if a common ingroup was made salient as a link between ingroup and outgroup. The results of Abele et al. (1998) and Forgas and Fiedler (1996) converge in that positive mood led to more intergroup differentiation in classical minimal group paradigms, unless participants were instructed that the categorization was related to important other personal and social features. So we might conclude that positive mood has detrimental effects for low relevance groups but ameliorating effects for high relevance groups, but only if the ingroup and the outgroup share at least some commonality like, for instance, a common ingroup.

However, in our recent study dealing with national groups as intergroup situation (Machunsky & Meiser, 2008), we found preliminary evidence that heuristic processing is also prevalent in highly meaningful groups. This effect is interesting in two respects: First, it shows that people in a heuristic processing mode might not only rely on category labels but recognize evaluative standards provided by the superordinate category – possibly because prototypicality-based evaluations may appear somewhat more legitimized (see Weber, Mummendey, & Waldzus, 2002). Second, in contrast to the studies by Dovidio et al. (1995, 1998) the presence of a superordinate category did not lead to an amelioration of intergroup judgments. The latter issue points to the conflicting predictions of the CIIM and the IPM. Further research should clarify under which conditions positive mood triggers the processes described by the CIIM, and under which conditions we have to expect the detrimental effects described by the IPM. The structural fit between the subordinate groups and the superordinate category might be a candidate for a moderator.

Considering the effects of negative mood on intergroup judgments, research revealed mainly detrimental effects, albeit for different reasons: Some studies relied on a motivational *mood repair* account (Esses & Zanna, 1995; Forgas & Fiedler, 1996), others on a cognitive *congruency* account (Kenworthy et al., 2003). An automatic process of concept activation can be assumed for mood congruency, whereas mood repair is most likely a motivational process, so that they can be considered as complementary processes that both lead to more ingroup bias.

To summarize, mood is an essential determinant of memory and cognitive processing style that moderates social judgments, including the highly relevant domain of intergroup judgments. In particular, happy and sad mood were shown to affect intergroup evaluations, even though not in a simple way. Research has instead revealed a complex interplay of personal factors (like category relevance) and group settings (like the salience of a common ingroup). Nevertheless, we may conclude that negative mood potentially jeopardizes efforts to enhance intergroup relations, whether it is a result of cognitive or of motivational processes. On the other hand, using elated mood to facilitate programs that aim at the amelioration of intergroup relations is a risky endeavor. Hence, the boundary conditions of the intergroup situation need to be considered carefully if one wants to take advantage of people's happiness.

References

Abele, A., Gendolla, G. H. E., & Petzold, P. (1998). Positive mood and in-group–out-group differentiation in a minimal group setting. *Personality and Social Psychology Bulletin, 24*, 1343–1357.

Bianchi, M., Mummendey, A., Steffens, M., & Yzerbyt, V. (2009). *What do you mean by Europeans? Evidence of spontaneous ingroup projection.* Manuscript submitted for publication.

Blaney, P. H. (1986). Affect and memory: A review. *Psychological Bulletin, 99*, 229–246.

Bless, H., Bohner, G., Schwarz, N., & Strack, F. (1990). Mood and persuasion: A cognitive response analysis. *Personality and Social Psychology Bulletin, 16*, 331–345.

Bless, H., Clore, G., Schwarz, N., Golisano, V., Rabe, C., & Wölk, M. (1996). Mood and the use of scripts: Does a happy mood really lead to mindlessness? *Journal of Personality and Social Psychology, 71*, 665–679.

Bless, H., Mackie, D. M., & Schwarz, N. (1992). Mood effects on attitude judgments: Independent effects of mood before and after message elaboration. *Journal of Personality and Social Psychology, 63*, 585–595.

Bodenhausen, G. V., Kramer, G. P., & Süsser, K. (1994). Happiness and stereotypic thinking in social judgment. *Journal of Personality and Social Psychology, 66*, 621–632.

Bolte, A., Goschke, T., & Kuhl, J. (2003). Emotion and intuition: Effects of positive and negative mood on implicit judgments of semantic coherence. *Psychological Science, 14*, 416–421.

Bower, G. H. (1981). Mood and memory. *American Psychologist, 36*, 129–148.

Chaiken, S. (1980). Heuristic versus systematic information processing and the use of source versus message cues in persuasion. *Journal of Personality and Social Psychology, 39*, 752–766.

Crisp, R. J., & Hewstone, M. (2000). Crossed categorization and intergroup bias: The moderating roles of intergroup and affective context. *Journal of Experimental Social Psychology, 36*, 357–383.

Crisp, R. J., & Hewstone, M. (2006). *Multiple social categorization: Processes, models, and applications.* Hove, UK: Psychology Press.

Dewhurst, S. A., & Parry, L. A. (2000). Emotionality, distinctiveness, and recollective experience. *European Journal of Cognitive Psychology, 12*, 541–551.

Dovidio, J. F., Gaertner, S. L., Isen, A. M., & Lowrance, R. (1995). Group representations and intergroup bias: Positive affect, similarity, and group size. *Personality and Social Psychology Bulletin, 21*, 856–865.

Dovidio, J. F., Gaertner, S. L., Isen, A. M., Rust, M., & Guerra, P. (1998). Positive affect, cognition, and the reduction of intergroup bias. In C. Sedikides, J. Schopler, & C. A. Insko (Eds.), *Intergroup cognition and intergroup behavior* (pp. 337–366). Hove, UK: Lawrence Erlbaum Associates Ltd.

Dreisbach, G., & Goschke, T. (2004). How positive affect modulates cognitive control: Reduced perseveration at the cost of increased distractability. *Journal of Experimental Psychology: Learning, Memory, and Cognition, 30*, 343–353.

Eich, E., & Metcalfe, J. (1989). Mood dependent memory for internal versus external events. *Journal of Experimental Psychology: Learning, Memory, and Cognition, 15*, 443–455.

Esses, V. M., & Zanna, M. P. (1995). Mood and the expression of ethnic stereotypes. *Journal of Personality and Social Psychology, 69*, 1052–1068.

Fein, S., & Spencer, S. J. (1997). Prejudice as self-image maintenance: Affirming the self through derogating others. *Journal of Personality and Social Psychology, 73*, 31–44.

Fiedler, K. (1990). Mood-dependent selectivity in social cognition. *European Review of Social Psychology, 1*, 1–32.

Fiedler, K. (2001). Affective influences on social information processing. In J. P. Forgas (Ed.), *Handbook of affect and social cognition* (pp. 163–186). Mahwah, NJ: Lawrence Erlbaum Associates, Inc.

Fiedler, K., & Freytag, P. (2004). Pseudocontingencies. *Journal of Personality and Social Psychology, 87*, 453–467.

Forgas, J. P. (1992). Affect in social judgments and decisions: A multiprocess model. In M. Zanna (Ed.), *Advances in experimental social psychology* (pp. 227–275). New York: Academic Press.

Forgas, J. P. (1995). Mood and judgment: The affect infusion model (AIM). *Psychological Bulletin, 117*, 39–66.

Forgas, J. P. (1998). On being happy and mistaken: Mood effects on the fundamental attribution error. *Journal of Personality and Social Psychology, 75*, 318–331.

Forgas, J. P. (2001). Introduction: Affect and social cognition. In J. P. Forgas (Ed.), *Handbook of affect and social cognition* (pp. 1–24). Mahwah, NJ: Lawrence Erlbaum Associates, Inc.

Forgas, J. P. (2007). When sad is better than happy: Negative affect can improve the quality and effectiveness of persuasive messages and social influence strategies. *Journal of Experimental Social Psychology, 43*, 513–528.

Forgas, J. P., & Bower, G. H. (1987). Mood effects on person-perception judgments. *Journal of Personality and Social Psychology, 53*, 53–60.

Forgas, J. P., & Ciarrochi, J. V. (2002). On managing moods: Evidence for the role of homeostatic cognitive strategies in affect regulation. *Personality and Social Psychology Bulletin, 28*, 336–345.

Forgas, J. P., & Fiedler, K. (1996). Us and them: Mood effects on intergroup discrimination. *Journal of Personality and Social Psychology, 70*, 28–40.

Förster, J., & Strack, F. (1996). Influence of overt head movements on memory for valenced words: A case of conceptual–motor compatibility. *Journal of Personality and Social Psychology, 71*, 421–430.

Hertel, P., & Hardin, T. S. (1990). Remembering with and without awareness in a depressed mood: Evidence of deficits in initiative. *Journal of Experimental Psychology: General, 119*, 45–59.

Hertel, P., & Meiser, T. (2000). Capacity and procedural accounts of impaired memory in depression. In U. von Hecker, S. Dutke, & G. Sedek (Eds.), *Generative mental processes and cognitive resources: Integrative research on adaptation and control* (pp. 283–307). Dordrecht, The Netherlands: Kluwer Academic Publishers.

Isen, A. M. (1987). Positive affect, cognitive processes, and social behavior. In L. Berkowitz (Ed.), *Advances in experimental social psychology* (pp. 203–253). New York: Academic Press.

Isen, A. M., & Daubman, K. A. (1984). The influence of affect on categorization. *Journal of Personality and Social Psychology, 47*, 1206–1217.

Isen, A. M., Daubman, K. A., & Nowicki, G. P. (1987). Positive affect facilitates creative problem solving. *Journal of Personality and Social Psychology, 52*, 1122–1131.

Isen, A. M., & Means, B. (1983). The influence of positive affect on decision-making strategy. *Social Cognition, 2*, 18–31.

Isen, A. M., Niedenthal, P. M., & Cantor, N. (1992). An influence of positive affect on social categorization. *Motivation and Emotion, 16*, 65–78.

Josephson, B. R., Singer, J. A., & Salovey, P. (1996). Mood regulation and memory: Repairing sad moods with happy memories. *Cognition and Emotion, 10*, 437–444.

Kenworthy, J. B., Canales, C. J., Weaver, K. D., & Miller, N. (2003). Negative incidental affect and mood congruency in crossed categorization. *Journal of Experimental Social Psychology, 39*, 195–219.

Levine, L. J., & Bluck, S. (2004). Painting with broad strokes: Happiness and the malleability of event memory. *Cognition and Emotion, 18*, 559–574.

Machunsky, M., & Meiser, T. (2008). *The heuristic use of relative ingroup prototypicality information.* Manuscript in preparation, University of Marburg, Germany.

Machunsky, M., Meiser, T., & Mummendey, A. (in press). On the crucial role of the mental ingroup representation for ingroup bias and the ingroup prototypicality–ingroup bias link. *Experimental Psychology.*

Meiser, T., & Hewstone, M. (2004). Cognitive processes in stereotype formation: The role of correct contingency learning for biased group judgments. *Journal of Personality and Social Psychology, 87*, 599–614.

Meiser, T., & Hewstone, M. (2008). Cognitive factors in stereotype formation: Illusory and spurious correlations revisited. Manuscript in preparation, University of Marburg, Germany.

Miller, N., Urban, L. M., & Vanman, E. J. (1998). A theoretical analysis of crossed social categorization effects. In C. Sedikides, J. Schopler, & C. A. Insko (Eds.), *Intergroup cognition and intergroup behavior* (pp. 393–420). Hove, UK: Lawrence Erlbaum Associates Ltd.

Mummendey, A., & Wenzel, M. (1999). Social discrimination and tolerance in intergroup relations: Reactions to intergroup difference. *Personality and Social Psychology Review, 3*, 158–174.

Ochsner, K. N. (2000). Are affective events richly recollected or simply familiar? The experience and process of recognizing feelings past. *Journal of Experimental Psychology: General, 129,* 242–261.

Parrott, W. G., & Sabini, J. (1990). Mood and memory under natural conditions: Evidence for mood incongruent recall. *Journal of Personality and Social Psychology, 59,* 321–336.

Petty, R. E., Cacioppo, J. T., & Goldman, R. (1981). Personal involvement as a determinant of argument-based persuasion. *Journal of Personality and Social Psychology, 41,* 847–855.

Pratto, F., & John, O. P. (1991). Automatic vigilance: The attention-grabbing power of negative social information. *Journal of Personality and Social Psychology, 61,* 380–391.

Schaller, M., & O'Brien, M. (1992). "Intuitive analysis of covariance" and group stereotype formation. *Personality and Social Psychology Bulletin, 18,* 776–785.

Schwarz, N., & Clore, G. L. (1983). Mood, misattribution, and judgments of well-being: Informative and directive functions of affective states. *Journal of Personality and Social Psychology, 45,* 513–523.

Schwarz, N., & Clore, G. L. (1996). Feelings and phenomenal experiences. In E. T. Higgins & A. W. Kruglanski (Eds.), *Social psychology. Handbook of basic principles* (pp. 433–465). New York: Guilford.

Sedikides, C. (1994). Incongruent effects of sad mood on self-conception valence: It's a matter of time. *European Journal of Social Psychology, 24,* 161–172.

Spencer, S. J., Fein, S., Wolfe, C. T., Fong, C., & Dunn, M. A. (1998). Automatic activation of stereotypes: The role of self-image threat. *Personality and Social Psychology Bulletin, 24,* 1139–1152.

Urada, D. I., & Miller, N. (2000). The impact of positive mood and category importance on crossed categorization effects. *Journal of Personality and Social Psychology, 78,* 417–433.

von Hecker, U., & Meiser, T. (2005). Defocused attention in depressed mood: Evidence from source monitoring. *Emotion, 5,* 456–463.

Weber, U., Mummendey, A., & Waldzus, S. (2002). Perceived legitimacy of the intergroup status differences: Its predictions by relative ingroup prototypicality. *European Journal of Social Psychology, 32,* 449–470.

Wentura, D., Rothermund, K., & Bak, P. (2000). Automatic vigilance: The attention-grabbing power of approach- and avoidance-related social information. *Journal of Personality and Social Psychology, 78,* 1024–1037.

Wenzel, M., Mummendey, A., & Waldzus, S. (2008). Superordinate identities and intergroup conflict: The ingroup projection model. *European Review of Social Psychology, 18,* 331–372.

6 A self-regulation approach to group processes

Kai Sassenberg
Knowledge Media Research Center, Tübingen

Karl-Andrew Woltin
Université catholique de Louvain, Louvain-la-Neuve

While in many domains of psychology a process perspective on motivation has been dominant for a while (i.e., self-regulation; for an overview see Boekaerts, Pintrich, & Zeidner, 2000), intergroup research has for a long time exclusively focused on needs and motives as main constructs of motivation. The current chapter summarizes recent developments towards a self-regulation approach to group processes and intergroup behavior. Prior to discussing this research we summarize studies on the positive–negative asymmetry in social discrimination (see next paragraph for a definition), because this was one of the first fields concerning and applying self-regulation to the group level. Afterwards, self-regulation is defined and a framework for group-based self-regulation research is provided. Then, the research on self-regulation in the intra- and intergroup domain is summarized and differences between individual and group-based self-regulation are analyzed. Finally, the existing evidence is discussed focusing on the question of whether self-regulation can actually be truly group based.

The positive–negative asymmetry in social discrimination

While social discrimination in laboratory settings usually addressed less positive treatment of outgroup compared to ingroup members (Mummendey & Otten, 2004), in real-life settings social discrimination is generally thought of as clearly negative behavior directed at members of others groups. In 1992 Amélie Mummendey and colleagues (Mummendey et al., 1992) found that *negative* outcomes (e.g., noise, unpleasant tasks) were equally allocated to ingroup and outgroup members in the minimal group paradigm (Tajfel, Billig, Bundy, & Flament, 1971), whereas more positive outcomes (e.g., rewards, pleasant tasks) were allocated more to ingroup than to outgroup members. Additional research replicated this so-called positive–negative asymmetry in social discrimination: Social discrimination is stronger or exclusively present when positive outcomes are being distributed among in- and outgroup members, and is weaker or absent concerning the allocation of negative outcomes (for a summary see Mummendey & Otten, 1998). Amélie Mummendey and her colleagues proposed three explanations for this effect. First, the *normative explanation* suggests that social discrimination with negative outcomes is seen as normatively less appropriate than social discrimination with positive outcomes (Blanz, Mummendey, & Otten, 1997). Second, the *cognitive explanation* suggests that a negative outcome, just like negative information in general, attracts more attention and therefore leads to more thorough information processing. This will in turn lead to less discrimination as long as the social groups do not have features justifying discrimination (Forgas & Fiedler, 1996; Otten, Mummendey, & Buhl, 1998). Finally, the *categorization explanation* suggests that dealing with negative outcomes reduces the salience of social categorizations, which diminishes social discrimination, especially within minimal groups (Mummendey, Otten, Berger, & Kessler, 2000).

Given that three proposed factors (i.e., norms, thorough information processing, and diminished categorization) have proven to contribute to the phenomenon, one might be highly satisfied and end research in this domain. However, all three explanations listed above have a limitation in common: They only explain why social discrimination with negative outcomes is reduced or does not occur, and therefore they require an additional explanation for the existence of social discrimination in general. A more parsimonious model would explain why social discrimination with positive outcomes occurs *and* why social discrimination with negative resources does not occur (or is reduced). As negative versus positive outcomes address the issue of valence in outcome allocations, Amélie Mummendey and her colleagues (including the first author) sought to provide such a parsimonious explanation by applying self-regulation theories to the group level. The rationale behind this approach is that theories in this domain address valence as appraisals resulting from information processing rather than as features of the environment, and allow us to explain the positive–negative asymmetry in social discrimination as well as the opposite effect at the same time (for details see below). Having been successfully applied to the positive–negative asymmetry in social discrimination, research on group-based self-regulation was adapted to other domains and phenomena central to intergroup research. In the remainder of this chapter this research on group-based self-regulation, going far beyond the explanation of the positive-negative asymmetry in social discrimination, is summarized.

The concept of self-regulation

"Self-regulation comprises the volitional and cognitive processes individuals apply to reach a (subjectively) positive state" (Sassenberg & Woltin, 2008, p. 127). Self-regulation thus differs from traditional approaches to motivation in groups such as social identity theory (Tajfel & Turner, 1979, see Spears et al., chapter 2 in this volume) or optimal distinctiveness theory (Brewer, 1991, see Brewer, chapter 1 in this volume) by focusing on mental processes during motivated action rather than on needs or motivational states initiating action. In other words, self-regulation approaches focus on the processes of motivation, whereas the need-based approaches focus on a specific content of motivation. As self-regulation may take place in an automatic or controlled manner, it is important to note that in this chapter the term "self-control" is used to indicate self-regulation processes that are controlled and reflective; the label self-regulation is reserved for automatic and impulsive processes (see also Förster, Liberman, & Friedman, 2007, for this distinction).

A lot of domains have profited from incorporating a self-regulation approach to earlier motivational approaches and thus gained a better understanding of individuals' motivation (for summaries see Baumeister & Vohs, 2004; Boekaerts et al., 2000). This endeavor has only recently started in research on group processes and intergroup relations, where the regulation of the group social self has been addressed. Just as in other domains the benefit of applying a self-regulation approach to group processes is that motivational processes can be understood to a larger extent. To give an example, rather than predicting that the need for positive distinctiveness elicits social discrimination (as done by social identity theory), self-regulation approaches predict why and under which conditions showing social discrimination has a positive valence for group members. As will become evident below, this also applies to the case of the positive–negative asymmetry in social discrimination.

In what follows, the key steps that are necessary to apply self-regulation approaches to self-regulation when social identity is salient are discussed. This includes aspects that can be transferred from research on individual self-regulation as well as those requiring alterations and extensions. However, before this is done, the basic assumptions of self-regulation research relevant for the current context are outlined (see Figure 6.1). Self-regulation approaches assume that events elicit affect in individuals if they are related to individuals' goals (i.e., desired end-states) and standards (i.e., values and beliefs based on which individuals evaluate their own behavior). Positive affect results from events indicating success in goal striving, whereas negative affect results from events indicating failure. Depending on the activated

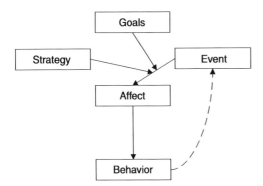

Figure 6.1 A basic self-regulation model. Arrows represent self-regulation processes, except for the dashed line, which is part of the environmental dynamics.

self-regulation strategy (i.e., the motivational state) the specific resulting affect differs. For example, individuals with an approach strategy (i.e., striving to reach a goal such as being among the top three candidates in a competition) show anger in response to a negative event (e.g., being fourth). In contrast, individuals with an avoidance strategy (i.e., striving not to fail reaching a goal, such as not being among the candidates other than the top three) respond to the same situation with fear and tension. It is important to keep in mind that the same goal may thus be pursued with either an approach or an avoidance strategy. In turn, the behavioral responses also differ: Individuals with an approach strategy are more likely to act against the source of the negative event, whereas individuals with an avoidance strategy are more likely to withdraw (Carver, 2004). The next section summarizes research applying these basic assumptions from individual self-regulation to the regulation of the social self.

Regulating the social self

Different self-categorization

Smith (2002) suggested that "since self-regulatory systems [. . .] operate at individual, relational, and group levels, this [self-regulatory] process should operate in conceptually the same way at each level" (Smith, 2002, p. 33). This should be the case as all three levels involve the same mental systems. In other words, when social identity is salient, the same processes should apply, but the agent of regulation differs: Higgins and May (2001) argue that given a salient social identity, "we" becomes the agent of self-regulation and "us" the target. To be more precise, the salience of social identity implies that not only events that are relevant to an individual and his or her goals but also events that are relevant to the entire group or other ingroup members determine the affective response of an individual. In line with this assumption, research on intergroup emotions has shown that events occurring to other members of a salient ingroup result in the same emotions and action tendencies as when these events occur to the target person personally (Mackie, Devos, & Smith, 2000; see also Yzerbyt & Kuppens, chapter 8 in this volume).

When comparing the individual to the group level, besides the range of events impacting on self-regulation, the goals and standards also differ. Whereas personal goals and standards guide individual self-regulation, group goals and group norms guide group-based self-regulation. Furthermore, the more strongly group members identify with a group and the more salient the respective social category is, the more they adhere to group norms and engage in actions favoring group interests (e.g., Sassenberg, 2002; Stürmer & Simon, 2004).

In a study we tested the impact of group members' deviations from ingroup standards on affect and well-being (Sassenberg, 2004). Participants had to provide their current characteristics concerning a group membership (their regional identity) as well as standards and goals shared within their group (ingroup standards) and within a relevant outgroup (outgroup standards). Discrepancies between the actual self and ingroup standards as well as outgroup standards were coded. At the individual level, discrepancies between standards and the current self have been shown to lead to more negative affective states and lower levels of well-being (Strauman & Higgins, 1987, 1988). Derived from these findings, we expected that, especially for highly identified group members, discrepancies concerning ingroup but not outgroup standards should lead to negative affect and lower levels of well-being. Indeed, we found that higher discrepancies concerning ingroup but not outgroup standards led to more negative affect and less well-being for highly identified group members – but not for less strongly identified group members. These findings indicate that if the self-concept is dominated by a group membership (i.e., if a person identifies highly with a group), ingroup standards have the same function as individual level goals when personal identity is salient. Thus, they provide evidence for the assumption that while the different levels of self-categorization come with different goals to regulate, the processes stay the same, because discrepancies pertaining to either the personal or the social self influence affect and well-being in the same way. The next section summarizes research that focused on demonstrating that self-regulatory processes known from research on the individual self can be transferred to the social self.

Same processes

Self-discrepancy theory

Three domains of the self are distinguished by self-discrepancy theory (Higgins, 1987). Attributes an individual currently possesses are represented within the *actual self*. Attributes an individual would ideally like to possess (i.e., hopes, aspirations, and wishes) are represented within the *ideal self*. Finally, attributes of which an individual thinks he or she should or ought to be possessed (i.e., duties, obligations, and responsibilities) are represented within the *ought self*. The most important prediction of self-discrepancy theory pertains to emotions: Discrepancies between the actual self and the ideal self are supposed to lead to more dejection-related emotions (sadness, disappointment) and fewer cheerfulness-related emotions (happiness, enthusiasm); discrepancies between the actual self and the ought self are supposed to lead to more agitation-related emotions (tension, nervousness) and fewer quiescence-related emotions (calmness, relaxedness).

The first research applying self-discrepancy theory to the social self was conducted by Bizman, Yinon, and Krotman (2001). They looked at how discrepancies between the actual group self (i.e., the perceived current state of the ingroup) and perceived ingroup ideals and oughts impact on emotions experienced as a group member (i.e., group-based emotions). In line with self-discrepancy theory, group-based actual-ideal discrepancies indeed led to more group-based dejection, but not group-based agitation. Conversely, group-based actual-ought discrepancies led to more group-based agitation and fear of negative evaluations, but not to group-based dejection. In both cases the effects remained reliable even after controlling for individual level self-discrepancies that had been separately assessed. Overall, discrepancies between domains of the group self have thus been shown to have a similar impact on group-based affect as discrepancies between domains of the individual self have on individual level affect.

Petrocelli and Smith (2005) argued that the effects found by Bizman et al. (2001) – but generally all emotional reactions stemming from self-discrepancies – should be moderated by attributions (internal vs. external)[1] concerning the discrepancies' causes and, central to the current reasoning, by social identification. Participants were instructed to list attributes of the type of group they would ideally like to see Americans (i.e. their ingroup) to be, as well as attributes that describe what they think Americans ought to be like. These were then presented back to them and participants had to judge to what extent Americans as a social group currently possessed these ideal and ought attributes. Causal attributions for group discrepancies were assessed via items measuring the extent to which participants believed that external vs. internal factors were responsible for the discrepancies. Indeed Petrocelli and Smith (2005) found that higher levels of group-based actual–ideal discrepancies led to higher levels of dejection the more individuals identified with their ingroup (and the more its discrepancies were attributed internally). Higher levels of group-based actual–ideal discrepancies also led to higher levels of discontent the more individuals were identified (and the more the ingroup's discrepancies were attributed externally). Likewise, perceived actual–ought discrepancies of the ingroup resulted in higher levels of agitation and anger the more strongly participants identified with their ingroup (and to the extent that these discrepancies were regarded as stemming from external rather than internal causes). Overall, the influence of ingroup level self-discrepancies on group-based emotions was thus found to increase with group members' social identification.

Together with Bizman et al. (2001) these studies demonstrate that ingroup level self-discrepancies lead to the same emotional outcomes as individual level self-discrepancies, and even more so when individuals are highly identified with their ingroup.

Regulatory focus theory

Regulatory focus theory (Higgins, 1997) developed out of self-discrepancy theory. Rather than exclusively focusing on interindividual differences, regulatory focus theory also targets situational variations in self-regulation strategies. It suggests that two regulatory foci exist: a promotion focus and a prevention focus. In a *promotion focus* individuals are guided by ideals, they apply eagerness means during goal striving (e.g., taking risks, avoiding missing an opportunity), they perceive events as gains versus non-gains, and they respond to success and failure with cheerfulness and dejection, respectively. In contrast, in a *prevention focus* individuals are guided by oughts and obligations, they apply vigilance means during goal striving (e.g., following rules, trying to avoid errors), they perceive events as non-losses and losses, and they respond to success and failure with quiescence and agitation, respectively. There is ample evidence supporting regulatory focus theory (for summaries see Higgins & Spiegel, 2004; Molden, Lee, & Higgins, 2008). However, until recently research on regulatory focus emphasized "self-regulation with 'I' as agent and 'me' as target, but a more complete model of self-regulation incorporating the group level would include 'we' as agent and 'us' as target" (Higgins & May, 2001, p. 64).

The initial attempt at applying regulatory focus theory to the regulation of the social self (Bizman et al., 2001; Petrocelli & Smith, 2005; Sassenberg, 2004) focused on the positive–negative asymmetry in social discrimination (Sassenberg, Kessler, & Mummendey, 2003). We reasoned that social discrimination while distributing positive outcomes should be stronger than social discrimination while distributing negative outcomes, but in a promotion focus only (i.e., not in a prevention focus), because positive outcomes are valued more in a promotion focus compared to a prevention focus (Idson, Liberman, & Higgins, 2000). In contrast, group members in a prevention focus should show more discrimination while distributing negative outcomes than while distributing positive outcomes (compared to group members in a promotion focus), because individuals in a prevention focus try to circumvent losses. Furthermore, because the social self is regulated (i.e., the ingroup), regulatory focus was expected to only impact on the allocations of outcomes to the ingroup but not on the allocation of outcomes to the outgroup.

In two minimal-group experiments, in which we assessed and manipulated regulatory focus, this prediction was tested. To avoid the impression among participants that they themselves could profit from the resource allocation, they ostensibly had to allocate the compensation for participants in the next experimental session and they were informed that their compensation was already fixed. This served two purposes. First, the allocations were thus relevant to the social self but not to the individual self. Second, the critique that allocations in minimal groups are guided by expectations concerning the behavior of others affecting participants' personal outcomes (e.g., Rabbie, Schot, & Visser, 1989) does not apply to the current procedure. To vary the type of outcomes, participants allocated either increases or decreases of the monetary compensation. In line with the hypothesis, the positive–negative asymmetry of social discrimination was replicated among participants with a promotion focus (i.e., participants showed higher levels of discrimination with positive than with negative outcomes). However, participants in a prevention focus discriminated more when allocating negative outcomes than when allocating positive outcomes. Also in line with our expectations, differences in resource allocation only affected the ingroup but not the outgroup. Proving further evidence for the regulation of the social self, the effects reported before were limited to participants perceiving a fit between their self-concept and the minimal categorization.

Taken together, the results clearly indicate that the mechanisms suggested by regulatory focus theory do not only apply to the individual but also to the social self. Moreover, they suggest that the positive–negative asymmetry found in various studies on social discrimination is a result of participants' promotion focus in these studies. As this regulatory mode is indeed predominant in western societies (Lee, Aaker, & Gardner, 2000), and as all published work on the positive–negative asymmetry was conducted in these societies, this explanation is quite plausible.

In an additional line of research we studied the impact of regulatory focus in victims of social discrimination (Sassenberg & Hansen, 2007). Our expectation was that social discrimination would result in negative affective responses and the willingness to act against the discriminating group, especially for group members with a prevention focus. This effect was furthermore predicted to be particularly strong when social discrimination was based on negative outcomes (compared to positive outcomes). This was expected because responses to negative events are stronger among individuals in a prevention focus (Idson et al., 2000), and experiencing social discrimination always is a negative event. A line of experiments varying whether the outgroup was perceiving the ingroup as being less positive, more negative or similar to themselves, and measuring as well as manipulating regulatory focus, supported these predictions. Depending on participants' prevention strength, agitation, anger, and the willingness to act against the discriminating outgroup were stronger following discrimination. This pattern was particularly strong when social discrimination was based on negative outcomes. No effect of promotion strength was found. When regulatory focus was induced the three dependent variables were only elevated after discrimination in the prevention condition, not in the promotion condition.

In sum, this research provides additional evidence that regulatory focus theory applies to the regulation of the social self. More precisely, it demonstrates that, provided a salient social identity, events relevant to the ingroup elicit the same affect and action intentions as events relevant to the individual, when personal identity is salient.

Implementation intentions

To provide more convincing evidence that the social self is actually regulated similarly to the individual self, two further criteria should be fulfilled: (a) the applicability of self-regulation mechanisms other than regulatory focus/self-discrepancies that are known from research on individual self-regulation to the social self, and (b) the automatic nature of the regulation of the social self. Research addressing both criteria is summarized in the current section.

So-called implementation intentions provide a context that allows addressing these criteria. Implementation intentions are action plans in the form of "if x happens, then I will do y". Forming this kind of plan improves goal achievement by increasing the likelihood that goal striving is initiated. The effects result (among other things) from the fact that situational cues included in the if-component automatically activate action tendencies included in the then-component of the implementation intention (Gollwitzer & Sheeran, 2006). Hence, while implementation intentions are formed intentionally, they result in automatic goal striving (i.e., self-regulation).

In our own research (Wieber & Sassenberg, 2006) we demonstrated that implementation intentions can also be successfully formed for ingroup goals. More interestingly, if an implementation intention is formed in relation to a specific outgroup (e.g., "If I see a member of group A, I will treat this person well") and the situational cue from the if-condition appears in the context of another outgroup (e.g., a member of group A shows up in a room while interacting with a member of group B), the intended behavior is also shown toward the members of this second outgroup (e.g., the member of group B is treated well). Thus, implementation intentions concerning an outgroup generalize to other outgroups, if a cue pointing to the first group is present. If an implementation intention is formed in relation to the ingroup (e.g., "If I see a member of my group, I will treat the person well") this ingroup related goal is more likely to be reached. Hence, implementation intentions also foster the achievement of ingroup goals. In addition, if the situational cue for the ingroup related implementation intention (e.g., an ingroup member) appears in the context of an outgroup (e.g., while talking to an outgroup member), a contrast effect occurs. In the case of the above example this will lead to the outgroup member being treated badly. Hence, implementation intentions are automatically generalized beyond one group. In the case of an outgroup related implementation intention, the presence of this outgroup when dealing with a member of another outgroup leads to the application of the implementation intention to this second outgroup member. However, implementation intentions also lead to automatic contrast effects when the self (in this case the ingroup) is part of the context or the target of the judgment – just like other automatic processes (e.g., Schubert & Häfner, 2003). In sum, this work indicates that the social self is regulated automatically and that other self-regulation phenomena beyond regulatory focus and self-discrepancies apply to the regulation of the social self, including unintended side effects.

Mindsets

Further research demonstrated that mindsets (i.e., goal striving strategies) activated at the individual level also transfer to the group level. Sassenberg, Moskowitz, Jacoby, and Hansen (2007b) studied the impact of a competition mindset on group evaluations. Participants either thought about an interpersonal competition or actually went through an interpersonal competition before evaluating unrelated outgroups. In control conditions participants either thought about cooperation, were involved in a situation in which their outcomes depended on their own and others' performance, or were in a situation in which their outcomes were independent of others' performance. Participants in the competition mindset evaluated outgroups more negatively (compared to the control conditions). This effect was mediated neither by frustration nor by negative affect resulting from the competition. Rather more, it was an outcome of the application of the information processing strategy (i.e., the mindset) that was activated in the interpersonal context but had an impact in the intergroup context. These findings provide additional evidence for the application of individual level self-regulation strategies to an intergroup context.

The action phase model

Whereas the studies reviewed so far all addressed *spontaneous* self-regulation processes at the group level, Woltin and Sassenberg (2008) focused on *controlled* group-based self-regulation, namely the reflective choice of means. This is to say, we investigated group members' behavioral and mental strategies employed on behalf of group goals (see Förster et al., 2007, for a distinction between automatic and controlled self-regulation). The action phase model (Heckhausen, 1999) describes individual control strategies directed at changing either the external world or inner states. These strategies are differently adaptive given a pre- or a post-deadline phase of individual goal pursuit. This is to say, depending on whether many or only severely limited opportunities for reaching one's goal are present, different control strategies should be applied. We reasoned that these strategies should not only apply to individual goal pursuit (i.e., when personal identity is salient). In line with Smith's (2002) assumption that the social and personal self are regulated following the same principles, we predicted these strategies to also hold at the group level, namely for group goals and group deadlines. We thus hypothesized that the more an individual identifies with the ingroup, the more important the group goal should be to the social self, which in turn should lead to enhanced phase-adequate control strategy usage during group goal pursuit (i.e., adaptive group-based self-control).

Manipulating and measuring both social identification as well as the deadline phase (e.g. by means of time left to reach the group goal) we indeed found that especially highly identified group members of both natural and laboratory groups adaptively engaged in controlled self-regulation on behalf of their respective groups. To give an example, highly identified group members in the pre-deadline condition spent more time on the group task than highly identified group members in the post-deadline condition; for less strongly identified individuals, effort did not differ between conditions.

Furthermore, two studies ruled out the alternative explanation that group members made an effort because of individual outcome considerations by means of having only the group, but not the individual participant, benefit from successful goal achievement. These results point to the fact that theories of individual controlled self-regulation can also be applied to (inter)group contexts.

The impact of the social self on self-regulation processes

The literature reviewed in the previous section pointed to the fact that, compared to the individual level, self-regulation processes at the group level remain basically the same, but a different content is regulated: the social and not the individual self. One might thus ask what is specific about self-regulation at the group level. This question pertains to the effects that ingroups may have on self-regulation strategies. A line of research therefore treats self-regulation strategies as the outcome of intergroup contexts by investigating the impacts of various features of intergroup contexts (especially threat) on self-regulatory strategies (mainly regulatory focus). Thus, this research investigates the possibility of an (inter)group context to elicit specific self-regulation strategies.

An important group level feature that has been shown to impact on self-regulation strategies is the composition of the group context (the presence of ingroup vs. outgroup members), for example in performance situations. Derks, van Laar, and Ellemers (2006) investigated the effects of an ingroup compared to an outgroup context (i.e., only in- or only outgroup members present during performance, respectively) and of contextual emphasis (of dimensions on which the ingroup vs. outgroup excels vs. no dimension emphasized) on low-status members' focus on hope for success (i.e., a focus on gains vs. non-gains) versus a focus on fear of failure (i.e., a focus on losses vs. non-losses). They found that compared to ingroup contexts, stigmatized group members in an outgroup context expecting to perform badly on a task in which the outgroup excels, feel more agitated following negative performance feedback (the emotional reaction congruent with a focus on fear of failure; Study 1). However, independent of either in- or outgroup contexts, stigmatized group members felt more cheerful concerning the upcoming task (the emotional reaction congruent with a focus on hope for success; Study 2) when the importance of a dimension on which the *in*group excels was emphasized – and their social identity could thus be protected. The research by Derks et al. (2006) thus shows an elicitation of self-regulation strategies among low-status group members depending on the group context and the task type.

The elicitation of self-regulation strategies in intergroup encounters from the perspective of high-status group members has also been investigated and shows similar effects. Trawalter and Richeson (2006) had white participants expect an interracial interaction to take place and told them to try to avoid prejudice (thus inducing a prevention focus), to try to have a positive interracial exchange (thus inducing a promotion focus), or gave them no instructions (control condition). Compared to participants in the promotion condition, participants in the prevention and the control condition performed worse on a subsequent Stroop color-naming task. Trawalter and Richeson (2006) explain this drop in executive attentional task performance in terms of vigilant monitoring of thoughts and behavior (congruent with a prevention focus self-regulation strategy), depleting inhibitory task performance necessary for the Stroop task. The fact that anticipated interracial encounters apparently elicit a prevention focus (as indicated by participants in the control and the prevention focus condition performing equally badly) is thus another example of an intergroup feature having an impact on the self-regulation strategy pursued.

Minimizing the context to mere expectations, Seibt and Förster (2004) argue that activated self-stereotypes can induce specific self-regulation strategies, and in turn can have an influence on the manner in which individuals attempt to solve a task. They found that being confronted with a negative stereotype induces a state of vigilance (congruent with a prevention focus), whereas being confronted with a positive ingroup stereotype induces a state of eagerness (congruent with a promotion focus). This was demonstrated by the participants confronted with negative stereotypes being slower (an indicator of less eagerness, respectively more vigilance) on word selection and dot-connection tasks than participants in a control group not being confronted with a stereotype. On the contrary, participants confronted with positive stereotypes were faster than the control group. However, for accuracy (an indicator of vigilance), the pattern reversed. Their research thus shows how mere ingroup stereotypes (i.e., an ingroup-based feature of an intergroup context) elicit self-regulation strategies. Reducing the influence of the context even further, Oyserman, Uskul, Yoder, Nesse, and Williams (2007, Experiments 1 & 2) could show that merely making a stigmatized low status group membership salient suffices to elicit specific self-regulation strategies, namely a prevention focus. Furthermore, contrary to the studies reported so far, Oyserman et al. (2007) could show these effects on direct measures of self-regulation strategies (rather than by behavioral or emotional indicators, only).

Yet another way in which self-regulation may influence the behavior and experienced emotions of group members is by forming part of the group norm. Such a norm in line with one of the two foci has been called "*collective regulatory focus*". Faddegon, Scheepers, and Ellemers (2008) induced such a "collective regulatory focus" by presenting group mottos to participants – either expressing a preference for promotion (e.g., "If there is a will, there will be a way") or prevention strategies (e.g., "An ounce of prevention is worth a pound of cure"). Overall, "collective regulatory focus" impacted on the behavior and emotions of group members in terms of bringing both in line with the regulatory focus associated with their ingroup (e.g., a more liberal bias in task performance given a collective promotion focus compared to a collective prevention focus). In a second study Faddegon et al. (2008) also manipulated the strength of participants' identification with the task group and demonstrated that social identification moderated the influence of the groups' "collective focus" on members' emotions. The research also provides first evidence concerning the social sharedness of self-regulation: Group members tend to adopt the self-regulation strategy of their ingroup members when they experience them having a certain self-regulation strategy.

The social sharedness of self-regulation strategies has also been addressed by Levine, Higgins, and Choi (2000), who studied the influence of group members' regulatory focus on the formation of a group norm. Levine et al. (2000) had participants work on a recognition task in three-person-groups. Regulatory focus was manipulated and group members' convergence towards a liberal or conservative bias while responding out loud to the trial items was measured. Levine et al. (2000) indeed found members of collaborating groups to influence each other concerning their self-regulation strategy: Groups converged over time towards a liberal bias when group members had a promotion focus and towards a conservative bias when group members had a prevention focus. Florack and Hartmann (2007) demonstrated similar effects for investment decisions in groups.

The interplay between the social self and self-regulation processes

The two foregoing sections allow drawing the conclusions that (a) self-regulation strategies impact on intergroup behavior, and (b) intergroup context impacts on self-regulation strategies. This almost inevitably leads to the question of what happens if the intergroup context elicits a self-regulation strategy that is not compatible with the one held by a group member. The regulatory fit hypothesis (Higgins, 2000) allows us to derive an answer to this. It states that individuals prefer behavior that fits their regulatory needs (holding the outcomes constant). For example, individuals in a prevention focus will like searching for errors in a text more than writing a new text (given that both types of behavior can lead to the same reward). As a consequence positive valence is transferred from behavioral preferences to objects allowing them to show this behavior (in the example above, the text). From the regulatory fit hypothesis we derived that social groups allowing individuals to show behavior that fits their activated needs (implied by their regulatory focus) will be preferred over groups that do not allow for this. We tested this prediction in the context of group power. Groups high in power are generally expected to provide freedom to follow one's interest, whereas members of lower power groups have to follow rules and worry about their safety and security (for a similar argument see Keltner, Gruenfeld, & Anderson, 2003). Hence, high power groups have a better fit with promotion strategies, and low power groups have a better fit with prevention strategies. Therefore, individuals with a promotion focus should like higher power groups more than individuals with a prevention focus (who should prefer lower power groups more than individuals in a promotion focus). The preference for a high versus low power group results from the fact that one's preferred behavioral strategies implied by one's regulatory focus can be more easily applied in these groups differing in power.

Indeed a series of studies supports this prediction concerning group preference and our reasoning that this effect results from the feeling that the group fits in terms of behavioral options, allowing group members to fulfill their personal needs implied by their regulatory focus. Additional studies demonstrated that individuals in a prevention focus actually show a more positive spontaneous affective response to lower power ingroups than to higher power ingroups (Sassenberg, Jonas, Shah, & Brazy, 2007a). These results were also replicated using gender as a proxy for power: Men experience more positive affect concerning their own gender in a promotion focus than in a prevention focus, whereas women preferred their gender more and even identified more strongly with their own gender in a prevention compared to a promotion focus (Sassenberg, Brazy, Jonas, & Shah, 2006).

Taken together, the regulatory fit of an ingroup determines its evaluation. If the self-regulation strategy suggested by the intergroup context and the strategy held by a group member do not fit, group members will affectively distance themselves from the group, and in extreme cases even dis-identify. Hence, self-regulation can have an impact on the self-concept. Another example of this kind of effect occurs during the integration of a new group membership into the self-concept. Matschke and Sassenberg (2008) demonstrated that new group members who are applying approach versus avoidance strategies during their integration into the new group respond differently to their treatment by the group. The stronger individuals' approach strategy is, the stronger their identification will be after getting positive feedback from the group. The stronger individuals' avoidance strategy is, the more they will distance themselves from the group after experiencing rejection. Taken together, the self-regulation strategy applied during the integration into a new group influences the resulting changes of the self-concept in terms of identification with the new group.

Conclusion: Can self-regulation really be group based?

In this chapter, we have given an overview on research investigating (1) the application of self-regulation strategies at the group level, (2) some differences between individual and group level self-regulation, (3) the effects of group level features on self-regulation, and (4) the interplay between self-regulation strategies and the intergroup context. It is important to note that self-regulation pertains exclusively neither to the personal nor the social self – simply because it is a motivational process and not an element of the representation of the self (i.e., the self-concept).

Beyond the mere application of self-regulation approaches established for the individual self to the social self, the work summarized here clearly demonstrates that the self-concept neither has primacy over self-regulation nor does the reverse case apply. Just as activated aspects of the self-concept influence goals targeted in self-regulation, they can be an outcome of self-regulation (in terms of which self-concept is being activated).

In order to claim that the studies summarized above provide examples of truly group-based self-regulation – situations in which "we" is the subject and "us" or "they" are the target of self-regulation as Higgins and May (2001) stated – criteria for evaluating this claim are needed. In developing these criteria Sassenberg and Woltin (2008) drew an analogy to four criteria for truly group-based emotions (i.e., group-based emotions being different from individual level emotions; depending on individuals' levels of group identification; contributing to motivating and regulating intra- and intergroup attitudes and behavior; and being socially shared) set forth by Smith, Seger, and Mackie (2007). Instead of demanding that all criteria need to be fulfilled for judging a finding as an effect of group-based self-regulation, we rather see evidence supporting all four criteria across different studies as a prerequisite for assuming group-based self-regulation to exist as a phenomenon. While none of the studies presented here fulfills all criteria, all studies fulfill some of them. Along with each criterion we will give an example from one of the studies reported above in order to clarify the respective criterion. The following four criteria should be fulfilled for truly group-based self-regulation:

1 *Ingroup variables (e.g., ingroup appraisals) should contribute to the effects of self-regulation beyond individual level variables.*
   A precondition for ingroup variables to have an effect is an appraisal of the current situation in terms of self-categorizing as a group member. In general, the first criterion holds when the impact of a group-level variable remains even when controlling for its counterpart at the individual level. Bizman et al. (2001) demonstrated that group-based actual–ideal discrepancies predict group-based dejection (but not agitation), and that group-based actual–ought discrepancies predict group-based agitation and fear (but not dejection). Importantly, the effect of group-based discrepancies remained intact even when controlling for personal (individual level) self-discrepancies. Thus, the found associations between group discrepancies and group-based emotions cannot be accounted for only by their relation to personal self-discrepancies.

2 *The effects of self-regulation should be the more pronounced the more strongly a group member is identified with the group.*
   Like criterion 1, this criterion is also based on the reasoning that thinking of oneself as a group member is a prerequisite for any kind of group-based self-regulation to occur. The level of identification with the group should further fuel this process because the situation/action should be more important to the social self, which should in turn lead to an amplification of self-regulation effects. Using minimal groups Sassenberg et al.

(2003) found regulatory focus to affect allocations of positive outcomes towards the ingroup. However, only participants who found the minimal categorization to be in line with their self-perception (i.e., who perceived the ingroup as their social self and thus identified with the group) showed the described effects. A further example of criterion 2 being fulfilled is the fact that Petrocelli and Smith (2005) found all their effects to be moderated by social identification (i.e., they were stronger the more group members were identified).

3   *Self-regulation should be functional for the group, rather than the individual, and guide intra- and intergroup behavior.*

Self-regulation of one's behavior is assumed to be functional, for example in terms of attaining goals. If self-regulation is to be group-based, functionality should accordingly pertain to the group. An example of behavior having implications that are functional for the group but not for the individual is provided by Levine et al. (2000), who found group members to converge in their liberal or conservative biases on a performance task according to manipulated regulatory focus. This convergence did not benefit individual but rather group performance tied to monetary compensation. However, in most studies mentioned above the behavior investigated did serve a symbolic function – meaning that it had an impact on the social standing of the group.

4   *The effects of self-regulation should be socially shared within the group.*

This criterion states that the effects will go beyond the response of a single individual in terms of group members in general responding equally (e.g., experiencing the same emotions, showing equal strategies in their behavior). Faddegon et al. (2008; but see also Florack & Hartmann, 2007; Levine et al., 2000) provide evidence for this in terms of group characteristics (an induced "collective regulatory focus") having an impact on group members' emotional and behavioral reactions.

In sum, the existing evidence justifies the conclusion that the concepts concerning self-regulation at the individual level set forth and investigated can also be applied to the social self. This is to say that group-based self-regulation exists. The process of group-based self-regulation is collective in nature because of individuals' group memberships having an impact on psychological processes, as mentioned in the four criteria. In this way it follows the same reasoning as motivational approaches to intergroup relations that are based on needs (for an overview see Brewer, chapter 1 in this volume). However, while need-based approaches address the question of *what* group members are striving for, this approach focuses on strategies applied to the pursuit of group goals (and therefore on *how* group members are pursuing a goal). Thus, for a more complete understanding of the role of motivation in intergroup phenomena, both approaches are of different, but equal, value.

The particular bonus gained by the group-based self-regulation approach is twofold: First, self-regulation approaches render possible more specific predictions, for example concerning social discrimination with positive versus negative resources. In turn the approach sheds more light on intergroup phenomena such as the positive–negative asymmetry in social discrimination (Mummendey & Otten, 1998). To give another example, regulatory focus also explains individuals' general tendency to prefer groups high or low in power. A second bonus is that the group-based self-regulation approach also has the potential to integrate different lines of research working with different theories and models: Several studies treating regulatory focus as a dependent variable have identified joint psychological processes underlying different intergroup phenomena (e.g., stereotype threat). Thus, the group-based self-regulation approach is a prime candidate for contributing to a more parsimonious and at the same time more general explanation of intergroup phenomena.

Note

1 Appraisal theories of emotions (Roseman, 1991; Weiner, 1986) state that external compared to internal sources of an event have different implications for emotional consequences: Internally attributed events are assumed to result in agitation and dejection, externally attributed events are assumed to result in discontent and anger. In line with this reasoning, Petrocelli and Smith (2005) assumed actual–ideal discrepancies to especially lead to dejection when they are attributed internally, and also actual–ought discrepancies to especially lead to agitation when they are attributed internally. Contrary to this, higher levels of discontent and anger were expected with stronger external attributions concerning the respective discrepancy. Their results supported their prediction for individual level discrepancies and actual–ideal discrepancies at the group level. However, for group-based actual–ought discrepancies their assumptions were not supported. For the context of this chapter, Petrocelli and Smith's (2005) focus on the impact of attributions will thus not be further addressed.

References

Baumeister, R. F., & Vohs, K. D. (Eds.). (2004). *Handbook of self-regulation: Research, theory, and applications*. New York: Guilford.

Bizman, A., Yinon, Y., & Krotman, S. (2001). Group-based emotional distress: An extension of self-discrepancy theory. *Personality and Social Psychology Bulletin, 27*, 1291–1300.

Blanz, M., Mummendey, A., & Otten, S. (1997). Normative evaluations and frequency expectations regarding positive and negative outcome evaluations between groups. *European Journal of Social Psychology, 27*, 165–176.

Boekaerts, M., Pintrich, P. R., & Zeidner, M. (Eds.). (2000). *Handbook of self-regulation*. San Diego, CA: Academic Press.

Brewer, M. B. (1991). The social self: On being the same and different at the same time. *Personality and Social Psychology Bulletin, 17*, 475–482.

Carver, C. S. (2004). Negative affects deriving from the behavioral approach system. *Emotion, 4*, 3–22.

Derks, B., van Laar, C., & Ellemers, N. (2006). Striving for success in outgroup settings: Effects of contextually emphasizing ingroup dimensions on stigmatized group members' social identity and performance styles. *Personality and Social Psychology Bulletin, 32*, 576–588.

Faddegon, K., Scheepers, D., & Ellemers, N. (2008). If we have the will, there will be a way: Regulatory focus as a group identity. *European Journal of Social Psychology, 38*, 880–895.

Florack, A., & Hartmann, J. (2007). Regulatory focus and investment decisions in small groups. *Journal of Experimental Social Psychology, 43*, 626–632.

Forgas, J. P., & Fiedler, K. (1996). Us and them: Mood effects on intergroup discrimination. *Journal of Personality and Social Psychology, 70*, 28–40.

Förster, J., Liberman, N., & Friedman, R. (2007). Seven principles of goal activation: A systematic approach to distinguishing goal priming from priming of non-goal constructs. *Personality and Social Psychology Review, 11*, 211–233.

Gollwitzer, P. M., & Sheeran, P. (2006). Implementation intentions and goal achievement: A meta-analysis of effects and processes. *Advances in Experimental Social Psychology, 38*, 69–119.

Heckhausen, J. (1999). *Developmental regulation in adulthood: Age-normative and sociostructural constraints as adaptive challenges.* New York: Cambridge University Press.

Higgins, E. T. (1987). Self-discrepancy: A theory relating self and affect. *Psychological Review, 94*, 319–340.

Higgins, E. T. (1997). Beyond pleasure and pain. *American Psychologist, 52*, 1280–1300.

Higgins, E. T. (2000). Making a good decision: Value from fit. *American Psychologist, 55*, 1217–1229.

Higgins, E. T., & May, D. (2001). Individual self-regulatory functions. It's not "we" regulation, but it's still social. In C. Sedikides & M. B. Brewer (Eds.), *Individual self, relational self, collective self* (pp. 47–67). New York: Psychology Press.

Higgins, E. T., & Spiegel, S. (2004). Promotion and prevention strategies for self-regulation: A motivated cognition perspective. In R. F. Baumeister & K. D. Vohs (Eds.), *Handbook of self-regulation: Research, theory, and applications* (pp. 171–187). New York: Guilford.

Idson, L. C., Liberman, N., & Higgins, E. T. (2000). Distinguishing gains from nonlosses and losses from nongains: A regulatory focus perspective on hedonic intensity. *Journal of Experimental Social Psychology, 36*, 252–274.

Keltner, D., Gruenfeld, D. H., & Anderson, C. (2003). Power, approach, and inhibition. *Psychological Review, 110*, 265–284.

Lee, A. Y., Aaker, J. L., & Gardner, W. L. (2000). The pleasures and pains of distinct self-construals: The role of interdependence in regulatory focus. *Journal of Personality and Social Psychology, 78*, 1122–1134.

Levine, J. M., Higgins, E. T., & Choi, H.-S. (2000). Development of strategic norms in groups. *Organizational Behavior and Human Decision Processes, 82*, 88–101.

Mackie, D. M., Devos, T., & Smith, E. R. (2000). Intergroup emotions: Explaining offensive action tendencies in an intergroup context. *Journal of Personality and Social Psychology, 79*, 602–616.

Matschke, M. C., & Sassenberg, K. (2008). *Goals and motivation as moderators of the integration of a new group membership into the self-concept.* Unpublished manuscript, Knowledge Media Research Center, Tübingen, Germany.

Molden, D. C., Lee, A. Y., & Higgins, E. T. (2008). Motivations for promotion and prevention. In J. Y. Shah & W. L. Gardner (Eds.), *Handbook of motivation science* (pp. 169–187). New York: Guilford.

Mummendey, A., & Otten, S. (1998). Positive–negative asymmetry in social discrimination. In W. Stroebe & M. Hewstone (Eds.), *European review of social psychology* (Vol. 9, pp. 107–143). New York: Wiley.

Mummendey, A., & Otten, S. (2004). Aversive discrimination. In M. B. Brewer & M. Hewstone (Eds.), *Emotion and motivation* (pp. 298–318). Malden, MA: Blackwell Publishing.

Mummendey, A., Otten, S., Berger, U., & Kessler, T. (2000). Positive–negative asymmetry in social discrimination: Valence of evaluation and salience of categorization. *Personality and Social Psychology Bulletin, 26*, 1258–1270.

Mummendey, A., Simon, B., Dietze, C., Grünert, M., Haeger, G., Kessler, S., et al. (1992). Categorization is not enough: Intergroup discrimination in negative outcome allocations. *Journal of Experimental Social Psychology, 28*, 125–144.

Otten, S., Mummendey, A., & Buhl, T. (1998). Information processing and social discrimination: Accuracy in information processing and positive–negative assymetry in social discrimination. *Revue Internationale de Psychologie Sociale, 11*, 69–96.

Oyserman, D., Uskul, A. K., Yoder, N., Nesse, R. M., & Williams, D. R. (2007). Unfair treatment and self-regulatory focus. *Journal of Experimental Social Psychology, 43*, 502–512.

Petrocelli, J. V., & Smith, E. R. (2005). Who I am, who we are, and why: Links between emotions and causal attributions for self- and group discrepancies. *Personality and Social Psychology Bulletin, 31*, 1628–1642.

Rabbie, J. M., Schot, J. C., & Visser, L. (1989). Social identity theory: A conceptual and empirical critique from the perspective of a behavioural interaction model. *European Journal of Social Psychology, 19*, 171–202.

Roseman, I. J. (1991). Appraisal determinants of discrete emotions. *Cognition and Emotion, 5*, 161–200.

Sassenberg, K. (2002). Common bond and common identity groups on the Internet: Attachment and normative behavior in on-topic and off-topic chats. *Group Dynamics: Theory, Research, and Practice, 6*, 27–37.

Sassenberg, K. (2004). *When the ingroup guides self-regulation: The impact of self-discrepancies concerning ingroup goals on affect and well-being.* Unpublished manuscript, Knowledge Media Research Center, Tübingen, Germany.

Sassenberg, K., Brazy, P. C., Jonas, K. J., & Shah, J. Y. (2006). *Fitting with one's genes: The regulatory fit of gender.* Unpublished manuscript, Knowledge Media Research Center, Tübingen, Germany.

Sassenberg, K., & Hansen, N. (2007). The impact of regulatory focus on affective responses to social discrimination. *European Journal of Social Psychology, 37*, 421–444.

Sassenberg, K., Jonas, K. J., Shah, J. Y., & Brazy, P. C. (2007a). Regulatory fit of the ingroup: The impact of group power and regulatory focus on implicit intergroup bias. *Journal of Personality and Social Psychology, 92*, 249–267.

Sassenberg, K., Kessler, T., & Mummendey, A. (2003). Less negative = more positive? Social discrimination as avoidance and approach. *Journal of Experimental Social Psychology, 39*, 48–58.

Sassenberg, K., Moskowitz, G. B., Jacoby, J., & Hansen, N. (2007b). The carry-over effect of competition: The impact of competition on prejudice towards uninvolved outgroups. *Journal of Experimental Social Psychology, 43*, 529–538.

Sassenberg, K., & Woltin, K.-A. (2008). Group-based self-regulation: The role of regulatory focus. *European Review of Social Psychology*, *19*, 126–164.

Schubert, T. W., & Häfner, M. (2003). Contrast from social stereotypes in automatic behavior. *Journal of Experimental Social Psychology*, *39*, 577–584.

Seibt, B., & Förster, J. (2004). Stereotype threat and performance: How self-stereotypes influence processing by inducing regulatory foci. *Journal of Personality and Social Psychology*, *87*, 38–56.

Smith, E. R. (2002). Overlapping mental representations of self and group: Evidence and implications. In J. P. Forgas & K. D. Williams (Eds.), *The social self. Cognitive, interpersonal, and intergroup perspectives* (pp. 21–35). New York: Psychology Press.

Smith, E. R., Seger, C. R., & Mackie, D. M. (2007). Can emotions be truly group level? Evidence regarding four conceptual criteria. *Journal of Personality and Social Psychology*, *93*, 431–446.

Strauman, T. J., & Higgins, E. T. (1987). Automatic activation of self-discrepancies and emotional syndromes: When cognitive structures influence affect. *Journal of Personality and Social Psychology*, *53*, 1004–1014.

Strauman, T. J., & Higgins, E. T. (1988). Self-discrepancies as predictors of vulnerability to distinct syndromes of chronic emotional distress. *Journal of Personality*, *56*, 685–707.

Stürmer, S., & Simon, B. (2004). Collective action: Towards a dual-pathway model. In W. Stroebe & M. Hewstone (Eds.), *European review of social psychology* (Vol. 15, pp. 59–99). Hove, UK: Psychology Press/Taylor & Francis.

Tajfel, H., Billig, M. G., Bundy, R. P., & Flament, C. (1971). Social categorization and intergroup behaviour. *European Journal of Social Psychology*, *1*, 149–178.

Tajfel, H., & Turner, J. C. (1979). An integrative theory of intergroup conflict. In W. G. Austin & S. Worchel (Eds.), *The social psychology of intergroup relations* (pp. 33–47). Monterey, CA: Brooks/Cole.

Trawalter, S., & Richeson, J. A. (2006). Regulatory focus and executive function after interracial interactions. *Journal of Experimental Social Psychology*, *42*, 406–412.

Weiner, B. (1986). *An attributional theory of motivation and emotion*. New York/Berlin: Springer-Verlag.

Wieber, F., & Sassenberg, K. (2006). *Benefits without costs? Implementation intention induced overgeneralization and contrast effects in social judgments.* Unpublished manuscript, University of Jena, Germany.

Woltin, K.-A., & Sassenberg, K. (2008). *Group-based self-control: The influence of social identification on individual control strategies.* Unpublished manuscript, University of Jena, Germany.

7 Go to Hell!

Determinants of motivated social exclusion

Immo Fritsche
Friedrich-Schiller-University of Jena

Thomas W. Schubert
ISCTE

People exclude. They ignore others in everyday interactions, prevent them from entering private circles. Or they even actively drive them out of their country or their moral community, which might be accompanied by additional punishment or persecution. Often social exclusion hurts the excluded and is clearly aversive. In some cases such aversive exclusion is considered legitimate by society (e.g., imprisoning war criminals), in others it is not (e.g., denying human rights to prisoners). It can be either explicit (e.g., exclusion from a political party) or implicit (e.g., being not invited to take part in common activities), can be justified by individual attributes (e.g., exclusion of a sportsman who used illegal substances) or by membership in an excluded group (e.g., exclusion of a sportsman whose national sporting association does not obey international anti-doping rules). In this chapter we review social psychological research on the question of how social exclusion of others is motivated.

Motivated social exclusion

People belong to certain social groups and categories and they do not belong to others. Although people are always excluded or exclude themselves from certain groups, that usually does not pose a problem. It even might be considered beneficial for social identity concerns to be a member of distinct (Jetten, Spears, & Postmes, 2004), and thus exclusive (Brewer, 1991; see also Brewer, chapter 1 in this volume), groups as this allows us a clear understanding of who we are (Hogg, 2000). On the other hand, assigning others to different social categories enables efficient information processing and action on the side of the observer (e.g., Macrae, Milne, & Bodenhausen, 1994). However, problems occur when the categorized other does not agree with being included in one category (categorization threat; Branscombe, Ellemers, Spears, & Doosje, 1999) or being excluded from another. That is, in many cases social exclusion would be considered aversive by the excluded and therefore elicits social conflict.

Although socially excluding others is often likely to involve psychological costs (e.g., social conflict), people are sometimes inclined to exclude others from a shared social category, indicating social exclusion motivation. We define *motivated social exclusion* as the intended implicit or explicit attempt to psychologically or physically remove an individual or a group from a shared social ingroup or to refuse their entry.

According to this definition, the chapter focuses on intended rather than accomplished exclusion. That is, instead of focusing on the question of when social exclusion becomes factual reality for both the excluding and the excluded party, we rather conceive of social exclusion as an individual or collective behavioral inclination on the side of the excluding party. This inclination might not only be expressed in cognition or behavior explicitly indicating exclusion, such as not categorizing others as ingroup members or denying entry in ingroup assemblies. However, more implicit forms of exclusion attempts are also conceivable, such as ascribing attributes that are incompatible with those of the ingroup or ignoring others in conversations. Furthermore, social exclusion can either occur in psychological (e.g., defining others as being not of our kind) or physical form (e.g., denying entry to ingroup buildings or residence in ingroup territories), or in both.

In our definition of motivated social exclusion we consider lacking inclusion as conceptually equivalent to exclusion and thus use both synonymously. Although being excluded from a group one has belonged to might be of different subjective severity than being not allowed to enter an aspired group, determinants and consequences should have a high overlap for both phenomena. In addition, social exclusion always implies that change has occurred, or would occur. Either an existing category breaks up and gives way to another, less inclusive one, or an inclusion is hindered and prevented. In any case, social exclusion always has its impact through its association with its contra-factual opposite, inclusion.

It is also important to note that motivated social exclusion refers to exclusion of both individuals and groups. According to self-categorization theory (Turner, Hogg, Oakes, Reicher, & Wetherell, 1987), individuals can be categorized as members of nested social groups. For social exclusion this means that individuals can be excluded from groups and groups can be excluded from superordinate groups or categories.

Social exclusion has also become a prominent term in other social sciences such as sociology, economy, and political science. However, in these disciplines the term social exclusion is often equated with economic discrimination (e.g., Hills, Le Grand, & Piachaud, 2002). In our approach we take a broader and more basic scope, conceiving of social exclusion as exclusion from social categories. Although social exclusion might result in restricted access to resources and services, it does not necessarily have to. There might be different and also more basic psychological consequences. However, of course, investigating the determinants of motivated social exclusion is then of foremost societal importance when it leads to aversive consequences on the side of the excluded, and for sure, social exclusion can be both determinant and justification (e.g., Bandura, 1999) of treating others badly.

Group membership implies shared attributes and interaction rules among its members. This is important for understanding social exclusion phenomena in two ways. First, those who are in the group are considered as sharing common attributes and are treated in line with shared interaction rules, but those who are outside the group are not. This can have serious consequences for people who are excluded from moral communities[1] as they might have to fear non-moral treatment. However, second, those who are seen as not sharing group-related attributes and as not complying with shared rules of conduct run the risk of being excluded from the group. It is the aim of this chapter to shed some more light on the interplay of ingroup norms and deviance to explain social exclusion. Furthermore we focus on motivational conditions on the side of the observer that lead to the inclination to socially exclude others. However, first we briefly look at consequences of social exclusion.

Consequences of social exclusion

An increasing amount of research in social psychology addresses the aversive consequences of social exclusion. In their famous ostracism experiments, Kipling Williams and his colleagues (for overviews see Williams, 2007; Williams & Zadro, 2005) investigated participants' reactions to being excluded from a ball tossing game. After having tossed the ball for a few times, ostracized individuals were excluded from the game by not receiving the ball anymore for about five minutes. This paradigm has also been transferred to a computer mediated communication ("cyberball"; Williams & Jarvis, 2006). Compared to those who were not excluded, those participants who were excluded in the ball tossing game increased activities directed at face-saving, control restoration and social (re-)inclusion and initially reported lower self-esteem, control, sense of belonging, and sense of meaningful existence. Most interestingly, the latter effects occurred even when cyberball participants had been told that they were playing with members of a despised outgroup (Gonsalkorale & Williams, 2007) or with simulated players that were scripted regarding what to do in the game (Zadro, Williams, & Richardson, 2004). This lends support to the authors' notion that people dispose of a highly sensitive system to detect indications of social exclusion in order to be able to counteract possible exclusion early. Indications of aversive exclusion seem to pose a threat to basic human needs, and those individuals whose basic needs (e.g., the need for control) are threatened anyway should be particularly affected by ostracism experiences. In line with this notion Warburton, Williams, and Cairns (2006) showed that ostracism in the ball tossing paradigm increased aggressive behavior only in those participants who had not been able to control the onset of blasts of aversive noise in a previous task compared to those who had control.

Social exclusion consistently results in lowered self-esteem (Leary, 2005). Building on this evidence, Leary and Baumeister (2000) proposed a heuristic monitoring process that detects when social inclusion is endangered. Following their sociometer theory, individuals' self-esteem serves as a global indicator of whether or not they are included, which is proposed to lead to self-esteem motivation and protection.

Determinants of excluding individuals and groups

In contrast to the intense research on the (negative) consequences of social exclusion, systematic research on the factors that determine whether or not individuals are excluded from groups is rather rare and unsystematic. In the following, we try to reduce this gap by summarizing social psychological theories and evidence that might contribute to explain why and when we exclude individuals and groups.

Social exclusion of individuals

Inclusion of new individuals or whole new groups of people into groups, and also exclusion of individuals or sub-groups from groups, are common and normal events in each group's life cycle, as scholars such as Sani (2005) and Levine, Moreland, and Hausmann (2005) noted. In particular, the latter authors argued that groups improve their performance by actively managing their membership in terms of including and excluding people. Similarly, individuals manage their membership in groups actively according to their needs and motives. Entry into a group and exit from a group are complemented by changes of roles individuals take on while they are members in the group and thus under the influence of the group's socialization processes, or in divergence with the group's goals. From this perspective, inclusion and exclusion can be understood as role transitions that follow rules of fulfillment of both the individual's and the group's goals, and are managed by communication. Yet the questions arise: Which specific functions underlie social exclusion? Which motives and goals are precisely at work? And which cognitive processes underlie the transitions of inclusion and exclusion?

Evolutionary considerations

Social exclusion is a phenomenon that is not unique to humans, but is also known in the animals' realm. For several other species it has been observed that single individuals are expelled from the collective in certain circumstances. Thus, it can be assumed that exclusory behavior has evolved because of its function for evolutionary success. Kurzban and Leary (2001) proposed that for social species it is important to differentiate between those other individuals who make sociality beneficial for one's own fitness, those who do not, and those who even cause fitness costs to the socially living individual.

The latter two might be subject to motivated social exclusion. The authors specify a broad variety of specific evolutionary functions social exclusion might have and that may explain exclusory behavior towards particular individuals and collectives. A first set of functions is said to be related to disease avoidance. It is assumed that others are avoided or even actively excluded from interactions when they exhibit signs associated with infectious diseases. As costs of not detecting infected individuals are potentially high (contagion and perhaps death), and signs of infection might not be detected easily, evolutionary theorists assume that exclusory tendencies are not only directed against people who carry clear indications of infection but also against those carrying features that are correlated with infectious disease only to a minor degree (such as physical asymmetries). As exemplary evidence for this approach Schaller, Park, and Faulkner (2003) have found that the more people felt vulnerable to diseases the less likely they were to have friends with physical disabilities. In addition, research on disease avoidance theory (Schaller et al., 2003) has predicted and found that perceived vulnerability to disease was negatively correlated with attitudes towards immigration of members of unfamiliar outgroups compared to those of familiar outgroups. This is explained by increased risk of contagion in contact with previously unknown populations because of diseases for which one has not acquired immunity, and by non-familiar or subjectively non-appropriate health care customs of non-local cultures.

A second set of evolutionary functions Kurzban and Leary (2001) identify are those related to ensuring the benefits of dyadic cooperation in reciprocal exchange relationships and friendships. It is proposed that exclusory tendencies have developed towards those people who are not likely to be benefit providers in exchange or friendship relations. These are (a) people who act in unpredictable ways or are at least associated with unpredictability because of individual characteristics (e.g., some of the mentally ill) or unexpected and non-normative behavior (e.g., sexual preference minority groups, suicidal persons). In addition, (b) people with a poor potential to increase their interaction partner's well-being (e.g., the homeless) and (c) known cheaters (e.g., convicted criminals) should decrease fitness in exchange or friendship relations and thus are assumed to be targets of social exclusion.

Third, Kurzban and Leary (2001) propose that in the course of human evolution, mechanisms were selected that preserve both intra-group cooperation and outgroup exploitation, and excluding non-beneficial ingroup members and not including outgroup members is one of them. In more detail, social exclusion is expected towards "those who defect against the group, violating the group rules that preserve the interests of individual group members" (p. 196). Furthermore, outgroup exclusion is assumed to reflect the general tendency in groups to exploit subordinate outgroups. Here exclusion is seen manifested in restricted mating opportunities for subordinate outgroup men, and exclusion of the outgroup from economic and societal benefits that are reserved for members of the superordinate ingroup.

The intergroup perspective

As highlighted in the evolutionary approaches, the tendency to protect the integrity of a social ingroup seems to be part of our species' ancestral design that still unfolds its effects on human behavior. However, besides providing individuals with both social interaction partners to cooperate with and those to exploit, social groups are also understood as fulfilling basic cognitive and motivational functions. According to social identity theory (Tajfel & Turner, 1979) group membership gives individuals a sense of who they are and that they have value. For a social ingroup to exist, similarity between their members should exceed similarity between ingroup members and outgroup members (Turner et al., 1987). This implies that ingroup members who are different from other ingroup members, and perhaps more similar to outgroup members, might pose a threat to the clarity of what the group is like and whether it is positive. As a consequence, social exclusion of these group members should protect both a clear ingroup image as well as a positive ingroup evaluation, which is what people are striving for according to social identity theory. There are various approaches that explain motivated social exclusion on the ground of such an intergroup account.

Members only: Keeping groups exclusive

Social categories help one to orient oneself in the social environment. Here, those groups one belongs to are of particular importance to individuals because they help one to understand the self and to define it in positive terms. A descriptive and prescriptive prototype of the ingroup informs us about our own attributes and our own position in the world, which is of basic importance for effective action. In addition, being part of positively distinct social groups should be an important basis for high self-esteem. Hence, from a social identity perspective (Tajfel & Turner, 1979; Turner et al., 1987) defending a distinct and positive image of the ingroup is highly desirable, which is expressed in a pervasive tendency to favor ingroup over outgroup members when allocating positive resources (for an overview see Hewstone, Rubin, & Willis, 2002). Another way of ingroup defense is to take care that ingroup members contribute to the positive distinctiveness of the ingroup. This can be reached by means of inclusion and exclusion. Both tendencies have been described in the intergroup literature as ingroup over-exclusion (Leyens & Yzerbyt, 1992), negative treatment of impostors (Hornsey & Jetten, 2003), and black sheep effects (Marques & Yzerbyt, 1988).

The ingroup over-exclusion effect has been described by Leyens and Yzerbyt (1992), who assumed that people are more reluctant to categorize unknown individuals as ingroup members than as outgroup members. Experimental evidence shows that Belgian participants who had to decide whether each of a list of target persons belonged to the Walloon ingroup or to the Flemish outgroup, categorized more targets as outgroup than as ingroup members. In addition, they asked for more information about the target when the target appeared to be stereotypical for the ingroup than when it was not. Obviously, people are particularly concerned about avoiding errors when including others in the ingroup. This has also been demonstrated in a second experiment by Yzerbyt, Leyens, and Bellour (1995). Here, both Walloon (French speaking group) and Flemish (Dutch speaking group) Belgians were asked to decide whether each of a list of either Walloon or Flemish target speakers belonged to their ethnic ingroup or to the outgroup. The central result was that participants were more accurate in categorizing true outgroup members as outgroup than in categorizing true ingroup members as ingroup. However, this was only true when the ingroup speakers had been talking in the language of the outgroup (i.e., in an ambiguous situation) but not when they had been talking in the ingroup's language. Following the social identity approach, people should be especially inclined to avoid "contamination" of their ingroup by non-fitting members in cases where this ingroup defines their self to a great extent, that is, when they are highly identified with the group. If the ingroup over-exclusion effect is indeed rooted in ingroup defense motivation, the effect should be more pronounced in high than in low identifiers. Castano, Yzerbyt, Bourguignon, and Seron (2002) investigated this assumption by asking North Italians to indicate whether each of several depicted target persons was North Italian or South Italian. The target pictures were generated by morphing faces having been identified as North Italian with those having been identified as South Italian, resulting in targets representing different degrees of ingroup relative to outgroup features. The results revealed the importance of participants' identification with the North Italian ingroup for the over-exclusion effect to occur: High but not low identifiers categorized more targets as outgroup than as ingroup members and needed longer to decide on group membership the closer targets came to the ingroup prototype. In a related study, Castano (2004) showed that a mortality salience treatment, which is known to increase social identification with potentially death-transcending ingroups (Castano & Dechesne, 2005), also enhanced the tendency to include only members who looked like the ingroup prototype, and to exclude persons who looked like the outgroup prototype. This demonstrates the motivational dynamics behind the process of ingroup over-exclusion.

Social exclusion of intragroup deviants

We have seen that there is a basic tendency to keep the ingroup exclusive and to be cautious about including individuals in the ingroup. This might reflect a desire for positive distinctiveness of the ingroup. But what if individuals who had been included in the ingroup before turn out to deviate from the ingroup prototype? Research on the treatment of ingroup impostors and "black sheep" provides evidence for negative treatment towards deviants that could be interpreted as reflecting a desire to exclude deviants from the ingroup.

Impostors are "people who make public claims to an identity while disguising their failure to fulfil key criteria for group membership" (Hornsey & Jetten, 2003, p. 639). That is, impostors are those people who would not have been likely to be included in the group if their true nature had been known when categorizing them, and confirming inclusion would blur group boundaries and group definition. In an initial study on the treatment of impostors, Hornsey and Jetten (2003; Study 1) asked vegetarians and non-vegetarians to evaluate a target person who claimed to be a vegetarian towards others but in one condition was described to eat meat occasionally while in the other he was said to never eat meat. As a result, both vegetarians and non-vegetarians rated the impostor as more damaging for the vegetarian cause than the authentic target. However, interestingly, only vegetarians but not non-vegetarians expressed more negative affect towards the impostor versus the authentic target. In line with the basic idea of social identity defense, impostors should lead to negative reactions only if they have smuggled themselves into a group that is critical for defining one's identity. This has been shown more directly in two additional studies by Hornsey and Jetten (2003; Studies 2 and 3) where those vegetarians who were more strongly identified with their group indicated more negative affect towards an impostor than those who were less strongly identified. In addition, before high identifiers got to know that the allegedly vegetarian target was an impostor, they liked him/her more than low identifiers did. However, after reading about the true nature of the target, high identifiers' likeability ratings no longer differed from those of low identifiers. That is, the high identifiers seemed to remove a bonus in likeability from the target he or she had received after being held as an ingroup member. This might be interpreted as a removal of group membership status. What might also support this interpretation is that in these studies, likeability was measured by items reflecting desired personal contact and friendly interaction. Thus, reduced likeability expressed an increased tendency to exclude the impostor from pleasant interpersonal interactions, which is motivated social exclusion.

A black sheep is an ingroup member who deviates from ingroup norms in a negative direction. According to the "black-sheep effect" hypothesis (Marques, Yzerbyt, & Leyens, 1988), a negative ingroup member should be evaluated more negatively than a negative outgroup member. This tendency has been shown in various experiments (for an overview see Abrams, de Moura, Hutchison, & Viki, 2005). In one of the first black sheep experiments, Marques et al. (1988; Study 1) asked the participants of their study to assign positive and negative traits to three members of the ingroup (Belgians) and three members of the outgroup (North Africans). Each of them was described as either likeable, unlikeable, or had received no description. As a result, unlikeable targets received more negative evaluations when they were members of the ingroup than when they were members of the outgroup. Conversely, likeable ingroup members were evaluated more positively than likeable outgroup members. No difference occurred between neutral in- and outgroup targets. These results have been explained by the subjective group dynamics model (e.g., Abrams et al., 2005).

As has also been stated in the above mentioned research on the treatment of impostors, reactions towards black sheep are assumed to be a consequence of identity defense motivation. More specifically, the subjective group dynamics model proposes that people not only strive for clarity of group definition but also for validation of prescriptive ingroup norms (for suggestions for a moderating role of actual motivation for uncertainty reduction vs. ingroup enhancement see Hogg, Fielding, & Darley, 2005). This explains why in the initial black sheep experiment, Marques et al. (1988) did not only find more negative reactions to negative ingroup members than to negative outgroup members, but also more positive reactions to positive ingroup members than to positive outgroup members: Positivity of ingroup members proves that the ingroup must be right. Abrams, Marques, Bown, and Henson (2000) found more elaborate evidence for validation of ingroup norms in two experiments. They showed that the degree of deviance from an ingroup prototype did not reliably predict the evaluation of deviating ingroup members. In contrast, it was more important whether ingroup members deviated into the direction of the group norm (pro-norm deviance; e.g., a woman who is particularly feminine) or opposed to the group norm (anti-norm deviance; e.g., a woman who is particularly masculine). Although all deviants were evaluated more negatively than non-deviants in their first but not in their second experiment, pro-norm deviants received better ratings than anti-norm deviants in both experiments. In addition, the authors found a tendency to view anti- but not pro-norm deviants as less typical for the ingroup in the second experiment, which might point to a subtyping strategy used to deal with ingroup deviants who are not excluded from the main category.

Neither the work on treatment of impostors nor the literature on the black-sheep effect provides direct evidence that non-normative group members are excluded from the group. Abrams et al. (2005) propose that many other strategies than social exclusion are conceivable for dealing with ingroup deviants, including education and marginalization (see Levine et al., 2005). It is important to note that marginalization might rather represent subtyping of and negative attitudes against those ingroup members who violate the norms. However, it remains an open question in this literature if – and if yes, when – deviant ingroup members are excluded from the norm-setting group.

Social exclusion of groups

Schisms

The previous examples dealt with exclusion from an ingroup of those individuals who lacked sufficient properties indicating their legitimate membership in the ingroup category. However, as in many ways a reverse phenomenon also exists, namely the secession of ingroup members or a group of ingroup members from their ingroup. Such schisms have been investigated by Sani and colleagues (Sani 2005, Sani & Reicher, 1998, 1999; Sani & Todman 2002). Sani et al. investigated two cases in particular: The secession of a faction of the former Italian communist party after it changed its program and name, and the secession of members of the Church of England after it started to ordain women as priests. In both cases, the results showed that leaving the ingroup was associated with the perception that the group's essential features had changed, and the identity of the ingroup subverted. Sani et al. emphasize that the understanding of a changed value as a fundamental and essential one is an outcome of communicative and constructive processes. Leaving the ingroup seems to be mediated by feelings of agitation and dejection, by a loss of identification with the ingroup, and by a loss of perceived entitativity of the ingroup.

Even though Sani et al. do not investigate this fact, it is interesting to note that in both described cases the seceding members do not simply form smaller groups, but construct themselves as connected to larger social entities: The seceding faction of Italian communists see themselves as upholding the communist tradition and as inheriting the status as the authentic Italian communists, and thus as still belonging to the previous, larger, and "true" ingroup. Likewise, the seceding members of the Church of England construct themselves as connected to the Catholic Church and actually view the changing Church of England as leaving this superordinate category, and becoming a sect. It is in this sense possible that secession or self-exclusion from an ingroup is often bolstered by the construction of a sustained membership in a superordinate category, and the self-exclusion is actually perceived as an exclusion of the ingroup's majority from the superordinate category, to which the seceding subgroup still belongs. However, it remains open whether this is typical of schisms, or is just a common feature of the two cases described by Sani et al.

Moral exclusion

Recently, one of the authors was duped by his 4-year-old son refusing to keep on eating his delicious roast hare while crying out, "Poor bunny! – *You* don't want to be eaten either!" Obviously, people often do not apply the same moral standard to all categories of living beings. This has the advantage of being able to eat hares, which is good for meat-loving gourmets. However, it is of course bad for hares.

Different standards of just treatment apply within different superordinate categories. Whereas on the level of species it might be acceptable that we kill animals, it is not acceptable that we kill humans. Although as a consequence of human moral universalism basic rights have been established for all humans in most contemporary societies, there are also more or less explicit differences in moral obligations towards members of different human groups. For example, it is the right of every university student to have access to the university's resources such as internal library services or taking part in student sports courses, whereas this is prohibited for non-students. Conflict over whether this kind of broadly accepted exclusion is illegitimate is likely to be rather rare. However, there are other examples more prone to conflict, such as the practice that citizenship status in a country implies a variety of rights and benefits that are not attainable by non-citizens. Excluding groups or individuals from superordinate categories means that standards of conduct that apply to members of the category do not apply to the excluded. This can have severe consequences for those who are excluded, and thus it would be in their best interest to share one moral community with antagonistic groups and to avoid being excluded.

Research by Susan Opotow (1995) has investigated the determinants of moral exclusion, which she defined as excluding groups and individuals from one's scope of justice. In research on land-use conflicts between people and a population of beetles as well as on adolescents' peer conflicts, she found that the tendency to morally exclude adversaries increased with conflict severity. Interestingly, similarity to the other party only then decreased moral exclusion when conflict severity was low, but *increased* it when conflict severity was high. Manipulating perceived utility of the beetles for humans showed that although participants were more inclined to protect the beetles when they were perceived as being beneficial rather than harmful, utility did not decrease moral exclusion. This pattern of findings suggests an instrumental explanation of moral exclusion that is in line with historic research on the development of persecuting societies (e.g., in the Middle Ages; Moore, 1987). Following that notion, the combination of being in some regard dependent on the outgroup (e.g., under conditions of perceived utility), but simultaneously striving for ingroup dominance over the outgroup, might be the most fertile ground for moral exclusion to grow.

In such cases, moral exclusion might not only determine but also legitimize negative treatment of others. As a consequence, perpetrators might not only use morally excluding statements as justifications of harm doing (e.g., Bandura, 1999) but might even be freed from the obligation to justify their behavior at all. Enjoying roast hare does not require moral discourse at the lunch table if everybody agrees about hares being game and not belonging to the children's realm of human-like Easter bunnies and cuddly toys.

Infra-humanization and de-humanization

Basic human rights or ethical codes of conduct are widely shared and exist to protect humans from arbitrary mistreatment by others. However, most tragically, history is full of examples of blatant cruelty against groups of people, which might raise serious doubts that standards of humanity have ever existed. But they of course have and still do. So, how was it possible that European colonists treated the inhabitants of occupied territories as animals or sold them as slaves, that marauding troops devastated Central Europe during the Thirty Years War and that Nazi Germany committed industrialized murder of millions of Jews, political opponents and other minority people? Calling these cruelties "inhumane" not only describes their quality but perhaps also a psychological process that made them possible. That is, inhumane treatment of victims can be made possible and justified by not seeing them as humans.

Jacques-Philippe Leyens and colleagues (e.g., Leyens et al., 2003; see also Leyens & Demoulin, chapter 11 in this volume) have shown in their research on infra-humanization that tendencies to exclude social outgroups from the human category determine intergroup relations. According to their theorizing, ingroup dominance can be established or defended by infra-humanization, which is the combination of human essence attribution to the ingroup and reluctance to attribute likewise to the outgroup. Most extensively, this phenomenon has been demonstrated for the ascription of secondary emotions (specific to humans) and primary emotions (not specific to humans). For instance, Leyens et al. (2001) asked students of a Canary Islands university and Spanish mainland students to select from a list of four secondary emotions (nostalgia, compassion, pride, and remorse) and four primary emotions (courage, astonishment/fear, exaltation, and surprise) those emotions that they considered typical characteristics of either Canary Islands or Spanish mainland students. Pre-tests had revealed that secondary and primary emotions did not differ in valence. As predicted by the infra-humanization hypothesis, when describing the ingroup, participants selected more secondary – that is uniquely human – emotions than when they were asked to describe the outgroup. No differences occurred for the attribution of primary emotions. This basic effect has been replicated several times not only for explicit but also for implicit measures of emotion attribution. In this vein, Paladino, Leyens, Rodriguez-Perez, Rodriguez-Torres, and Gaunt (2002) have shown in an IAT paradigm (Implicit Association Test; Greenwald, McGhee, & Schwartz, 1998) that secondary emotions were more strongly associated with the ingroup and primary emotions were more strongly associated with the outgroup than the reverse combination. Viki, Winchester, Titshall, Chisango, Pina, and Russell (2006) demonstrated infra-humanization beyond the ascription of secondary emotions by measuring the association of the in- and outgroup with words related to humans or to animals. In four studies the authors could show that human- but not animal-related words were more strongly associated with the ingroup than with the outgroup on both implicit and explicit measures. Behavioral consequences of infra-humanization have been found for cases in which in- or outgroup members expressed either secondary or primary emotions (Vaes, Paladino, Castelli, Leyens, & Giovanazzi, 2003): When expressing secondary emotions ingroup members were approached faster than outgroup members, but outgroup members who expressed secondary emotions were more quickly avoided than ingroup members. Avoidance might be an indirect indicator of social exclusion tendencies.

However, as research by Nick Haslam (Haslam, 2006) shows, denial of humanness not only occurs by likening others to animals, but also by likening others to machines or automata. He proposes that animalistic de-humanization involves denying the civility, refinement, moral sensibility, rationality, and maturity of others, whereas in mechanistic de-humanization emotional responsiveness, interpersonal warmth, cognitive openness, agency, individuality, and depth are denied. Although both kinds of de-humanization finally result in exclusion of individuals or groups from the human category, according to Haslam (2006) they might be accompanied by different emotions. While disgust and contempt might go along with animalistic de-humanization, mechanistic de-humanization might instead elicit disregard and indifference.

As has been suggested for moral exclusion, infra-humanization and de-humanization also seem to be instrumental for people. Paladino, Vaes, Castano, Demoulin, and Leyens (2004) found the infra-humanization effects only for high- but not for low-identifiers, and Castano and Giner-Sorolla (2006) showed that outgroup infra-humanization was increased when participants were made to reflect on mass killing of the outgroup for which the ingroup was perceived responsible. Obviously, conceiving of the outgroup as less human than the ingroup is fueled by motives of ingroup identity protection and enhancement, which is particularly important for highly identified individuals and when a positive group image is under threat. Then, thinking of outgroup members as being less human can both make the representation of the ingroup relatively more positive in intergroup comparison, and can be hoped to justify or at least qualify earlier cruelties against outgroup people.

Summary and future directions for research

Why do people exclude? Whereas the negative consequences of social exclusion for the excluded have been explicitly addressed in recent social psychological research (e.g., Williams, 2007), research on determinants of social exclusion is still rare and less explicit in its scope. In the previous sections of this chapter we reviewed research that contributes to a better understanding of the functions and motivations of social exclusion. From an evolutionary perspective, social exclusion might serve to avoid possible fitness costs implied in humans' high degree of sociality by differentiating between beneficial and non-beneficial contacts. More specific in scope, the intergroup perspective emphasizes a motivation for positive and distinct collective identities, which is reflected in a host of special motives such as the one to have a valid worldview. These motives then imply a certain reluctance to include others in the ingroup (ingroup over-exclusion effect; Leyens & Yzerbyt, 1992), and negative reactions towards individuals deviating from the (positive) attributes of the ingroup. Whether these negative reactions always lead to social exclusion attempts is not clear, neither theoretically (e.g., Abrams et al., 2005) nor empirically. Nevertheless, indirect indicators of social exclusion inclinations towards deviant group members can be found in the literature, such as reduced personal contact with ingroup impostors (Hornsey & Jetten, 2003). Collective social exclusion is the exclusion of a social outgroup from a superordinate category shared with the ingroup. Basically the same motivational forces seem to be at work for the exclusion of individuals from ingroups, and the exclusion of whole subgroups from a common ingroup. With the exception of work on group schisms where subgroups purposely exclude themselves (e.g., Sani, 2005), research has focused on cases in which collective exclusion can have serious negative consequences for those excluded, and hence is likely to be accompanied by conflict. This is particularly the case when groups of individuals are excluded from the human category, which has been investigated in research on moral exclusion (Opotow, 1995), infra-humanization (Leyens et al., 2003), and de-humanization (Haslam, 2006). Interestingly, exclusion from the human category might not only foster inhumane treatment of those excluded, but might also be utilized to justify negative treatment afterwards (e.g., Castano & Giner-Sorolla, 2006).

Individual or collective deviance has been proposed to be a precursor of motivated social exclusion. However, deviance should not always lead to social exclusion. Often, people who deviate from the ingroup prototype are just treated less positively, and negative treatment or even social exclusion are rather rare events (e.g., Mummendey, Otten, Berger, & Kessler, 2000). Ongoing research by Amélie Mummendey and colleagues (Fritsche, Kessler, Mummendey, & Neumann, in press; Kessler, Neumann, Mummendey, Schubert, & Waldzus, 2007) addresses the conditions under which deviance leads to motivated social exclusion. Departing from the notion that ingroup and outgroup evaluations are based on their relative proximity to the prototype of a superordinate category (Mummendey & Wenzel, 1999), it is claimed that there are different types of deviation from the features of the superordinate category. In particular, it is argued that it should make a difference whether groups deviate from minimal or from maximal goals, which can both be part of the superordinate category's representation. In *minimal goals* a threshold is specified that marks whether the goal has been attained or not (e.g., "Immigrants should have at least basic knowledge of their host society's language") and not reaching the threshold is evaluated negatively. In *maximal goals* an ideal reference value is defined (e.g., "Immigrants should have as much knowledge of their host society's language as possible"), and goal attainment is judged in a gradual fashion where increasing distance from the reference value is evaluated with decreasing positivity. Whereas maximal goals are proposed to give group behavior direction, minimal group goals are thought to define fixed boundaries of conduct. Hence, in other words, minimal group goals might define the moral boundaries of groups. Therefore, people who violate minimal goals – but not those who violate maximal goals – might be considered as standing outside the group. This should make motivated social exclusion more likely, as violation of minimal group goals poses a threat to the normative consensus within (superordinate) groups, and might thus even threaten group existence. In line with this reasoning, for instance, Fritsche et al. (in press) found that the more people were inclined to form minimal goals rather than to have maximal goals, the more they suggested excluding norm-breaking individuals and members of deviant social categories from the moral community. For example, minimal goal orientation increased demands for suspending the licenses of drivers who moderately violated traffic regulations, or for excluding members of a national team from the Olympic Games whose national sports association had failed to conform to international anti-doping standards. This shows that the more people are inclined to interpret norm violations as deviation from minimal rather than from maximal goals, the more they exclude deviants from the group. They should do so because violation of the collective normative boundaries poses a threat to group definition and integrity.

Motivated social exclusion can lead to severe conflict between individuals and groups when those who are to be excluded are reluctant to leave the category. Although the targets of social exclusion may agree with their exclusion in certain circumstances, there is a general tendency to resist exclusion, nevertheless. This is so because social exclusion is basically aversive and people have a desire to avoid exclusion in most cases. This desire might be a result of actual self-categorization processes, but can be increased in cases when groups serve as social resources (e.g., Correll & Park, 2005) providing a sense of meaningful belonging, self-esteem, control, or epistemic or self-concept certainty. The pervasiveness of exclusion avoidance is well illustrated in schism research, where even in cases of collective *self*-exclusion from a former ingroup, people seem to strive to continue to be included in a legitimate superordinate category from which the remaining members of the former ingroup can now be excluded in turn. That is, to psychologically buffer self-exclusion, a group (rather than self-excluding individuals) has the opportunity to turn the tables and to exclude rather than being excluded. This might be the starting point for severe intergroup conflicts over which party is the one excluded.

Divergent perspectives on the legitimacy of collective exclusion lay the ground for severe intergroup conflict. This is particularly likely to be the case if the group that is the target of social exclusion perceives collective mobility as being low, that is when the group does not perceive any other place to be than within the disputed superordinate category. This might be true for confessional groups facing attempts to exclude them from their broader religious community (e.g., when the Roman Catholic Church claims that Protestant churches are no church), or native populations that are no longer allowed to inhabit the territories they live in. In such cases intergroup conflict on social exclusion might be about group existence.

Note

1 The term "moral community" has been used to describe "who is inside or outside our psychological boundary for justice" (Clayton & Opotow, 2003, p. 301).

References

Abrams, D., de Moura, G. R., Hutchison, P., & Viki, G. T. (2005). When bad becomes good (and vice versa): Why social exclusion is not based on difference. In D. Abrams, M. A. Hogg, & J. M. Marques (Eds.), *The social psychology of inclusion and exclusion* (pp. 161–189). New York: Psychology Press.

Abrams, D., Marques, J. M., Bown, N., & Henson, M. (2000). Pro-norm and anti-norm deviance within and between groups. *Journal of Personality and Social Psychology, 78*, 906–912.

Bandura, A. (1999). Moral disengagement in the perpetration of inhumanities. *Personality and Social Psychology Review, 3*, 193–209.

Branscombe, N. R., Ellemers, N., Spears, R., & Doosje, B. (1999). The context and content of social identity threat. In N. Ellemers & R. Spears (Eds.), *Social identity: Context, commitment, content* (pp. 35–58). Oxford: Blackwell Science.

Brewer, M. (1991). The social self: On being the same and different at the same time. *Personality and Social Psychology Bulletin, 17*, 475–482.

Castano, E. (2004). In case of death, cling to the ingroup. *European Journal of Social Psychology, 34*, 375–384.

Castano, E., & Dechesne, M. (2005). On defeating death: Group reification and social identification as immortality strategies. *European Review of Social Psychology, 16*, 221–255.

Castano, E., & Giner-Sorolla, R. (2006). Not quite human: Infrahumanization in response to collective responsibility for intergroup killing. *Journal of Personality and Social Psychology, 90*, 804–818.

Castano, E., Yzerbyt, V. Y., Bourguignon, D., & Seron E. (2002). Who may enter? The impact of in-group identification on in-group/out-group categorization. *Journal of Experimental Social Psychology, 38*, 315–322.

Clayton, S., & Opotow, S. (2003). Justice and identity: Changing perspectives on what is fair. *Personality and Social Psychology Review, 7*, 298–310.

Correll, J., & Park, B. (2005). A model of the ingroup as a social resource. *Personality and Social Psychology Review, 9*, 341–359.

Fritsche, I., Kessler, T., Mummendey, A., & Neumann, J. (in press). Minimal and maximal goal orientation and reactions to norm violations. *European Journal of Social Psychology.*

Gonsalkorale, K., & Williams, K. D. (2007). The KKK won't let me play: Ostracism even by a despised outgroup hurts. *European Journal of Social Psychology, 37*, 1176–1186.

Greenwald, A. G., McGhee, D. E., & Schwartz, J. L. K. (1998). Measuring individual differences in implicit cognition: The implicit association test. *Journal of Personality and Social Psychology, 74*, 1464–1480.

Haslam, N. (2006). Dehumanization: An integrative review. *Personality and Social Psychology Review, 10*, 252–264.

Hewstone, M., Rubin, M., & Willis, H. (2002). Intergroup bias. *Annual Review of Psychology, 53*, 575–604.

Hills, J., Le Grand, J., & Piachaud, D. (2002). *Understanding social exclusion*. Oxford: Oxford University Press.

Hogg, M. A. (2000). Subjective uncertainty reduction through self-categorization: A motivational theory of social identity processes. In W. Stroebe & M. Hewstone (Eds.), *European review of social psychology* (Vol. 11, pp. 223–255). Chichester, UK: Wiley.

Hogg, M. A., Fielding, K. S., & Darley, J. (2005). Fringe dwellers: Processes of deviance and marginalization in groups. In D. Abrams, M. A. Hogg, & J. M. Marques (Eds.), *The social psychology of inclusion and exclusion* (pp. 191–210). New York: Psychology Press.

Hornsey, M. J., & Jetten, J. (2003). Not being what you claim to be: Impostors as sources of group threat. *European Journal of Social Psychology, 33*, 639–657.

Jetten, J., Spears, R., & Postmes, T. (2004). Intergroup distinctiveness and differentiation: A meta-analytic integration. *Journal of Personality and Social Psychology, 86*, 862–879.

Kessler, T., Neumann, J., Mummendey, A., Schubert, T., & Waldzus, S. (2007). *Minimal versus maximal orientations as determinants of negative treatment of others.* Unpublished manuscript.

Kurzban, R., & Leary, M. R. (2001). Evolutionary origins of stigmatization: The functions of social exclusion. *Psychological Bulletin, 127*, 187–208.

Leary, M. R. (2005). Varieties of interpersonal rejection. In K. D. Williams, J. P. Forgas, & W. von Hippel (Eds.), *The social outcast: Ostracism, social exclusion, rejection, and bullying* (pp. 35–51). New York: Psychology Press.

Leary, M. R., & Baumeister, R. F. (2000). The nature and function of self-esteem: Sociometer theory. In M. P. Zanna (Ed.), *Advances in experimental social psychology* (Vol. 32, pp. 1–62). San Diego, CA: Academic Press.

Levine, J. M., Moreland, R. L., & Hausmann, L. R. M. (2005). Managing group composition: Inclusive and exclusive role transitions. In D. Abrams, M. A. Hogg, & J. M. Marques (Eds.), *The social psychology of inclusion and exclusion* (pp. 137–160). New York: Psychology Press.

Leyens, J.-P., Cortes, B., Demoulin, S., Dovidio, J. F., Fiske, S. T., Gaunt, R., et al. (2003). Emotional prejudice, essentialism, and nationalism: The 2002 Tajfel Lecture. *European Journal of Social Psychology, 33*, 703–717.

Leyens, J.-P., Rodriguez-Perez, A., Rodriguez-Torres, R., Gaunt, R., Paladino, M.-P., Vaes, J., et al. (2001). Psychological essentialism and the differential attribution of uniquely human emotions to ingroups and outgroups. *European Journal of Social Psychology, 31*, 395–411.

Leyens, J.-P., & Yzerbyt, V. Y. (1992). The ingroup overexclusion effect: Impact of valence and confirmation on stereotypical information search. *European Journal of Social Psychology, 22*, 549–569.

Macrae, C. N., Milne, A. B., & Bodenhausen, G. V. (1994). Stereotypes as energy-saving devices: A peek inside the cognitive toolbox. *Journal of Personality and Social Psychology, 66*, 37–47.

Marques, J. M., & Yzerbyt, V. Y. (1988). The black sheep effect: Judgmental extremity towards ingroup members in inter- and intra-group situations. *European Journal of Social Psychology, 18*, 287–292.

Marques, J. M., Yzerbyt, V. Y., & Leyens, J.-P. (1988). The "Black Sheep Effect": Extremity of judgments towards ingroup members as a function of group identification. *European Journal of Social Psychology, 18*, 1–16.

Moore, R. I. (1987). *The formation of a persecuting society*. Cambridge, MA: Blackwell.

Mummendey, A., Otten, S., Berger, U., & Kessler, T. (2000). Positive–negative asymmetry in social discrimination: Valence of evaluation and salience of categorization. *Personality and Social Psychology Bulletin, 26*, 1258–1270.

Mummendey, A., & Wenzel, M. (1999). Social discrimination and tolerance in intergroup relations: Reactions to intergroup difference. *Personality and Social Psychology Review, 3*, 158–174.

Opotow, S. (1995). Drawing the line: Social categorization, moral exclusion, and the scope of justice. In B. B. Bunker & J. Rubin (Eds.), *Conflict cooperation, and justice: Essays inspired by the work of Morton Deutsch* (pp. 347–369). San Francisco: Jossey-Bass.

Paladino, M.-P., Leyens, J.-P., Rodriguez-Perez, A., Rodriguez-Torres, R., Gaunt, R., & Demoulin, S. (2002). Differential association of uniquely and non uniquely human emotions with the ingroup and the outgroup. *Group Processes and Intergroup Relations, 5*, 105–117.

Paladino, M.-P., Vaes, J., Castano, E., Demoulin, S., & Leyens, J.-P. (2004). Emotional infra-humanization in intergroup relations: The role of national identification in the attribution of primary and secondary emotions to Italians and Germans. *Cahiers de Psychologie Cognitive, 22*, 519–536.

Sani, F. (2005). When subgroups secede: Extending and refining the social psychological model of schism in groups. *Personality and Social Psychology Bulletin, 31*, 1074–1086.

Sani, F., & Reicher, S. (1998). When consensus fails: An analysis of the schism within the Italian Communist Party (1991). *European Journal of Social Psychology, 28*, 623–645.

Sani, F., & Reicher, S. (1999). Identity, argument, and schism: Two longitudinal studies of the split in the Church of England over the ordination of women to the priesthood. *Group Processes and Intergroup Relations, 2*, 279–300.

Sani, F., & Todman, J. (2002). Should we stay or should we go? A social psychological model of schisms in groups. *Personality and Social Psychology Bulletin, 28*, 1647–1655.

Schaller, M., Park, J. H., & Faulkner, J. (2003). Prehistoric dangers and contemporary prejudices. *European Review of Social Psychology, 14*, 105–137.

Tajfel, H., & Turner, J. C. (1979). An integrative theory of intergroup conflict. In W. G. Austin & S. Worchel (Eds.), *The social psychology of intergroup relations* (pp. 33–47). Monterey, CA: Brooks/Cole.

Turner, J. C., Hogg, M. A., Oakes, P. J., Reicher, S. D., & Wetherell, M. S. (1987). *Rediscovering the social group. A self-categorization theory*. Oxford: Basil Blackwell.

Vaes, J., Paladino, M. P., Castelli, L., Leyens, J.-P., & Giovanazzi, A. (2003). On the behavioral consequences of infrahumanization: The implicit role of uniquely human emotions in intergroup relations. *Journal of Personality and Social Psychology, 85*, 1016–1034.

Viki, G. T., Winchester, L., Titshall, L., Chisango, T., Pina, A., & Russell, R. (2006). Beyond secondary emotions: The infrahumanization of outgroups using human-related and animal-related words. *Social Cognition, 24*, 753–775.

Warburton, W. A., Williams, K. D., & Cairns, D. R. (2006). When ostracism leads to aggression: The moderating effects of control deprivation. *Journal of Experimental Social Psychology, 42*, 213–220.

Williams, K. D. (2007). Ostracism. *Annual Review of Psychology, 58*, 425–452.

Williams, K. D., & Jarvis, B. (2006). Cyberball: A program for use in research on interpersonal ostracism and acceptance. *Behavior Research Methods, 38*, 174–180.

Williams, K. D., & Zadro, L. (2005). Ostracism: The indiscriminate early detection system. In K. D. Williams, J. P. Forgas, & W. von Hippel (Eds.), *The social outcast: Ostracism, social exclusion, rejection, and bullying* (pp. 19–34). New York: Psychology Press.

Yzerbyt, V. Y., Leyens, J.-P., & Bellour, F. (1995). The ingroup overexclusion effect: Identity concerns in decisions about group membership. *European Journal of Social Psychology, 25*, 1–16.

Zadro, L., Williams, K. D., & Richardson, R. (2004). How low can you go? Ostracism by a computer is sufficient to lower self-reported levels of belonging, control, self-esteem, and meaningful existence. *Journal of Experimental Social Psychology, 40*, 560–567.

Part III

Emotions and intergroup relations

8 Group-based emotions
The social heart in the individual head

Vincent Yzerbyt and Toon Kuppens
Université catholique de Louvain,
Louvain-la-Neuve

In a classic study, Minard (1952) examined racial interactions between white and black coal miners inside and outside the Pocahontas Coal Field of McDowell, West Virginia, USA. Although this research was conducted when segregation was still legal in many states, its message directly relates to a number of recent research efforts in the realm of group-based emotions. Minard found that whereas white coal miners treated black co-workers as equals in the context of the mine, they also dealt with them as social inferiors in the outside world. These data are often presented as evidence that the situational and normative pressures constrain the manifestation of people's behavior, especially in the realm of intergroup relations, and obscure the impact of more enduring aspects of people such as attitudes. In short, one should not expect people's prejudice to materialize in discrimination in any straightforward way. Only by taking some distance from any particular context and by averaging over many behaviors should researchers expect to observe a decent level of correspondence between attitude and behavior.

In this chapter, we take issue with a popular interpretation of such a discrepancy. For many observers, the particular settings people find themselves in entail a series of obstacles that simply stand in the way of the actualization of their dispositional penchant. Our understanding of this mismatch between otherwise chronic attitudes and behaviors in specific situations is very different. We take issue with the view that people somehow remain the same but negotiate with the context. In fact, we argue that people change in radical and indeed essential ways from one situation to another! Similarly, attitudes are not stable representations stored somewhere in our head. Rather, they are created again every time an evaluation is considered necessary. We argue that attitudes are inherently flexible and that this explains why they can be so context-sensitive (Smith & Conrey, 2007). Therefore we should not expect intergroup attitudes to be directly related to discriminatory behavior unless both are measured in the same context and with the same object (outgroup) in mind (for a discussion on this topic, see Mackie & Smith, 1998).

Building on social identity theory (SIT, Tajfel & Turner, 1979) and self-categorization theory (SCT, Turner, Hogg, Oakes, Reicher, & Wetherell, 1987), but also on research in social cognition, we argue that specific features of the context alter who people are in very fundamental ways. Temporary and short-lived as they may be, the viewpoints adopted by individuals are nonetheless experienced as authentic and permanent. Such modifications are responsible for a drastic alteration in individuals' appraisal of the situation, in their emotional reaction to it, and, eventually, in their behavioral response. Crucially, this means that what individuals think, feel, and do when confronted with people and events around them can be much more flexible than is generally thought.

Building on this general argument, this chapter focuses on group-based emotions. Specifically, we examine how emotional reactions are sensitive to the social landscape with which people are confronted. In the first section, we provide a quick overview of "intergroup emotion theory" (IET, Smith, 1993) as well as a series of other theoretical approaches pertaining to emotions in the intergroup domain. We also present early empirical work showing that people can and do experience emotions not on a strict individual basis but on behalf of the group to which they belong. In the second section, we detail our own strategy to study what we call group-based emotions. We then dwell on a series of illustrative empirical findings. Our third and final section presents some intriguing consequences of social identity changes on the perception of group threats. We conclude by delineating a number of open questions and we propose new directions for future research. The key idea, and indeed the backbone of this chapter, is that people experience different emotions as a function of their salient social identity. This is what makes these emotional episodes group-based.

From generalized prejudice to intergroup emotions

In the field of intergroup relations, no concept has been more central than the concept of prejudice (Allport, 1954). Prejudice can be simply defined as the affective reaction that people experience when they are confronted with another group or one of its members. Obviously, prejudice would hardly preoccupy the scientific community if it were always or even mostly positive. Unfortunately, the gut reaction that people feel when they meet with members of another group is more often than not of a definite negative nature. Over the years, researchers have come to use the concept of prejudice to refer to a host of unflattering emotional responses such as anxiety, disgust, fear, envy, contempt, and so on (Stephan & Stephan, 2000). Not surprisingly, these various negative reactions are thought to be linked to the opinions people hold about groups and to translate into behavioral reactions. This trinity of prejudice, stereotypes, and discrimination lies at the heart of the vast majority of research efforts on intergroup attitudes (Fiske, 1998; Schneider, 2004).

The way prejudice is being conceptualized in the domain of intergroup relations has been considerably modified since Smith (1993), in an insightful contribution, proposed combining self-categorization theory (Turner et al., 1987) and appraisal theories of emotion (Frijda, Kuipers, & ter Schure, 1989;

Lazarus, 1991; Scherer, 1988). Doing so allowed Smith (1993) to address several limitations of the traditional approaches to prejudice. Specifically, the dominant perspectives have a hard time accounting for some discrepancies between people's beliefs about other groups (i.e., their stereotypes), and their affective reactions (i.e., their prejudice). One example is that some groups seem to possess positive qualities but do not seem to be liked much. Moreover, although prejudice has traditionally been posited to be the key factor shaping stereotypes and discrimination, many observations suggest that it is the information one has about groups that feeds into emotional reactions and these affective responses, in turn, shape people's behaviors. Appraisal theories of emotion (e.g., Lazarus, 1991) are particularly well equipped to account for these phenomena. Although the specifics of the different theories vary, the underlying rationale is constant. A stimulus, be it an object, a situation, a person, or, of course, a group, is evaluated along a number of meaningful dimensions. This triggers a specific pattern of emotional reactions. Eventually, behavioral tendencies and specific actions ensue.

One limitation of appraisal theories is that emotional phenomena are conceptualized at the individual level. Building on self-categorization theory (Turner et al., 1987) and his own work on the overlap between the definition of the self and the ingroup (Smith, Coats, & Walling, 1999; Smith & Henry, 1996), Smith (1993, 1999) proposed that people were also likely to appraise situations, experience emotions, and express behaviors as members of social groups rather than as individuals. In other words, people's cognitive evaluation is conducted from the perspective of the group member. Situations are appraised, not for their relevance to the individual, but for their relevance to the group to which the individual belongs. This depersonalization process is crucial in order to understand what the appropriate stakes are vis-à-vis the stimulus: People do not function anymore as unique individuals but as interchangeable exemplars of their relevant ingroup in the comparative context. Just like people turn to their ingroup in order to settle on what their beliefs and behaviors should be, a phenomenon at the heart of referent informational theory (Turner, 1991), they can be seen as relying on their group identity to work out the fundamental characteristics of the situation, react emotionally to them, and take appropriate action.

In an early test of Smith's (1993) intergroup emotion theory (IET), Mackie, Devos, and Smith (2000) reasoned that the strength of the ingroup position should influence group members' emotions and action tendencies. Appraisal theories of emotion hold that anger (fear) emerges when people face a negative event, such as a conflict, and realize that they do (do not) have the necessary means to withstand a fight and, eventually, prevail. Anger (fear) will then translate into action tendencies aimed at confronting (avoiding) the source of conflict. In the scenario used by Mackie et al. (2000), participants are asked to specify whether they are members of a group that supports or opposes some controversial issue. They are then presented with information suggesting that their own group enjoys substantial (versus little) collective support, whereas the other group can count on little (versus substantial) support. The key dependent measures concern emotional reactions and action tendencies.

In one of their studies, Mackie et al. (2000, Experiment 2) had participants read and evaluate a list of 19 headlines supposedly taken from newspapers and related to the issue of whether homosexual couples in long-term relationships should benefit from the same legal rights as married heterosexuals. Whereas the vast majority of headlines (16 out of 19) supported the ingroup in the "strong ingroup" condition, only a minority of headlines (3 out of 19) supported the ingroup in the "weak ingroup" condition. There was also a control condition in which participants were not presented any headlines. In line with IET, participants made to believe that the ingroup was in a strong (weak) position felt more (less) angry and wanted to oppose the outgroup more (less). As expected, anger proved to be a mediator of the impact of collective support on the tendency to confront the outgroup. Unfortunately, and replicating earlier findings (Mackie et al., 2000, Experiment 1), feelings of fear and defensive action tendencies remained impervious to the manipulation.

Interesting as they may be, empirical demonstrations such as these suffer from a number of limitations (for a detailed discussion, see Yzerbyt, Dumont, Mathieu, Gordijn, & Wigboldus, 2006). One is that IET is mainly, if not solely, concerned with people's emotional reactions as group members *toward groups*, be it the ingroup or outgroups. That is, the ambition is to understand and predict how people may react emotionally and, as a consequence, initiate certain behaviors, based on a particular appraisal of the groups that are salient in the intergroup situation (for a similar analysis, see Parkinson, Fischer, & Manstead, 2005, and Iyer & Leach, 2008, as well as the contributions of Brown and Otten, chapters 10 and 9 in this volume). In contrast, we would argue that the targets of so-called intergroup emotions can be much more diverse and do not need to be groups per se. In its emphasis on group and group members as the target of emotions, IET is highly similar to a number of other perspectives that have been proposed in recent years.

For instance, the *stereotype content model* (Cuddy, Fiske, & Glick, 2007; Fiske, Cuddy, Glick, & Xu, 2002; Fiske, Xu, Cuddy, & Glick, 1999) proposes that the nature of the intergroup relations determines the stereotypes of the outgroup. Two dimensions of the intergroup relations are considered essential: perceived status and competition. Perceived status predicts competence stereotypes: high (low) status groups are considered competent (incompetent). Perceived competition predicts warmth stereotypes (warmth stereotypes being associated with an absence of competition). Warmth and competence are seen as core dimensions of group perception and are hypothesized to lead to specific emotions (Cuddy et al., 2007; Judd, James-Hawkins, Yzerbyt, & Kashima, 2005; Phalet & Poppe, 1997; Yzerbyt, Provost, & Corneille, 2005). Similarly, Neuberg and Cottrell's (2002) *biocultural or sociofunctional model* sees cognitive appraisals of intergroup relations as the first step in a causal chain that ultimately leads to behavior. These authors argue that important threats from an outgroup to ingroup resources or group functioning elicit specific intergroup emotions. We examine the sociofunctional model in more detail later.

Having said this, the idea that perceivers undertake a cognitive evaluation of the various groups that they are confronted with constitutes a most valuable development in research on intergroup relations. Indeed, the link between this work and the stereotyping literature is obvious and promises to improve our understanding of the factors that play a role in intergroup contact. Moreover, providing evidence for the social nature of these evaluations is a real benefit. Recent empirical evidence suggests that the appraisal of specific groups is indeed likely to be shared with other members of the same group (Smith, Seger, & Mackie, 2007), confirming the impact of group membership on people's assessment of the relationships (Yzerbyt, Dumont, Wigboldus, & Gordijn, 2003).

If one examines the research conducted under the IET umbrella, it is interesting to note that Smith and colleagues adopted only one of two possible strategies aimed at providing evidence for the existence of emotions that rest on group membership. As a matter of fact, their approach consists in changing the (alleged) objective conditions faced by the group to which people belong in the hope that this will change their subjective evaluation of the outgroup, and directly influence their feelings and action tendencies as group members. Rather than concentrating on the appraisal side of the coin, the alternative strategy, and the one we decided to implement in our research, directly addresses the social identity aspect of the phenomenon. What we have been doing is to modulate the specific social identity that is made salient. Because this strategy capitalizes on the earliest stage of the process, it tends to facilitate the examination of a wider variety of stimulus objects (not only groups) while retaining the essential feature that the emotional experience is grounded in the group. This is why we much prefer the label *group-based emotions* (GBE). The key idea is that when people are confronted with specific events, how they appraise the situation will be crucially influenced by the salient social identity, which provides the lens through which the situation is being seen.

A distinct advantage of focusing on social identity in order to elicit group-based emotions is that it clarifies the distinction between the individual and the group level. Changing the objective conditions faced by the group may also change the conditions of the individual, possibly leading to a change in individual appraisals and emotions. Therefore, it is not always certain that a manipulation of group conditions affects only group-based emotions and not individual emotions. Manipulating the social identity avoids this interpretational problem because it unambiguously moves the identity from the personal to the group level. The next section is devoted to the underlying rationale of our GBE approach.

The impact of social context on group-based emotions

A basic assumption underlying self-categorization theory (SCT) is that people can function at different levels of identity (Turner et al., 1987). SCT makes a distinction between personal and social identity. Still, both of these levels of self-categorization are seen as valid and authentic definitions of the self. That is, people are both individual persons and members of various groups, and operating at the personal or group level is, psychologically speaking, equally real. However, it remains that the forces guiding people's behavior at one or the other level may not be the same. At the personal level, behavior is shaped by individual differences. Unique characteristics such as traits, attitudes, and the like are at the forefront and combine with situational constraints to shape people's responses. In contrast, when working at the group level, people come to perceive themselves as interchangeable exemplars of their group, and their beliefs and actions should be aligned on their understanding of those features that define their group as opposed to a salient outgroup in the comparative context.

One illustration of the power of this mechanism can be found in a study by Verkuyten and Hagendoorn (1998). These authors reasoned that prejudice (measured by the social distance of their Dutch participants towards Turks living in The Netherlands) should be influenced by individual-level versus group-level factors as a function of whether the context emphasizes personal versus national identity. As predicted, authoritarianism, an individual difference variable, influenced prejudice when personal identity was made salient. In sharp contrast, the ingroup stereotypes of Dutch about Turkish people were related to prejudice when national identity was activated.

Research outside the SCT tradition similarly illustrates the sensitivity of people's behavior to the identity under which they operate. Over the last decade, an impressive number of studies have documented the fact that performance in a domain is hindered when individuals feel that a group to which they belong is negatively stereotyped in that domain, a phenomenon called "stereotype threat" (Steele & Aronson, 1995). In an intriguing study, Shih, Pittinsky, and Ambady (1999) capitalized on the cultural stereotypes that quantitative skills are superior among Asians than among other ethnic groups, but are inferior among women than among men. Indeed, participants, all Asian females, performed better than a control condition when their ethnic identity had been made salient, but their performance was depressed when their gender identity was activated. In these studies, people's behavior changes in significant ways simply because one social identity among many possible others has taken precedence as a result of subtle contextual changes. Our initial studies similarly rest on this idea that social identities can be somehow "selected" so as to influence people's reactions and emotions.

In one of our early demonstrations of the role of social categorization on group-based emotions (Gordijn, Wigboldus, & Yzerbyt, 2001), we confronted students from the University of Amsterdam with a newspaper article.

The story reported a conflict involving students from Leiden University and the professors and board at that same university. The latter wanted to implement new policies restricting access to the university. Leiden students had not been consulted and strongly opposed the decisions. Mobilization was on its way. Our University of Amsterdam students could receive the story in a number of ways, namely as students, as people enrolled in Amsterdam, or even as individual observers. We decided to channel the way to approach this conflict by warning experimental (but not control) participants that we were interested in comparing either the reactions of people belonging to different universities or the reactions of students and professors. Crucially, this manipulation took place *before* participants were presented with the newspaper article.

To the extent that participants see themselves as belonging to the same group as the students of Leiden, a reaction we hoped would be set off in the condition comparing "students versus professors", they should adopt a perspective similar to the one found among the Leiden students and feel the emotions presumably experienced by these students. In contrast, we expected participants in the condition comparing "different universities" to see themselves and the Leiden students as members of different groups. As a consequence, the emotions felt would be less akin to those presumably experienced by the victims. Our dependent variables comprised measures of anger, happiness, anxiety, and also a measure of similarity to the Leiden students.

As predicted, participants felt angrier and less happy when the study allegedly was aimed at comparing reactions of students to those of professors compared to what was observed in the other experimental condition. There was no impact of our manipulation on anxiety, another negative emotion. Interestingly, participants in the control condition spontaneously tended to distance themselves. In spite of the fact that control participants had reasons to embrace the student identity, similarity ratings showed that they contrasted away from the victims. Clearly, thus, we were able to generate divergent patterns of emotional reactions by encouraging observers of some event to draw particular contours in their social landscape.

This initial success allowed us turn to our attention to a number of additional issues. Because group-based emotion theory holds that people's emotional reactions should mediate the impact of our manipulation on action tendencies, a *first question* was whether we could extend our argument about the impact of the categorization to include the issue of action tendencies and actual behavior. A *second issue* concerns the role of identification. Although we observed that the temporary salience of one identity over another affects the chain of reactions, we wanted evidence that the impact of the contextually salient category would be moderated by the degree of chronic identification with the salient category, further establishing the group-based nature of emotions. A *third question* is whether we could find cases in which an emotion other than anger, say fear, would show the predicted pattern. *Fourth*, and finally, a convincing demonstration of the influence of social as opposed to personal identity on cognitive appraisals, emotions, and action tendencies would be provided if one could encourage observers to embrace either the perspective of the victims or the perspective of the perpetrators. The remainder of this section deals with these four issues.

In order to address the mediating role of emotions on action tendencies and the moderating role of identification, we (Yzerbyt et al., 2003) conducted a study in which French-speaking students at the University of Louvain in Louvain-la-Neuve, Belgium, learned about a conflict between Dutch-speaking students of the University of Ghent and their university authorities. The alleged clash revolved around the unexpected decision to impose English as the language for all Master-level classes. Again, we activated one of several social identities in our participants *before* they were confronted with the critical event. Also, before we presented them with the newspaper article, we measured participants' level of chronic identification with the group they were associated with in their specific condition, namely students in general (as compared to professors) or students from Louvain-la-Neuve (as compared to students from other universities). After they had read the article, participants reported their emotional reactions (anger, sadness, fear, and happiness) as well as the related action tendencies (offensive tendencies, absence of reaction, avoidance tendencies, mocking tendencies).

As hypothesized, people's emotional reactions were not only higher on anger than on any other emotion, but anger was also the only emotion that proved sensitive to our independent variables. Moreover, as predicted, the simultaneous presence of high identification and a group membership emphasizing the similarity with the victims was conducive to higher levels of anger than any of the three other combinations. Turning to action tendencies, the specific categorization imposed on participants through the comparison context combined with their chronic identification led to the production of a pattern that was consistent with expectations. That is, participants manifested the strongest offensive action tendencies when they had been thrown in the same category as the victims and had initially expressed strong levels of identification with this category. No differences emerged among the three other combinations. Importantly, our mediational hypothesis was confirmed: The stronger offensive action tendencies of the participants who were led to see themselves as belonging to the same category as the victims (i.e., students in general) and identified highly with this category, were fully mediated by the participants' emotional reactions of anger. In sum, this study strongly supports our approach to studying GBE.

It should be noted that the categorization manipulation used here relied on sub-categorization rather than cross-categorization. Participants were either put in the shoes of students in general or in the shoes of only a subset of students, namely students from their university. In line with other work showing the impact of broadening group boundaries on social behavior and inter-group relations (Gaertner & Dovidio, 2000; Gaertner, Dovidio, Anastasio, Bachman, & Rust, 1993), our findings underscore the importance of making salient a common ingroup for the emergence of GBE and action tendencies similar to those of the victims.

The above empirical demonstrations all focused on anger as the key emotion. Moreover, no evidence was provided for the impact of context on actual behaviors. These two issues were addressed in a series of studies that took advantage of the infamous terrorist attacks against the World Trade Center on September 11, 2001 (Dumont, Yzerbyt, Wigboldus, & Gordijn, 2003). One of these studies (Dumont et al., Experiment 2) was conducted just 1 week after the events. After having received a full-page picture of the burning Twin Towers, participants were given one of two rationales for the study. Half of the participants were informed that the study aimed at comparing European and Arab respondents. The remaining participants learned that their responses as Europeans would be compared with those of American respondents. The identity manipulation was thus quite subtle: Whereas the first condition presented Europeans and Americans as belonging to the same group of non-Arabs, the second put forth a distinction between Europeans and Americans. Interestingly, we observed no impact of our manipulation on the identification with Europeans. As well as a series of questions aimed at tapping participants' emotional reactions and action tendencies, we also measured several behaviors.

Results confirmed that sadness and anger were strongly reported by participants, but that these emotions remained unaffected by our subtle identity manipulation. In contrast, and as predicted, making salient a context that linked participants with victims of the harmful behavior in a common ingroup led them to report more fear than when the context had participants categorize the victims as outgroup members. Moreover, we obtained clear evidence that the manipulation influenced behavioral tendencies. Informing participants that their answers would be compared to Arab respondents elicited stronger tendencies to seek information about the events and its developments, stronger tendencies to provide support and help to the victims, and stronger tendencies to talk about the events with other persons than when they thought they would be compared to American respondents. Finally, our manipulation also affected significant behaviors such as communicating personal data in order to later receive information about terrorist networks, about how to support and help the victims, or about demonstrating for NATO's intervention. These behaviors would be most relevant if one wished to reduce one's level of uncertainty, regain some subjective control over the situation, and improve self-protection, which are all possible behavioral reactions to fear.

In addition to showing that emotions other than anger prove sensitive to categorization and identity changes elicited by the context, these findings also indicate that the impact of the context extends to behavioral intentions and actual behaviors. In this respect, we can mention another interesting study that used a method very similar to ours. Levine, Prosser, Evans, and Reicher (2005) set out to explore the impact of social categorization on real-life helping behavior. In their first study, they recruited male Manchester United soccer club fans as participants and confronted them with an emergency incident. During the first part of the experiment, participants' identity as Manchester United fans was made salient. While walking to another building for the second part of the experiment, a confederate jogged in front of the participants and ostensibly twisted his ankle while shouting out in pain. The victim's group membership was manipulated by means of his clothing: He was either wearing a Manchester United shirt, a Liverpool FC shirt, or an unbranded sports shirt. As predicted, participants were much more likely to offer help when the victim was wearing a Manchester United shirt.

In a clever follow-up study, Levine and colleagues (2005) used the same procedure, but made a more inclusive social category salient to the participants, the superordinate category of football fans in general. This means that both Liverpool FC and Manchester United fans could now be seen as belonging to the participants' ingroup. Indeed, participants were now much more inclined to offer help when the jogger was wearing a football shirt (either Manchester United or Liverpool FC), as compared to a neutral sports shirt. The large effect of social categorization in these studies is remarkable given the history of intense rivalry between the two teams. Even though no information was collected regarding participants' appraisals and emotional reactions, these results bear striking similarity to our own work.

The fourth and final issue of this section discusses another attempt to emphasize the role of social categorization in the emergence of emotions. We wanted to show that the same observers could be led to see themselves as victims or perpetrators of a particular event, and to feel angry or content as a function of the particular "social" shoes they were led to walk in. Of course, we also intended to trigger systematic differences in people's appraisal of the very same situation as well as in their behavioral intentions.

Addressing this question allowed us to establish a direct link with fascinating research conducted over recent years on collective guilt. Specifically, this work examined the conditions under which people experience guilt and shame with respect to harmful behavior perpetrated by members of the ingroup on members of other groups. In one telling study (Doosje, Branscombe, Spears, & Manstead, 1998, Experiment 2), Dutch participants first completed an identification questionnaire pertaining to their identity as Dutch people. They were then confronted with one of three sets of information about the conduct of Dutch people in one of their former colonies. Depending on conditions, the information was either consistently negative, both negative and positive, or consistently positive.

Not surprisingly, whereas participants in the negative conduct condition felt guilty and very much wanted to compensate for their ancestors' misbehavior, the reverse pattern emerged in the positive conduct condition. The most interesting data, however, concern the ambiguous condition. When the behaviors of the Dutch colonial forces turned out to be both positive and negative, only those participants who were not strongly identified expressed guilt and agreed to compensate. In contrast, high identifiers expressed significantly less guilt and were not ready to offer compensation for the way their ancestors acted. These findings suggest that identification very much orients people's interpretation of events, even distant ones, thereby shaping their emotional reactions and willingness to engage in specific actions.

In one of our studies (Gordijn, Yzerbyt, Wigboldus, & Dumont, 2006), the goal was to show that the *very same* people could be led into reacting either like victims or like perpetrators simply by taking advantage of the existence of social identities linking people to either one of these two kinds of protagonist in some conflict. This time, we took advantage of the particular situation with which US universities are confronted, whereby out-of-state students pay more than their in-state colleagues to attend classes. We informed in-state students from the University of Colorado at Boulder that their state house representatives had decided to raise the tuition by 35% for out-of-state students. This information was conveyed *right after* we had indicated to our participants that we wanted their opinion and reactions on a series of newspaper articles either *as students* (allegedly in order to compare them with non-students) or *as Colorado residents* (allegedly in order to compare them with people from other states), and had asked them to complete a scale tapping their identification with the relevant category. We then measured participants' appraisals of the policy adopted by Colorado state house representatives as well as their emotional reactions and action tendencies. Note here that we had never directly examined appraisals before. We were thus very interested to look at the perception of legitimacy and justice associated with the policy as a function of the particular social identity we imposed on participants.

Replicating our previous findings, we confirmed that participants thinking of themselves as connected to the victims through the salient identity (students) reported more anger when they had initially indicated that they were strongly rather than weakly identified with the category of students. Importantly, a mirror pattern emerged for participants in the condition where their identity associated them to the perpetrators (Colorado residents). The more these participants identified with their state, the less angry they felt about the policy adopted by their state house representatives. As far as appraisals and action tendencies are concerned, there were interesting effects of identification within each social identity condition. Participants induced to think of themselves as linked to the victims saw the decision as less acceptable and reported a stronger willingness to take action against the proposal as a function of their identification with the group of victims. In contrast, in the condition where similarities with the perpetrators were made salient, participants now saw the situation as less wrong and expressed more support for the decision when they identified more with the perpetrators.

Finally, a most compelling piece of evidence regarding the viability of the proposed links between categorization, appraisals, GBE, and action tendencies comes from evidence that the interactive impact of categorization and identification on participants' action tendencies was mediated by how illegitimate they perceived the situation, which was itself mediated by how angry they felt. These data provide very strong support for the validity of our approach to GBE. They nicely complement the findings reported by Doosje and colleagues (1998) in showing that people can be manipulated into approaching a situation from very different perspectives. Depending on the specific social landscape that was activated in their particular case, observers understood the same events, reacted emotionally to them, and intended to do something about them in ways that varied dramatically. A recent study by Pennekamp, Doosje, Zebel, and Fischer (2007) further suggests that different perspectives associated with different social identities also seem to be able to exert their influence within one person. For Surinamese who have migrated to The Netherlands, Surinamese identification had a positive relation with the perceived relevance of the past slavery, which led to more group-based anger, whereas identification with The Netherlands was related to putting the slavery in a historical perspective and was associated with less group-based anger.

Drawing on our argument regarding the impact of categorization on group-based emotions (Yzerbyt, Dumont, Gordijn, & Wigboldus, 2002), Wohl and Branscombe (2004) conducted an internet study in which Jewish participants assigned more or less collective guilt for the Holocaust to Germans, expressed more or less willingness to forgive Germans, and judged genocide as being more or less pervasive as a function of the specific identities that were activated at the outset of the questionnaire, either Jews (versus Germans) or human beings. Again, the message here is that there is definitely more than one identity that observers can embrace when they approach a situation.

Clearly, our efforts, and now other people's work, show that, rather than leaving it all up to the observers, one can channel the social identity they adopt so as to orient their subsequent appraisals, emotions, action tendencies, and indeed behaviors. In the next section, we turn to our latest empirical work, illustrating once more how changes in social identity have non-trivial consequences in the kinds of appraisals and emotions experienced by people.

The power of group-based emotions

The studies presented in the previous section emphasize the fact that emotions such as anger or even fear can be modulated by the specific social landscape that is being promoted in the situation and the particular social identity endorsed by the perceivers. We thought it useful to provide even more unambiguous evidence to this effect. Therefore we decided to show that people's salient social identity can change the entire profile of appraisals and emotions that people experience. To test this hypothesis, we decided to draw on the work by Neuberg and Cottrell (2002) and once again show the versatility of people's group-based emotions.

In their biocultural (or sociofunctional) theoretical model of group-based emotions, Neuberg and Cottrell (2002; Cottrell & Neuberg, 2005) argue that certain specific intergroup threats are related to the experience of specific intergroup emotions and specific behavioral tendencies toward the outgroup. According to the authors, our dependence on the group during our evolutionary history has made us sensitive to threats to group-level resources and obstructions to efficient group functioning. Intergroup emotions are a response to those group-level threats, and they help us to effectively deal with them by bringing about adaptive behavioral intentions (although the reported data are limited to threats and emotions while behavioral tendencies are not discussed). Interestingly enough, Cottrell and Neuberg (2005) have not at all incorporated the theories of social identity and self-categorization into their model. In other words, they fail to take into account the flexibility of people's identity that is emphasized in these approaches. In our view, however, the same intergroup situation can be interpreted differently depending on the contextually salient social identity. If one social identity is more salient than another, this should have an impact on relevant emotions and behavioral tendencies.

We investigated this idea using Muslims as the target outgroup and young female students as participants. In general and across studies, all participants completed the same questionnaire, but we manipulated the salient social identity as in previous studies. The first study (Kuppens & Yzerbyt, 2008) had three social identity conditions. In one condition, respondents were asked for their opinion as *women*. They were told their responses would be compared to those of men, and were asked to answer some questions about identification with other women. In a second condition, respondents were asked for their opinion as *young persons*, and the salience of that identity was manipulated in the same way as in the woman condition. There was also a control condition in which respondents were asked for their opinion with no further instruction.

From Neuberg and Cottrell's (2002) sociofunctional model, we selected seven intergroup threats to be included in our study. Some of these were deemed especially relevant to the woman social identity. Indeed, the public discourse about Muslims often emphasizes their supposedly very different cultural background. One of the differences that is most discussed is the allegedly subordinate position of women in the Muslim community. We therefore considered "threat to personal freedoms and rights" and "threat to group values" to be particularly relevant for women. Furthermore, Muslims are associated with street violence and harassment. Women are physically weaker than men so we considered "threat to physical safety" to be particularly relevant for women as well. As irrelevant threats, we chose "threat to trust relations", "threat to reciprocity relations", "threat to the perception of the ingroup's morality", and "threat to health via contagion". We do not claim that women do not experience these threats, but that they are not *especially* relevant to women (i.e., more relevant to women than to men). We predicted that female students in the woman condition would report higher threat appraisals for the relevant threats but not for the irrelevant threats.

Furthermore, using the theoretical connections between threats and emotions put forward in the sociofunctional model, fear and disgust should be linked to the relevant threats and thus should also be higher in the woman condition. Pity and guilt are not linked to any of the relevant threats, so no differences were expected for these two emotions. The results of this first study largely confirmed our expectations: The differences between the "woman condition" and the control condition were significantly larger for relevant threats and emotions than for irrelevant threats and emotions. Respondents in the "young person" condition generally did not differ much from the control condition. Interestingly, and confirming the general idea of the sociofunctional model, the impact of the social identity manipulation on fear and disgust was fully mediated by the relevant threat appraisals.

In a follow-up study (Kuppens & Yzerbyt, 2008), we dropped the young person condition and thus only had a control condition and a woman condition. In the control condition, we told participants that we were interested in individual differences regarding the attitude toward Muslims and we explicitly asked them for their personal opinion. In addition to the relevant (fear, disgust) and irrelevant (guilt, pity) emotions from the first study, we now also included a measure of envy as additional irrelevant emotions. Results replicated our first study. As predicted, the differences between the woman condition and the control condition were significantly larger for relevant threats and emotions than for irrelevant ones.

The sociofunctional model also addresses behavioral tendencies. Cottrell and Neuberg (2005) proposed behavioral tendencies that are directly aimed at removing the relevant group-based threat. For instance, the proposed behavioral reaction to a threat to group values is to "maintain and confirm the value system", and the proposed reaction to endangered physical safety is to "protect self and valued others". However, these authors report no data that support their contention. We included measures of the behavioral tendencies proposed by Cottrell and Neuberg (2005) in both our studies. Moreover, as the relevant emotions in our studies (fear and disgust) could theoretically lead to a more general avoidance behavioral intention, we also included items that tap the general intention to avoid Muslims. None of the behavioral intentions proposed by Cottrell and Neuberg (2005) proved sensitive to our social identity manipulation. In contrast, participants in the women condition in the second study reported a stronger intention to avoid Muslims, compared to the control condition (in the first study there was a nonsignificant trend in the same direction).

Taken together, these two studies provide most encouraging support for the idea that the sociofunctional model of intergroup emotions can be fruitfully integrated with the self-categorization approach to produce findings that are fully in line with our group-based emotion model. The contextually relevant social identity clearly has an impact on perceived threats and reported emotions and behavioral tendencies. These results strengthen the support for a flexible view on group-based emotions, even when applying a model based on evolved reactions to intergroup threats. Furthermore, although previous studies had already shown the influence of social identity manipulation on group-based anger and fear, these studies add to earlier findings by showing an effect for disgust.

Conclusion

We started this chapter with a reminder about the attitude–behavior discrepancy, a well-known concern among social psychologists. It is our view that this issue is generally presented in a problematic way. The traditional view is that people have a certain personality and hold attitudes that persist across time, but that they are confronted with a number of obstacles and constraints in various situations that lead them to behave in "discrepant" ways. We propose an alternative view based on self-categorization theory, namely that people are more often than not changed in essential ways because of the situations that they find themselves in. To the extent that social perceivers endorse different identities, whether at a personal or social level, or one social identity versus another, they are likely to appraise the world around them in radically different ways. These divergent but nevertheless authentic experiences of the environment trigger different emotional experiences and materialize in different behaviors.

After presenting the theoretical arsenal and empirical strategy underlying most contemporary perspectives that deal with so-called intergroup emotions, we detailed our own strategy for establishing the significance of group-based emotions. The innovative character of our approach resides in our directly manipulating the salient social identity of participants. As a set, our research findings offer a most convincing demonstration that emotional reactions and their associated behaviors are indeed grounded in the social identity of perceivers. By promoting a particular approach to the social landscape, social perceivers can be shown to manifest radically different emotions and behaviors. The bottom-line message of our work is thus that in order to change people's emotions, it may be worth trying to change who people are and to do so by engineering the way they define their social environment in the salient comparative context. Such a modification may be greatly facilitated to the extent that one fully understands how people change as a function of whom they associate with at a psychological level.

In our view, a series of fascinating questions emerge from our research on group-based emotions and definitely deserve to be investigated. First and foremost, we would like to suggest that people remain generally blind to the fact that they would be likely to react differently, sometimes in dramatic ways, if they had been led to approach the environment with a different social identity. This is most intriguing because it means that people remain generally unable to appreciate the importance and consequences of the construal of a situation. If people were able to do this better, they may find themselves in a better position to appreciate the perspective of another person and avoid misunderstandings (Demoulin, Leyens, & Dovidio, 2008). This relative inability to embrace a different perspective for oneself would seem to be related to the difficulty of showing consideration for the views of others. We are currently interested in the relation that may or may not exist between these two skills.

To date, our work on group-based emotions has always examined the impact of identity on the emotional experience (for a review, see Yzerbyt et al., 2006). Another issue that deserves closer attention concerns the reverse causal link (see also Kessler & Hollbach, 2005). Is it the case that emotions may guide the adoption of specific identities? In other words, is it possible that people end up endorsing one social identity more easily than another as a function of the specific emotion that they feel on being confronted with some new event involving different people belonging to various groups?

It is important to emphasize that our research program takes a decidedly unusual perspective regarding the variability of human behavior, in particular when it comes to stereotyping, prejudice, and discrimination. As a matter of fact, we argue that it is much easier to provide an account for the stability by of human behavior capitalizing on flexibility than to explain flexibility from stability. This viewpoint leads us to propose that people who want to modify intergroup behavior could do so by trying to see how it is possible to vary the specific vantage point that individual perceivers adopt rather than trying to change social groups in their entirety (Yzerbyt, 2006). Although we quite realize that this angle has seldom attracted the attention of policy makers, it would nevertheless seem to be a most promising avenue.

References

Allport, G. W. (1954). *The nature of prejudice*. Cambridge, MA: Addison-Wesley.

Cottrell, C. A., & Neuberg, S. L. (2005). Different emotional reactions to different groups: A sociofunctional threat-based approach to "prejudice". *Journal of Personality and Social Psychology, 88*, 770–789.

Cuddy, A. J. C., Fiske, S. T., & Glick, P. (2007). The BIAS map: Behaviors from intergroup affect and stereotypes. *Journal of Personality and Social Psychology, 92*, 631–648.

Demoulin, S., Leyens, J.-P., & Dovidio, J. F. (Eds.). (2008). *Intergroup misunderstandings: Impact of divergent social realities*. New York: Psychology Press.

Doosje, B., Branscombe, N. R., Spears, R., & Manstead, A. S. R. (1998). Guilty by association: When one's group has a negative history. *Journal of Personality and Social Psychology, 75*, 872–886.

Dumont, M., Yzerbyt, V. Y., Wigboldus, D., & Gordijn, E. H. (2003). Social categorization and fear reactions to the September 11th terrorist attacks. *Personality and Social Psychology Bulletin, 29*, 1509–1520.

Fiske, S. T. (1998). Stereotyping, prejudice, and discrimination. In D. T. Gilbert, S. T. Fiske, & G. Lindzey (Eds.), *The handbook of social psychology* (4th ed., Vol. II, pp. 357–411). Oxford: Oxford University Press.

Fiske, S. T., Cuddy, A. J. C., Glick, P., & Xu, J. (2002). A model of (often mixed) stereotype content: Competence and warmth respectively follow from perceived status and competition. *Journal of Personality and Social Psychology, 82*, 878–902.

Fiske, S. T., Xu, J., Cuddy, A. J. C., & Glick, P. (1999). (Dis)respecting versus (dis)liking: Status and interdependence predict ambivalent sterotypes of competence and warmth. *Journal of Social Issues, 55*, 473–489.

Frijda, N. H., Kuipers, P., & ter Schure, E. (1989). Relations among emotion, appraisal, and emotional action readiness. *Journal of Personality and Social Psychology, 57*, 212–228.

Gaertner, S. L., & Dovidio, J. F. (2000). *Reducing intergroup bias: The common ingroup identity model.* Hove, UK: Psychology Press.

Gaertner, S. L., Dovidio, J. F., Anastasio, P. A., Bachman, B. A., & Rust, M. C. (1993). The common ingroup identity model: Recategorization and the reduction of intergroup bias. In M. Hewstone & W. Stroebe (Eds.), *European Review of Social Psychology* (Vol. 4, pp. 1–26). Chichester, UK: Wiley.

Gordijn, E. H., Wigboldus, D., & Yzerbyt, V. (2001). Emotional consequences of categorizing victims of negative outgroup behavior as ingroup or outgroup. *Group Processes and Intergroup Relations, 4*, 317–326.

Gordijn, E. H., Yzerbyt, V. Y., Wigboldus, D., & Dumont, M. (2006). Emotional reactions to harmful intergroup behavior. *European Journal of Social Psychology, 36*, 15–30.

Iyer, A., & Leach, C. W. (2008). Emotion in inter-group relations. In M. Hewstone & W. Stroebe (Eds.), *European review of social psychology* (Vol. 19, pp. 86–125). Chichester, UK: Wiley.

Judd, C., James-Hawkins, L., Yzerbyt, V. Y., & Kashima, Y. (2005). Fundamental dimensions of social judgment: Understanding the relations between judgments of competence and warmth. *Journal of Personality and Social Psychology, 89*, 899–913.

Kessler, T., & Hollbach, S. (2005). Group-based emotions as determinants of ingroup identification. *Journal of Experimental Social Psychology, 41*, 677–685.

Kuppens, T., & Yzerbyt, V. (2008). *Group-based emotions: The impact of social identity on appraisals, emotions, and behaviors.* Manuscript submitted for publication. Université Catholique de Louvain at Louvain-la-Neuve, Belgium.

Lazarus, R. S. (1991). *Emotion and adaptation.* Oxford: Oxford University Press.

Levine, M., Prosser, A., Evans, D., & Reicher, S. (2005). Identity and emergency intervention: How social group membership and inclusiveness of group boundaries shape helping behavior. *Personality and Social Psychology Bulletin, 31*, 443–453.

Mackie, D. M., Devos, T., & Smith, E. R. (2000). Intergroup emotions: Explaining offensive action tendencies in an intergroup context. *Journal of Personality and Social Psychology, 79*, 602–616.

Mackie, D. M., & Smith, E. R. (1998). Intergroup relations: Insights from a theoretically integrative approach. *Psychological Review, 105*, 499–529.

Minard, R. D. (1952). Race relationships in the Pocahontas coal fields. *Journal of Social Issues, 8*, 29–44.

Neuberg, S. L., & Cottrell, C. A. (2002). Intergroup emotions: A sociofunctional approach. In D. M. Mackie & E. R. Smith (Eds.), *From prejudice to intergroup emotions: Differentiated reactions to social groups* (pp. 265–283). New York: Psychology Press.

Parkinson, B., Fischer, A. H., & Manstead, A. S. R. (2005). *Emotion in social relations. Cultural, group, and interpersonal processes.* New York: Psychology Press.

Pennekamp, S. F., Doosje, B., Zebel, S., & Fischer, A. H. (2007). The past and the pending: The antecedents and consequences of group-based anger in historically and currently disadvantaged groups. *Group Processes and Intergroup Relations, 10,* 41–55.

Phalet, K., & Poppe, E. (1997). Competence and morality dimensions of national and ethnic stereotypes: A study in six eastern-European countries. *European Journal of Social Psychology, 27,* 703–723.

Scherer, K. R. (1988). Cognitive antecedents of emotions. In V. Hamilton, G. H. Bower, & N. H. Frijda (Eds.), *Cognitive perspectives on emotion and motivation* (pp. 89–126). Dordrecht, The Netherlands: Kluwer.

Schneider, D. J. (2004). *The psychology of stereotyping.* New York: Guilford.

Shih, M., Pittinsky, T. L., & Ambady, N. (1999). Stereotype susceptibility: Identity salience and shifts in quantitative performance. *Psychological Science, 10,* 80–83.

Smith, E. R. (1993). Social identity and social emotions: Toward new conceptualizations of prejudice. In D. M. Mackie & D. L. Hamilton (Eds.), *Affect, cognition, and stereotyping: Interactive processes in group perception* (pp. 297–315). San Diego, CA: Academic Press.

Smith, E. R. (1999). Affective and cognitive implications of a group becoming part of the self: New models of prejudice and of the self-concept. In D. Abrams & M. A. Hogg (Eds.), *Social identity and social cognition* (pp. 183–196). Malden, MA: Blackwell.

Smith, E. R., Coats, S., & Walling, D. (1999). Overlapping mental representations of self, in-group, and partner: Further response time evidence and a connectionist model. *Personality and Social Psychology Bulletin, 25,* 873–882.

Smith, E. R., & Conrey, F. R. (2007). Mental representations are states, not things. Implications for implicit and explicit measurement. In B. Wittenbrink & N. Schwarz (Eds.), *Implicit measures of attitudes: Procedures and controversies* (pp. 247–264). New York: Guilford.

Smith, E. R., & Henry, S. (1996). An ingroup becomes part of the self: Response time evidence. *Personality and Social Psychology bulletin, 22,* 635–642.

Smith, E. R., Seger, C. R., & Mackie, D. M. (2007). Can emotions be truly group level? Evidence regarding four conceptual criteria. *Journal of Personality and Social Psychology, 93,* 431–446.

Steele, C. M., & Aronson, J. (1995). Stereotype threat and the intellectual test performance of African Americans. *Journal of Personality and Social Psychology, 69,* 797–811.

Stephan, W. G., & Stephan, C. W. (2000). An integrated threat theory of prejudice. In S. Oskamp (Ed.), *Reducing prejudice and discrimination* (pp. 23–45). Mahwah, NJ: Lawrence Erlbaum Associates, Inc.

Tajfel, H., & Turner, J. (1979). An integrative theory of intergroup conflict. In W. G. Austin & S. Worchel (Eds.), *The social psychology of intergroup relations.* Monterey, CA: Brooks/Cole.

Turner, J. C. (1991). *Social influence.* Milton Keynes: Open University Press.

Turner, J. C., Hogg, M. A., Oakes, P. J., Reicher, S. D., & Wetherell, M. S. (1987). *Rediscovering the social group: A self-categorization theory.* Oxford: Basil Blackwell.

Verkuyten, M., & Hagendoorn, L. (1998). Prejudice and self-categorization: The variable role of authoritarianism and in-group stereotypes. *Personality and Social Psychology Bulletin, 24,* 99–110.

Wohl, M. J. A., & Branscombe, N. R. (2004). Importance of social categorization for forgiveness and collective guilt assignment for the holocaust. In N. R. Branscombe & B. Doosje (Eds.), *Collective guilt: International perspectives*. Cambridge: Cambridge University Press.

Yzerbyt, V. Y. (2006). From subtle cues to profound influences: The impact of changing identities on emotions and behaviors. In P. A. M. van Lange (Ed.), *Bridging social psychology: Benefits of transdisciplinary approaches* (pp. 391–396). Mahwah, NJ: Lawrence Erlbaum Associates, Inc.

Yzerbyt, V. Y., Dumont, M., Gordijn, E., & Wigboldus, D. (2002). Intergroup emotions and self-categorization: The impact of perspective-taking on reactions to victims of harmful behavior. In D. Mackie & E. Smith (Eds.), *From prejudice to intergroup emotions* (pp. 67–88). Philadelphia: Psychology Press.

Yzerbyt, V. Y., Dumont, M., Mathieu, B., Gordijn, E. H., & Wigboldus, D. (2006). Social comparison and group-based emotions. In S. Guimond (Ed.), *Social comparison processes and levels of analysis: Understanding cognition, intergroup relations, and culture* (pp. 174–205). Cambridge: Cambridge University Press.

Yzerbyt, V. Y., Dumont, M., Wigboldus, D., & Gordijn, E. H. (2003). I feel for us: The impact of categorization and identification on emotions and action tendencies. *British Journal of Social Psychology, 42*, 533–549.

Yzerbyt, V. Y., Provost, V., & Corneille, O. (2005). Not competent but warm . . . Really? Compensatory stereotypes in the French-speaking world. *Group Processes and Intergroup Relations, 8*, 291–308.

9 Social categorization, intergroup emotions, and aggressive interactions

Sabine Otten
University of Groningen

Group membership shapes the way we perceive and interpret our social world. Knowing which group a person belongs to, and whether he or she is "one of us" or "one of them", provides us with heuristics on how to give meaning to certain events, and on what to expect in the further interaction. This should definitely also apply to the way we perceive and react in aggressive interactions. For example, imagine a soccer fan standing in line to get into the soccer arena. All of a sudden somebody from behind bumps into him, and a moment later he feels a substantial amount of liquid running down his back. Instantaneously, our soccer fan turns around and sees a guy behind him, who is holding a beer glass that is half empty. Will it matter whether our soccer fan identifies the source of his trouble as a supporter of his own team, or as a supporter of the other team? Will he be more convinced that the others had bad intentions, will he be more angry, and will he choose a more destructive reaction when facing an outgroup member rather than an ingroup member?

As the example above illustrates, social categorization can matter in aggressive interactions. In the present chapter, I summarize theoretical and empirical evidence showing such influence. More specifically, I address how social categorization of the opponents can affect the interpretation, emotional reactions, and subsequent behavioral tendencies in social conflicts. Combining two traditions of research, the one focusing on intergroup processes, the other focusing on aggression, is an endeavor that was certainly strongly inspired and influenced by Amélie Mummendey. Her passion for contributing to a better understanding of negative phenomena in our society – such as aggression and social discrimination – turned out to be very infectious. As my mentor and the promoter of my PhD project, she helped me take the first steps into this undoubtedly still highly relevant field of research (Mummendey & Otten, 1993; Otten, Mummendey, & Wenzel, 1995).

The following survey on the impact of social categorization starts with a part dealing with the definition of aggression, thereby emphasizing the role of subjective interpretation of contextual conditions. Subsequently, theoretical and empirical evidence for both relatively more favorable as well as more harsh reactions to ingroup rather than outgroup perpetrators in aggressive interactions are reported, and perceived ambiguity of hostile intentions is introduced as a crucial moderator herein. In the final section of this chapter, I specifically focus on the role of group-based emotions in social conflicts, and on their mediating role for reactions to ingroup and outgroup perpetrators.

Defining aggressive interactions

Before discussing how social categorization can affect aggressive interactions, it is relevant to clarify the defining features of this type of social behavior. Aggressive interactions involve an actor/offender performing a certain problematic behavior, and a recipient, experiencing (or at least observing) the negative consequences of this action. According to the widely shared definition by Baron (1977), "aggression is any form of behavior directed toward the goal of harming another living being who is motivated to avoid this treatment" (p. 7). When we talk about aggression, this typically implies that we consider the behavior as norm-deviation and as meant to do harm. Interestingly, the actual harm that results from the behavior is a less important criterion for defining an action as aggressive than its inappropriateness, and its intentionality (Mummendey, Linneweber, & Löschper, 1984). Both features, however, norm-deviation and hostile intent, cannot be objectively identified, but are recognized as the result of an evaluative process. To give an extreme example: Killing a cruel dictator will be seen as aggressive by his followers, but not by those who hoped that the regime would come to an end.

Accordingly, as clearly stated in several publications by Amélie Mummendey and her co-workers, *subjective and context-specific interpretation* is a defining element of aggressive interactions (e.g., Mummendey et al., 1984; Mummendey & Otten, 1989). Whether an observer or the recipient of a certain harmful behavior will experience this episode as intended to do harm, and as norm-deviation deserving retaliation and punishment is not fully determined by the behavior in itself but rather is dependent on his or her subjective, context-specific perception, interpretation and evaluation. Typically, an aggressive act does not occur in isolation, but is part of a sequence of actions and re-actions, which both opponents typically structure in such a way that they themselves were not responsible for the onset of the conflict (Mummendey & Otten, 1989). Consequently, cognitive appraisals and affective reactions to actual or perceived provocations by others do play a relevant role when we want to understand aggressive interactions and their (de)escalation (e.g., Lindsay & Anderson, 2000; Mummendey et al., 1984; Otten & Mummendey, 2002a).

Importantly, among others things, the context-specificity of aggressive interactions implies that it is worthwhile to analyze the impact of the social categorization of the parties involved in the conflict (i.e., the group affiliations of actor, recipient, and, possibly, observer). While researchers such as Sherif (e.g., 1966) and Tajfel (e.g., 1982) still had to argue that it is worthwhile to distinguish interpersonal and intergroup behavior, in the meantime there is ample research revealing that categorizing oneself and others as members of certain groups can have a powerful impact on perception, affective responses, and behavioral tendencies (e.g., Brewer, 2003; Brewer & Brown, 1998; Brown, 2000). Specifying whether and how aggressive interactions are affected by categorizing the perpetrator and/or victim as either ingroup or outgroup members is the aim of the present chapter.

Social categorization in aggressive interactions – some basic thoughts

What happens when people categorize the opponents in a social conflict as members of certain groups, and when they think about the protagonists not as unique individuals, but in terms of (one of) us versus (one of) them? It is at the heart of social identity theory (Tajfel & Turner, 1979) and self-categorization theory (Turner, Hogg, Oakes, Reicher, & Wetherell, 1987) that once a certain group membership becomes psychologically relevant, this will affect perception, attitudes, and behavior. Therefore, when investigating the influence of salient social categorization in aggressive interaction, it is very plausible to expect that people's reactions will differ when being confronted with either an ingroup or an outgroup perpetrator's negative, harmful behavior.

A plausible hypothesis that we could derive from social identity theory (Tajfel & Turner, 1979) and its prediction that people strive for a positive distinctiveness of their own group as compared to other groups, is that we should find *ingroup bias* when comparing reactions to ingroup and outgroup perpetrators: People should react less negatively when becoming a target of (or merely witnessing) negative, harmful behavior performed by a member of their own group (ingroup) rather than by a member of another group (outgroup). There is plenty of evidence revealing that group members tend to show positive bias towards their ingroup and its members, such that they evaluate ingroup members more positively than outgroup members, or that they favor them in allocation decisions (e.g., Brown, 2000; Hewstone, Rubin, & Willis, 2002). In the case of negative conduct by ingroup members, biased perception and biased reactions could still help to reduce the possible damage to the ingroup's reputation, thereby helping to protect positive ingroup distinctiveness. Conversely, reacting especially harshly towards an ingroup member showing negatively deviant behavior would not be functional; condemning outgroup aggression, however, could – as a byproduct – even reveal the ingroup's moral superiority.

Moreover, becoming target of an *outgroup* member's aggressive behavior may, besides the direct harm that has (or could have) resulted, also imply that the relevant social identity was disrespected: "They think they can do these things to us." Wenzel (see chapter 4 in this volume) elaborates in detail on the ways that unjust behavior does not only offend ideas about entitlements, but can, when social categorization is salient, have implications for one's identity. In the same vein, according to Tedeschi and Felson (e.g., 1994) restoring (social) identity is one of the functions that aggressive (re-)actions can have. An outgroup perpetrator's harm-doing towards an ingroup member might be perceived as an action intended to express the outgroup's superiority over the ingroup, or, at least, as challenging the ingroup's position relative to the outgroup. For example, aggression between fans from different soccer teams can acquire such symbolic meaning; an attack does not only cause physical harm, but can also signal the club's defeat. In such situations, retaliation can become highly relevant in order to restore positive ingroup distinctiveness. Together, this reasoning suggests that reactions to outgroup offenders can be expected to be harsher than those to ingroup offenders.

Finally, rather than assuming strategic, motivational forces driving relatively more positive reactions to ingroup as compared to outgroup perpetrators, such bias could also just be the result of positive affect that is, by default, and automatically, associated with the ingroup. Otten and collaborators (Otten & Moskowitz, 2000; Otten & Wentura, 1999) have shown that such an automatic positive affect is even linked to ingroups that were formed on an arbitrary basis in the laboratory. Therefore, it is likely that such automatic ingroup bias will also exert an influence on social conflicts: Identifying a person, who caused harm either to the individual or to a third person, as an ingroup member should activate positive affect and, thereby, temper negative reactions; for reactions toward an outgroup protagonist, whose group is associated with neutral or even negative affect, however, there is no such buffer. Empirical evidence in line with this account was recently provided by Jacoby, Otten, and Sassenberg (2008), and is reported in more detail later in this chapter.

There are, however, at least two arguments suggesting that ingroup favoritism is not the only possible outcome when comparing reactions to ingroup versus outgroup offenders: First of all, research on the *positive–negative asymmetry in social discrimination* (e.g., Mummendey & Otten, 1998) implies that people are less prone to show ingroup bias on negative comparison dimensions (such as negative evaluations or the distribution of punishments) than on positive comparison dimensions (positive evaluations, distribution of benefits). Given that reactions in aggressive interaction typically imply judgments on negative dimensions, be it the degree of perceived inappropriateness, the degree of anger or sadness about the event, or the harshness of punishment that is considered an appropriate reaction to negative dimensions, we might infer that ingroup bias should be weak or even absent.

However, there is much more powerful and direct evidence questioning that a comparison between reactions to either an ingroup or an outgroup perpetrator should reveal ingroup bias. Research on the so-called *black sheep effect* suggests that a striving for positive ingroup distinctiveness as mentioned in the previous paragraph may not only enhance ingroup bias, but could also instigate the opposite judgmental bias, namely comparatively more harsh reactions to ingroup rather than outgroup members showing negatively deviant behavior (Marques & Paez, 1994; Marques & Yzerbyt, 1988; Marques, Yzerbyt, & Leyens, 1988). Meanwhile there is ample empirical evidence revealing that when an ingroup member offends norms that are highly relevant to the ingroup and its reputation, reactions tend to be more negative than when the same offence was done by an outgroup member. Such judgmental bias is assumed to buffer the possible damage to the ingroup's positive identity by creating a distance between the deviant and the group as a whole, and by reinstating the group's commitment to the norm that was offended (Abrams, Marques, Brown, & Henson, 2000; Marques, Abrams, & Serôdio, 2001).

Obviously, there are two radically opposing possibilities regarding the way reactions to ingroup and outgroup perpetrators could differ, namely ingroup bias (favoring the ingroup perpetrator), on the one hand, and the black sheep effect (a bias that implies a disadvantage for the ingroup perpetrator), on the other. And obviously, there is empirical evidence supporting both predictions. How can this be? Before solving this puzzle by introducing ambiguity of hostile intent as a relevant moderator variable, I first summarize some research revealing ingroup bias in aggressive interactions.

Empirical evidence for ingroup favoritism in aggressive interactions

One of the first demonstrations revealing differential reactions to ingroup and outgroup members showing problematic behavior was provided by Duncan (1976). In his experiment, White student participants watching a videotape depicting negative behavior (an ambiguous shove) showed biased reactions in the way they explained the harm-doer's behavior: When the perpetrator was Black, participants gave mostly personal attributions for the behavior (i.e., he is aggressive), thereby underlining his responsibility, whereas in the conditions with a White perpetrator, situational attributions attenuating responsibility and hostile intent were more probable.

In a similar vein, Sagar and Schofield (1980) provided evidence for White school children's ingroup bias when being confronted with ambiguously hostile behavior by either an ingroup (White) or an outgroup member (African-American). Finally, there is evidence for ingroup favoritism in *reactions to provocations*: Rogers and Prentice-Dunn (1981) report that White participants reacted more negatively to a provocation by a Black perpetrator as opposed to a White perpetrator. Common to these experiments is, however, that they cannot be straightforwardly interpreted as demonstrations of ingroup favoritism, but also in terms of mere stereotyping effects (i.e., just determined by characteristics commonly associated with the groups in questions, and not by more general us–them distinctions). Hence, the question arises as to whether the biased reactions of the European-American participants would also have arisen if the outgroup perpetrator had, for example, been Asian-American rather than African-American.

To a much lesser extent this interpretational ambiguity – stereotyping or mere categorization effect – applies to research that we conducted during the European Soccer Championships in 2004 (Otten & Jacoby, 2004): We first verified in a pilot study with Dutch students that there were no systematic differences in the extent to which soccer supporters from the two nations that we referred to in our study, Germany and The Netherlands, were seen as stereotypically aggressive. Thus, effects we found in our main study with respect to the social categorization of the perpetrator (German vs. Dutch) could not be plausibly interpreted as revealing differences in the degree to which the respective categories were stereotyped as aggressive, but signaled ingroup–outgroup differences per se. Moreover, the study is interesting as it also reveals that for observers' reactions to aggressive events, not only the perpetrator's group membership, but also the *victim's group membership* can matter. In an online survey with Dutch soccer fans, we manipulated both the categorization of the perpetrator and that of the victim (Dutch vs. German, respectively). We asked participants to imagine a conflict between two soccer fans: in a crowded restaurant, the one badly stumbles over the other's foot while carrying a tray full of food; whether the foot was in the way accidentally or intentionally was unclear. When the victim was an ingroup member, there were clearly more favorable judgments (i.e., less perceived hostility; less perceived intentionality) for an ingroup member rather than an outgroup member causing the trouble. If, however, the victim was introduced as an outgroup member, the harsh reactions towards an outgroup perpetrator vanished and were even less negative than those towards the ingroup perpetrator.

Otten and Stapel (2007) provided *implicit evidence for a positive bias towards aggressively acting ingroup members*, or, to put it differently, we showed that categorizing a person as an ingroup member can function as a buffer against associations with aggressiveness. In this research, we used a well-established design from research on priming effects on person perception, namely the famous "Donald paradigm", by Srull and Wyer (1979). First, participants were unconsciously primed with the concept aggression: They were asked to unscramble sentences, some of which related to aggressive behavior. Then, allegedly as an unrelated task, they rated a target person's trait aggressiveness based on an ambiguous person description. We manipulated social categorization by introducing the target person either as an ingroup member (i.e., a Dutch person born in The Netherlands) or as an outgroup member (i.e., either with a Moroccan or with a Surinamese cultural background). Our results strongly revealed that subconscious aggression priming had a negative effect on outgroup targets but not on ingroup targets in the person perception task. Thus, the findings indicate that ingroup membership of a person who shows potentially problematic behavior can serve as a buffer against associations with aggressiveness.

Importantly, in these studies by Otten and Stapel (2007) not only a target person from an outgroup that – in The Netherlands – is typically stereotyped as aggressive (i.e., the Moroccans), but also a target from the typically non-aggressive outgroup (Surinamese) was vulnerable to aggression priming effects. This finding indicates that not only negative stereotypes, but also social categorization per se (us versus them) can lead to biases in the perception of (potentially) aggressive behavior. Thereby the results add to early studies (e.g., Duncan, 1976; Rogers & Prentice-Dunn, 1981), whose results can be explained as merely a result of (negative) stereotyping rather than as a social categorization effect. Yet, even though negative outgroup stereotypes are not a necessary condition for finding ingroup bias in reactions to negative behavior, they nonetheless enhance people's willingness to perceive an outgroup person as aggressive and his or her conduct as inappropriate. This finding is further supported by a field study conducted in several Dutch neighborhoods with a considerable percentage of inhabitants with Moroccan or Turkish background (Ufkes, Otten, Giebels, & van der Zee, 2008). The degree to which indigenous Dutch inhabitants were negatively prejudiced towards the respective group predicted how inappropriate and annoying they perceived deviant behavior of an outgroup neighbor (positive correlation) and the tendency to seek versus avoid a confrontation (positive and negative correlation, respectively).

Finally, a study by Jacoby et al. (2008) revealed some initial evidence for the mechanism that may (at least in part) account for ingroup bias in reaction to negative conduct. In this study, which dealt with evaluative and punishment reactions to negatively deviant behavior (cheating in an exam), they did find ingroup bias. However, when statistically controlling for the degree to which the ingroup and the outgroup, respectively, were evaluated positively in general, the evaluative advantage towards an ingroup deviant as opposed to an outgroup deviant vanished. Hence, the evaluative advantage that the ingroup perpetrator's behavior has, as compared with an outgroup perpetrator's behavior, can be traced back to the more general evaluative bias towards ingroup members. Interestingly, the second study by Otten and Stapel (2007) – though indirectly – also supports this interpretation. In that study, we inhibited the typical positive evaluative default for the ingroup by priming not only the concept of aggression, but also an association of this negative concept with either the ingroup (the indigenous Dutch) or an outgroup (the Moroccans). Not surprisingly, in the condition priming associations of aggression with Moroccans, a Moroccan target was perceived much more aggressively in the subsequent person perception task than a Dutch target. The opposite pattern, however, emerged when "Dutch + aggression" were primed in combination, thereby rendering the typically positive automatic associations with the ingroup ineffective (Otten & Moskowitz, 2000): In this case, a Dutch target was rated as even more aggressive than a Moroccan target.

Ingroup favoritism versus black sheep effect:
The role of ambiguity

As stated earlier in the text, there are both theoretical as well as empirical arguments in support of two opposing effects of social categorization (i.e., the distinction between ingroup and outgroup) on reactions to harmful behavior, namely ingroup bias or the black sheep effect. Interestingly, in most of the studies revealing ingroup bias in reactions to negative behavior, the perpetrator's intention to do harm is ambiguous (e.g., Duncan, 1976; Otten & Jacoby, 2004; Otten & Stapel, 2007; Sagar & Schofield, 1980). This is a relevant observation, given that the perception of behavior as aggressive is, as outlined earlier in this chapter, based on the perception that the perpetrator had the intention to do harm. Therefore, in the following, I summarize research investigating how the (non-)ambiguousness of hostile intent moderates reactions to ingroup and outgroup perpetrators.

A plausible interpretation for ingroup bias in response to ambiguous hostile conduct is that ambiguity about the ingroup actor's (but not the outgroup actor's) negative intentions can be resolved by interpreting his/her behavior in line with the general positive attitude towards the ingroup and its members ("Oh, it was one of us. Then, (s)he certainly did not mean to harm me"). Hence, with ambiguous hostile intent the information about the perpetrator's affiliation with the ingroup can be used as a cue to interpret the behavior, thereby making it less probable that the behavior will be seen as bad and aggressive. Thus, the ingroup perpetrator's behavior implies little damage to the ingroup's reputation and its positive regard. What, however, if there is no doubt that the ingroup perpetrator intended to do harm to an ingroup member? In that case, an important condition for the black sheep effect (e.g., Abrams et al., 2000; Marques et al., 2001) is met: A relevant norm is offended, as deliberately turning against and harming a fellow ingroup member clearly and considerably violates the (positive) expectations directed at ingroup members. Therefore, denying the negative quality of the offence is not feasible; rather, clearly rejecting the ingroup perpetrator's conduct becomes the best option to protect the ingroup's integrity and reputation. Bringing both arguments together, we expected that in ambiguous situations in which the ingroup actor's intention to do harm was doubtful, reactions should reveal a positive bias towards the ingroup. If the hostile intention of the perpetrator was obvious, however, an ingroup perpetrator should receive especially harsh reactions. Thus, we hypothesized that the ambiguity of hostile intent would moderate whether ingroup favoritism or the black sheep effect would emerge in aggressive interactions.

In research conducted in both Germany and The Netherlands, my collaborators and I could provide ample evidence in line with these hypotheses. For example, in one study we confronted Dutch school students (grades 9–10) from a larger school center with shared facilities for several schools with a scenario describing negatively deviant behavior (a painful shove) enacted by either somebody from their own school, or by somebody from the other school (Knuijver, Kornfeld, Ravensbergen, Timmer, & Witteman, 2006). When reading and evaluating the scenario, participants were instructed to take the victim's perspective. With respect to the intention to do harm, the shove was either ambiguous or unambiguous. Results revealed an interaction of the two manipulated variables on perceived inappropriateness and on the degree to which the participants felt annoyed: When the intention to do harm was ambiguous, there was ingroup bias, but when the intention to do harm was beyond doubt, the outgroup perpetrator got relatively more favorable judgments than ingroup perpetrators.

Other experiments based on the same design supported the interactive effect of the ambiguity of hostile intention and social categorization, not only for evaluative reactions (inappropriateness, annoyance) to a negative event, but also for behavioral reactions in a computer-simulated interaction: Using an adaptation of the "hot sauce paradigm" (Lieberman, Solomon, Greenberg, & McGregor, 1999), Braun and collaborators (Braun, Otten, & Gordijn, 2008a; see also Ekker, Otten, & Gordijn, 2007) showed the hypothesized moderating impact of the ambiguity of hostile intent also for a measure of retaliatory aggression. Allegedly as part of an unrelated experiment on gender differences in taste experience, participants who were previously confronted with non-cooperative behavior from an ingroup or an outgroup interaction partner, were asked to choose for this person from a sample of drinks that were sorted from "tasty" to "very disgusting" (allegedly, this classification was based on prior pilot work). Also for this measure we found strong effects of the ambiguity variable, such that it was only when hostile intention in the provocation episode was unambiguous that the most disgusting drink was chosen for the ingroup member, whereas there was clear evidence for ingroup favoritism in the condition with ambiguous hostile intention. Besides providing converging evidence for the moderating role of ambiguity of hostile intent, altogether this set of studies also adds to the earlier research on ingroup favoritism in aggressive interactions: The findings from studies using various types of social categories provide further evidence that such biases do not necessitate the existence of negative outgroup stereotypes.

Though the research did not focus on aggressive interactions, the relevant role of interpretational ambiguity for reactions to negatively deviant behavior by either ingroup or outgroup members was also corroborated by research by van Prooijen (2006). He asked his participants to take the role of a judge and to evaluate and determine the punishment for ingroup or outgroup suspects whose guilt (e.g., with respect to a charge for theft) was more or less probable. When guilt probability was low, there was evidence for ingroup favoritism, but when guilt probability was high, the black sheep effect emerged: Judgments and punishments were more harsh for the ingroup suspect. Importantly, different from the studies summarized in the previous paragraph, in van Prooijen's (2006) studies participants did not have the role of a victim who experienced (or at least observed) harm-doing to him- or herself, but that of a third party (the judge). Moreover, while "guilt probability" referred to the ambiguity of whether the person accused of negative conduct was in fact the perpetrator (who caused the harm?), in the research reported earlier (Braun et al., 2008a; Knuijver et al., 2006; Otten & Jacoby, 2004), the ambiguity referred to the intentionality and, relatedly, the norm-deviance of the behavior (was it meant to do harm?), while the person causing the victim's harm is clearly identified. Given the consistency of findings in both paradigms, together these lines of research clearly support the relevant role of ambiguity – whether it is about the source or the intention – of harmful behavior as moderating variable determining the occurrence of either ingroup bias or the black sheep effect in social conflicts.

The finding that in the unambiguous conditions, ingroup favoritism vanishes and even reverses, fits with findings from intergroup research showing that ingroup bias is not unconditional but sensitive to reality constraints (e.g., Ellemers, van Rijswijk, Roelfs, & Simons, 1997): If there is information that clearly challenges the positive associations with the ingroup and its members, this information is taken into account and can even result in contrast effects (e.g., pronouncedly negative reactions). Such reasoning suggests that the black sheep effect in the unambiguous conditions is the result of conscious, elaborate information processing. This assumption was supported in recent research by Braun, Otten, and Gordijn (2008b); two studies revealed that the strongly negative reactions to ingroup deviants rely on sufficient cognitive capacity. In this research we manipulated cognitive load. In the load conditions, while reading and evaluating the scenario, participants either had to remember an 8-digit number, or a complicated audio-taped text, which they allegedly should remember later on in the experiment. In both studies, cognitive load affected reactions to the unambiguously hostile episode. It was only without cognitive load that participants responded with the enhanced levels of anger, and with the more negative appraisals to ingroup perpetrators, that we found in earlier research. With load, however, the effect of ambiguity on reactions to an ingroup actor vanished. These findings suggest that turning against the negatively deviant ingroup actor, and overriding the typical positive bias toward the ingroup and their members, is a cognitively effortful process that does not function automatically.

Aggressive interactions in intergroup contexts: The role of group-based emotions

In the previous sections we have been mostly dealing with the more general question of whether there is evidence for significant differences in reactions to negative and harmful behavior enacted by either ingroup or outgroup members. In the remainder of this chapter, we go beyond the mere demonstration of such significant ingroup–outgroup differences, and introduce research suggesting that emotions linked to the respective groups have a relevant function for the effects of social categorization in aggressive interactions.

Intergroup emotions theory

According to appraisal theories of emotions (Frijda, 1986), certain appraisals of a situation (e.g., perception of control or certainty or threat) elicit certain emotions, and, subsequently, corresponding behavioral tendencies. For example, interpreting a situation as threatening should elicit fear and lead to flight and avoidance reactions. In intergroup emotion theory (Smith, 1993; Mackie, Devos, & Smith, 2000; Mackie & Smith, 2002), this reasoning is combined with ideas from theories on intergroup behavior, and applied to group contexts. Once an individual self-categorizes in terms of a certain group membership, he or she can experience emotions on behalf of that group. International soccer championships give very illustrative examples of group-based emotions: People in front of their TV sets can experience enormous joy if their own country's national team has scored a goal and has won a match, but they will also feel anger, frustration, or sadness, in the case where the national team has lost. Importantly, such group-based emotions do not even necessitate the presence of other group members; the decisive factor is the identification with the group membership at stake.

The emotional experiences linked to group membership vary according to the situation, but also according to characteristics of the intergroup relation. For example, Mackie and collaborators (2000) showed that the perceived strength of the individual's own group in relation to the other group mattered for both emotional experiences and subsequent action tendencies: In their studies, people were categorized based on their opinion about a controversial issue (homosexual marriage), and then confronted with arguments from the group of people with the opposing point of view. Participants who were led to believe that the group of people sharing their opinion would only be a minority, reacted with less anger to the outgroup's argument, and they were less eager to confront the outgroup members than participants who thought that a majority of people would share their opinion on the controversial issue. More generally, this research implies that the status of one's group as either majority or minority and the power associated with this status will translate into different emotions – anger versus fear – and different behavioral tendencies: approach or avoidance.

Social categorization and emotional experience in social conflicts

A study by Gordijn, Wigboldus, and Yzerbyt (2001) impressively demonstrated how category salience affects emotional reactions in intergroup conflict. In this research, Gordijn and her collaborators took advantage of the cross-categorization principle. They investigated emotional reactions to the very same event, a journal article stating that professors at the Dutch Leiden University were planning to make the selection criteria, exams, and study load tougher for their students, but varied the extent to which participants felt part of the victim group or not. Either the study was introduced as wanting to compare the reactions of "students at Leiden University" (which was not the participants' home university) with those of "students from other universities in The Netherlands", or it was said that the study would investigate how "students" would react to such plans. As predicted on the basis of intergroup emotions theory, in the latter, inclusive condition, anger was significantly higher, indicating that because of cross-categorization, participants felt negatively affected by the Leiden professors' behavior. More recently, the same principle was demonstrated by Dumont, Yzerbyt, and Wigboldus (2003), who investigated Dutch and Belgian people's emotional and behavioral reactions to the horrible events of 9/11. When the terrorist attacks were framed as directed against the United States, participants reacted to pictures of the burning Twin Towers with significantly less fear than when the events were framed as revealing the conflict between western societies on the one hand, and Muslim societies on the other. Hence, both studies consistently reveal that when included in the broader "we" defining the target group, at which certain harm has been or might be directed, emotional reactions and action tendencies intensify (see also Gordijn, Yzerbyt, Wigboldus, & Dumont, 2005, for further evidence in line with these findings).

Studies conducted in the cross-categorization paradigm (e.g., Dumont et al., 2003; Gordijn et al., 2001) manipulate whether either the ingroup or a psychologically less relevant group, which does not include the self, is seen as negatively affected by an outgroup's actions or action plans. As summarized above, this research shows that both anger and fear can increase when harm is seen as directed against an ingroup. In a similar way, Gordijn and collaborators used the cross-categorization principle in order to confront people with the same conflict, but having them either share a social category with the perpetrator group or with the victim group (Gordijn et al., 2005). The results of this research reveal effects of the categorization procedure that fully resemble perpetrator–victim differences as known from the aggression literature (e.g., Mummendey et al., 1984; Mummendey & Otten, 1989): When social categorization made people feel part of the perpetrator group they experienced less anger and were less interested in taking action than those who felt part of the victim's group.

In a different line of research, we (e.g., Braun et al, 2008a; Kamans, Otten, & Gordijn, 2007; Vogelzang & Otten, 2006) further focused on the effect of social categorization on emotional reactions to perpetrators; we made salient the same social categorization of the participants (e.g., as soccer supporters) in all conditions, and looked at group-based emotions and their link to action tendencies when the *source* of the harm was portrayed as either an ingroup member or an outgroup member (e.g., supporter of their own versus an opposing soccer team). Thus, these studies extend the earlier reflection on conditions for ingroup versus outgroup bias in aggressive interactions to the analysis of group-based emotions in social conflicts. This line of research includes studies in which participants were reacting from the role of an observer not directly involved in the conflict (e.g. Vogelzang & Otten, 2006), studies in which participants were asked to take the perspective of the victim and to imagine as vividly as possible that they themselves would be involved in the described conflict (e.g. Braun et al., 2008a, 2008b; Kamans et al., 2007), and, finally, a study in which the participants did in fact experience harm themselves (Braun et al., 2008a). In all these studies the question was whether the type of emotions experienced in response to a negative action, and its mediating effect on subsequent action tendencies, would differ as a function of social categorization.

Us versus them, and shame versus anger: Matching emotions and categorization

In a first step, we investigated whether harmful behavior enacted by either an ingroup or an outgroup member elicited different emotions in an observer, who was not directly hurt, but to whom the relevant social categorization was psychologically meaningful. In a questionnaire study conducted with first-year psychology students (Vogelzang & Otten, 2006), we tested this idea. Participants were confronted with a faked newspaper article describing that either a psychology student (ingroup) or an economics student (outgroup), who had been drinking on a popular terrace in the city, was arrested by the police after he had brutally hit and injured a woman who had passed by the pub and had commented on young people's drinking. After reading the scenario, participants reported the degree to which they felt various emotions (such as anger, disappointment, sadness, shame, and unease). From this list, only anger and shame were affected by the categorization of the perpetrator as either ingroup or outgroup: An ingroup member's misconduct elicited significantly more shame than an outgroup member's misconduct, whereas anger was stronger in reaction to an outgroup actor rather than to an ingroup actor. Note that feelings of guilt were not included in the list of emotions; therefore, our findings unfortunately cannot speak directly to the shame versus guilt distinction, as carefully elaborated on in the chapter by Rupert Brown included in this volume (see chapter 10). Yet, we assume that given the typically high levels of identification of students with their study major, negative deviance of an ingroup member should reflect negatively on the self-concept, thereby making the emotional reaction of shame especially probable.

Based on the results of their first study, Vogelzang and Otten (2006) in a second study primed the two critical emotions, shame and anger, via an auto-biographical memory task (see e.g., Bodenhausen, Sheppard, & Kramer, 1994). Besides the emotion priming, we again varied the perpetrator's group membership. Herewith we wanted to show more straightforwardly that reactions to ingroup and outgroup harm-doers are differentially affected by self-related emotions such as shame, and by other-related emotions such as anger. The data clearly corroborated the idea that shame is a more relevant emotion in shaping reactions to an ingroup member's rather than an outgroup member's misconduct, whereas the opposite pattern applies to anger. In the shame priming condition, the ingroup member elicited more negative reactions than the outgroup member: He was seen as having caused more damage to his group's reputation, and there was a stronger wish that he should be punished. In the anger-priming condition, however, the data pattern reversed, and revealed significant ingroup bias in punishment reactions. Thus, somewhat parallel to the findings for ambiguity of a hostile event, the situationally most relevant emotion (anger and shame, respectively) can determine whether we will find ingroup favoritism or a black sheep effect in observers' responses to other group members' negatively deviant behavior.

Group-based emotions as mediating variable in social conflicts

The results by Vogelzang and Otten (2006) reveal that manipulating emotions has an effect on how social categorization impacts on reactions to negative, harmful behavior. In further studies we measured rather than manipulated emotions, thereby focusing directly on the mediating role of group-based emotions as suggested by intergroup emotions theory (Smith, 1993). Moreover, we manipulated the ambiguity of hostile intent or, as is discussed in the following paragraph, characteristics of the intergroup relation (relative power).

As summarized above, manipulating the ambiguity of the perpetrator's hostile intention had an especially polarizing effect on ingroup actors, resulting in relative ingroup bias in the condition when hostile intent was ambiguous, and in the black sheep effect in the condition when hostile intent was unambiguous. Importantly, in the previously mentioned study by Braun and collaborators (Braun et al., 2008a), the strength of anger turned out to mediate the effect of ambiguity versus non-ambiguity of hostile intention on punishment reactions towards *ingroup perpetrators*: Compared with the ambiguous condition, non-ambiguous hostile intent of an ingroup perpetrator elicited more anger, which, in turn, predicted more negative behavioral reactions For *outgroup actors*, however, the ambiguity manipulation did not affect the strength of anger reactions. Note that this analysis focused on anger as the mediating variable for the effects of ambiguity on reactions to harmful behavior by ingroup and outgroup offenders. It did not address the differential impact of anger on reactions to ingroup versus outgroup perpetrators, respectively, as shown in the research by Vogelzang and Otten (2006): Even though anger was hypothesized and shown to be a stronger *moderator* of responses to outgroup rather than to ingroup deviants, variations in the degree of anger still can have a *mediating* impact on subsequent behavior toward targets of either group. Importantly, the findings by Braun et al. (2008a) reveal that this mediation by anger does significantly contribute to the ambiguity effects on ingroup punishment, thereby suggesting that it is worthwhile to take into account emotions as relevant variables for predicting whether we will find ingroup bias or the black sheep effect in reaction to group members' negatively deviant behavior.

Power as moderator of reactions to negative intergroup behavior

According to intergroup emotions theory, the relative power of one's group will determine whether a certain situation will elicit fear and avoidance behavior, or rather anger and approach behavior (e.g. Mackie et al., 2000). We further tested this assumption in studies wherein the participants either imagined being the victim of harmful behavior, or actually experienced a verbal offence and unfair treatment by an outgroup member (Kamans et al., 2007); relative power was manipulated by placing the participant in either a majority or a minority group. In line with previous findings, we found that participants categorized as member of a powerless group experienced more fear than those who were part of a more powerful group. However, different from previous research (e.g. Mackie et al., 2000), we found that members of powerless groups also experienced more anger (!) than the powerful. Depending on the *kind of threat* characterizing the conflict (Cottrell & Neuberg, 2005), emotions translated into action. Fear led to more avoidance behavior by powerless group members in the case of a physical conflict (threat of being physically harmed), whereas their anger translated – at least for high identifiers – into negative approach behavior when valuable resources were at stake, and the outgroup formed an obstacle to keeping or getting access to these resources.

Together, these findings corroborate the results reported by Mackie and collaborators (2000) by revealing that relative group power can moderate the link between appraisals, emotions, and action tendencies in social conflicts. However, they also differ from and add to this earlier research in several important ways by revealing that the kind of threat involved moderates low power groups' emotional and behavioral reactions in social conflicts, and by showing that anger and fear are emotions that can not only operate in opposition to each other, but also in conjunction. If low power groups experience a conflict such that the other group blocks their striving to implement certain values (e.g., homosexuals' right to marry, such as in the research by Mackie et al., 2000), they might overcome their fear and might well be willing to act in line with their anger and confront the opponent group. If, however, the powerful outgroup poses a physical threat, then fear as the more functional emotion and not anger will determine the subsequent action tendencies.

Summary and conclusions

Altogether, there is a lot of evidence both on a theoretical and on an empirical level suggesting that it is worthwhile to consider social categorization as a relevant variable in social conflicts. Moreover, it seems necessary to take emotional reactions into account, as they can both moderate and mediate differences in evaluative and behavioral reactions to negative, harmful conduct enacted by or directed at either ingroup or outgroup members. Importantly, the findings reported in this chapter reveal that the influence of social categorization is not a simple one, such as ingroup membership *always* leading to biased reactions in social conflicts. Rather, we were alerted to several relevant moderating variables such as the ambiguity of the event initiating the conflict, the power relation between the relevant groups involved, the type of emotion experienced in reaction to the initiating event, and the type of threat implied by this event. Also, as typical for basically all effects of social categorization, the strength of identification with the relevant ingroup is a relevant moderator in many instances.

Ingroup bias is a response to social situations that can be generated outside awareness, but this automatic response, which was in fact found in the research by Otten and Stapel (2007) reported in this chapter, can clearly be overridden by other reactions. I assume that this is especially the case when the positive valence automatically associated with one's own group (Otten & Moskowitz, 2000; Otten & Wentura, 1999) is exceeded by the negative valence associated with the critical behavior. This should especially be the case if the self is in the role of a victim, if highly relevant norms were broken (such as harming somebody deliberately) and/or if ingroup identification is low. Once negative valence dominates, automatic processing becomes less probable, and responses will probably become more strategic. So far, there are only some very preliminary findings in line with this reasoning (Braun et al., 2008b), but it will be certainly worthwhile to further investigate the link between category-based responses in social conflict and information processing modes.

Obviously, by investigating the role of social categorization in social conflicts, we can enrich theory and research for both domains: the study of intergroup relations and the study of social conflicts/aggressive interactions (Otten & Mummendey, 2002b). But the research presented in this chapter certainly also has applied relevance: Understanding how social categorization can both fuel and temper emotional and behavioral reactions in social conflicts can be used in anti-aggression training. For example, just as perspective-taking is used to alert actors of negative behavior to the bad consequences of their conduct, cross-categorization techniques might be used to instigate reinterpretation processes of problematic situations. Finally, in the domain of conflict mediation by third parties (e.g., Giebels & Janssen, 2005), it seems especially worthwhile to consider the effects of social categorization. Particularly in intergroup conflicts, the mediator's group affiliation should strongly and differentially determine the trust experienced by the parties involved, and the emotional and behavioral reactions to mediation attempts.

References

Abrams, D., Marques, J. M., Brown, N., & Henson, M. (2000). Pro-norm and anti-norm deviance within and between groups. *Journal of Personality and Social Psychology, 78*, 906–912.

Baron, R. A. (Ed.). (1977). *Human aggression.* New York: Plenum Press.

Bodenhausen, G. V., Sheppard, L. A., Kramer, G. P. (1994). Negative affect and social judgment: The differential impact of anger and sadness. *European Journal of Social Psychology, 24*, 45–62.

Braun, B. M., Otten, S., & Gordijn, E. H. (2008a). *Ingroup favoritism or black-sheep effect? The role of group affiliations and ambiguity of negative intentions in aggressive interactions.* Unpublished manuscript, University of Groningen, The Netherlands.

Braun, B. M., Otten, S., & Gordijn, E. H. (2008b). *Ingroup versus outgroup bias in aggressive interaction: The interactive role of cognitive load and ambiguity of negative intentions.* Unpublished manuscript, University of Groningen, The Netherlands.

Brewer, M. B. (2003). *Intergroup relations* (2nd ed.). Buckingham, UK: Open University Press.

Brewer, M. B., & Brown, R. J. (1998). Intergroup relations. In D. T. Gilbert, S. T. Fiske, & G. Lindzey (Eds.), *The handbook of social psychology* (4th ed.) (pp. 554–594) New York: McGraw-Hill.

Brown, R. (2000). Social identity theory: Past achievements, current problems and future challenges. *European Journal of Social Psychology, 30*, 745–778.

Cottrell, C., & Neuberg, S. (2005). Different emotional reactions to different groups: A sociofunctional threat-based approach to "prejudice". *Journal of Personality and Social Psychology, 88*, 770–789.

Dumont, M., Yzerbyt, V., & Wigboldus, D. (2003). Social categorization and fear reactions to the September 11th terrorist attacks. *Personality and Social Psychology Bulletin, 29*, 1509–1520.

Duncan, B. L. (1976). Differential social perception and attribution of intergroup violence: Testing the lower limits of stereotyping of Blacks. *Journal of Personality and Social Psychology, 34*, 590–598.

Ekker, B. M., Otten, S., & Gordijn, E. H. (2007). Was het een van ons? Groepslidmaatschap en ambiguïteit als determinanten van reacties op schadelijk gedrag [Was it one of us? Group membership and ambiguity as determinants of reactions to harmful behavior]. In C. Van Laar, R. Ruiter, J. Karremans, W. Van Rijswijk, & F. Van Harreveld (Eds.), *Jaarboek Sociale Psychologie 2006* (pp 135–144). Groningen: ASPO pers.

Ellemers, N. van Rijswijk, W. Roelfs, M., & Simons, C. (1997). Bias in intergroup perceptions: Balancing group identity with social reality. *Personality and Social Psychology Bulletin, 23*, 186–198.

Frijda, N. H. (1986). *The emotions.* Cambridge: Cambridge University Press.

Giebels, E., & Janssen, O. (2005). Conflict stress and reduced well-being at work: The buffering effect of third-party help. *European Journal of Work and Organizational Psychology, 14*, 137–155.

Gordijn, E. H., Wigboldus, D., & Yzerbyt, V. (2001). Emotional consequences of categorizing victims of negative outgroup behavior as ingroup or outgroup. *Group Processes and Intergroup Relations, 4*, 317–326.

Gordijn, E. H., Yzerbyt, V., Wigboldus, D., & Dumont, M. (2005). Emotional reactions to harmful intergroup behavior. *European Journal of Social Psychology, 36*, 15–30.

Hewstone, M., Rubin, M., & Willis, H. (2002). Intergroup bias. *Annual Review of Psychology, 53* 575–604.

Jacoby, J., Otten, S., & Sassenberg, K. (2008). *Not so black sheep: When positive ingroup valence eliminates the black sheep effect.* Unpublished manuscript. Knowledge Media Research Center, Tübingen, Germany.

Kamans, E., Otten, S., & Gordijn, E. (2007). Machteloos maar boos! De invloed van dreiging op emoties en gedragsneigingen van machteloze groepen [Powerless but angry! The effect of threat on emotions and action tendencies in low power groups]. In C. Van Laar, R. Ruiter, J. Karremans, W. Van Rijswijk, & F. Van Harreveld (Eds.), *Jaarboek sociale psychologie 2006* (pp. 215–224). Groningen: ASPO pers.

Knuijver, S., Kornfeld, A., Ravensbergen, L., Timmer, C., & Witteman, J. (2006). *Aggression and social identities.* Unpublished bachelor thesis, University of Groningen, The Netherlands.

Lieberman, J. S., Solomon, S., Greenberg, J., & McGregor, H. A. (1999). A hot new way to measure aggression: Hot sauce allocation. *Aggressive Behavior, 25*, 331–348.

Lindsay, J. A., & Anderson, C. A. (2000). From antecedent conditions to violent actions: The general affective aggression model. *Personality and Social Psychology Bulletin, 20*, 34–44.

Mackie, D. M., Devos, T., & Smith, E. R. (2000). Intergroup emotions: Explaining offensive action tendencies in an intergroup context. *Journal of Personality and Social Psychology, 79*, 602–616.

Mackie, D. M., & Smith, E. R. (2002). Intergroup emotions and the social self. Prejudice reconceptualized as differential reactions to outgroups. In J. P. Forgas & K. D. Williams (Eds.), *The social self. Cognitive, interpersonal and intergroup perspectives* (pp. 309–326). New York: Psychology Press.

Marques, J., Abrams, D., & Serôdio, R. G. (2001). Being better by being right: Subjective group dynamics and derogation of ingroup deviants when generic norms are undermined. *Journal of Personality and Social Psychology, 81*, 436–447.

Marques, J. M., & Paez, D. (1994). The black sheep effect: Social categorization, rejection of ingroup deviates, and perception of group variability. In W. Stroebe & M. Hewstone (Eds.), *European Review of Social Psychology*, (Vol. 5, pp. 37–68). Chichester, UK: Wiley.

Marques, J. M., & Yzerbyt, V. Y. (1988). The black sheep effect: Judgmental extremity towards ingroup members in inter- and intragroup situations. *European Journal of Social Psychology, 18*, 287–292.

Marques, J. M., Yzerbyt, V. Y., & Leyens, J. P. (1988). The "black sheep effect": Extremity of judgments towards ingroup members as a function of group identification. *European Journal of Social Psychology, 18*, 1–16.

Mummendey, A., Linneweber, V., & Löschper, G. (1984). Actor or victim of aggression: Divergent perspectives – divergent evaluations. *European Journal of Social Psychology, 14*, 297–311.

Mummendey, A., & Otten, S. (1989). Perspective-specific differences in the evaluation of aggressive interaction sequences. *European Journal of Social Psychology, 19*, 23–40.

Mummendey, A., & Otten, S. (1993). Aggression: Interactions between individuals and social groups. In R. B. Felson & J. T. Tedeschi (Eds.), *Aggression and violence* (pp. 145–167). Washington, DC: American Psychological Association.

Mummendey, A., & Otten, S. (1998). Positive–negative asymmetry in social discrimination. In W. Stroebe & M. Hewstone (Eds.), *European Review of Social Psychology* (*Vol. 9,* pp. 107–143). New York: Wiley.

Otten, S., & Jacoby, J. (2004). Perceived aggression by Dutch and German soccer supporters during the European championships 2004. Unpublished data, University of Groningen, The Netherlands.

Otten, S., & Moskowitz, G. B. (2000). Evidence for implicit evaluative ingroup bias: Affect-biased spontaneous trait inference in a minimal group paradigm. *Journal of Experimental Social Psychology, 36,* 77–89.

Otten, S., & Mummendey, A. (2002a). Sozialpsychologische Theorien aggressiven Verhaltens [Social-psychological theories of aggressive behaviour]. In D. Frey (Hrsg.), *Theorien der sozialpsychologie* (2, völlig überarbeitete Auflage) [Theories of social psychology (2nd completely revised edition)] (pp. 198–216). Bern: Huber.

Otten, S., & Mummendey, A. (2002b). Social discrimination and aggression: A matter of perspective-specific divergence? In W. Kallmeyer & C. F. Graumann (Eds.), *Perspecitivity and perspectivation in discourse* (pp. 233–250). Wilrijk: John Benjamins Publishers.

Otten, S., Mummendey, A., & Wenzel, M. (1995). Evaluation of aggressive interactions in interpersonal and intergroup contexts. *Aggressive Behavior, 21,* 205–224.

Otten, S., & Stapel, D. A. (2007). Who is this Donald? How social categorization shapes aggression priming effects. *European Journal of Social Psychology, 37,* 1000–1015.

Otten, S., & Wentura, D. (1999). About the impact of automaticity in the minimal group paradigm. Evidence from an affective priming task. *European Journal of Social Psychology, 29,* 1049–1071.

Rogers, R. W., & Prentice-Dunn, S. (1981). Deindividuation and anger-mediated interracial aggression: Unmasking regressive racism. *Journal of Personality and Social Psychology, 41,* 63–73.

Sagar, H. A., & Schofield, J. W. (1980). Racial and behavioral cues in black and white children's perceptions of ambiguously aggressive acts. *Journal of Personality and Social Psychology, 39,* 590–598.

Sherif, M. (1966). *In common predicament: Social psychology of intergroup conflict and cooperation.* Boston: Houghton-Mifflin.

Smith, E. R. (1993). Social identity and social emotions: Toward new conceptualizations of prejudice. In D. M.Mackie & D. L. Hamilton (Eds.), *Affect, cognition, and stereotyping: Interactive processes in group perception* (pp. 297–315). San Diego, CA: Academic Press.

Srull, T. K., & Wyer, R. S. (1979). The role of category accessibility in the interpretation of information about persons: Some determinants and implications. *Journal of Personality and Social Psychology, 37,* 1660–1672.

Tajfel, H. (1982). Social psychology of intergroup relations. *Annual Review of Psychology, 33,* 1–39.

Tajfel, H., & Turner, J.C. (1979). An integrative theory of intergroup conflict. In W. G. Austin, & S. Worchel (Eds.), *The social psychology of intergroup relations* (pp. 33–47). Monterey, CA: Brooks/Cole.

Tedeschi, J. T., & Felson, R. B. (Eds.). (1994). *Aggression and coercive action: A social interactionist perspective.* Washington, DC: American Psychological Association.

Turner, J. C., Hogg, M. A., Oakes, P. J., Reicher, S. D., & Wetherell, M. S. (1987). *Rediscovering the social group: A self-categorization theory.* Oxford: Blackwell.

Ufkes, E. G., Otten, S., Giebels, E., & van der Zee K. I. (2008). *Categorization processes and conflicts in neighborhoods.* Paper presented at the 21st Annual IACM Conference, Chicago, July 3–6, 2008.

van Prooijen, J.W. (2006). Retributive reactions to suspected offenders: The importance of social categorizations and guilt probability. *Personality and Social Psychology Bulletin, 32,* 715–726.

Vogelzang, L., & Otten, S. (2006). *Wij = schaamte, zij = woede. Een onderzoek naar de invloed van categorisatie en emoties op de beoordeling van daders* [We = shame, they = anger. A study on the impact of categorization and emotions on judgments about perpetrators]. Unpublished manuscript, University of Groningen, The Netherlands.

10 From both sides now

Perpetrator and victim responses to intergroup transgressions

Rupert Brown
Sussex University

From its beginning to its end, the history of the twentieth century, like others before it, was stained with instances of genocide and bloody intergroup conflicts. From the slaughter of Armenians in 1915 to the massacres in Rwanda and Bosnia in the 1990s, the capacity for groups to inflict suffering and death on each other on large scales seems tragically not to have diminished. The twenty-first century has started no more auspiciously as events in Afghanistan, Darfur and Iraq reveal. Nevertheless, despite all this appalling bloodshed, one encouraging feature has been the emergence of political debate over the desirability of perpetrator groups accepting responsibility for what they have done, and offering material reparations or other symbols of collective remorse to the victims of their misdeeds (Barkan, 2000; Buruma, 1994; Steele, 1990). Within social psychology this debate has instigated theory and research into the social psychological antecedents and consequences of such emotions as group-based guilt and shame that may be experienced by members of *"perpetrator"* groups (e.g., Branscombe & Doosje, 2004; Leach, Snider, & Iyer, 2002), and parallel, though less extensive, investigations into the emotions and attitudes of *"victim"* groups towards perpetrators (Hewstone, Cairns, Voci, McLernon, Niens, & Noor, 2004; Nadler & Liviatan, 2004; Wohl & Branscombe, 2005). In this chapter I review some of our[1] recent work which has been variously concerned with both sides of this perpetrator–victim relationship.

I begin with conceptual questions: What do we mean by group-based emotions, and especially collective guilt and shame? I also attempt to clarify the meaning of intergroup forgiveness. This conceptual discussion gives way to a brief consideration of measurement issues as I outline our attempts to develop reliable and valid indicators of collective guilt and shame, and intergroup forgiveness. The heart of the chapter then presents summaries of our several studies on the antecedents and consequences of guilt, shame and forgiveness in intergroup contexts as varied as indigenous–non-indigenous relations in Chile and post-conflict relationships in Bosnia Herzegovina and Northern Ireland. The chapter concludes with a discussion of some key issues for future research.

Conceptual issues

Let me begin by noting that the emotional responses with which I am concerned in this chapter are reactions by group members as *group members*, not necessarily to things that they have done or experienced personally but to actions or experiences that they believe others in their group have committed or had. In this sense, they are collective or group-based reactions, and they are possible with one simple precondition: that those group members have at least some level of minimal identification with their ingroup (the social category that is contextually or contemporaneously relevant for them). To make this point might seem to be trivial, redundant even, in this tribute volume to Amélie Mummendey, someone for whom the notion of social identification has been so central to most of her work. Still, it is an assumption that I believe is not universally shared throughout the discipline of social psychology, at least to judge from the content of the majority of articles in our premier journals. The credit for first recognising the possibility of group-based emotions is often attributed to Smith (1993). While that chapter is certainly well cited and has proved highly influential, in fact, of course, the notion that people can feel good or bad, happy or sad, about their group's (mis)fortunes more properly derives from the much earlier Social Identity Theory (Tajfel & Turner, 1979). Indeed, the very essence of the concept of social identity as articulated in that theory is that the ingroup's concerns can become individual group members' concerns, independently of their own personal standing or well-being.

Here I am concerned with two classes of group-based reactions in particular: how members of groups that have perpetrated illegitimate actions against members of another group respond emotionally to the knowledge of those misdeeds; and how members of victim groups respond to those who have perpetrated violence against them.

With regard to the former, two possible emotions (among others) that may be felt are guilt and shame. Although these emotions are often used synonymously in everyday parlance, within social psychology they have quite specific meanings. Following Lewis (1971) and Tangney (1991), several commentators argue that in feeling collective guilt, group members focus primarily on their group's wrongdoings and their consequences for the harmed group: "we did these bad things to that group, who suffered as a result" (Branscombe, Slugoski, & Kappen, 2004; Leach et al., 2002; Lickel, Schmader, & Barquissau, 2004). Shame, on the other hand, is marked more by a focus on the implications of the wrongdoing for the ingroup's sense of itself or its reputation: "we did those bad things to that group and thus we are (seen to be) a bad group" (Branscombe et al., 2004; Lickel et al., 2004). Because of these different emphases, the consequences of feeling guilty or ashamed are also thought to differ. Guilt, with its focus more on the ingroup's actions and their consequences, is normally believed to lead to some form of restitution to the victim group (e.g., apology, reparation);

shame, with its greater ingroup focus, is predicted to lead to avoidance of or even, in some cases, some reactive hostility towards the outgroup (Branscombe et al., 2004; Lickel et al., 2004). As we shall see, there is some empirical support for these hypotheses, even if the story is a little more complicated than they suggest.

From the victim group's side, the emotions are likely to be different. Fear, anger and the feeling of being victimised are all plausible reactions. What we have been interested in are the perceptions and emotions which might be associated with the first tentative steps towards intergroup forgiveness by members of victim groups. This interest is connected to our broader concern with factors that can promote (or hinder) intergroup reconciliation in post-conflict situations. But what is meant by intergroup forgiveness? In the sense in which we have been using it, forgiveness is a prosocial orientation whose aim is the restoration of a relationship with an outgroup who has harmed or violated the ingroup in some way. It involves a constellation of reduced feelings of revenge, anger and mistrust and enhanced intentions to understand and approach the outgroup (Cehajic, Brown, & Castano, 2008; Noor, Brown, & Prentice, 2008b). Just as in the case of perpetrator emotions, this conceptualisation draws on work in interpersonal forgiveness (e.g., Scobie & Scobie, 1998). However, note that, once again, it is not necessary for members of victim groups to have been actually harmed themselves; it is enough that they identify sufficiently with their ingroup to experience other ingroup members' suffering vicariously (Hewstone et al., 2004). Similarly, any forgiveness that they may come to feel may not be directed towards the literal perpetrators of the malfeasances but may often be towards the perpetrator group as a whole. In this sense it is *intergroup* forgiveness.

Measurement issues

The study of collective guilt and shame is a relatively young field, initiated empirically by Doosje, Branscombe, Spears, and Manstead (1998). In that study and those that followed it (e.g., Branscombe et al., 2004; Iyer, Leach, & Crosby, 2003; Pederson, Beven, Walker, & Griffiths, 2004; Swim & Miller, 1999), scales were developed to assess people's feelings of group-based guilt. In contrast, group-based shame has attracted much less attention. Both Harvey and Oswald (2000) and Lickel, Schmader, Curtis, Scarnier, and Ames (2005) devised scales of shame that relied on the endorsement of emotion words like "ashamed" "embarrassed" and "humiliated" (and other synonyms of "shame"). Despite the face validity conferred by such techniques, they suffer from the potential problem that the ordinary language usage of these words often overlaps with "guilt" and its synonyms.

Accordingly, we felt the need to develop measures of collective guilt and shame that were both relevant to the contexts of our research (indigenous–non-indigenous relations in Chile, post-conflict Bosnia Herzegovina), and derived as closely as possible from their theoretical formulations (see previous section). After several iterations in different studies we arrived at the two scales presented in Table 10.1. Notice how the guilt items tend to highlight the misdeeds of the perpetrator group (in this case non-indigenous Chileans) and some of the consequences of these for the victim group, the Mapuche (e.g., loss of their language and customs). The shame items, on the other hand, tend to focus on the reputation of the ingroup (e.g., "bad image in the eyes of the world") or some inherent defect in the ingroup (e.g., "intolerant by nature"). These scales, or variants of them, have good internal reliability (Brown & Cehajic, 2008; Brown, Gonzalez, Zagefka, Manzi, & Cehajic, 2008) and, as we shall see, also have some predictive utility.

The literature on intergroup forgiveness is smaller still. Studies by Wohl and Branscombe (2005) and Hewstone et al. (2004) provided useful pointers for the development of our measure of intergroup forgiveness that we have

Table 10.1 Collective guilt and shame measures (from Brown et al., 2008)

Collective guilt	*Collective shame*
• I feel guilty for the manner in which the Mapuche have been treated in the past by non-indigenous Chileans • When I think how non-indigenous have stolen the Mapuche lands, I feel guilty • I feel very bad when I realise what we the non-indigenous Chileans have contributed to the loss of Mapuche language and customs • Sometimes I feel guilty for the things that non-indigenous Chileans have done to the Mapuche • When I think what non-indigenous Chileans have done to the Mapuche, I feel guilty • Even if I have done nothing bad, I feel guilty for the behaviour of non-indigenous Chileans toward the Mapuche • I feel guilty for the bad living conditions of the Mapuche • To think how we Chileans show intolerance, by refusing to offer job contracts to Mapuche people, makes me feel guilty	• I feel bad because the behaviour of non-indigenous Chileans towards the Mapuche people has created a bad image in the eyes of the world • I feel bad when I see an international report on the treatment received by the Mapuche on the part of non-indigenous Chileans • Sometimes it shames me how others can think of us for the manner in which we have harmed the Mapuche • To think how Chile is seen for its treatment of the Mapuche makes me feel ashamed • I feel humiliated when I think of the negative manner that Chile is seen by the rest of the world for how it has treated the Mapuche • I feel shame when I think how non-indigenous Chileans have behaved towards the Mapuche • I feel ashamed to be a non-indigenous Chilean for the way we have treated the Mapuche • I feel ashamed for the damage done to the Mapuche by non-indigenous Chileans • I feel ashamed for the racist tendency of non-indigenous Chileans • It shames me when I realise that non-indigenous Chileans could be intolerant by nature

Table 10.2 Intergroup forgiveness measure (from Noor et al., 2008a)

- I would like my community not to hold a grudge against the other community for the things they've done to us
- I would encourage my community to let the other community off for the things they've thought of us
- Getting even with the other community for treating us badly is not important to me
- I would like to ask my community to forgive the other community for their acts of violence
- I would urge my community not to hold feelings of resentment towards the other community for their sectarianism
- I would encourage my community not to have ill thoughts about the other community's motives
- I would like my community to seek ways of forgiving the other community so that our lives are not dominated by bitterness

used in contexts as diverse as Bosnia, Chile and Northern Ireland. Again, the scale has undergone small refinements as our research has evolved and the best version to date is presented in Table 10.2. It, too, has good internal reliability (Cehajic et al., 2008; Noor, Brown, Gonzalez, Manzi, & Lewis, 2008a; Noor et al., 2008b).

Antecedents and consequences of collective guilt, shame, and forgiveness

Our principal interest in guilt, shame and forgiveness lies not so much in the emotions per se but in understanding what else they might lead to and in discovering whence they came. I begin by reviewing our recent work on guilt and shame. Then I turn to forgiveness.

Antecedents and consequences of collective guilt and shame

To my knowledge, the first attempt to study the effects of collective guilt empirically was made by Doosje et al. (1998). In one of the studies in that paper findings were reported of the effects of presenting Dutch participants with historical accounts of the Dutch colonial (mis)treatment of Indonesia in the previous century. Despite the fact that these participants could have no direct involvement with these events, they reported measurable amounts of guilt and a desire to compensate Indonesia, and guilt and compensation were positively correlated. Similar associations between guilt and reparation have been reported in other contexts (Iyer et al., 2003; McGarty, Pederson, Leach, Mansell, Waller, & Bliuc, 2005; Swim & Miller, 1999), although more recent findings suggest that these associations may only hold up for generalised reparation attitudes rather than behavioural intentions to make reparation (Iyer, Schmader, & Lickel, 2007; Leach, Iyer, & Pederson, 2006). In regard to the latter, it has been suggested that anger is a better predictor since anger is thought to be a more active energising emotion than guilt (Iyer et al., 2007; Leach et al., 2006).

Little of the above work was concerned with collective shame. Harvey and Oswald (2000) sought to induce guilt and shame experimentally and found that both showed similar relationships with measures of outgroup compensation. Lickel et al. (2005) asked respondents to recall misdeeds committed by friends, family members or fellow ethnic group members and to record the emotions that such misdeeds evoked in them, the respondents. Feelings of guilt were, as usual, correlated with motives to apologise or repair, while shame was linked more to motives to distance oneself from the perpetrator or the situation.

The fact that so few studies had sought to investigate the consequences of both collective guilt and shame in the same study and that, moreover, the majority had also relied on cross-sectional designs led us to conduct two longitudinal studies in which we could examine both the short-term (contemporaneous) and longer term (longitudinal) correlates of guilt and shame (Brown et al., 2008). The studies were set in the context of relations between the non-indigenous majority and the indigenous minority in Chile. The latter group has experienced a long history of oppression and discrimination by the majority and was thus a plausible target group for feelings of collective guilt and shame. We measured these feelings of the majority group with versions of the scales presented in Table 10.1 and correlated them with attitudes towards various reparation policies then under discussion in Chilean society (e.g., economic benefits for the indigenous group, public apologies). The time-lag in Study 1 was 8 weeks; in Study 2 it was 6 months. Across both studies there were two consistent findings: at a cross-sectional level, *both* guilt and shame were positively correlated with reparation; however, in the longitudinal analyses, in which Time 1 values of the dependent measure (reparation) were controlled, *only* collective guilt was predictive of later reparation. Moreover, in Study 2 there was also a moderation of the longitudinal effects of guilt by shame such that a stronger (and significant) link between guilt and reparation was found for low shame participants; for high shame participants the guilt reparation correlation was non-significant (see Figure 10.1).

It seemed to us that these findings were noteworthy for three reasons. First, we confirmed for the first time in a longitudinal study that guilt – but not shame – was predictive of a desire to endorse reparation attitudes. Second, the data revealed that guilt and shame can interact, the latter seeming to "inhibit" the otherwise prosocial consequences of guilt. Finally, and initially rather perplexingly from a theoretical point of view, contemporaneously *both* emotions were positively correlated with reparation. Existing theory did not predict such an association, even if empirically there were already intimations of its existence (Harvey & Oswald, 2000; Schmader & Lickel, 2006).

Accordingly, in a third Chilean study, we sought to uncover what might mediate the shame–reparation link (Brown et al., 2008). We speculated that one clue might lie in the reputational aspect of shame. If that aspect of shame

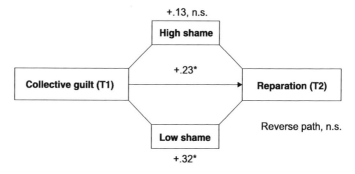

Figure 10.1 Longitudinal effects of collective shame and collective guilt on reparation (from Brown et al., 2008, Study 2).

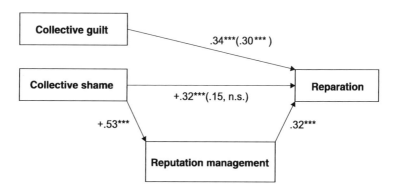

Figure 10.2 Reputation management mediates the relationship between shame and reparation (from Brown et al., 2008, Study 3).

predominated then, we argued, it could be alleviated by a desire to improve the reputation of the ingroup that had been tarnished by its historical wrong-doings. Such reputation management motive could lead to respondents wanting to (be seen to) make some reparation to the outgroup. Therefore, we included a reputation management measure as a potential mediator in a further cross-sectional study. As we had predicted, this measure did mediate the shame–reparation link while it had little discernible effect on the guilt–reparation association (see Figure 10.2). One other noteworthy result from this study was that the correlations between guilt, shame and reparation, and the mediation effect of reputation management, held up even when controlling for anger. This was interesting in view of findings from very different contexts that suggested that the effects of guilt disappeared once anger was controlled (Iyer et al., 2007; Leach et al., 2006). Although there were many differences between these various studies, one key difference might be that, as noted earlier, in the Iyer et al. (2007) and Leach et al. (2006) studies behavioural *intentions* were the dependent measure, while we were examining reparation *attitudes*.

In two other studies, set in the very different context of post-conflict Bosnia, we investigated further potential mediators of the relationships between guilt, shame and reparation (Brown & Cehajic, 2008). Here, we were concerned with any feelings that young Bosnian Serbs might have about the atrocities meted out by Serbs to Bosnian Muslims in the 1992–1995 war. Since feelings of guilt are theorised to focus mostly on the ingroup's misdeeds and their consequences for the outgroup, we hypothesised that these might be linked to reparation via empathy, an other-centred emotional orientation. Shame, on the other hand, is more inwardly directed and so we wondered if it might be more associated with self-pity and hence with reparation in an attempt at alleviation.

This might especially be the case if the reparation is to be made public and can thus serve to ameliorate the ingroup's reputation. In other words, we speculate that temporary relief from that inner distress may be achieved by some reparative gestures to the victim. Although such a process had not been investigated in the collective domain, Tangney (1991) had earlier found a correlation between individual shame-proneness and personal distress.

Including both empathy and self-pity as mediators in our analyses mostly confirmed our hypotheses. The guilt–reparation association was significantly mediated by empathy, even if only partially, and not at all by self-pity. In contrast, the shame–reparation link was partially mediated by self-pity and also, surprisingly, by empathy. Our admittedly speculative explanation for the latter result is that it may reflect some of the same impression management strategy that we observed in Chile: our Serb participants may have been attempting to portray their group in a more favourable light by claiming some empathy with the Muslim outgroup.

So far, I have considered the consequences of group-based shame and guilt: what of their *antecedents*? It is clear, first of all, that both emotions require that group members have some awareness that their group has done something wrong. One presumably cannot feel either emotion without first perceiving that the group was responsible for some misdeeds. However, merely perceiving their group's involvement in the wrongdoing is not the same as *personally accepting* some responsibility for that group's actions and their consequences. It is the latter appraisal, we believe, which is the key antecedent of guilt. Some prior research already supports this idea. Iyer et al. (2003) found that white Americans who were asked to focus on their group's responsibility for ethnic discrimination in their country tended to feel guilty. Likewise, Leach et al. (2006) found that recognising that non-indigenous Australians were responsible for the plight of Aboriginal Australians was correlated with guilt.

The antecedents of collective shame are likely to differ however. After an initial perception of the ingroup's responsibility, it is possible that an appraisal may be made that such misdeeds threaten the ingroup's public image. It is this threatened image that will probably lead to shame. Iyer et al. (2007) found that shifting the appraisal of one's country's war-time transgressions to a concern about the country's reputation increased shame but not guilt.

This comment from a young Bosnian Serb captures this process well: "for me personally, Srebenica is a big shame. I cannot believe that we have allowed it to happen . . . Srebenica is the biggest black mark in Serbian history. It has created a bad image of us in the world" (Cehajic & Brown, 2008, p. 200).

These considerations led us to conduct two further studies in Bosnia Herzegovina, focusing on Bosnian Serbs (Cehajic & Brown, 2007). In these studies we sought to manipulate the appraisal focus on the ingroup's negative behaviour. Serb participants read abstracts of interviews with young Serbs talking about war crimes. Sometimes these interviews heightened Serbian responsibility for the crimes; sometimes they emphasised more the damage done to the Serbian reputation (e.g., as in the quotation above); in a control group there was no interview abstract. Although these manipulations were only efficacious in the first study, in both the subsequent appraisals that we sought to influence were reliably correlated with their respective emotions. Thus, acceptance of group-based responsibility led only to guilt and not shame; a threatened group image led only to shame and not guilt.

Much remains to be done for an adequate understanding of what leads to guilt or shame or even no emotion at all following ingroup transgressions. One particularly thorny issue is denial (Cohen, 2001). There is no doubt that in many contexts group members are rather reluctant to recognise that their group has done anything wrong, perhaps to protect themselves from these discomforting emotions (Iyer, Leach, & Pederson, 2004). Indeed, the absolute levels of guilt and shame reported by our Bosnian Serb participants were typically rather low (typically 3.0 or less on a 7-point scale; Brown & Cehajic, 2008; Cehajic & Brown, 2007). Yet, in other contexts the same emotions may be rather more readily admitted. For example, in two studies in Chile the mean levels were 3.0 or more on a 5-point scale (Brown et al., 2008). Was it the differential seriousness of the misdeeds, the different time-lag between the misdeeds and the assessment of emotion or some other factor that inhibited the emotions in the first case rather more than it appeared to in the second? These are just some of the questions to which we need answers.

Antecedents and consequences of intergroup forgiveness

Perpetrators may feel guilt or shame or neither, but how do members of "victim" groups respond to acts of violence against them? The word "victim" is in quotation marks because in many intergroup conflicts there is no one obvious group that has objectively experienced more oppression than the other, whatever claims to the contrary are made by their members (Noor,

Brown, & Prentice, 2008c). Northern Ireland would be a case in point. In other contexts the objective victimhood of one group is beyond question, except to the most extreme deniers. Thus, in the genocides in Nazi Germany or, more recently, in Bosnia some groups clearly have suffered more than others. Still, in both kinds of context it is a psychologically interesting and politically important question to ponder what might motivate groups in a post-conflict era to consider forgiving the other party and to begin the process of intergroup reconciliation.

Most work on forgiveness has been conducted in the interpersonal sphere (e.g., Enright, 1991; Karremans, Van Lange, & Holland, 2005; McCullough, Worthington, & Rachal, 1997; Scobie & Scobie, 1998). Although this work was useful in providing pointers as to likely mediating processes, it may not be safe to assume a direct parallelism between the interpersonal and intergroup domains (Noor et al., 2008c). Most work on intergroup forgiveness has focused on its antecedents. Thus, Hewstone et al. (2004) found that the amount and quality of intergroup contact in Northern Ireland was predictive of forgiveness, apparently because the contact was linked to outgroup trust. Indeed as we shall see, trust turns out to be an important antecedent of forgiveness perhaps because to contemplate forgiveness is to place oneself (or one's group) in a vulnerable position, and some degree of trust may thus be required for this to occur (Nadler & Liviatan, 2004). Another key determinant of intergroup forgiveness may be how the members of victim groups construe the situation in categorical terms. Consistent with the Common Ingroup Identity Model (Gaertner & Dovidio, 2000), Wohl and Branscombe (2005) found that Jewish participants, who were induced to think of themselves as "human", instead of the less inclusive category "Jew", were more inclined to forgive Germans for the Holocaust. In the studies I describe below, these two factors, trust and superordinate identification, play a large role in predicting forgiveness, alongside other factors.

Earlier, I described some of our work concerning the feelings that young Bosnian Serbs might have about what had happened in the 1992–1995 war. In the war's aftermath, what might predispose young Bosnian Muslims, the victim group in that conflict, to begin to forgive Serbs, and what then might follow from that forgiveness? We have recently been exploring the answers to these questions (Cehajic, Brown, & Castano, 2008). Following Hewstone et al. (2004), we reasoned that frequent and good quality contact with the outgroup (Serbs) would be a primary antecedent of intergroup forgiveness. How might it have its effects? One potential mediator could be heightened outgroup trust, as I noted above. Another, and related to trust, was increased empathy for the outgroup. There are several studies that link contact to empathy and thence to improved intergroup attitudes (see Brown & Hewstone, 2005). If we regard forgiveness as a favourable intergroup attitude, it seems likely that empathy for the outgroup, a greater awareness of the world from its point of view, could serve as a mediator of the presumed contact–forgiveness link. A third potential mediator is perceived outgroup heterogeneity. If members of victim groups can come to see the perpetrators as more variable, this may facilitate forgiveness since the "really guilty" members of the outgroup may by subtyped as different from the majority. Moreover, there is good evidence that contact is positively associated with perceived outgroup heterogeneity (Islam & Hewstone, 1993; Voci & Hewstone, 2003), thus completing the possible mediating chain.

In view of Wohl and Branscombe's (2005) finding that superordinate identification can stimulate forgiveness, this seemed another obvious variable to explore. In Bosnia the "Bosnian Muslim" (or "Bosniak) subgroup and the "Bosnian" superordinate identities are rather closely related, but not completely synonymous. Thus we speculated that the most appropriate measure of a "common ingroup identity" would be a "Bosniak-free" Bosnian identity – that is, the residual variance from regressing Bosnian identification on Bosniak identification. This variable was then included as one of the exogenous variables in our structural equation model.

Finally, we were interested to discover whether holding more forgiving attitudes would be associated with approach tendencies towards the outgroup (e.g., for Bosnians, wanting to participate in an exchange programme with Serbs; entertaining the possibility of working in Republica Srpska (the Serbian entity of Bosnia Herzegovina).

Including these various predictors, mediators, and outcomes of forgiveness in the same hypothesised structural equation model provided a reasonable approximation of the inter-relationships observed in our data set derived from a survey of Bosniak adolescents. Some 45% and 51% respectively of the variance in forgiveness and approach tendencies was explained by the model (see Figure 10.3). As expected, trust in and empathy for the outgroup, together with perceived outgroup heterogeneity, mediated the relationship between contact and forgiveness. Common ingroup identification was a direct

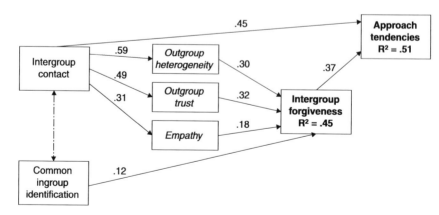

Figure 10.3 Antecedents and consequences of intergroup forgiveness (from Cehajic et al., 2008).

predictor of forgiveness, and forgiveness predicted approach tendencies. Although this was only a cross-sectional survey, thus rendering causal inferences difficult, alternative models with different possible causal ordering of the variables did not fit the data as well as that presented in Figure 10.3.

We then sought to extend our investigations of intergroup forgiveness to other ethno-political contexts, namely post-Pinochet Chile and Northern Ireland in the wake of the 1998 peace agreement (Noor et al., 2008a; Noor et al., 2008b). In these intergroup situations, although there is no denying the history of bloodshed and suffering, there is less consensus as to who contributes the "victim group". In fact, not only is there less consensus but there may even be some competition to be seen to have suffered the most. We term this orientation "competitive victimhood" and, following Nadler and Saguy (2003), we hypothesised that it would be inversely related to forgiveness. We also included variables that we already identified as being important antecedents of forgiveness in Bosnia – namely, empathy, trust and group identification (Cehajic et al., 2008). In two studies in Northern Ireland and one in Chile we found striking confirmation of our hypotheses. In all three studies, competitive victimhood proved to be a strong negative correlate of forgiveness, while common ingroup identification, empathy and trust were positive predictors.

These studies, like most in the field, were cross-sectional surveys with the usual qualifications about causal inference. Furthermore, we could guess, but not be certain, that intergroup forgiveness might lead to reconciliation attitudes. Accordingly, in a third study in Northern Ireland we included a longitudinal element to the design (time-lag 4–6 weeks), together with a measure of reconciliation attitude (e.g., "my community and the other need to change our relationship with each other", "my community needs to talk with the other community about issues that divide us"; Noor et al., 2008a, Study 3). Our goal was to discover whether forgiveness would, in fact, predict reconciliation longitudinally. Using a conventional cross-lagged regression analysis in which reconciliation at time 2 was regressed onto forgiveness at time 1, controlling for time 1 reconciliation attitudes, we found, indeed, that forgiveness was a reliable predictor of reconciliation. There is some basis, therefore, for assuming that forgiveness and reconciliation are causally related to each other.

Conclusions and future prospects

There seems little doubt from the work presented in this chapter that the emotions that may be felt by perpetrator groups and the reactions of victim groups are all important ingredients in post-conflict intergroup situations. Nevertheless, their precise role in predicting intergroup behaviour remains ambiguous. In part, this is for methodological reasons. The vast majority of the work in this field – including most presented here – has been correlational in nature. Although we have sought to overcome some of the limitations of such correlational designs by including a longitudinal component in some of our studies, strong causal interpretation is still problematic. Moreover, our outcome measures (e.g., reparation, forgiveness) have been attitudinal in nature and it is uncertain how these will translate into actual behaviours aimed at rebuilding damaged intergroup relationships. Our first conclusion, therefore, is to call for more experimental work in which hypothetical ante-cedents (e.g., guilt, shame, victimhood) are manipulated and where some prosocial intergroup behaviours – or at the very least, behavioural intentions – are assessed. We have made some first steps in this direction but much still remains to be done (Brown & Chatfield, 2007; Brown & Coen, 2007).

This raises another theoretical matter, especially in relation to collective guilt. Leach et al. (2006) and Iyer et al. (2007) have argued that guilt, being essentially an introverted and dysphoric emotion, is unlikely to be sufficiently progressive to motivate people to reparative *action*. It may well predict repa-rative attitudes, but the step to reparative behaviour may be a step too far. Instead, argue these authors, a more extraverted emotion like anger may be necessary to generate reparative action intentions (and behaviour itself). They provide some evidence for this in the context of attitudes and behavioural intentions in relation to the current Iraq War and the situation of Australian Aborigines. However, this issue is far from settled. Until we have the kind of experimental evidence alluded to above, examining behaviour (and inten-tions) in a range of contexts where collective guilt may be being felt – about both contemporary and historical injustices – it would be prudent to suspend a definitive judgement on this issue.

Finally, in this chapter I have considered the actions and reactions of perpetrator and victim groups separately. However, in real intergroup situations they will be reciprocally linked – the behaviour and emotion of one group will affect the other, which will then respond, setting in train a new sequence of intergroup interactions. This seems like an obvious new research direction to pursue. We made a start on this in a scenario study in which we elicited "victims' " responses to perpetrator offers of reparation (or not), accompanied by various supposed emotions (guilt, shame, none) (Giner-Sorolla, Castano, Espinosa, & Brown, 2008). The fictitious scenario was an environmental disaster caused by the negligence of a large corporation. The chief executive of this corporation was described as making offers of resti-tution and simultaneously expressing his dysphoric emotions about what had happened. Participants playing the role of members of the community who had been affected by the disaster were invited to express their (dis)satisfaction with the chief executive's stance. Interestingly, the most favourable response was observed in the condition where the chief executive offered reparation and expressed shame. Offering reparation and showing guilt was viewed less favourably, more or less the same as if he had expressed no emotion at all. We plan to follow up this preliminary work by examining the responses of real victim groups in a current intergroup conflict situation. A central goal of this new research will be to identify the critical mediating processes that govern victim groups' reactions, and to explore which of these will be linked to intergroup forgiveness and reconciliation. In this way, we hope to reach a better understanding of how intergroup emotions can be harnessed for socially reconstructive ends.

Note

1 I gratefully acknowledge the contributions of many others to the work that I report in this chapter. They are, in alphabetical order: Emanuele Castano, Sabina Cehajic, John Chatfield, Sharon Coen, Pablo Espinosa, Roger Giner-Sorolla, Roberto Gonzalez, Jorge Manzi, Masi Noor and Hanna Zagefka. It is by no means a conventional platitude to say that the research would simply not have been possible without their collective efforts.

References

Barkan, E. (2000). *The guilt of nations*. London: Johns Hopkins University Press.

Branscombe, N. R., & Doosje, B. (2004). *Collective guilt: International perspectives*. New York: Cambridge University Press.

Branscombe, N. R., Slugoski, B., & Kappen, D. M. (2004). The measurement of collective guilt: What it is and what it is not. In N. Branscombe & B. Doosje (Eds.), *Collective guilt: International perspectives* (pp. 16–34). Cambridge: Cambridge University Press.

Brown, R., & Cehajic, S. (2008). Dealing with the past and facing the future: Mediators of the effects of collective guilt and shame in Bosnia Herzegovina. *European Journal of Social Psychology*, *38*, 669–684.

Brown, R., & Chatfield, J. (2007). *Shame on us: Social consequences of a group based dysphoric emotion*. Unpublished manuscript, University of Sussex.

Brown, R., & Coen, S. (2007). "Questione di feeling": Il ruolo delle emozioni nel miglioramento degli atteggiamenti intergruppi. ["Question of feeling": The role of emotions in the improvement of intergroup attitudes]. In R. Brown, D. Capozza, & O. Licciardello (Eds.), *Immigrazione, acculturazione, modalita' di contatto* [*Immigration, acculturation, modality of contact*] (pp. 50–66). Milano: Franco Angeli.

Brown, R., Gonzalez, R., Zagefka, H., Manzi, J., & Cehajic, S. (2008). Nuestra culpa: Collective guilt and shame as predictors of reparation for historical wrong-doing. *Journal of Personality and Social Psychology*, *94*, 75–90.

Brown, R., & Hewstone, M. (2005). An integrative theory of intergroup contact. *Advances in Experimental Social Psychology*, *37*, 255–343.

Buruma, I. (1994). *The wages of guilt: Memories of war in Germany and Japan*. London: Jonathan Cape.

Cehajic, S., & Brown, R. (2007). *"The burden of our times": Antecedents of group-based guilt and shame*. Under review.

Cehajic, S., & Brown, R. (2008). Not in my name: A social psychological study of antecedents and consequences of acknowledgement of ingroup atrocities. *Genocide Studies and Prevention*, *3*, 195–211.

Cehajic, S., Brown, R., & Castano, E. (2008). Forgive and forget? Antecedents, mediators and consequences of intergroup forgiveness in Bosnia and Herzegovina. *Political Psychology*, *29*, 351–367.

Cohen, S. (2001). *States of denial: Knowing about atrocities and suffering*. Oxford: Polity Press.

Doosje, B., Branscombe, N. R., Spears, R., & Manstead, A. S. R. (1998). Guilty by association: When one's group has a negative history. *Journal of Personality and Social Psychology, 75*, 872–886.

Enright, R. D. (1991). The moral development of forgiveness. In W. Kurtines & J. Grerwitz (Eds.), *Handbook of moral behaviour and development*. Hillsdale, NJ: Lawrence Erlbaum Associates, Inc.

Gaertner, S., & Dovidio, J. (2000). *Reducing intergroup bias: The common ingroup identity model*. Hove, UK: Psychology Press.

Giner-Sorolla, R., Castano, E., Espinosa, P., & Brown, R. (2008). Shame expressions reduce the recipients's insult from outgroup reparations. *Journal of Experimental Social Psychology, 44*, 519–526.

Harvey, R. D., & Oswald, D. L. (2000). Collective guilt and shame as motivation for White support for Black programs. *Journal of Applied Social Psychology, 30*, 1790–1811.

Hewstone, M., Cairns, E., Voci, A., McLernon, F., Niens, U., & Noor, M. (2004). Intergroup forgiveness and guilt in Northern Ireland: Social psychological dimensions of "The Troubles". In N. Branscombe & B. Doosje (Eds.), *Collective guilt: International perspectives* (pp. 193–215). Cambridge: Cambridge University Press.

Islam, M. R., & Hewstone, M. (1993). Dimensions of contact as predictors of intergroup anxiety, perceived outgroup variability, and outgroup attitude: An integrative model. *Personality and Social Psychology Bulletin, 19*(6), 700–710.

Iyer, A., Leach, C. W., & Crosby, F. (2003). White guilt and racial compensation: The benefits and limits of self-focus. *Personality and Social Psychology Bulletin, 29*, 117–129.

Iyer, A., Leach, C. W., & Pederson, A. (2004). Racial wrongs and restitutions: The role of guilt and other group based emotions. In N. Branscombe & B. Doosje (Eds.), *Collective guilt: International perspectives* (pp. 262–283). Cambridge: Cambridge University Press.

Iyer, A., Schmader, T., & Lickel, B. (2007). Why individuals protest the perceived transgressions of their country: The role of anger, shame and guilt. *Personality and Social Psychology Bulletin, 33*, 572–587.

Karremans, J. C., Van Lange, P. A. M., & Holland, R. W. (2005). Forgiveness and its associations with prosocial thinking, feeling and doing beyond the relationship. *Personality and Social Psychology Bulletin, 31*, 1315–1326.

Leach, C., Iyer, A., & Pederson, A. (2006). Anger and guilt about ingroup advantage explain the willingness for political action. *Personality and Social Psychology Bulletin, 32*, 1232–1245.

Leach, C. W., Snider, N., & Iyer, A., (2002). "Poisoning the consciences of the fortunate": The experience of relative advantage and support for social equality. In I. Walker & H. Smith (Eds.), *Relative deprivation: Specification, development and integration* (pp. 136–163). Cambridge: Cambridge University Press.

Lewis, H. B. (1971). *Shame and guilt in neurosis*. New York: International Universities Press.

Lickel. B., Schmader, T., & Barquissau, M. (2004). The evocation of moral amotions in intergroup contexts: The distinction between collective guilt and collective shame. In N. Branscombe & B. Doosje (Eds.), *Collective guilt: International perspectives* (pp. 35–55). Cambridge: Cambridge University Press.

Lickel, B., Schmader, T., Curtis, M., Scarnier, M., & Ames, D. R. (2005). Vicarious shame and guilt. *Group Processes and Intergroup Relations, 8*, 145–157.

McCullough, M. E., Worthington, E. L., & Rachal, K. C. (1997). Interpersonal forgiving in close relationships. *Journal of Personality and Social Psychology, 73*, 321–336.

McGarty, C., Pederson, A., Leach, C. W., Mansell, T., Waller, J., & Bliuc, A.-M. (2005). Group-based guilt as a predictor of commitment to apology. *British Journal of Social Psychology, 44*, 659–680.

Nadler, A., & Liviatan, I. (2004). Intergroup reconciliation processes in Israel: Theoretical analysis and empirical findings. In N. Branscombe & B. Doosje (Eds.), *Collective guilt: International perspectives* (pp. 216–235). Cambridge: Cambridge University Press.

Nadler, A., & Saguy, T. (2003). Reconciliation between nations: Overcoming emotional deterrents to ending conflicts between groups. In H. Langholtz & C. E. Stout (Eds.), *The psychology of diplomacy* (pp. 29–46). Westport, CT: Praeger.

Noor, M., Brown, R., Gonzalez, R., Manzi, J., & Lewis, C. A. (2008a). On positive psychological outcomes: What helps groups with a history of conflict to forgive and reconcile with each other? *Personality and Social Psychology Bulletin, 34*, 819–832.

Noor, M., Brown, R., & Prentice, G. (2008b). Precursors and mediators of intergroup reconciliation in Northern Ireland: A new model. *British Journal of Social Psychology, 47*, 481–495.

Noor, M., Brown, R., & Prentice, G. (2008c). Prospects for intergroup reconciliation: Social-psychological predictors of intergroup forgiveness and reparation in Northern Ireland and Chile. In A. Nadler, T. E. Malloy, & J. D. Fisher (Eds.), *The social psychology of intergroup reconciliation* (pp. 97–114). Oxford: Oxford University Press.

Pederson, A., Beven, J., Walker, I., & Griffiths, B. (2004). Attitudes toward indigenous Australians: The role of empathy and guilt. *Journal of Community and Applied Social Psychology, 14*, 233–249.

Schmader, T., & Lickel, B. (2006). Stigma and shame: Emotional responses to the stereotypic actions of one's ethnic group. In S. Levin & C. van Laar (Eds.), *Stigma and group inequality: Social psychological approaches*. New York: Lawrence Erlbaum Associates, Inc.

Scobie, E. D., & Scobie, G. E. W. (1998). Damaging events: The perceived need for forgiveness. *Journal for the Theory of Social Behaviour, 28*, 373–401.

Smith, E. R. (1993). Social identity and social emotions: Toward new conceptualizations of prejudice. In D. M. Mackie & D. L. Hamilton (Eds.), *Affect, cognition and stereotyping* (pp. 297–315). San Diego, CA: Academic Press.

Steele, S. (1990). *The content of our character: A new vision of race in America*. New York: St Martin's Press.

Swim, J. K., & Miller, D. L. (1999). White guilt: Its antecedents and consequences for attitudes toward affirmative action. *Personality and Social Psychology Bulletin, 25*, 500–514.

Tajfel, H., & Turner, J. (1979). An integrative theory of intergroup conflict. In W. G. Austin & S. Worchel (Eds.), *The social psychology of intergroup relations* (pp. 33–47). Monterey, CA: Brooks & Cole.

Tangney, J. P. (1991). Moral affect: The good, the bad, and the ugly. *Journal of Personality and Social Psychology, 61*, 598–607.

Voci, A., & Hewstone, M. (2003). Intergroup contact and prejudice towards immigrants in Italy: The mediational role of anxiety and the moderational role of group salience. *Group Processes and Intergroup Relations, 6*, 37–54.

Wohl, M. J. A., & Branscombe, N. (2005). Forgiveness and collective guilt assignment to historical perpetrator groups depend on level of social category inclusiveness. *Journal of Personality and Social Psychology, 88*, 288–303.

11 Hierarchy-based groups

Real inequalities and essential differences

Jacques-Philippe Leyens and Stéphanie Demoulin
Université catholique de Louvain, Louvain-la-Neuve

One of the most popular studies in social psychology is certainly the Stanford Prison Experiment (SPE, Haney, Banks, & Zimbardo, 1973). One summer in the early 1970s, Zimbardo recruited volunteers to participate for 2 weeks in a simulated prison. Participants were randomly assigned to the role of guards and prisoners. The latter were simply told about the date of the beginning of the simulation. Guards received instructions and were screened for personality problems. The day the study started, prisoners were arrested at their home and thrown in real police cars with howling sirens. They were conducted to a police station where they went through the usual routine and, then, were sent to the simulated prison where guards were expecting them. Problems immediately started. Guards behaved increasingly aggressively, if not sadistically, and prisoners became completely apathetic. Some prisoners were so disturbed that they had to be replaced, and, finally, it was decided to stop the study after 6 days.

Thirty years after the SPE, Reicher and Haslam (2006) conducted a somewhat similar study in the UK, sponsored by the BBC: the BBC prison experiment. However,

> The aim of the study was not to simulate a prison (. . .) but rather to create an institution that in many ways resembled a prison (. . .) as a site to investigate the behaviour of groups that were unequal in terms of power, status, and resources.
>
> (Reicher & Haslam, 2006, p. 7)

Still, participants were distributed into prisoners and guards, who were said to have superior skills. The study was to last 8 days. A major difference from the SPE is that everybody was informed that, on the third day of confinement, one prisoner with the required skills would be promoted to become a guard. Some other changes were also introduced, all inspired by social identity theory (see below). For instance, after the promotion, the experimenters told everybody that skills did not differentiate the two groups. Contrary to what happened in Stanford, prisoners immediately identified with their group, more than did guards, and this identification with the group of prisoners became especially marked after the promotion of one prisoner to the role of guard. From this moment on, the prisoners commanded the prison! An example: "late on the evening of Day 6, the prisoners in Cell 2 broke out of their cell and occupied the guards' quarters. At this point, the guards' regime was seen by all to be unworkable and at an end" (Reicher & Haslam, 2006, p. 21).

What is relevant for the present purpose is that, in the SPE, the dominated group accepted its status and respected the rules of the dominants, even to the point that some members were so traumatized that they had to be taken care of. In the BBC prison experiment, nothing of this sort happened. As time went on, the dominated group increased in cohesion, to the point of challenging the orders of the guards, and finally taking the position of the dominant group. Opposition of behaviors cannot be greater, as is the opinion of the different authors about each other's work: "these authors have insisted on using the Stanford Prison Experiment (SPE) as their 'straw situation' to give visibility and conceptual legitimacy to their scientifically irresponsible 'made-for-TV-study' " (Zimbardo, 2006, p. 47). Why such opposition?

This chapter is devoted to scrutinizing the reactions of dominated groups in front of dominant ones. The problem is touchier than it could appear at first sight. It is controversial. Because of space limits, the present essay is not meant to be exhaustive. Rather, it presents the contributions that appear most illustrative of such controversy.

Dominant and dominated groups may (re)act differently because they precisely occupy different positions in the society and because this society presents specific characteristics. If dominated members react, it is in order to change the *reality* of their individual or group status. In the first part of this chapter, we review the main theories that have dealt with the problem of changing or not of the "shared reality" of the society. Is inequality between groups fate or a transient state? Besides the relative positions within society because of structural factors, groups may react against others because of fundamental perceived *differences* between them. What may be important for dominant and dominated groups is not only the fact that they occupy various positions in society, but also the fact that they feel essentially different. This substantial difference implies consequences that we examine in the second section of this chapter. In summary, in the first part of the chapter, we defend the idea that groups, especially dominated ones, react as a function of inequalities inscribed in societal structural factors. These factors motivate dominated groups to justify, reduce, or abolish differences. In the second part, we propose that perceived differences between groups, dominant or dominated, lead them (or not) to experience the other groups as less human or more animal than the ingroup in a rather automatic way. These two perspectives are not opposed but complement each other. It is true that "real" inequalities exist between groups and elicit different behaviors. It is also true that groups sometimes perceive essential differences with other groups and react symbolically, and, eventually, behaviorally.

Recognizing, accepting, and rejecting the ingroup's status

One of the studies that we like was conducted by Ellemers, van den Heuvel, de Gilder, Maass, and Bonvini (2004). They worked with female university professors who recognized that conditions were harder for them than for their male colleagues who more often had a companion and children. Helped partly by the feminist revolution that made university authorities recognize that females are under-represented as professors (in our university there was a rule until the late 1960s that no woman could become professor), some female researchers have been appointed professors at their university. When asked by Ellemers et al. (2004) what they thought about their graduate students, these female university teachers favored more male graduates than did their male colleagues. This section should help with understanding of these findings.

Hierarchy of groups

Probably in every society, there are dominant and dominated groups (e.g., men and women, respectively). One does not need to be a social psychologist to make this observation. There is however a gap between this observation and potential theories about it. When we say dominant versus dominated, it could mean various things. The difference could lie in the power, the status, the resources, the education, and so on. Power is not status, and resources are not education. This chapter does not make such distinctions because they do not matter for the analysis. It is why we speak similarly of dominant versus dominated or stigmatized groups, of high- versus low-status groups.

When one says that there are dominant and dominated groups in a society, it means that there is, at least, a tacit consensus about the hierarchy. Even if they do not agree with their position, groups recognize their relative ranking. Stated otherwise, dominant members know that they are part of the top of the hierarchy, that they have more "power"; on the other hand, dominated members recognize their status at the bottom of the hierarchy even though they may question its legitimacy, as feminists did relative to men (Zelditch, 2001). For what follows, it is important to remember that the hierarchy of groups in a given society is not only a mirror of objective reality but also the result of shared views about this reality. This sharing is important for at least two reasons. First, it gives a meaning to the theories that are presented. Second, it prevents misinterpretations of the data that were obtained.

For social identity theory (SIT) (Tajfel, 1981), categorization into groups and comparison between them leads to more or less positive social identities. When they consider themselves members of a given group, people do not only have a personal identity (i.e., I as Philippe) but a social one (i.e., I as male). The positivity of the latter one will depend on the ranking of the ingroup in the hierarchy. Thus, for SIT, inequalities between groups are at the core of the theory, and as we will see soon, social dominance theory (SDT) (Sidanius & Pratto, 1999) explicitly focuses on group-based hierarchies. "All human societies tend to be structured as systems of *group-based-hierarchies*. At the very minimum, this hierarchical social structure consists of one or a small number of dominant and hegemonic groups at the top and one or a numerous of subordinate groups at the bottom" (Sidanius & Pratto, 1999, p. 31; italics in the original). Dominant groups are said to have more positive social value than subordinate ones. This social value corresponds to a consensus in the society. Third, the last theory to be examined in this section, system-justification theory (SJT) (Jost & Banaji, 1994), also relies on the observation that society, the system, is composed of groups that differ in their amount of power, prestige, status, and so on.

The three theories cited above (SIT, SDT, and SJT) agree that dominant groups will do all they can to maintain, and even improve, their position. Again, this reaction is not surprising. Everybody is accustomed to right wing (conservative) political parties that are supported by the wealthiest people, and that always claim more privileges only for these well-off individuals; they also claim that women should have children and stay home. The three theories agree with the fact that dominant groups try to maintain the status quo in society. SIT, for instance, has experimentally illustrated situations analogous to the one with the political parties. Even groups that have a highly positive social identity continue to favor their ingroup; such a reaction has become known as "ingroup favoritism bias" (Mullen, Brown, & Smith, 1992). Another everyday example may illustrate this ingroup bias. Rich regions, and not poor ones, want their autonomy in several European countries (e.g., Belgium, Italy, Spain). The claim for autonomy relies on the will of rich regions to become wealthier even if it means that poor regions will become even poorer.

SDT researchers have developed the SDO (social dominance orientation) questionnaire to measure the desire for a hierarchy with superior groups dominating inferior ones (see for a review Sidanius & Pratto, 1999). Here are some items: "Some groups of people are simply inferior to other groups", "To get ahead in life, it is sometimes necessary to step on other groups", "Inferior groups should stay in their place." Members of dominant groups score higher on this questionnaire than those who belong to dominated groups. SDT has also verified that members of dominant or superior groups make a great use of "hierarchy-enhancing legitimizing myths" (HE-LM), such as racism, nationalism, classism, Protestant work ethic, and so on. These myths or beliefs legitimize or justify social dominance. "We are superior because we are Whites, Americans, aristocrats, hard-working, etc."

Similarly to the previous theories, SJT predicts that members of dominant groups think and act in a way that sustains the status quo in society. Like SDT, SJT defends the idea that high-status groups justify or rationalize their privileges through a series of means. "Stereotypes of the working class (or immigrants or Gypsies) as lazy, irresponsible, and unintelligent allow people to blame these groups for their own poverty and to deflect blame from the system. Ideological beliefs associated with individualism, meritocracy, belief in a just world, and the Protestant ethic presumably serve the same function" (Jost & Hunyady, 2002, p. 112).

Shaking or respecting the consensus

If there is a recognized hierarchy of groups, and if dominant groups do all they can to maintain their superiority, what do dominated groups do? The three theories, which were consensual up to now, offer different answers. According to SDT, dominated groups may react against the situation, as do feminists. Otherwise, there would never be tensions between groups, and one knows these exist. Alongside the HE-LM, there are hierarchy-attenuating legitimizing myths (HA-LM) such as multiculturalism or Universal Rights of Man. Reactions would then depend on the situation, but Sidanius and Pratto insist on the fact that the search for domination is greater than the one for change. In other words, members of high-status groups feel more positively about their own group than members of low-status groups feel about their group. One possible explanation for this difference of legitimization may come from what people think about their group and what they think others think about their group. Luthanen and Crocker (1992) speak of private and public collective self-esteem. Private collective self-esteem refers to personal appreciation of the ingroup, while public collective self-esteem is a meta-appreciation, a belief about the appreciation of the group by outsiders. Given what we said earlier about the consensus concerning relative dominance or domination, it is not surprising that the two types of self-esteem correlate (Luthanen & Crocker, 1992). However, consensus might be more easily accepted by some groups than by others, and this difference may explain why members of stigmatized groups do not necessarily suffer in their social identities. For instance, Crocker, Luthanen, Blaine, and Broadnax (1994) have not found a positive relation between private and public collective self-esteem among Black US citizens. It follows that HE-LM are strongly endorsed by dominant groups, but that HA-LM should not be absent among dominated groups (see Federico & Levin, 2004).

The position of SJT resembles the one of SDT, because it also insists on legitimization, but it is much more drastic. According to this theory, members of both dominant and dominated groups maintain the status quo in society. The last assertion is original and takes its roots into the ideology of "false consciousness", erroneously attributed to Marx (rather than to Engels). It means that dominated groups are trapped by the ideology of the society, do not realize the forces of relations between classes, and believe they act in their own interest. In fact, for Marx, all classes (but for different reasons) participate in the same ideology, and this is the thesis defended by SJT.

This theory has had great success but it has also received extensive and severe criticisms (see Reicher, 2004; Rubin & Hewstone, 2004). We concentrate on some of the empirical weaknesses that are most relevant for our purpose. The first experiments tested directly whether there were differences of reactions among dominant and dominated groups (for a review see Jost & Hunyady, 2002). There were two kinds of general design. In the first one, Jost and colleagues gave "objective" information about the higher or lower status of the participants' group compared to an outgroup. For instance, they told university students that alumni from another university earned more or less money than people from the ingroup university. In their answers, participants from both (manipulated) low- and high-status groups reproduced the hierarchy. All students reported that those alumni pertaining to the university that led to more money were better educated and more intelligent. In the second type of experiments, Jost and his collaborators worked with real-life lower and higher status groups, such as students from notoriously prestigious and non-prestigious universities. Again, the participants reproduced the hierarchy. In our opinion, these experiments do not show that low-status groups accept their position, but simply recognize the existing reality, already noted by SIT and SDT. In these experiments, groups with various statuses, manipulated or natural, show the expected consensus. They repeat what the experimenter just said, or comply with well-established facts. In fact, it is extremely important that low-status groups recognize their low status. Recognition does not mean *acceptance*, but *recognition* is necessary for potential reaction (see for instance, Wright and Lubensky, in press).

Jost, Pelham, and Carvallo (2002, Study 1) have also tried to show that low-status groups accept their status implicitly, without awareness. To this end, they used the Implicit Association Task (IAT, Greenwald, McGhee, & Schwarz, 1998), a test that compares the time taken to make compatible associations between the ingroup and the outgroup with respective characteristics (e.g. ingroup–book, outgroup–beer) and the time needed for incompatible associations (e.g., ingroup–beer, outgroup–book). Results showed ingroup bias for students of a prestigious university, but they did not show the expected outgroup bias from students of a non-prestigious university. This absence of outgroup bias is important because its presence would have meant that the dominated group accepted the values of the dominant one (see Livingston, 2002). In summary, SJT is much more radical than SDT as regards dominated groups, but the empirical evidence is not as convincing as one would like. SJT is better at showing recognition than acceptance of dominated group members (but see Jost, Banaji, & Nosek, 2004).

Note that the behaviors of guards and prisoners in the SPE correspond to the predictions of SJT. Guards become aggressive and prisoners turn out spineless. Zimbardo (2007), however, offers another explanation. According to him, it is the situation that is crucial because it creates roles and people conform to them.

SIT also considers the co-existence of dominant and dominated groups, but it does with many more nuances, and more precise predictions, than SDT and SJT. It postulates that group members want a positive social identity. If such a positive identity is not available, two ways of dealing with thus are possible: social (or more precisely individual) mobility, and social change. In the first case, individuals from a dominated group will try to pass into the dominant one (e.g., Michael Jackson and his change of skin color). In the second case, group members will adopt strategies to improve the state of their dominated group (e.g., women vs. men). For Tajfel (1981), these strategies have to take into account the global context. Three variables are considered of utmost importance. First, the state of groups can be considered stable or unstable, that is, will remain as they are or may change. Second, the relative ranking may be viewed as legitimate or not, meaning that legitimacy or illegitimacy reigns over the hierarchy. Third, and finally, the frontiers between groups can be impermeable or permeable, implying that it is possible or not to go from one group to another. The more the situation is stable, legitimate, and permeable, the more people will adopt social mobility, which means that when a solution exists for passing into the other group, people will do it as individuals. One can speak of "outgroup bias" on the part of members of dominated groups who adopt this strategy. It was clearly the case in the study by Ellemers et al. (2004) summarized at the beginning of this section. The female professors sacrificed their personal life to achieve the rank of professor and adopted a "macho" position by derogating female graduate students relative to male ones. By contrast, instability, illegitimacy, and impermeability constitute conditions that may lead to social change. In this last case, people change the value of comparison ("Black is beautiful") or start to oppose the dominant group. This solution is the one chosen by the prisoners in Reicher and Haslam BBC prison experiment after the promotion of a single prisoner into the camp of the guards. The authors had staged this promotion especially to manipulate permeability (before the promotion)/ impermeability (after the promotion). Also, revelation by the experimenters that skills did not differentiate the groups of guards and prisoners was meant to make the situation illegitimate and increase the chance of a collective action.

SIT is much older than the two previous theories and an innumerable number of studies have been conducted to test its hypotheses (see Ellemers, Spears, & Doosje, 2002). Mullen et al. (1992) conducted a meta-analysis on ingroup bias, which was followed by a more extensive one by Bettencourt, Charlton, Dorr, and Hume (2001). Both sets of data allow us to conclude that groups are clearly aware of which is on top and which is the "underdog". This recognition has an impact on the value that the groups attribute to different dimensions. These dimensions may be relevant or irrelevant for the intergroup situation. It is clear that dominant groups rate themselves higher on relevant dimensions, and are rated as such by dominated groups. However, the status effect is substantially decreased in the case of irrelevant dimensions. Stated otherwise, dominated groups seem to experience less difficulties in affirming their group's value on these dimensions (e.g., sociability) than on relevant ones (e.g., competence). Interestingly, in the cases of permeability and illegitimacy, dominated groups were less likely to admit the superiority of dominant groups on relevant dimensions, and to need to express their own value on irrelevant dimensions. Dupont (2004, p. 22, italics in the original) gives the following conclusion:

> Given the importance of dimensions relevance put forth in both meta-analyses, these results are inconsistent with the idea of low-status being resilient to the negative view of their group. However, it is important to remain explicit on the meaning that should be attributed to these results: Low-status group members actually *do* display preference for the in-group, but the matter is that they tend to do so to a *lesser extent* than the high-status ones. Hence, they cannot be said to favor the out-group or to derogate the in-group in the primary sense of the terms. Clearly, what seems to best differentiate low- and high-status group members is the *confidence* with which they claim their superiority.

Much more could be said about SIT but there is no need since this theory is exposed, sometimes extensively, in several chapters of this book. These other chapters will certainly make clear that SIT wanted to go beyond realistic conflict (LeVine & Campbell, 1972) and to show that discrimination does not need material resources to show up. There can be symbolic conflicts. However, it is important to note that SIT does not consider that group members satisfy themselves uniquely with symbolic solutions. As individuals or as groups they look for a positive identity provided by the relative ranking of groups in the society.

Summary

Societies are replete with groups that differ in terms of objective or, at least "shared" realities: power, status, and/or resources. When saying "shared realities", it means that groups agree that they are unequal in terms of power, status, and/or resources. What becomes interesting is to see how dominant and dominated groups react to these inequalities. The three theories reviewed above agree that dominant groups do their best to maintain their privileged position. Nuances and even opposition appear when dominated groups are concerned. SJT and SDT give great importance to dominant groups since they rely on ambient ideology. According to SJT, this ideology defends the status quo, and, therefore, dominated groups accept their inferiority. For SDT, there are ideologies that accentuate and attenuate inequalities. Behavior will follow as a function of the chosen ideologies but the most frequently selected ones are in favor of legitimizing those at the top of the group hierarchy. Contrary to the preceding theories, SIT is especially interested in the reactions of members of dominated groups. It makes predictions as to how and when these members will behave. The "how" has to do with the strategy, individual or group. The "when" is the conditions (im/permeability, il/legitimacy, in/stability), linked to structural factors in the society, which lead to specific strategies. Choosing an individual strategy means acceptance of the dominant norms. Opting for a group policy implies refusal of dominant values and a fight, pacific or not, for recognition of one's group.

Again, we would like to emphasize that the three perspectives deal with objective, in the sense of consensual, dimensions such as power, status, or financial resources. Dominant and dominated groups agree about their ranking on those dimensions; it is acceptance that may vary.

The perception of outgroups as infra-humanized

Up to now, we have considered that the idea of a hierarchy of groups in society requires a consensus. This consensus does not mean immobility, but it requires recognition. In fact, it might even be advantageous for dominated groups to increase the gap between them and the dominant group, in order to augment the potential perception of illegitimacy.

Consensus implies reality, objective or at least shared perception, and while it has to be recognized, it may lead to acceptance or reaction. In the rest of this chapter, we defend the idea that, in addition to the strategies developed in the first part, dominant and dominated groups alike look for an essential distinction that is not consensual but alien to so-called objective "shared realities". While the concept crucial for the reactions reviewed in the first part was "objective inequalities" between groups, here the concept that prompts the distinction between groups is the one of "essential differences". Dominant and dominated groups react not only because there is a gap in status (power, resources), but because they perceive walls of differences between them (Leyens, Demoulin, Vaes, Gaunt, & Paladino, 2007). This perception may involve dominant versus dominated groups, as well as dominant and dominated groups among themselves. Faced with a fundamental difference, group members conceive their group as substantially superior and derogate the outgroup because they attribute more humanity to the ingroup than to many outgroups. We call this phenomenon infra-humanization (Leyens et al., 2000, 2003). We first examine the basis of the infra-humanization model and its main hypotheses before discussing societal implications. We end by defending the idea that infra-humanization, unlike other more classical types of biases, is not dependent on structural factors in the society but results from an unmediated phenomenal perception.

Before developing the infra-humanization model, we insist that it is not meant to nuance, oppose, or improve the theories reviewed so far. People do not only fight to maintain or abolish inequalities, they also react to essential differences that they translate in degrees of humanity. Great Britain and Germany are two important, high-status countries, and nevertheless British students infra-humanize German ones (Viki, Winchester, Titshall, Chisango, Pina & Russell, 2006).

Ingroups are more human than outgroups

About 10 years ago, our team (Leyens et al., 2000) started a research program with the idea that people imagine that groups possess different essences. Essentialism is the belief that people are what they are by substance, and not by contingencies. This conception of human groups opposes nature to culture. Groups are what they are by nature, and not by culture. It means that group differences do not imply cultural, historical, accidental factors, but that there are discontinuities in humanity, even if the idea of a single human species is accepted. Besides the uniqueness of the human species, other characteristics contribute to *essential* disparities. The differences in biology, language, or religion, for instance, are not considered accidents but foundations of insuperable distinctions.

Essentialism is an old concept in sociology and anthropology, for instance, but the idea of its application in social psychology was introduced only in 1992, by Rothbart and Taylor. Because of the quasi-universality of ethnocentrism (Jahoda, 1999; Sumner, 1906), we postulated that the ingroup would have a more human essence than (certain) outgroups. It followed that the human essence should be constituted by particular characteristics linked to humanity, and that ingroups should possess them more than most outgroups.

The starting point was to find the specific human characteristics. Recently, Haslam (2006; Haslam, Bain, Douge, Lee, & Bastian, 2005) has developed a model of dehumanization where he distinguishes between two kinds of humanity. On the one hand, one may compare humanity with what is not humanity, bestiality for instance. Or, one may try to find what is typical of human nature. Curiosity, for instance, is typical of humans but it is not restricted to them. While Haslam has mainly worked with this second kind of (mechanistic) dehumanization, we have worked with the first one and have asked people to rank-order characteristics that were uniquely human. This comparative way to envisage humanity was more suitable for our purpose than a definition in terms of what is most common to human beings. Indeed, unique humanness directly focuses on differences, on what makes "us" and "them". Rather than speaking of dehumanization, which means, etymologically, completely deprived of humanity, we opted for the neologism "infrahumanization", implying than others are *less* humans, or more animals.

The first test consisted of finding uniquely human characteristics. When we asked students to rank-order uniquely human characteristics, the consensus was incredible: almost everyone stated intelligence, language, and "sentiments" (in French). The French word "émotions" almost never appeared. In conformity with our desire to avoid societal structural factors, we decided to work with "sentiments" versus "émotions". Because the distinction between these two words is specific to Latin languages, Demoulin, Leyens, Paladino, Rodriguez, Rodriguez, and Dovidio (2004a) conducted a cross-cultural study in four countries with five different languages. Participants rated emotional terms on a series of features, one of them being "very exclusive to humans", versus "not at all exclusive to humans". Other features included visibility, locus of agency, intensity, duration, age of appearance, morality, and so on. The results were again consensual and allowed us to make the distinction between primary non-uniquely human emotions/"émotions" (e.g., fear, anger, joy, surprise) and secondary uniquely human emotions/ "sentiments" (e.g., guilt, shame, love, optimism). Secondary emotions were rated as less visible, intense, caused internally, lasting longer, appearing later in life, and more associated with morality. This cross-cultural study allowed us to test the link between humanity and specific characteristics.

A large number of tests have been conducted to test the second link between the specific human characteristics and ingroup versus outgroup (see Demoulin et al., 2004b; Leyens et al., 2003; Leyens et al., 2007). We summarize here only two of them. In one experiment (Boccato, Cortes, Demoulin, & Leyens, 2007, Experiment 1), participants were subliminally primed with the words "Belgian" or "Arab" and they had to decide as quickly as possible if what appeared on the screen of their computer was a word or a non-word. The words were positive and negative primary and secondary emotions as well as words not related to the emotional domain. As expected, people were quicker to react to secondary emotions when primed by the word "Belgian" than when primed with "Arab". As also expected, there were no differences for primary emotions because these belong to everybody, including animals. Also, there was no effect of valence; indeed, positive *and* negative secondary emotions are uniquely human emotions. Humanity is not restricted to positive items. The latter result differentiates infra-humanization from a simple ingroup bias *à la* SIT.

The second approach to test infra-humanization utilized a questionnaire. Traditionally, the first page asked for ingroup identification or presented the research about perceptions concerning groups in order to make inter-group relations salient. The second page consisted of 26 words. Six were secondary emotions, six were primary emotions, and the other 14 words were fillers mostly related to competence and sociability. Half of each category contained positive words and the other half contained negative ones. Valence across emotions and competence–sociability was kept equal. In addition, two words were also included, that is, intelligence and talent (remember that intelligence was rated as the most uniquely human characteristic). Participants were asked to select about 10–12 characteristics that were most prototypical of the ingroup/outgroup. The comparisons between ingroup and outgroup were made between participants (e.g., Leyens et al., 2001) or within them (e.g., Cortes, Demoulin, Rodriguez, Rodriguez, & Leyens, 2005). The main dependent variables were the number of primary and secondary emotions chosen for the ingroup and the outgroup, and the results supported the hypothesis. More positive and negative secondary emotions were attributed to the ingroup than to the outgroup. This pattern of data was not replicated for primary emotions. Such findings have been repeated with multiple ingroups and outgroups time and again (e.g., see Delgado, 2008). Concerning the words "intelligence" and "talent", it should be noted that high-status groups rated themselves significantly superior. Low-status groups, on the other hand, afforded competence to high-status groups but rated "intelligence" and "talent", that is, uniquely human characteristics, to the same degree. Stated otherwise, although status moderated the results for competence and sociability in general, it did not impact the attribution of uniquely human emotions, or the attribution of other uniquely human features, such as intelligence and talent.

The latter link was to test the humanity of the ingroup. To this end, Boccato, Capozza, Falvo, and Durante (2008) subliminally primed Northern Italian students with a human or a monkey and subsequently gave a lexical decision task. The critical words were names from the North or the South of Italy. Participants were quicker at responding for Northern names when they had first been primed by a human face. Interestingly, there was no difference for the animal priming. In other words, the ingroup responded faster when humanity, rather than bestiality, had been evoked. In another study, the same authors primed the ingroup versus the outgroup and looked at responses linked to humanity (human face) or not (ape). The results show that the link between humanity and the ingroup is bi-directional.

These examples of studies (see also Demoulin et al., 2004b; Leyens et al., 2007) support the main hypotheses of the infra-humanization model. To address the question of status, we first focus on some of the implications of infra-humanization that have relevance for this question.

Infra-humanization and status

Infra-humanization has serious implications for harmony between groups. The more Blacks (Whites) infra-humanize White (Black) victims of the 2005 Katrina Hurricane, the less they intend to help them (Cuddy, Rock, & Norton, 2007). The more Portuguese students infra-humanize Turkey, the more opposed they are to the adhesion of Turkey to Europe (Pereira, Vala, & Leyens, 2007). The more British infra-humanize Muslims, the more they are indifferent to the ill-treatment of these people (Viki, Zimmerman, & Ballantyne, 2007; Zimmerman, Viki, Adams, Zebel, & Doosje, 2007). The more Catholics and Protestants in Northern Ireland infra-humanize the outgroup, the less willing they are to forgive (Tam, Hewstone, Cairns, Tausch, Maio, & Kenworthy (2007).

In spite of the above examples, a series of studies have shown that conflict is *not* a necessary condition for infra-humanization to occur. In other words, ingroup love and outgroup hate can occur independently of any conflicting situation between the groups. Such observation reinforces the idea that infra-humanization is independent of the societal reality where some groups stigmatize other ones.

Some researchers misinterpret infra-humanization research because they believe the phenomenon will occur in every case. In fact, the question of which outgroups will be infra-humanized is still under scrutiny. We suggest that groups are likely to infra-humanize each other when they are involved in fate or behavioral control (Kelley, 1979). Behavioral control means that the two groups are interdependent, such as when political parties have to form a coalition, or when nations want to form a social Europe. Fate control intervenes when the actions of one group (e.g., Polish proposals for the death penalty) have consequences for others (e.g., the European Union). Indeed, if there is no relation between groups, the differences probably mean nothing. Groups must be relevant for each other in order to elicit infra-humanization.

Relevance explains why French-speaking Belgians did not infra-humanize Parisians, although they did not like them; and they did not infra-humanize Praguois to whom they were indifferent (Cortes et al., 2005). Canarians did not infra-humanize Poles and Indians even though they were more favorable to the latter than to the former (Delgado, 2008). To know which groups were least or most likely to be infra-humanized, Delgado (2008) asked Spanish students to ascribe primary and secondary emotions to one of a series of countries (e.g., Germany), regions of the world (e.g., South America), and continents (e.g., Europe). Other students rated the different groups in terms of similarity, friendship, information, and status. As expected, none of these variables predicted primary emotions. By contrast, the more the countries, regions of the world, and continents were perceived as similar, the more they received secondary emotions. Importantly for our purpose, status did not predict secondary emotions.

In all the studies that have been conducted so far, status did not play a role (for a review, see Leyens et al., 2007). Dominant groups infra-humanized dominated and other dominant groups, while dominated groups infra-humanized dominant and other dominated groups. The research program that has most systematically taken components of status into account was conducted by Vaes and Paladino (2007). In a first pre-test on Northern Italian students, outgroups were selected on the basis of the Stereotype Content Model (Fiske, Cuddy, Glick, & Xu, 2002). This model distinguishes groups according to two orthogonal dimensions: competence and warmth. Three groups were chosen because they were high in competence and low in warmth. Three other groups were high in warmth and low in competence, and finally the last three groups were low in both dimensions. In a second pre-test, Northern Italian students gave auto-stereotypes of their groups and stereotypes of one of the outgroups. The same procedure (auto-stereotypes/stereotypes) was conducted for each of the outgroups because the auto-stereotypes may vary according to the comparison group. The "real" participants were asked to rate each of the stereotypes on four dimensions (balanced for order): prototypicality for the ingroup, prototypicality for the outgroup, perceived humanity, and valence. Findings show that the stereotypes' prototypicality for the ingroup (i.e., North Italy) is predicted by perceived humanity, controlling for valence. The difference of typicality between ingroup and outgroup is also predicted overall by perceived humanity, showing therefore infra-humanization. An interesting result appears for the groups low in both competence and warmth. The more characteristics are judged typical of these groups, the less human the characteristics are perceived to be (see also Harris & Fiske, 2006).

One could argue that the Stereotype Content Model considers the ingroup as having the highest status because it is high on both competence and warmth. Nevertheless, it would be difficult to consider that Northern Italians have an objectively higher status than US citizens, Japanese and Germans (the outgroups rated as high in competence and low in warmth). In other words, this research program indicates, once again, that groups infra-humanize outgroups that are higher or lower than themselves. One word of caution is necessary. Not everyone in a group necessarily infra-humanizes outgroup members. A minimum amount of ingroup identification is necessary. If people do not care at all for their group, it would be meaningless to infra-humanize. In the studies conducted so far (Demoulin et al., in press; Paladino, Vaes, Castano, Demoulin, & Leyens, 2004; Rohmann, Niedenthal, Brauer, Castano, & Leyens, 2005; Viki, 2005), high-identifiers always infra-humanized the most, whereas, depending on the situation, low-identifiers infra-humanized less or not at all.

The phenomenal experience of infra-humanization

In the first part of this chapter, we have seen that groups react or not towards one another as a function of elements exterior to them, the societal structural factors being the most important of these elements. As illustrated above, this is not the case for infra-humanization. Outgroups that are fundamentally different from the ingroup are phenomenally experienced as less human, or more animal. The system, capitalist or Marxist for instance, in which those groups exist is alien to such perception, and so is the justification of such system. Of course, the presence of a slight conflict with a given outgroup may facilitate its infra-humanization, but, to paraphrase Asch (1952), it is the outgroup that changes and not the judgment about the outgroup. To show this invariance, we have up to now only indirect evidence.

First, if infra-humanization works besides material elements contributing to the hierarchy of groups, it should not be related to realistic threat (Stephan & Stephan, 2000). To the contrary, if fundamental differences matter, it is symbolic threat, dealing with values (customs, traditions) that should be associated with infra-humanization. Two studies have measured both realistic and symbolic threats (Pereira et al., 2007; Viki et al., 2007). In both cases, there was no relation between infra-humanization and realistic threat, as expected, but, also as predicted, there was one with symbolic threat. The greater the infra-humanization, the greater the values pertaining to the outgroup were perceived as threatening. These findings consolidate the thesis that infra-humanization by dominant or dominated groups has little to do with the acceptance or rejection of one's status, with accepting or increasing self-esteem as a tool for other goals. Infra-humanization is not linked to things that people can loose or gain (money, jobs), but it is associated with customs, values, differences. Greater infra-humanization is related to greater perception of differences on value symbols.

Second, if differences are of utmost importance, they should particularly matter in the case of races considered biologically different, independently of potential prejudice linked to theses races. Williams and Eberhardt (2008) constructed a neutral questionnaire about the (social or biological) conceptions of races. It contained items as innocuous at first sight as "It's natural to notice the racial group to which people belong", or "A person's race is fixed at birth". White and Asian US students answered this questionnaire, as well as another one on racial disparities and several others on prejudice. Even when prejudice was taken into account, the more people conceived race as biological, the more they accepted racial disparities. Other studies manipulated the social and biological beliefs about race and the same results were obtained. In other words, the more one sees a group as different, the more this outgroup is regarded as inferior, independently of any prejudice towards it. The difference suffices.

Third, the context can influence the perception of infra-humanization. In a pre-test, Delgado (2008) verified that Canarian participants had no negative reaction towards India (there are many Indian shop-keepers in the Canary Islands). In another pre-test, she selected positive and negative primary and secondary emotions, and measured the degree of their morality. Valence was of course controlled. Experimental participants had to undertake a lexical decision task with subliminal priming of Indian versus Canarian. In the control condition, the task was preceded by a short movie without relevance and there was no infra-humanization. In an animal violence condition, the movie depicted cruelty among animals, and there was no infra-humanization. In the third, human violence condition, participants saw scenes of aggression between humans alien to Indians and Canarians before completing the lexical decision task. This time, there was infra-humanization of India. The more moral the uniquely human emotions were, the greater was the infra-humanization. Such results have been duplicated and show that the reactions of participants do not depend on structural factors between the groups, but on the way the outgroup is experienced by ingroup members.

Fourth, and finally, if infra-humanization is the direct phenomenal perception of outgroups, this perception should not be influenced by motivational factors and mediated by other variables. Contrary to what we have sometimes written or implied in earlier publications (Demoulin, Leyens, Rodriguez, Rodriguez, Paladino, & Fiske, 2005), we never obtained direct evidence of a motivational basis for infra-humanization. Also, a perception is a direct experience and there should thus be no mediation between group membership and infra-humanization. The perception is unmediated. In fact, we found in only one study that the source for categorizing individuals into artificial groups and infra-humanization was mediated by essentialism and ingroup identification. This mediation appeared in the particular context of minimal groups where people had to give a (essential) meaning to the situation, and actually, they infra-humanized when they could give such meaning and identified with their artificial ingroup. In no other occasion, with real groups, have we reproduced these results. Once it "exists" (and does not need to be constructed), the perception of the outgroup is a given.

Summary

Alongside the fact that groups occupy unequal positions in society, and eventually react to change the existing hierarchy, groups also position themselves in terms of fundamental differences that are irrelevant to their ranking. Group members believe their ingroup has a more human essence than (some) outgroups. This infra-humanization, which is simultaneous ingroup love and outgroup hate (Blantz, Mummendey, & Otten, 1995; Brewer, 1999) does not relate to immediate material benefits or changes in the societal structure. It influences, however, the harmony between groups. Relations may deteriorate as a function of infra-humanization.

What is fundamentally divergent with the approach exposed in the first part is the non-importance of status. Rather, infra-humanization seems to appear as the result of a direct, immediate perception of outgroups. This perception may change with the context because the context changes the groups. It is thus useless to try incorporating this perspective with the previous one. They are complementary.

Conclusions

In this chapter, we examined and discussed the reactions of dominant and dominated groups towards one other. Two perspectives were adopted. According to the most classical one, status and therefore the ranking of groups are a matter of consensus in society, but consensus does not mean status quo. Different theories propose divergent solutions about this consensus. For SJT, all groups, dominant or dominated ones, strive to maintain the status quo. Whereas this function is reasonable for dominant groups, it is less understandable for dominated groups. If the latter remain passive, it is because they have not yet developed strong legitimizing "myths" towards equality, according to SDT, contrary to dominant groups that make use of lots of legitimizing "myths" towards inequity. The conditions of recourse to these myths remain an open question for SDT. Socio-structural factors of society have been explicitly investigated by SIT to determine when people who are part of dominated entities will react as individuals or as group members. For this latter theory, therefore, dominated people react but they may adopt different strategies, individual or collective, and among the collective strategies, they still have the choice between various options going from challenging the standards of comparison, for instance, to collective action.

Our reading of the literature is that dominated people, in general, are not satisfied with their present situation. If they do not react as a group, they do it as individuals who indeed improve the general situation. These reactions have to be understood by their motives. People look for improvement in their resources and/or their general esteem. These two goals are the motor of the consensus within society. If neither of them is activated, consensus will remain as it is; if one of them or both are stimulated, perception of consensus and, ultimately, objective reality may change. What is important for the perspective adopted by the three theories is that a change in society first needs recognition of consensus. This recognition is a requisite for potential change. Some researchers, however, have confounded recognition with acceptance.

One may look at the relations between groups, dominant or dominated, from an additional and different angle that complements the previous one. Groups may relate not only on the basis of what they may gain in terms of resources of general self-esteem, but also on their perception of the others, a perception that is based on *essential* differences. People believe that groups have different essences. An essence is what makes someone what he or she is. It is thus not difference per se that matters. It is likely that many people never bothered about the notion of Islamism before September 11, but that they now make a great difference (an *essential* one) between Muslims and Christians. Here, difference has to be understood as a difference of irreconcilable values, an essence that not only distinguishes but also classifies into another category. As a matter of fact, people classify in terms of humanity and, obviously, given universal ethnocentrism, they attribute to their ingroup the full human essence. Others are less human or more animal than the ingroup.

This classification is called infra-humanization and this chapter has summarized a number of tests of various hypotheses derived from the general model. It has been shown that there are no differences in terms of status, and that conflict is unnecessary for the occurrence of infra-humanization. For instance, also, infra-humanization does not correlate with realistic (material) threat, but it does with a symbolic one (values). In this sense, the phenomenon is entirely different from the one envisaged in the first part of the chapter. Structural factors of society are alien to the reaction of infra-humanization. What matters is what is uniquely human (or what is animal); consensus about group hierarchies is silent about the humanity dimension.

This chapter did not discuss racism. This topic could have been included in the chapter because it is a typical reaction of dominant groups towards dominated ones. We did not speak about it because the subject is too vast for part of a chapter. What we would like to say in the conclusions is that infra-humanization by dominant groups towards dominated ones is not equivalent to racism even if tests of Subtle Racism (Pettigrew and Meertens, 1995) insist on – explicit – differences of values and habits. Spanish people from the Canary Islands who infra-humanize Spanish from the mainland are probably not racist towards them. French-speaking Belgians are probably not racist towards the French, and yet they infra-humanize them. It may very well be that infra-humanization and racism sometimes reach the same targets (Christians towards Arabs, for instance, or vice versa), and both will be implicit, that is, without people's awareness. However, racism is likely to be a more complex phenomenon, involving prejudice, discrimination, and sometimes stereotyping, than infra-humanization. In this sense, racism is not alien to the theories reviewed in the first part of the chapter. A more elaborate connection between infra-humanization and racism might culminate in integrating perspectives that are now presented in parallel.

References

Asch, S. E. (1952). *Social psychology*. Englewoods Cliffs, NJ: Prentice-Hall.

Bettencourt, B. A., Charlton, A., Dorr, N., & Hume, D. L. (2001). Status differences and in-group bias: A meta-analytic examination of the effects of status stability, status legitimacy, and group permeability. *Psychological Bulletin, 127*, 520–542.

Blantz, M, Mummendey, A., & Otten, S. (1995). Positive–negative asymmetry in social discrimination: The impact of stimulus valence and size and status differentials on intergroup evaluations. *British Journal of Social Psychology, 34*, 409–419.

Boccato, G., Capozza, D., Falvo, R., & Durante, F. (2008). The missing link: Ingroup, outgroup, and the human species. *Social Cognition, 26*, 224–234.

Boccato, G., Cortes, B., Demoulin, S., & Leyens, J. Ph. (2007). The automaticity of infrahumanization. *European Journal of Social Psychology, 37*, 987–999.

Brewer, M. B. (1999). The psychology of prejudice: Ingroup love or outgroup hate? *Journal of Social Issues, 55*, 429–444.

Cortes, B. P., Demoulin, S., Rodriguez, R. T., Rodriguez, A. P., & Leyens, J. Ph. (2005). Infra-humanization or familiarity? Attribution of uniquely human emotions to the self, the ingroup, and the outgroup. *Personality and Social Psychology Bulletin, 31*, 243–253.

Crocker, J., Luthanen, R., Blaine, B., & Broadnax, S. (1994). Collective self-esteem and psychological well-being among White, Black, and Asian college students. *Personality and Social Psychology Bulletin, 20*, 503–513.

Cuddy, A. J. C., Rock, M. S., & Norton, M. I. (2007). Aid in the aftermath of Hurricane Katrina: Inferences of secondary emotions and intergroup helping. *Group Processes and Intergroup Relations, 10*, 107–118.

Delgado, N. (2008). *Dependencia contextual de la infra-humanización [Contextual dependence of infrahumanization]*. Doctoral thesis, Universidad de La Laguna, Tenerife.

Demoulin, S., Cortes, B. P., Viki, T. G., Rodriguez, A. P., Rodriguez, R. T., Paladino, M. P., et al. (in press). The role of ingroup identification in infra-humanization. *International Journal of Psychology*.

Demoulin, S., Leyens, J. Ph., Paladino, M. P., Rodriguez, R. T., Rodriguez, A. P., & Dovidio, J. F. (2004a). Dimensions of "uniquely" and "non-uniquely" emotions. *Cognition and Emotion, 18*, 71–96.

Demoulin, S., Leyens, J. Ph., Rodriguez, R. T., Rodriguez, A. P., Paladino, M. P., & Fiske, S. T. (2005). Motivation to support a desired conclusion versus motivation to avoid an undesirable conclusion: The case of infra-humanization. *International Journal of Psychology, 40*, 416–428.

Demoulin, S., Rodriguez, R. T., Rodriguez, A. P., Vaes, J., Paladino, M. P., Gaunt, R., et al. (2004b). Emotional prejudice can lead to infra-humanisation. In M. Hewstone & W. Stroebe (Eds.), *European review of social psychology* (Vol. 15, pp. 259–296). Hove, UK: Psychology Press.

Dupont, E. (2004). *Facing others' prejudice: Self-protective and threatening implications*. Doctoral dissertation, Université Catholique de Louvain, Belgium.

Ellemers, N., Spears, R., & Doosje, B. (2002). Self and social identity. *Annual Review of Psychology, 53*, 161–186.

Ellemers, N., van den Heuvel, H., de Glider, D., Maass, A., & Bonvini, A. (2004). The underrepresentation of women in science: Differential commitment or the queen bee syndrome? *British Journal of Social Psychology, 43*, 315–338.

Federico, C. M., & Levin, S. (2004). Intergroup biases as a function of reflected status appraisals and support for legitimizing ideologies: Evidence from the USA and Israel. *Social Justice Research, 17*, 47–73.

Fiske, S. T., Cuddy, A. J. C., Glick, P., & Xu, J. (2002). A model of (often mixed) stereotype content: Competence and warmth respectively follow from perceived status and competition. *Journal of Personality and Social Psychology, 82*, 878–902.

Greenwald, A. G., McGhee, D. E., & Schwarz, J. L. K. (1998). Measuring individual differences in implicit cognition: The Implicit Association Test. *Journal of Personality and Social Psychology, 74*, 1464–1480.

Haney, C., Banks, C., & Zimbardo, P. G. (1973). Interpersonal dynamics in a simulated prison. *International Journal of Criminology and Penology, 1*, 69–97.

Harris, L. T., & Fiske, S. T. (2006). Dehumanizing the lowest of the low: Neuroimaging responses to extreme out-groups. *Psychological Science, 17*, 847–853.

Haslam, N. (2006). Dehumanization: An integrative review. *Personality and Social Psychology Review, 10*, 252–264.

Haslam, N., Bain, P., Douge, L., Lee, M., & Bastian, B. (2005). More human than you: Attributing humanness to self and others. *Journal of Personality and Social Psychology, 89*, 937–950.

Jahoda, G. (1999). *Images of savages: Ancient roots of modern prejudice in western culture*. Florence, KY: Taylor & Frances/Routledge.

Jost, J. T., & Banaji, M. R. (1994). The role of stereotyping in system-justification and the production of false-consciousness. *Journal of Personality and Social Psychology, 33*, 1–27.

Jost, J. T., Banaji, M. R., & Nosek, B. A. (2004). A decade of system justification theory: Accumulated evidence of conscious and unconscious bolstering of the status quo. *Political Psychology, 25*, 881–920.

Jost, J. T., & Hunyady, O. (2002). The psychology of system justification and the palliative function of ideology. In M. Hewstone & W. Stroebe (Eds.), *European Review of Social Psychology* (Vol. 13, pp. 111–153). Hove, UK: Psychology Press/Taylor & Francis.

Jost, J. T., Pelham, B. W., & Carvallo, M. R. (2002). Non-conscious forms of system justification: Implicit and behavioral preferences for higher status groups. *Journal of Experimental Social Psychology, 38*, 586–602.

Kelley, H. H. (1979). *Personal relationships*. Hillsdale, NJ: Lawrence Erlbaum Associates, Inc.

LeVine, R. A., & Campbell, D. T. (1972). *Ethnocentrism: Theories of conflict, ethnic attitudes, and group behavior*. Oxford: Wiley.

Leyens, J. Ph., Cortes, B. P., Demoulin, S., Dovidio, J., Fiske, S.T., Gaunt, R., et al.

(2003). Emotional prejudice, essentialism, and nationalism. *European Journal of Social Psychology*, *33*, 703–717.

Leyens, J. Ph., Demoulin, S., Vaes, J., Gaunt, R., & Paladino, M.P. (2007). Infra-humanization: The wall of group differences. *Journal of Social Issues and Policy Review*, *1*, 139–172.

Leyens, J. Ph., Paladino, P. M., Rodriguez, R. T., Vaes, J., Demoulin, S., Rodriguez, A. P., et al. (2000). The emotional side of prejudice: The role of secondary emotions. *Personality and Social Psychology Review*, *4*, 186–197.

Leyens, J. Ph., Rodriguez, A. P., Rodriguez, R. T., Gaunt, R., Paladino, P. M., Vaes, J., et al. (2001). Psychological essentialism and the attribution of uniquely human emotions to ingroups and outgroups. *European Journal of Social Psychology*, *31*, 395–411.

Livingston, R. W. (2002). The role of perceived negativity in the moderation of African Americans' implicit and explicit racial attitudes. *Journal of Experimental Social Psychology*, *38*, 405–413.

Luthanen, R., & Crocker, J. (1992): A collective self-esteem scale: Self-evaluation of one's identity. *Personality and Social Psychology Bulletin*, *18*, 302–318.

Mullen, B., Brown, R., & Smith, C. (1992). Ingroup bias as a function of salience, relevance, and status: An integration. *European Journal of Social Psychology*, *22*, 103–122.

Paladino, M. P., Vaes, J., Castano, E., Demoulin, S., & Leyens, J. Ph. (2004). Emotional infra-humanization in intergroup relations: The role of national identification in the attribution of secondary emotions to Italians and Germans. *Cahiers de Psychologie Cognitive/Current Psychology of Cognition*, *22*, 519–536.

Pereira, C., Vala, J., & Leyens, J. Ph. (2007). *From infra-humanization to discrimination: Mediation of symbolic threat needs egalitarian norms.* Unpublished manuscript, ISCTE, Lisbon.

Pettigrew, T. F., & Meertens, M. W. (1995). Subtle and blatant prejudice in western Europe. *European Journal of Social psychology*, *25*, 57–75.

Reicher, S. (2004). The context of social identity: Domination, resistance, and change. *Political Psychology*, *25*, 921–945.

Reicher, S., & Haslam, S. A. (2006). Rethinking the psychology of tyranny: The BBC prison study. *British Journal of Social Psychology*, *45*, 1–40.

Rohmann, A., Niedenthal, P. M., Brauer, M., Castano, E., & Leyens, J. Ph. (2005). *The attribution of primary and secondary emotions to the ingroup and to the outgroup: The case of equal status countries.* Unpublished manuscript, University of Münster, Germany.

Rothbart, M., & Taylor, M. (1992). Category labels and social reality: Do we view social categories as natural kinds? In G. Semin & F. Fiedler (Eds.), *Language, interaction and social cognition.* London: Sage.

Rubin, M., & Hewstone, M. (2004). Social identity, system justification, and social dominance: Commentary on Reicher, Jost et al., and Sidanius et al. *Political Psychology*, *25*, 823–844.

Sidanius, J., & Pratto, F. (1999). *Social dominance: An intergroup theory of social hierarchy and oppression.* New York: Cambridge University Press.

Stephan, W. S., & Stephan, C. W. (2000). An integrated threat theory of prejudice. In S. Oskamp (Ed.), *Reducing prejudice and discrimination* (pp. 23–46). Mahwah, NJ: Lawrence Erlbaum Associates, Inc.

Sumner, W. G. (1906). *Folkways.* New York: Ginn.

Tajfel, H. (1981). *Human groups and social categories*. Cambridge: Cambridge University Press.

Tam, T., Hewstone, M., Cairns, E., Tausch, N., Maio, G., & Kenworthy, J. (2007). The impact of intergroup emotions on forgiveness in Northern Ireland. *Group Processes and Intergroup Relations, 10*, 119–136.

Vaes, J., & Paladino, M. P. (2007). *The human content of stereotypes: Subtle infrahumanization versus dehumanization.* Unpublished manuscript, University of Padova, Italy.

Viki, G. T. (2005). Unpublished raw data. University of Kent, UK.

Viki, G. T., Winchester, L., Titshall, L., Chisango, T., Pina, A., & Russell, R. (2006). Beyond secondary emotions: The infrahumanization of outgroups using human-related and animal-related words. *Social Cognition, 24*, 753–775.

Viki, G. T., Zimmerman, A., & Ballantyne, N. (2007). *Dehumanization and attitudes towards the ill-treatment and social exclusion of Muslims: The mediating role of perceived symbolic threat.* Unpublished manuscript, University of Kent, UK.

Williams, M. J., & Eberhardt, J. L. (2008). Biological conceptions of race and the motivation to cross racial boundaries. *Journal of Personality and Social Psychology, 94*(6), 1033–1047.

Wright, S. C., & Lubensky, M. E. (in press). The struggle for social equality: Collective action versus prejudice reduction. In S. Demoulin, J. Ph. Leyens, & J. F. Dovidio (Eds.), *Intergroup misunderstandings: Impact of divergent social realities.* New York: Psychology Press.

Zelditch, M. Jr. (2001). Theories of legitimacy. In B. Major & J. T. Jost (Eds.), *The psychology of legitimacy: Emerging perspectives on ideology, justice, and intergroup relations.* (pp. 33–53). New York: Cambridge University Press.

Zimbardo, P. G. (2007). *The Lucifer effect: How good people turn evil.* New York: Random House.

Zimbardo, P. G. (2006). On rethinking the psychology of tyranny: The BBC prison study. *British Journal of Social Psychology, 45*, 47–53.

Zimmermann, A., Viki, G. T., Abrams, D., Zebel, S., & Doosje, B. (2007). *Reconciliation and the war on terror: Implications of dehumanization and moral responsibility.* Unpublished manuscript, University of Amsterdam, The Netherlands.

Part IV

Motivated change in intergroup relations

12   To be is to do is to be

Collective identity and action

Bernd Simon
Christian-Albrechts-University Kiel

Introduction

At first glance the title "To be is to do is to be" may seem somewhat cryptic, but I hope that, as the chapter unfolds, it will become clear that it expresses the common thread that runs through and connects the different parts of the chapter. The subtitle "Collective identity and action" also deserves a few words of explanation and specification. Just as collective identity derived from one's group membership(s) goes beyond less inclusive self-interpretation or self-definition as a unique or independent single individual, the actions dealt with in this chapter pursue goals or projects that transcend people's narrow individual interests. In other words, I examine in this chapter the relationship between collective identity derived from membership in social groups and action that serves the collective or common interest of one's ingroup.

My interest in the relationship between collective identity and action has been motivated by the conviction that an understanding of this relationship is crucial for any attempt to find an answer to the more comprehensive question of "how the social gets into, and is in turn made possible by, the individual" (Mummendey & Simon, 1997). Collective identity is an important connection between the social and the individual and, in many ways, underlies the emergence of the individual as a social actor (Simon, 2004). For one, collective identity, like all forms of identity, takes shape during social interaction among people and in turn shapes their interactions (Stryker & Statham, 1985). Moreover, groups are social entities that usually have an internal structure (e.g., status hierarchies) and are themselves part of the larger social structure of intergroup relations. Collective identity derived from such group memberships thus imports (macro-level) social structure into the immediate (meso-level) interaction situation and eventually into the individual (micro-level) psyche (Stryker, 1987). For example, minority members' collective identity influences their interactions with the dominant majority as well as their individual self-perceptions and feelings (Lücken & Simon, 2005). However, collective identity as a (meso-level) social psychological process mediates not only people's experience of social structure (top-down impact from macro to micro), but also their efforts to change or preserve social structure (bottom-up impact from micro to macro) (Pettigrew, 1996; Turner, Hogg, Oakes, Reicher, & Wetherell, 1987). For example, collective identity possesses a strong mobilizing power in the context of social and political movements (Simon & Klandermans, 2001). In sum, collective identity, on the one hand, imports the social into the individual and, on the other hand, enables him or her to join a collective project and thus to act socially.

The remainder of the chapter is divided into three main sections. In each section I present a different line of empirical research examining novel aspects of the identity–action relationship. First, I examine how and why the experience of being respected operates as a powerful antecedent of the identity–action link. Next, I demonstrate the motivational power of collective identity as a reason for, or goal of, social action. In the third section, I turn to dual identity as a more complex variant of collective identity and examine its motivational role in politicization processes. This selection of issues is not exhaustive, but illustrates, in an exemplary fashion, why "to be is to do" and "to do is to be.".

Respect, collective identity, and intragroup cooperation

As mentioned above, collective identity typically takes shape during the interaction with other people. In fact, in a fundamental sense, identity ("to be") and the consciousness of one's own being requires the recognition of or by others (Hegel, 1970; Honneth, 1994). Interest in the role of social recognition in identity and associated behavior has recently been spurred on by the thriving career of the notion of *respect* in the social psychological literature. The increasing interest in respect has in turn been inspired and informed by research on procedural justice and authority relations that demonstrated that respectful (i.e., fair, trustworthy, and dignified) treatment by authorities strengthens commitment to the organization or group that the authority represents (Tyler & Blader, 2000; Tyler & Lind, 1992; see also Wenzel, chapter 4 in this volume). Meanwhile, the initial focus on vertical respect received from authorities has been extended also to include *horizontal* respect received from one's fellows (e.g., Branscombe, Spears, Ellemers, & Doosje, 2002; De Cremer, 2002). In our own research my co-workers and I are concerned with the effects of (dis)respectful treatment by ordinary ingroup members on group life, especially on collective identification and associated intragroup cooperation. We draw on the insight, derived from self-categorization theory (Turner et al., 1987) and related approaches to social justice (Wenzel, 2004), that shared group membership induces perceived interchangeability of ingroup members, which quickly translates into perceived entitlement to unbiased, trustworthy and dignified (i.e., respectful) treatment by fellow group members. Consequently, respectful (as opposed to disrespectful) treatment by fellow group members should reinforce the recipient's relationship with his or her group – a relationship that gives the recipient access to other desirable experiences, such as a sense of self or identity, but also entails obligations to the group and its goals. In short, respectful treatment should lead to stronger collective identification and greater willingness to engage in intragroup cooperation. In addition, in keeping with the insight that identity generally functions as "a social psychological mediator between input from and output in the social world" (Simon, 2004, p. 2), collective identification should mediate the effect of intragroup respect on intragroup cooperation.

We tested these predictions in a laboratory experiment with ad hoc (work) groups (Simon & Stürmer, 2003). Respectful versus disrespectful (intragroup) treatment was manipulated as the major independent variable by way of (dis)respectful comments made allegedly by fellow group members concerning the participant's contribution to a group task. In addition, we manipulated positive versus negative performance evaluation as a second independent variable in order to separate respect effects from evaluation effects. Our main dependent variables were identification with one's group and willingness to cooperate with the group.

Respect had the expected positive effects. Respectful as opposed to disrespectful treatment increased both collective identification and (intended) intragroup cooperation, although the latter was confined to the immediate group situation and did not generalize to cooperation outside the experimental session. Evaluation did not affect these aspects of group life, nor did it qualify the respect effects. As shown in Figure 12.1, respected group members identified more strongly with their group and were more willing to cooperate than disrespected group members *irrespective of whether their performance*

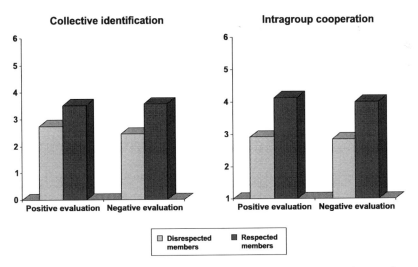

Figure 12.1 Collective identification and (intended) intragroup cooperation as a function of respect and evaluation.

Source: Simon and Stürmer, 2003, Figure 1. © The Society for Personality and Social Psychology 2003.

was positively or negatively evaluated. There was also support for the hypothesized role of collective identification as a mediating process. While collective identification at least partially mediated the *experimental* effect of respect on cooperation, a path analysis using the (manipulation check) measure of *perceived* respect as the predictor variable and the corresponding (manipulation check) measure of perceived evaluation as a control variable actually revealed a full mediation. As shown in Figure 12.2, the observed relationships suggest that the experience of being respected by fellow group members translates into identification with the entire group, which in turn fosters intragroup cooperation (for similar findings, see De Cremer, 2003).

So far it can be concluded that intragroup respect likely triggers a profitable sequence of increased collective identification and ensuing motivational gains that make action on behalf of one's group more likely (for a different view, see Sleebos, Ellemers, & de Gilder, 2006a, 2006b; for a critique of their work, see Simon, 2007). Moreover, in our experiment, intragroup respect was clearly more effective than explicit performance evaluation and it operated independently of such evaluation. Note that our social psychological distinction between intragroup respect and performance evaluation is very similar to Darwall's (1977) philosophical distinction between recognition respect and appraisal respect. Whereas evaluation or appraisal processes concerning the self traditionally have a prominent status in social psychological research (e.g., Sedikides & Strube, 1997), non-evaluative (recognition) respect is a relatively under-researched social psychological phenomenon that deserves more

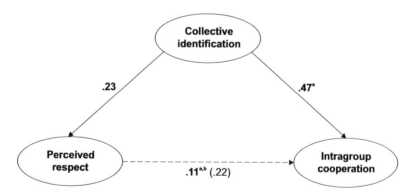

Figure 12.2 Path diagram (controlling for perceived evaluation) of the effect of perceived respect on (intended) intragroup cooperation mediated by collective identification.

Source: Simon and Stürmer, 2003, Figure 2. © The Society for Personality and Social Psychology 2003.

Notes:

Coefficients are standardized regression weights.

a Regression weights from the analysis with the mediator. The regression weight from the analysis without the mediator is given in parentheses.

b Nonsignificant regression weight. All other regression weights in the diagram are significant ($p \leq .05$).

attention. After all, our results suggest a strong link between such respect and group life so that to be respected or recognized as a group member is to identify and finally to act as a group member.

What is the active ingredient of respect?

So far, it seems safe to assume that (dis)respectful treatment is understood by the recipient as a gesture with symbolic meaning (Stryker & Statham, 1985) or, in other words, as an expressive performance (Sennett, 2003) on the part of one's fellows that conveys a specific social message concerning the self–(in)group relationship. However, while the message associated with respectful treatment obviously reinforces (or the message associated with disrespectful treatment undermines) the self–group relationship and related self-definitions and actions, it is less clear exactly what the specific content of this message is. In other words, the *active ingredient* of respect still needs to be discovered. The Simon and Stürmer (2003) experiment discussed above was a first step in that direction. We were able to demonstrate unique and robust effects of our respect manipulation *above and beyond* the influence of evaluation processes so that it is very unlikely that perceived (positive) evaluation is the active ingredient of respect. Of course, an exhaustive examination of all possible candidates for the role of active ingredient would be an unrealistic task. Still, my co-workers and I have scrutinized a number of prominent, and theoretically plausible, candidates in a series of additional laboratory experiments. In a first step, these experiments enabled us to ascertain "ex negativo" what respect or its active ingredient is *not*, but we were also able to muster "positive" evidence pointing to a very promising candidate.

We started our search of the active ingredient of (recognition) respect with perceived acceptance (Simon & Stürmer, 2005a). That is, we examined whether the effectiveness of respect could be traced back to the implicit message, possibly associated with respectful treatment, that one is accepted by, or included in, the social circle or group that extends the respectful treatment (De Cremer & Tyler, 2005). We again manipulated respect by confronting research participants with respectful or disrespectful remarks allegedly made by fellow group members. Acceptance was manipulated as a second independent variable after respect by way of contrived feedback as to whether fellow group members wished the participant to stay in the group or to leave the group. While collective identification and (intended) intragroup cooperation again served as the main dependent variables, we also measured perceived respect, perceived acceptance, and perceived liking (i.e., perceptions of being liked by one's fellow group members).

While we replicated the experimental effects of respect on collective identification and intragroup cooperation reported in Simon and Stürmer (2003), acceptance failed to qualify as the active ingredient of respect. Neither the experimental manipulation of acceptance nor the inclusion of the measure of perceived acceptance as a control variable could remove these effects. The supplementary liking measure equally failed to remove the experimental respect effects when included as a control variable, but it successfully removed an experimental acceptance effect on collective identification. Liking may thus underlie the effectiveness of acceptance, but certainly not the effectiveness of respect, which further underlines that respect and acceptance are quite different beasts, or better, quite different beauties. Finally, we secured additional evidence of the validity of the respect effects in that we could show that perceived respect actually mediated the effects of the experimental respect manipulation. Following the same logic in two other experiments (Simon & Stürmer, 2005b), we also found that neither attributions of intragroup status nor attributions of intragroup (personality-based) similarity qualify as active ingredient of respect. Obviously, the power of respect does not hinge on the implicit message that one is accepted, liked, or ascribed a high status in one's group, or that one shares a similar personality with one's fellow group members.

Now that we know better what respect or its active ingredient is *not*, it is time for some "positive" news. Our next step in the search for the active ingredient of (intragroup) respect was inspired by Richard Sennett's (2003, p. 208) suggestion that respect may function as an antidote in situations of inequality, in that respect helps humans "to reach across the boundaries of inequality." In line with prior work that suggested that respect is particularly valuable in situations in which the relationship between the self and the ingroup is strained (De Cremer, 2002), we reasoned that respect would be particularly welcome, and its effectiveness amplified, in a situation in which the recipient has only restricted rights and participation opportunities compared with fellow group members. We therefore carried out another experiment with two independent variables (Simon, Lücken, & Stürmer, 2006). First, (intragroup) equality was manipulated such that half the research participants were told that they would be withheld the right to vote in an upcoming group decision task, whereas their fellow group members would all be able to vote (restricted-rights condition). The remaining research participants learned that, whereas they personally could vote, another group member would be withheld the right to vote (full-rights condition). To avoid attributions of personal responsibility and blame, this inequality was introduced as a purely structural feature of the experimental setting. It was said to be necessary in order to avoid a stalemate in the group given the even number of people in the group, and it was allegedly implemented by a randomizing procedure. Otherwise, the procedure was basically the same as that in our previous work (Simon & Stürmer, 2003, 2005a). Respect was again manipulated by confronting research participants with respectful or disrespectful remarks allegedly made by their fellow group members, and collective identification and (intended) intragroup cooperation again served as dependent variables.

Manipulation check measures of perceived respect and perceived equality as a group member confirmed that both experimental manipulations were successful. Replicating our previous findings, we again found main effects of respect on both collective identification and intragroup cooperation. However, as expected and shown in Figure 12.3, we also found significant interaction effects such that the (simple) respect effects were stronger in the restricted-rights condition than in the full-rights condition (for a qualification concerning a measure of monetary donations to the group, see Simon et al., 2006). Viewed from a different perspective, once group members felt respected, differences in formal rights no longer mattered with regard to collective identification and intragroup cooperation. When respect was lacking, however, formal equality was an important determinant of these aspects of group life.

The finding that respect can heal the wounds of inequality suggests that respectful treatment conveys an *equality* message (i.e., the message that one is recognized as an equal). Indeed, an additional measurement of perceived equality after the respect manipulation indicated that respect was able to fully compensate for the initial deficit in self-perception caused by the structural inequality. These empirical observations are in line with the modern philosophical (Kantian) equality-based notion of respect. According to Kant (1974, p. 68), all persons deserve equal respect as a consequence of their equal possession of dignity, which further implies that people should never be treated merely as means to our own ends, but always also as ends in themselves (Kant, 1974, pp. 59–60). The convergence of social psychological research and philosophical thinking is encouraging and underpins the

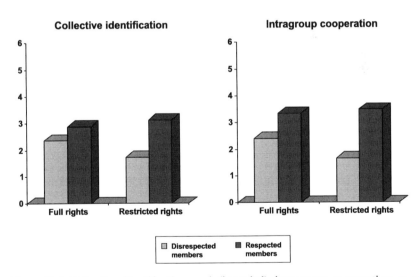

Figure 12.3 Collective identification and (intended) intragroup cooperation as a function of respect and structural (in)equality.

Source: Simon, Lücken, and Stürmer, 2006, Figures 1 and 2. © The British Psychological Society 2006.

hypothesis that (perceived) recognition of equality functions as the active ingredient of respect (for a more detailed integration of the various notions of respect, see Simon, 2007). Systematic examination of this hypothesis in future research will further deepen our understanding not only of the workings of respect, but also of the relationship between collective identity and action. For the time being, it certainly appears that to be (recognized as) an equal is to feel and to act as an equal (i.e., as a good, cooperative group member).

Affirmation of collective identity and social movement support

In the preceding section I have demonstrated that collective identity and action (or the motivation to act) on behalf of one's group are closely linked social psychological phenomena, and that intragroup respect is a potent trigger of the identity–action sequence – a trigger that operates at the meso-level of social interaction within the group. While knowing how the identity–action sequence can be set in motion in the first place is important, it is equally important to know how collective identity and action are linked to each other within this sequence or, in other words, *why* collective identity leads to action. In order to answer the latter question we need to turn to a more fine-grained analysis of the (micro-level) psychological processes mediating between collective identity and action.

Collective identity and the inner obligation to act

Evidence hinting at the motivational source of collective identity's mobilizing power comes from social movement research. More specifically, it has been argued in the social movement literature that an activist identity typically has specific implications for action embedded within it (Friedman & McAdam, 1992; Simon, 1998). Drawing on this argument, we hypothesized that the relationship between identification with a social movement and willingness to participate in pertinent social movement activities would be mediated by way of an inner obligation to behave as a "good" (i.e., active) member (Stürmer, Simon, Loewy, & Jörger, 2003). We tested this hypothesis in a questionnaire study conducted in the context of the US fat acceptance movement. Research participants were members of the National Association to Advance Fat Acceptance (NAAFA), which is an organization that fights against the oppression of fat people. As predicted, identification with NAAFA was related to willingness to participate in NAAFA's activities, and this relationship was fully mediated by way of an inner obligation to participate in such activities. In other words, with increasing collective identification, respondents felt increasingly obligated to act in terms of the mission or "raison d'être" of their organization, which in turn strengthened their willingness to act accordingly.

Collective identity as goal

We have seen that collective identification entails the obligation to act on behalf of one's ingroup or, in other words, the obligation to enact one's collective identity. Note that this obligation logically implies that the failure to act appropriately jeopardizes one's entitlement to the respective collective identity. Taking this reasoning one step further one could argue that the mobilizing power of collective identity derives at least partly from people's desire to assert or affirm their collective identity. Similar to their pursuit of individual identities (e.g., Steele, 1988; Wicklund & Gollwitzer, 1982), people may also aspire to possess a particular collective identity and may therefore engage in action that is indicative of the desired collective identity. Collective identity would then function not so much as a cause, but rather as a reason for, or goal of, one's action. That is, people may act in a particular way not only *because* they are members of a particular social group, but also *in order to* affirm their collective identity as a member of that group (or even in order to attain the particular collective identity in the first place). Thus, going to a demonstration organized by a particular social movement or donating money to that movement may serve as a means to attain or affirm the collective identity as a movement supporter.

To examine this line of reasoning we conducted a series of laboratory experiments in the context of the peace movement in Germany (Simon, Trötschel, & Dähne, 2008). Theoretically, we built on well-established insights into the psychology of goal-directed behavior in general and identity-directed behavior in particular. First, for a goal to exert a motivating force on one's behavior, the person must not completely or securely have attained the goal yet (Lewin, 1926). Second, identities are goals that are rarely, if ever, achieved completely or once and for all. Life with its changing circumstances and complex web of social interactions is a constant source of identity-relevant uncertainties, including self-doubts regarding identity possession as well as lack of identity recognition by others. Such experiences then invigorate a person's identity affirmation concerns to the extent to which he or she defines him- or herself in terms of the respective identity (Gollwitzer & Kirchhof, 1998; Lewin, 1926; Turner et al., 1987). Applied to the peace movement context, it follows that such affirmation processes should operate to the extent to which the person identifies with the peace movement (i.e., defines him- or herself as a movement supporter), but still has to deal with uncertainties as to whether he or she really possesses this identity – a state Wicklund and Gollwitzer (1982) referred to as incompleteness. Note that this reasoning also concurs with the self-verification perspective (e.g., Swann, Rentfrow, & Guinn, 2002). Although the self-verification perspective has so far been applied primarily to the analysis of identity processes in the interpersonal domain, its extension to the collective domain should produce comparable predictions. That is, in the face of identity-relevant uncertainties, people with high collective identification would be expected to be particularly motivated to verify their collective identity by performing identity-affirming behaviors (e.g., showing active social movement support).

The first experiment was a test of our basic assumption that social movement support serves an identity-affirming function. To this end we orthogonally manipulated identification with the peace movement and uncertainty of the possession of this collective identity as two independent variables. In line with self-categorization theory (Turner et al., 1987), collective identification was manipulated by instigating differentiation of self from either "a typical supporter of the peace movement" (low identification) or "a typical opponent of the peace movement" (high identification). Uncertainty of identity possession was manipulated using a forced-choice task in which participants were led to endorse statements that either did or did not raise doubts about their identity as a supporter of the peace movement. For this purpose each participant was presented with a set of four statements all of which reflected either a supportive attitude (low uncertainty) or a critical attitude toward the peace movement (high uncertainty). The participant then had to select those three statements with which "you could still agree to some extent, if at all possible, although they may not fully reflect your opinion." To further strengthen this manipulation, participants in the high-uncertainty condition were also asked to indicate whether they had participated in a particular peace demonstration that had allegedly taken place on campus in the previous year. Because, in reality, no such demonstration had taken place, research participants had to admit their non-participation in the (fictitious, but plausible) event, which added further doubt about identity possession. In the low-uncertainty condition, participants were asked to indicate whether they supported a rather uncontroversial political demand of the peace movement. As a measure of identity-affirming behavior, each participant was finally given the opportunity to support the peace movement by donating some portion of his or her payment (8 euros) as a research participant to the movement. We thus used *real* behavior as our main dependent variable. We predicted and found that, when people's collective identification was high, uncertain as opposed to certain possession of collective identity increased their donations. Also as expected, there was no effect of uncertainty of identity possession when collective identification was low and there was therefore no need for identity affirmation (see Figure 12.4).

In our second experiment we examined an implication of identity affirmation processes pertaining to the role of identity symbols. More specifically, we capitalized on the psychological phenomenon of substitution, which is an important hallmark of motivation and goal-directed behavior (Baumeister & Leary, 1995). Substitution refers to the possibility that one form of goal attainment can be replaced with another (e.g., eating bread with eating potato chips when one is hungry). Substitution can also involve symbols, especially in the social domain. Kurt Lewin (1926) alluded to the possibility that symbols can interfere with goal-directed behavior in that they encourage "unreal" attainment of the goal and thus reduce the energizing tension system (see also

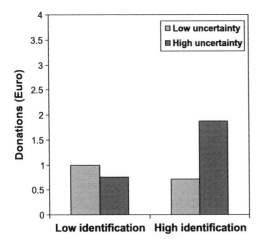

Figure 12.4 Monetary donations to the peace movement as a function of identification with the movement and uncertainty of identity possession.
Source: Simon, Trötschel, and Dähne, 2008, Figure 1. © John Wiley & Sons, Ltd. 2008.

Wicklund & Gollwitzer, 1982). Applied to the context of social movement participation, identity symbols, such as bumper stickers, badges, or pins symbolizing membership of or support for a particular movement, should reduce the psychological need to engage in personally more costly identity-affirming activities. Hence, we expected that possession of an identity symbol would serve as a substitute for, and thus undermine, more costly forms of movement support such as monetary donations, even though the latter are often more beneficial to the movement. We therefore included possession of an identity symbol as a third independent variable in our design. To this end, participants were instructed to wear either a pin showing the dove of peace (identity symbol) or a neutral pin showing a balloon (no identity symbol). The donation measure again served as the dependent variable.

The critical results can be summarized as follows. First, in line with the basic premise that identity affirmation processes require for their operation a certain level of identity strength or commitment (Gollwitzer & Kirchhof, 1998), all effects were restricted to the high-identification condition (see Figure 12.5). Second, the mobilizing effect of uncertainty of identity possession was replicated only when no identity symbol was available. Third, when an identity symbol was available, we even observed a reversed effect of uncertainty of identity possession. Participants wearing an identity symbol actually donated more money when they were certain as opposed to uncertain about their possession of the collective identity as a movement supporter. Note that the opposite effects of uncertainty of identity possession in the two different identity symbol conditions suggest that collective identity can play a role both as a *pull* factor and a *push* factor in movement

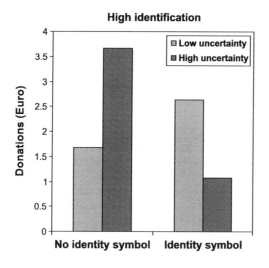

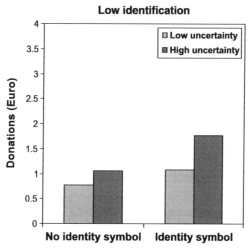

Figure 12.5 Monetary donations to the peace movement as a function of uncertainty of identity possession and possession of an identity symbol, separately for participants with high identification (upper panel) and participants with low identification (lower panel).

Source: Simon, Trötschel, and Dähne, 2008, Figure 2. © John Wiley & Sons, Ltd. 2008.

support (see the two middle bars in the upper half of Figure 12.5). From the perspective of traditional social identity or self-categorization research (Turner et al., 1987) one might expect collective-identity salience and associated self-stereotyping or conformity pressures to be particularly strong when collective identification is high, uncertainty of identity possession low, and an attention-grabbing identity symbol on one's chest. Hence, this combination likely maximized the power of collective identity as a push factor. Conversely, the combination of high collective identification, high uncertainty of identity possession, and missing identity symbol very likely maximized the power of collective identity as a pull factor.

To conclude this section, the observation that collective identity operates also as a goal that pulls people to collective action is a novel finding that complements prior work and helps to rectify the mostly tacit understanding of collective identity as primarily a push factor. Our research demonstrated that collective identity can have its origin as a pull factor in private experiences, such as self-generated doubts (Experiment 1), as well as in public experiences, such as other people's imputations (Experiment 2). In addition, a follow-up study to Experiment 2 confirmed that collective identity can exert its power as a pull factor both in public and private action contexts (Simon et al., 2008). Finally, collective-identity affirmation, especially in combination with the notion of substitution involving identity symbols, may provide an elegant explanation for the emergence of a "bumper sticker society" without enduring activism. It is indeed possible that sometimes people, especially those who are themselves not the direct victims of injustices, engage in political activism not so much because they want real (structural) social change, but mainly in order to affirm themselves. They may then fight less for the true victims of injustice and more for their own political or ideological opinions, attitudes, or identities. However, this does not imply that, in the final analysis, all political or collective action consists merely of fleeting and shallow acts of self-presentation or impression management (see Schlenker, 1980). On the contrary, a psychological mechanism like identity affirmation opens up the possibility that people not only enact identities that are thrust on them by their current living conditions (e.g., class identities and associated material interests), but also actively choose and pursue long-term identity projects that transcend those limiting conditions and thus acquire true moral depth. To act in order to be what one is not yet may very well set in motion a process of becoming what one has the potential to become but never imagined before.

Politicized collective identity and political involvement

In this section, I further examine the mobilizing role of collective identity in the context of political struggles. However, whereas in the preceding section the focus was on identity as a member or supporter of a group defined by its explicitly political mission (e.g., an activist group or a social movement), I now turn to identities associated with groups that do not necessarily have a political agenda to begin with (e.g., ethnic groups), but need to undergo a process of collective politicization first. The typical starting point of such politicization is group members' awareness of shared grievances for which they then blame some other party (e.g., a particular outgroup or "the system" in general). Collective politicization is in full bloom when group members "intentionally engage, as a mindful and self-conscious collective (or as representatives thereof), in . . . a power struggle knowing that it is the wider, more inclusive societal context in which this struggle takes place and needs to be orchestrated accordingly" (Simon & Klandermans, 2001, p. 323). This more inclusive context implies that the power struggle is not merely a bipolar conflict between ingroup and outgroup. Instead, the power struggle is usually tripolar or triangulated in that it also involves a third party (or at least an audience), such as the general public or more specific representatives thereof (e.g., the media, political parties, the government or other authorities), which the politicized group tries to force to take a stand in order to eventually enlist it as an ally for its own agenda ("You are either with us or with the bad guys!"). Note that all three parties (ingroup, outgroup, and third party) usually belong to the same superordinate or more inclusive political entity or polity (e.g., the nation-state or society at large), which brings identification with this entity into play as well. In fact, some sense of identification with the superordinate political entity seems to be a basic requirement for politicization in that it ensures that this entity is acknowledged as *one's own* political habitat or arena. More specifically, to the extent that one identifies with this entity, one should feel entitled to make political claims, because identity confers rights. Similarly, one should feel motivated to get actively involved in the political game, because it becomes one's own game, and one should feel encouraged to approach third parties as potential allies, because they can be viewed as ingroup members (at the superordinate level).

Group members thus adopt and enact a politicized collective identity (PCI) which involves a dual identity as both a member of the aggrieved (lower-level) ingroup and a member of the more inclusive (higher-level) political entity. This dual character of PCI concurs with Albert O. Hirschman's (1970) now classic analysis of exit, voice, and loyalty in firms, organizations, and states. He emphasized that loyalty to the firm, organization, or state is an important psychological prerequisite for any attempt on the part of dissatisfied customers, members, or citizens to change (voice option), rather than to escape from (exit option), the objectionable state of affairs in the firm, organization, or state. To borrow from Marxist terminology, PCI turns the aggrieved group from "a group of itself" into "a group of and for itself" in the political arena.

The general prediction derived from the above analysis is that dual identification with both the aggrieved ingroup and the larger political entity should foster political involvement among members of the aggrieved group. As a first test of this prediction Daniela Ruhs and I ran an experiment with students from various fields of study, but from the same university, as research participants. Participants' specific field of study provided the basis for the definition of the aggrieved ingroup, and the university served as the larger political entity (see Ruhs, 2008). Research participants were randomly assigned to one control and two experimental conditions. Whereas participants in the control condition underwent no identification manipulation whatsoever, participants in the two experimental conditions underwent manipulations of both the identification with their specific field of study and the identification with their university. More specifically, in the single-identity condition, identification with the specific field of study was experimentally strengthened, whereas identification with the university was experimentally weakened. In the dual-identity condition, both forms of identification were experimentally strengthened. In both experimental conditions, identification with the field of study was strengthened first. To this end participants were instructed to write down what they found particularly positive about their field of study. Identification with the university was then effected by requiring participants to write down either what they found particularly negative (single-identity condition) or what they found particularly positive (dual-identity condition) about the way in which the university had set up their particular field of study. Manipulation checks confirmed that the manipulations were successful. Subsequently, participants were informed that there were recurrent discussions in the university about changing its research and teaching priorities. This would entail a redistribution of the university's resources so that some fields of study would benefit at the expense of others. In fact, it was suggested that the participants' particular field of study could be negatively affected by this development, and they were then asked to indicate their willingness to protest against such changes. A composite index of political involvement (e.g., willingness to participate in demonstrations, willingness to complain to various university authorities) corroborated our prediction. Political involvement was significantly stronger in the dual-identity condition than in each of the two other conditions, which did not differ from each other. Identification with the aggrieved ingroup alone was obviously not sufficient to politicize group members, especially when identification with, or loyalty to, the larger political entity was missing. However, dual identification with both the aggrieved ingroup and the larger political entity seemed to foster the development and enactment of PCI as evidenced by group members' stronger willingness to engage in political action.

Collective politicization of migrants

The role of dual identification in political involvement was also confirmed in a more comprehensive field study in which we examined the politicization of Turkish (im)migrants in Germany (Simon & Ruhs, 2008). Turks are the largest migrant group of non-German descent in Germany. Since the late 1950s Germany sponsored their immigration as "guest workers" in response to labor shortages, until restrictive immigration controls were implemented and maintained in the wake of the economic crisis in the early 1970s. Owing to the understanding – widely shared both in the indigenous community and in the migrant community – that the "guests" would return to their homeland one day, official policies for integration were minimal. As a result, the about 2.6 million Turks that currently live in Germany clearly are a disadvantaged minority group relative to the German majority. Yet, for a long time, Turks in

Germany showed relatively little politicization, except for their involvement in homeland politics (e.g., De Wit & Koopmans, 2005). More recently, however, new integration policies together with a number of widely publicized debates over migration issues (e.g., the ban on headscarves in many German schools) seem to have created a climate much more conducive to politicization and the emergence of PCI among Turkish migrants. Thus, applying Simon and Klandermans's (2001) suggestion that PCI is a dual identity to this context, we expected that dual identification as both Turkish and German would predict political involvement of members of the Turkish minority in Germany.

To test the hypothesized role of dual identification, we collected data from an opportunity sample of 333 Turkish migrants in Germany using a paper-and-pencil as well as a web-based, electronic questionnaire that included several measures of collective identification and political involvement. Concerning collective identification, we measured identification with Turks, identification with Germany, dual identification as both Turkish and German, separatist identification as Turkish as opposed to German, and religious identification (mostly as Muslim). Concerning political involvement, we measured political claims making (e.g., demanding better education and training for Turkish youth in Germany), tendencies to involve society at large or representatives thereof (e.g., politicians or the media), and willingness to engage in political activity (e.g., participation in demonstrations, distribution of flyers). Because preliminary analyses yielded very similar results across measures, we combined the three measures into a single political involvement index for the main analysis. In addition, we measured a number of socio-demographic variables (gender, age, level of education, citizenship, and membership in a labor union) as well as political activity in the past. A multiple regression analysis with the identification measures as possible predictors, political involvement as the criterion, and the additional measurements as statistical control variables confirmed that dual identification was a significant and positive predictor of political involvement, as was separatist identification. Identification with Turks, identification with Germany, and religious identification had no (unique) predictive value. It is noteworthy that we simultaneously also included the statistical interaction of identification with Turks and identification with Germany as a possible predictor in the regression analysis. However, this alternative and arguably more mechanistic proxy of dual identification had no predictive value, quite unlike our more *direct* measurement of the psychological experience of dual identity (e.g., "I feel I belong to both the Turks and the Germans").

Given the cross-sectional nature of the above analysis, it was admittedly somewhat premature to speak of dual identification as a "predictor" of political involvement. Fortunately, 66 of the original respondents volunteered to complete a second questionnaire at least 6 months later thus enabling us also to conduct longitudinal analyses. More specifically, for this subgroup, we performed multiple regression analyses with all identification variables measured at Time 1 as possible predictors and political involvement reported at Time 2 (i.e., political involvement between the two points of measurement) as criterion. Socio-demographic variables and past political activity again served as statistical controls. None of the identification variables, including the interaction of identification with Turks and identification with Germany, predicted involvement in classical political action or "big politics" (e.g., participation in demonstrations or contact with members of the state or national parliament). However, for involvement in low-key political activities, such as involvement in neighborhood projects or exchange of migration-related political information with family and friends, dual identification was a significant and positive predictor. The other identification variables again had no predictive value. Moreover, the relationship between dual identification and Time 2 political involvement was fully mediated by Time 1 political involvement.

Together with the experimental results reported earlier, these cross-sectional and longitudinal findings converge to suggest a causal role of dual identification in political involvement. While this clearly supports the assumption that politicized collective identity is often a dual identity (Simon & Klandermans, 2001), there was also some indication (in the cross-sectional data) that separatist identification may play a politicizing role as well. However, lacking the pacifying effect of identification with the superordinate political or social entity (Gaertner & Dovidio, 2000), it stands to reason that politicization driven by separatist identification would tend to be more socially disruptive and prone to radicalization and violent escalation than politicization driven by dual identification. In fact, as long as dual identification ensures that politicization takes place within the superordinate normative frame or consensus, which in turn prescribes the rules of the political game including the spectrum of acceptable means and ends, politicization driven by dual identification should actually foster the social integration of political actors into the superordinate political entity. But make no mistake, such integration is no automatic or guaranteed outcome. It requires positive responsiveness on the part of the superordinate political entity or larger social system. Otherwise a growing sense of frustration or betrayal likely undermines dual identification and may initiate a shift to separatist identification which, in the long run, could result in radicalization and even violent action (Simon & Oakes, 2006, p. 128).

Conclusion

Having reached the end of the chapter, it is hoped that the title "To be is to do is to be" has become more intelligible as a summary statement of the relationship between identity and action. It was my objective to deepen our understanding of this relationship with particular emphasis on the collective realm. First, I demonstrated that to be respected or recognized as an equal by one's ingroup strengthens one's identification with that collective ("to be") which in turn increases one's willingness to act ("to do") as a good group member. I focused on the role of respect to exemplify the importance of meso-level variables and because of the novelty of social psychological research on respect, which is not to deny the potency of other (micro-, meso-, or macro-level) variables to initiate similar identity–action sequences. Second, I demonstrated that identity ("to be") functions not only as a cause of, but also as a reason for, or goal of, action ("to do in order to be"). Finally, I examined the relationship between "to be" and "to do" in the context of collective politicization. Again, identity – or more precisely a more complex combination or hybrid of sub- and superordinate collective identities – turned out to be an important causal antecedent of action. But the relevant action (i.e., political involvement) was also undertaken in order "to be", namely in order to be(come) an equal or respected member of the super-ordinate social entity (i.e., one's country of residence), thus completing the social psychological *identity–action–identity* cycle.

Acknowledgment

The research reported in this chapter was made possible by grants from the Deutsche Forschungsgemeinschaft.

References

Baumeister, R. F., & Leary, M. R. (1995). The need to belong: Desire for interpersonal attachments as a fundamental human motivation. *Psychological Bulletin, 117,* 497–529.

Branscombe, N. R., Spears, R., Ellemers, N., & Doosje, B. (2002). Intragroup and intergroup evaluation effects on group behavior. *Personality and Social Psychology Bulletin, 28,* 744–753.

Darwall, S. L. (1977). Two kinds of respect. *Ethics, 88,* 36–49.

De Cremer, D. (2002). Respect and cooperation in social dilemmas: The importance of feeling included. *Personality and Social Psychology Bulletin, 28,* 1335–1341.

De Cremer, D. (2003). Noneconomic motives predicting cooperation in public good dilemmas: The effect of received respect on contributions. *Social Justice Research, 16,* 367–377.

De Cremer, D., & Tyler, T. R. (2005). Am I respected or not? Inclusion and reputation as issues in group membership. *Social Justice Research, 18,* 121–153.

De Wit, T. D., & Koopmans, R. (2005). The integration of ethnic minorities into political culture: The Netherlands, Germany and Great Britain compared. *Acta Politica, 40,* 50–73.

Friedman, D., & McAdam, D. (1992). Collective identity and activism: Networks, choices, and the life of a social movement. In A. D. Morris & C. M. Mueller (Eds.), *Frontiers in social movement theory* (pp. 156–173). New Haven, CT: Yale University Press.

Gaertner, S. L., & Dovidio, J. F. (2000). *Reducing intergroup bias. The common ingroup identity model.* Philadelphia: Psychology Press.

Gollwitzer, P. M., & Kirchhof, O. (1998). The willful pursuit of identity. In

J. Heckhausen & C. S. Dweck (Eds.), *Motivation and self-regulation across the life span* (pp. 389–423). New York: Cambridge University Press.

Hegel, G. W. F. (1970). *Phänomenologie des Geistes [The phenomenology of spirit].* Frankfurt aM: Ullstein.

Hirschman, A. O. (1970). *Exit, voice and loyalty: Response to decline in firms, organizations, and states.* Cambridge, MA: Harvard University Press.

Honneth, A. (1994). *Kampf um Anerkennung [Struggle for recognition].* Frankfurt aM: Suhrkamp.

Kant, I. (1974). *Kritik der praktischen Vernunft [Critique of practical reason].* Frankfurt aM: Suhrkamp.

Lewin, K. (1926). Vorsatz, Wille und Bedürfnis [Intention, will, and need]. *Psychologische Forschung, 7,* 330–385.

Lücken, M., & Simon, B. (2005). Cognitive and affective experiences of minority and majority members: The role of group size, status, and power. *Journal of Experimental Social Psychology, 41,* 396–413.

Mummendey, A., & Simon, B. (Eds.). (1997). *Identität und Verschiedenheit: Zur Sozialpsychologie der Identität in komplexen Gesellschaften [Identity and diversity: The social psychology of identity in complex societies].* Göttingen: Verlag Hans Huber.

Pettigrew, T. F. (1996). *How to think like a social scientist.* New York: HarperCollins.

Ruhs, D. (2008). *Duale Identität: Konsequenzen und Antezedenzien im Kontext gesellschaftlicher Partizipation [Dual identity: Consequences and antecedents in the context of societal participation].* Unpublished doctoral dissertation, University of Kiel, Germany.

Schlenker, B. (1980). *Impression management: The self-concept, social identity, and interpersonal relations.* Monterey, CA: Brooks/Cole.

Sedikides, C., & Strube, M. J. (1997). Self-evaluation: To thine own self be good, to thine own self be sure, to thine own self be true, and to thine own self be better. In M. P. Zanna (Ed.), *Advances in experimental social psychology* (Vol. 29, pp. 209–269). New York: Academic Press.

Sennett, R. (2003). *Respect: The formation of character in a world of inequality.* Harmondsworth, UK: Penguin.

Simon, B. (1998). Individuals, groups, and social change: On the relationship between individual and collective self-interpretations and collective action. In C. Sedikides, J. Schopler, & C. Insko (Eds.), *Intergroup cognition and intergroup behavior* (pp. 257–282). Mahwah, NJ: Lawrence Erlbaum Associates, Inc.

Simon, B. (2004). *Identity in modern society.* Oxford: Blackwell.

Simon, B. (2007). Respect, equality, and power: A social psychological perspective. *Gruppendynamik und Organisationsberatung – Zeitschrift für angewandte Sozialpsychologie, 38,* 309–326.

Simon, B., & Klandermans, B. (2001). Politicized collective identity. A social psychological analysis. *American Psychologist, 56,* 319–331.

Simon, B., Lücken M., & Stürmer, S. (2006). The added value of respect: Reaching across inequality. *British Journal of Social Psychology, 45,* 535–546.

Simon, B., & Oakes, P. (2006). Beyond dependence: An identity approach to social power and domination. *Human Relations, 59,* 105–139.

Simon, B., & Ruhs, D. (2008). Identity and politicization among Turkish migrants in Germany: The role of dual identification. *Journal of Personality and Social Psychology, 95,* 1354–1366.

Simon, B., & Stürmer, S. (2003). Respect for group members: Intragroup determinants of collective identification and group-serving behavior. *Personality and Social Psychology Bulletin, 29,* 183–193.

Simon, B., & Stürmer, S. (2005a). In search of the active ingredients of respect: A closer look at the role of acceptance. *European Journal of Social Psychology, 35,* 809–818.

Simon, B., & Stürmer, S. (2005b). On the effectiveness of respect: Conditions and ingredients. Paper presented at the 14th General Meeting of the European Association of Experimental Social Psychology, Würzburg, Germany.

Simon, B., Trötschel, R., & Dähne, D. (2008). Identity affirmation and social movement support. *European Journal of Social Psychology, 38*(6), 935–946.

Sleebos, E., Ellemers, N., & de Gilder, D. (2006a). The carrot and the stick: Affective commitment and acceptance anxiety as motives for discretionary group efforts by respected and disrespected group members. *Personality and Social Psychology Bulletin, 32,* 244–255.

Sleebos, E., Ellemers, N., & de Gilder, D. (2006b). The paradox of the disrespected: Disrespected group members' engagement in group-serving efforts. *Journal of Experimental Social Psychology, 32,* 244–255.

Steele, C. M. (1988). The psychology of self-affirmation: Sustaining the integrity of the self. In L. Berkowitz (Ed.), *Advances in experimental social psychology* (Vol. 21, pp. 261–302). New York: Academic Press.

Stryker, S. (1987). Identity theory: Developments and extensions. In K. Yardley & T. Honess (Eds.), *Self and identity: Psychosocial perspectives* (pp. 89–103). New York: Wiley.

Stryker, S., & Statham, A. (1985). Symbolic interactionism and role theory. In G. Lindzey & E. Aronson (Eds.), *Handbook of social psychology* (3rd ed., pp. 311–378). New York: Random House.

Stürmer, S., Simon, B., Loewy, M., & Jörger, H. (2003). The dual-pathway model of social movement participation: The case of the fat acceptance movement. *Social Psychology Quarterly, 66,* 71–82.

Swann, W. B. Jr, Rentfrow, P. J., & Guinn, J. (2002). Self-verification: The search for coherence. In M. Leary & J. Tagney (Eds.), *Handbook of self and identity* (pp. 367–383). New York: Guilford.

Turner, J. C., Hogg, M. A., Oakes, P. J., Reicher, S. D., & Wetherell, M. S. (1987). *Rediscovering the social group. A self-categorization theory.* Oxford: Basil Blackwell.

Tyler, T. R., & Blader, S. L. (2000). *Cooperation in groups: Procedural justice, social identity, and behavioral engagement.* Philadelphia: Psychology Press/Taylor & Francis.

Tyler, T. R., & Lind, E. A. (1992). A relational model of authority in groups. In M. Zanna (Ed.), *Advances in experimental social psychology* (Vol. 25, pp. 115–191). New York: Academic Press.

Wenzel, M. (2004). A social categorization approach to distributive justice. In W. Stroebe & M. Hewstone (Eds.), *European review of social psychology* (Vol. 15, pp. 219–257). Hove, UK: Psychology Press.

Wicklund, R. A., & Gollwitzer, P. M. (1982). *Symbolic self-completion.* Hillsdale, NJ: Lawrence Erlbaum Associates, Inc.

13 Change in intergroup relations

Psychological processes accompanying, determining, and determined by social change

Thomas Kessler
University of Exeter

Nicole Syringa Harth
University of Jena

Imagine a person living her entire life in one country. After some time of increasing dissatisfaction of a majority of the people in this country, the economic, social, and political structure changes rather dramatically: The government of the country decides to merge with another country, which has been the wealthy neighbor for a long time. Facing this change, the person may experience joy, enthusiasm, and hope, because of the new opportunities. She may also experience insecurity, anxiety and threat, because of the uncertainty and the risk of becoming marginalized in her own country. Such a scenario happened during the unification of Germany in the late 1980s. After 40 years of separation, the two German countries merged into a new country. In the beginning, positive attitudes and expectations predominated throughout Germany. However, after the first enthusiasm, intergroup conflict between both groups (East Germans vs. West Germans) emerged. On the one side, many West Germans complained about the high costs of the unification, on the other side, many East Germans felt inferior and stigmatized by the West Germans. Thus, apart from the importance of this event for the people involved, German unification has been an excellent opportunity to test social psychological theories in the field as well as their applicability to social change. Amélie Mummendey and her colleagues – including the first author of this chapter – perceived this situation as a windfall for the scientific study of social change and worked on a large research grant examining change in intergroup relations in Germany.

Social change is a pervasive and fundamental characteristic of social life. It relates to large scale changes in social, political, and economic structures. Think of, for example, mergers of schools, organizations, or even states. Think of internationalization, with its increasing dispersal of social networks, contacts between people from various countries, traditions, and religions, as well as economic expansion of companies, and organizations. However, social change also relates to smaller scale issues, such as couples starting families, children starting school, or partners moving to a different country for better job opportunities. Generally, social change poses a fundamental challenge to all individuals involved, because they have to adapt repeatedly to new situations. This may be because of individual change (e.g., growth, development, aging) or environmental changes (e.g., globalization, war, migration). Environmental change affects individuals, but, conversely, they also actively act on and change their environment. We will argue that this bi-directionality precludes a simple linear sequence of response and adaptation to social change and the individual circumstances (Tajfel, 1972a). Taking this into account, social change poses one of the fundamental challenges to social sciences. Henri Tajfel once suggested that "ideally the central issue of social psychology should be the study of psychological processes accompanying, determining, and determined by social change" (Tajfel, 1972b, p. 4).

In this chapter, we first detail some aspects of social change. Then, we follow Tajfel's (1972b) logical distinction of psychological aspects of social change: First, we focus on psychological processes determined by social change. Here, we review research that demonstrates how change in status relations is experienced. In the following section, we report on psychological processes that either hinder or foster change, thereby focusing on coping strategies and behavior that aim at managing one's social position in relation to other groups. Finally, by referring to psychological processes accompanying social change, we call for a more dynamic understanding and investigation of social change. We conclude with some implications of the present view on social change.

Social change

Social change is a core issue that social sciences try to explain and understand. One might be interested in the explanation and description of broader societal change as sociology is, or one might focus on the content and meaning of evolving culture as historians and anthropologists do (Richerson & Boyd, 2005). Moreover, one might develop theories about social change in general, ranging from theories describing change as directed toward a certain goal, or equilibrium state, to evolutionary theories assuming change to be guided by chance and some general principles. However, as social psychologists, we focus on social change from a *psychological perspective*. This implies that we consider the broader social context, but take the individual as the unit of analysis. In particular, we focus on an individual's experiences, decisions, and behavior as influenced and shaped by the social context. In addition, we also focus on how the individual influences, or at least attempts to influence, the social environment.

The term "social change" has been used in a variety of ways. Here, we refer to social change as the *change in the relative position* of individuals and groups within a common society. Social change often includes changes in status relations through the emergence of new identities, and the negotiation and management of existing identities. The relative nature of change implies social comparisons between individuals or groups (Festinger, 1954; Tajfel, 1978). Typically, social change involves two groups, with additional groups as observers. Thus we have to consider several perspectives: For instance, how do people perceive and react to lower status in contrast to higher status? Depending on how this status relation is perceived, group members may see different opportunities to act, or even no necessity to do anything. Higher and lower status groups may actively resist or promote social change. Usually, higher status groups tend to resist change in order to maintain their status, whereas lower status groups tend to promote social change to gain some status advantage. However, we also observe different situations: At times, higher status group members seem to feel uncomfortable with their status, and lower status group members seem to perceive their status as acceptable. Hence, the challenge is to explain how group members differ in their status perception as well as in their actions taken in order to foster or prohibit social change.

Processes determined by social change

In this section we focus on processes that are determined by social change in status relations and the perception of relative status as a temporary product of change (as manipulated in experiments or assessed in survey studies). In particular, we detail how change in relative status is subjectively experienced, who the subject of this experience could be, and how lower and higher status are appraised.

Perception of status differences

When people experience some unexpected and negative change, they engage in an elaborate analysis of their situation (Klauer & Migulla, 1995). Such an analysis involves a complex sequence of appraisal and reappraisal processes triggering affective and emotional reactions as well as counterfactual and ruminative thoughts (Watkins, 2008). The importance of focusing on appraisal processes in contrast to objective reality has been promoted in early work on relative deprivation (Stouffer, Suchman, DeVinney, Star, & Williams, 1949) and in early emotion theories (Arnold, 1960; Sartre, 1939/1964). Generally, quantifiable differences in quality of life or economic conditions do not perfectly correspond to perceived life satisfaction and the perception of advantages and disadvantages (Taylor, 1998). In contrast, people with high income may complain about their economic opportunities, whereas others may be satisfied with much lower incomes. This illustrates that the perception of disadvantage does not mirror objective conditions, but arises from the discrepancy between what one thinks one deserves and what one actually has (see also Wenzel, chapter 4 in this volume). Work on relative deprivation tried to identify the necessary and sufficient conditions of the experience of relative disadvantage (Crosby, 1976; Gurr, 1970; Runciman, 1966). In her comprehensive review of studies, Crosby (1982) concluded that relative deprivation arises out of "frustrated wants and violated entitlements." In consequence, whether one's current status is perceived as an advantage or a disadvantage depends on the comparison between status quo and perceived entitlements.

Changes in status relations are often accompanied by strong emotions. Thus, Cook, Crosby, and Hennigan (1977) distinguished between the *perception* of disadvantage that is the cognitive component of relative deprivation and the *feeling* of disadvantage that is the emotional component of relative deprivation. The emotions people experience are determined by the appraisal of relative status and ongoing change (Smith, Cronin, & Kessler, 2008; Smith & Kessler, 2004). At this point relative deprivation theory allies with emotion theories assuming that the appraisal of a certain event on various appraisal dimensions determines the specific emotions (e.g., Frijda, Kuipers, & ter Schure, 1989; Roseman, Spindel, & Jose, 1990; see also chapter 8 by Yzerbyt & Kuppens in this volume). Noteworthy is the fact that researchers focused on the experience of status inequalities mainly from the perspective of disadvantaged groups: While the knowledge about the perception and emotions of relative deprivation grew, only a few scholars studied the perception and feelings associated with relative advantage. We return to this point later. First, we deal with perceiving and experiencing disadvantage.

Subject of perceived (dis)advantage

Already in 1966, Runciman proposed the important conceptual distinction between being relatively deprived because of (a) personal characteristics or (b) characteristics that one shares with other individuals. Individual or egoistic deprivation refers to comparisons between one's own conditions and those of other individuals, whereas collective or fraternal deprivation refers to being deprived on the group level (i.e., my group in relation to other groups). This distinction foreshadows the distinction between personal identity and social identity that was developed within social identity theory (SIT, Tajfel & Turner, 1979). Thus, whenever individuals perceive themselves as members of a social group their psychological frame of reference changes. When group membership is salient, they focus on their ingroup in relation to other groups. In contrast, when personal identity is salient, individuals locate themselves in relation to other individuals.

Personal identity refers to interpersonal comparisons, whereas social identity refers to intergroup comparisons. This difference also applies to perceived social discrimination and disadvantage, such as the person–group discrepancy of social discrimination (PGD; e.g., Crosby, 1982; Postmes, Young, Branscombe, & Spears, 1999). The PGD denotes the frequently found effect that members of lower status groups report less disadvantage or social discrimination against themselves individually compared to their group. For instance, East Germans perceive being less disadvantaged individually than

East Germans as a group. Kessler, Mummendey, and Leisse (2000) assumed that the assessment of personal disadvantage differs from a group-based assessment of disadvantage because they refer to different comparison contexts and, therefore, rely on different sets of comparison outcomes. In a survey study on perceived disadvantage in East Germany, Kessler et al. (2000) examined this hypothesis. In support of their reasoning, they showed that predominantly individual comparison outcomes (such as compared to their best friend) predict individual disadvantage, whereas intergroup comparison outcomes predominantly predict perceived collective disadvantages (such as compared to West Germans). Moreover, the results of this study demonstrate that the perception and evaluation of social change and status differences is dependent on whether one conceives of oneself as an individual or a group member.

Group-based perception of intergroup inequality: Integrating relative deprivation and social identity theory

Group members appraise the relative status of their ingroup by social comparisons with relevant outgroups (Tajfel & Turner, 1979). The comparison dimensions have to be important enough (relative to other possible comparison dimensions) to confer a value differentiation (either more positive or more negative) between the ingroup and the outgroup. However, group members further appraise given status information by assessing the permeability of group boundaries, and the stability and legitimacy of the status relation.

With regard to these dimensions, SIT shows some important parallels to the referent cognition theory (RCT; Folger, 1986, 1987; Olson & Roese, 2002), which is an influential theory of relative deprivation (RD). Both theories share, as a common theoretical basis, the assumption that a given situation is evaluated by comparing it to cognitive alternatives (see also Kahneman & Miller, 1986). In intergroup relations, the relative status of an ingroup is evaluated by simulating the legitimacy (*should* the status position change) and stability (*could* the status position change) of the status position (e.g., Turner & Brown, 1978). SIT adds to these features the assessment of permeability of group boundaries from the perspective of the individual (*could* the group membership be changed). According to RCT, three different aspects are evaluated by generating cognitive alternatives: First, *current status* is assessed by thinking about and generating alternatives to the current status position. If most of the generated alternatives are better than the current status then it will be evaluated as an unfavorable or low status. In contrast, if most of the generated alternatives are worse, the current status will be evaluated as favorable and high. Second, the *procedures* leading to the current situation are evaluated in a similar vein, triggering a judgment of legitimacy. Third, *future developments* or *future trends* are also evaluated by the simulation of alternatives, thereby the stability of the current situation is assessed and extrapolated to future trajectories. Taken together, RCT and SIT focus on similar appraisal dimensions for the evaluation of the group's position (stability and legitimacy). SIT adds the importance of perceived permeability of group boundaries, and relative deprivation adds the perceived alternatives to the current status position.

Central to both theories is the aspect of social identification for the experience of social inequality and related intergroup behavior. However, the two theories assume different mediating processes between these variables. Fundamental to SIT is ingroup identification that mediates the influence of the perceived situation on intergroup behavior (Kessler, Mummendey, & Waldzus, 2003). According to relative deprivation, the feeling of being disadvantaged, such as anger, resentment, or outrage is the important mediator (Smith & Ortiz, 2002). Again, the context of German reunification provided a good setting to test the integration of both theories (Mummendey, Kessler, Klink, & Mielke, 1999). First of all, both East Germans and West Germans consensually defined East Germans as the group with inferior status, which caused a particular strong feeling of being disadvantaged in the East German participants. Here, the inclusion of all appraisal dimensions (i.e., current status, stability and legitimacy, and permeability of group boundaries) improved the prediction of the emotions (e.g., anger and resentment). These emotions predicted the preference of collective intergroup behavior (i.e., social and realistic competition, see below). Moreover, the influence of ingroup identification on collective intergroup behavior was mediated by the feelings of disadvantage. Thus, the feeling of collective disadvantage was identified as a mediator of the association between the perception of intergroup relations and ingroup identification, thereby revealing that integrating SIT and RCT improves the prediction of intergroup behavior in response to changes in status relations. Clearly, these findings are important for our discussion of social change. The more the East Germans identified with their group, the more resentment they experienced about their situation, and, as a consequence, they were more willing to fight for future jobs, investments, and so forth in East Germany. We go more into detail on intergroup behavior as the result of perceived status relations after we introduce the perception of favorable status relations.

Perception of favorable status relations

Because of the abovementioned predominant focus on low status groups' perception, the perspective of the high status group is less well developed. How do people perceive their group's advantage in comparison to another group? Given that advantaged groups generally have more resources, such as power, access to the media, and so forth, their importance for social change should not be underestimated. In human history, there are numerous examples where advantaged groups posed either a barrier to change (e.g., prohibition of voting rights for women), or where members of advantaged groups advocated the social change attempts of the disadvantaged group (e.g., men who demanded and campaigned for women's rights). For example, in Germany quite recently many heterosexual people supported the request of homosexual couples for legal authentication of their partnership. There is good reason to assume that the way members perceive their group's better position will affect how they feel and what they would like to do about inequality.

Leach, Snider, and Iyer (2002) developed a conceptual model of the appraisals of and reactions to relative advantage. In line with current emotion research, they describe different ways in which relative advantage can be experienced, and argue that specific patterns of appraisals of intergroup inequality elicit specific emotions. The appraisals that they suggest to be important in this context are focus of comparison (ingroup vs. outgroup focus), perceived security (legitimacy and stability of advantage), and perceived control.

In a series of experiments, Harth and colleagues (Harth, Kessler, & Leach, 2008) examined the impact of two of these appraisals, focus and legitimacy, on group-based emotions such as pride, guilt, sympathy, and pity. In all studies, social inequality between social groups was made salient. To manipulate focus of comparison, participants were led to believe either that their ingroup was advantaged relative to an outgroup, or that the outgroup was disadvantaged relative to their ingroup. Moreover, the legitimacy of the status relation was manipulated by providing reasons for either legitimate or illegitimate status advantage versus disadvantage. In two studies, psychology students (ingroup) were told they had unequal job opportunities compared to social pedagogy students (outgroup), and in other studies, local students (ingroup) were said to have unequal access to facilities compared with immigrant adolescents (outgroup).

The results of these experiments showed that in the conditions with an ingroup focus, the perception of a legitimate higher status leads to more intense feelings of pride, and the perception of an illegitimate higher status leads to feelings of guilt. In the conditions with an outgroup focus, a more legitimate perception of status inferiority enhances pity, whereas the perception of an illegitimate status inferiority of the outgroup leads to feeling of sympathy. Important findings concerning social inequality and social change are that these emotions motivated different behavioral tendencies: Using various measures, participants showed most ingroup favoritism under ingroup focus and legitimate status superiority (pride), whereas they showed the lowest bias with outgroup focus and illegitimate status superiority (sympathy). Moreover, the experience of pride (but not guilt) and sympathy (but not pity) mediated the effect of the intergroup appraisal on ingroup-favoring behavioral tendencies: pride enhanced ingroup favoritism, whereas sympathy reduced it. Thus, even though the members of the high status group recognized their advantage, this did not necessarily lead to the support of equality. Only group-based sympathy stimulated support of the disadvantaged group and willingness to challenge inequality. Even though there was no clear-cut distinction between pity and sympathy on the semantic level,[1] these two emotions triggered different behavioral tendencies. While both apparently include a feeling of sorrow for other persons, feelings of sympathy triggered outgroup support, whereas feelings of pity motivated the advantaged to vote against sharing resources with the disadvantaged.

These studies indicate that higher status is not unequivocally associated with positive emotions. In addition, other studies showed that higher status is often connected with feelings of guilt (Doosje et al., 1998), and shame (Brown, Gonzalez, Zagefka, Manzi, & Cehajic, 2008; see also Brown, chapter 10 in this volume), or anger (Leach, Iyer, & Pedersen, 2007). Thus, higher ingroup status leads to various emotions (ranging from pride about the ingroup to sympathy toward the outgroup), which motivate a diversity of intergroup behavior.

To summarize, the experience of social change and status differences is not fully determined by objective circumstances. Rather, people add internal standards (e.g., entitlements) to assess whether they feel relatively advantaged or disadvantaged. Moreover, the subject of this experience could be either the individual or the group, depending on whether individual or social identity is salient. Although developed somewhat independently, different intergroup theories (i.e., SIT and RD) focus on similar intergroup appraisals (stability and legitimacy), and complement each other by referring to additional intergroup appraisals (e.g., SIT considers the permeability of group boundaries and RD emphasizes current status) to explain the experience of social change. Furthermore, the influence of identification on collective strategies is mediated by group-based emotions (e.g., anger and resentment). Thus, it is a beneficial development to integrate these theories in order to get a more comprehensive picture of status appraisal. The perception and experience of social change and, more generally, social structure lead to various intergroup behaviors implemented to change the intergroup relation.

Processes determining social change

After appraising social change and their ingroup's status relation, group members actively try to promote or to prevent further social change. As intergroup behavior is assumed to be functional in this respect, we review literature demonstrating the effects of these strategies. Broadly, SIT and RD focus on individual and collective strategies. For instance, individual and collective relative deprivation does not only have different antecedents, such as inter-individual and intergroup comparison outcomes, respectively, but also different consequences. In a meta-analysis, Smith and Ortiz (2002) showed that perceived collective disadvantage is positively related to *collective action*. In fact, RD was developed to explain people's engagement in public protest, social unrest, and rebellion (Gurr, 1970). In contrast, individual relative deprivation is not clearly related to intergroup behavior; more typical outcomes of individual relative deprivation are stress and health problems (Smith & Ortiz, 2002). However, one may speculate whether individuals who perceive their situation as unexpectedly negative may associate with a certain group in order to cope with this negative situation, to gain knowledge about the fate of other people, to connect with them, and to find norms about how to react to this situation (Hogg & Abrams, 1993).

Competitive strategies are the most obvious and intuitive factors fostering social change. We may distinguish between at least two forms of competition. *Social competition* refers to attempts to gain and demonstrate relative superiority on valued comparison dimensions. Thus, group members try to maximize the difference between their ingroup and a relevant outgroup. With social competition, group members establish ingroup distinctiveness, evaluative superiority, and ingroup reputation. In contrast to social competition, *realistic competition* refers to the attempts to gain tangible resources for the ingroup. Successful realistic competition would maximize the resources for the ingroup and would enhance the assertiveness of the ingroup, leading to a simultaneous disadvantage of the outgroup only in the case of negative interdependence between both groups. According to social identity theory, group members tend to prefer competitive strategies when they perceive the status relation as instable and illegitimate.

Sometimes, however, group members may acknowledge that outgroup superiority is stable and legitimate. Under such conditions, people tend to become socially creative (Tajfel & Turner, 1979): They are inclined to rearrange the frame of intergroup comparisons in order to gain a more favorable impression of their group. Typical creative strategies are the choice of alternative comparison groups, comparison dimensions, or the re-evaluation of comparison dimensions. A third category of identity management strategies suggested by Tajfel and Turner (1979) is individual mobility. When group members start to differentiate themselves from their group they may attempt to become a member of a more attractive group. Individual mobility and the associated ideology of social mobility (e.g., "a dishwasher can become a millionaire") tend to stabilize the relations (e.g., status differences) between the groups (Wright, Taylor, & Moghaddam, 1990). Thus, the ideology of social mobility can be seen as a strategic invention of higher status groups in order to defend their status superiority and to undermine collective attempts to change the status relation by status inferior groups.

These identity management strategies are assumed to be effective in that they change either the objective situation or its interpretation. So far, there are only very few empirical tests of their effectiveness. For example, the work of Schmitt and Maes (2002) provides a nice illustration of the "effectiveness" of prejudice, as one form of social competition. They assessed longitudinally the feeling of being disadvantaged of the East German participants, their prejudice against West Germans, and mental health indicators, such as emotional well-being, stress, and depression. The results revealed that East Germans, who perceived themselves as disadvantaged but reported being less prejudiced against West Germans, showed more health problems than East Germans who reported being more prejudiced. This indicates that prejudice can serve as a buffer against the negative effects of being disadvantaged. Similarly, in their studies on the rejection–identification model, Branscombe, Schmitt, and Harvey (1999) showed that perceived discrimination against an ingroup (a kind of negative comparison outcome) has a negative impact on well-being and health if the group members do not simultaneously increase their identification, which buffers against these negative effects of being discriminated against. How exactly the enhanced ingroup identification acts as a buffer is an open question. Enhanced identification may indicate more social support of the ingroup, or it may be an indicator for the application of identity management strategies (e.g., intergroup differentiation, see Jetten, Branscombe, Schmitt, & Spears, 2001).

The work of Reicher and Haslam (2006) showed how strong ingroup identification can empower lower status groups to subsequently implement changes in the social structure. They established a simulated prison with guards as the higher status group and the prisoners as the lower status group. In a well-planned sequence of events, they first established permeable group boundaries that prevented the prisoners from developing a common identity. After closing the group boundaries and introducing a person who initiated thinking about alternative social structures (alternatives to the current situation, instability and illegitimacy), the prisoners developed a strong identity that led them to resist the regime of the guards and finally enabled them to change the situation. In contrast, the guards did not develop a strong sense of identity and were therefore not very powerful in defending their situation. In fact, both subjective reports and physiological measures (i.e., enhanced cortisol level) revealed that the guards were more stressed than the prisoners (Haslam & Reicher, 2006). To our knowledge, this is the only study that clearly demonstrates the effectiveness of identity management strategies as a means to change the social system.

Changing the level of categorization may also be seen as a potentially effective way to cope with negative ingroup status. For instance, in the reunification process of East Germany and West Germany, individuals could self-categorize at various levels: as an individual, as East or West German, as German, or as a foreigner living in Germany. Basically, the categorization into an ingroup and an outgroup denotes potential intergroup conflict. Thus, the distinction between East Germans and West Germans implies potential conflict between these groups, whereas the distinction between Germans and foreigners living in Germany implies another potential intergroup conflict. Moreover, these two levels of categorization are closely related. According to the common ingroup identity model (CIIM; Gaertner, Dovidio, Anastasio, Bachman, & Rust, 1993), the re-categorization of two conflicting subgroups into a common ingroup reduces the conflict between these two subgroups (see also Wright, chapter 14 in this volume). Thus, East Germans (or West Germans) perceiving themselves as Germans may also perceive less conflict between the subgroups (East Germans and West Germans). Hence, the common ingroup (Germans) may have two different effects: On the one hand, it may reduce the conflict between the subgroups, and on the other hand, it may foster the conflict between the common ingroup and a new outgroup (i.e., foreigners). Kessler and Mummendey (2001) showed empirically that with each of the two levels of categorization, a specific intergroup conflict is associated. The stronger the categorization as East German (or West German) was, the stronger the conflict between these two groups was perceived to be. In addition, a stronger categorization as "German" leads to more xenophobia. Moreover, in line with the CIIM, individuals perceiving themselves as German tended to show less conflict at the subgroup level (i.e., between East Germans and West Germans).

From the social psychological perspective, this is not surprising. The impact of perceived relative deprivation on conflict between the inclusive category and a new outgroup could be explained as an intergroup version of triggered displaced aggression (Pedersen, Gonzales, & Miller, 2000). According to this approach, an initial provocation leads to the perception of a harmless trigger as additional provocation that instigates aggressive behavior. In the present context, the perception of collective disadvantage might be seen as the initial provocation and the presence of a salient outgroup as the triggering event. The presence of a new outgroup is perceived as an additional provocation in particular by individuals perceiving strong collective disadvantages. Hence, these conditions may lead to the observed endorsement of xenophobic attitudes.

This effect of the nested self-categorizations (ingroup/outgroup within a common ingroup related to a common outgroup) on the reduction and shift of intergroup conflict has also been replicated with adolescents in East Germany (Kessler, Noack, & Gniewosz, 2008b). Adolescents rated their identification as East German, German, and European. Moreover, they were asked to evaluate East and West Germans as well as Germans and Poles. The results revealed that each level of self-categorization is associated with specific bias: The categorization as East German enhanced bias against West Germans, and the self-categorization as German enhanced the bias against Poles. In addition, a common ingroup categorization reduced the conflict between the included groups (e.g., a self-categorization as German reduces the conflict between East and West Germans and a categorization as European reduces the conflict between Germans and Poles).

To summarize, we introduced social and realistic competition, social creativity and individual mobility as behavior in intergroup contexts. This behavior is assumed to be effective in producing or preventing social change. There is no systematic study of the effectiveness of intergroup behavior. However, examples show the effectiveness on psychological wellbeing and self esteem. Only a few studies focus directly on the change in the social system (e.g., Haslam & Reicher, 2006).

Social change as a dynamic phenomenon

One central aspect in the explanation of intergroup behavior is the time perspective. In theories of intergroup behavior these dynamics tend to be neglected (Kessler & Mummendey, 2002). For instance, it is often unclear whether we think of a clear sequence of processes or whether we assume bidirectional influences between the variables. In this section, we focus on psychological processes that accompany and reflect social change but may also develop their own dynamic.

While carefully reading this chapter, one might have come to the conclusion that social identity theory and the relative deprivation approach suggest a sequence of processes (see Kessler & Mummendey, 2002): First, the current ingroup status is evaluated by social comparison and simulation of alternatives based on the dimensions of relative status, stability and legitimacy of the status relation, and permeability of group boundaries. Both theories further predict that this evaluation of the intergroup relation shapes ingroup identification and triggers group-based emotions. Together, these variables are assumed to determine the preference of intergroup behavior such as identity management strategies. As also mentioned above, the influence of the evaluation of the intergroup relation on identity management strategies is mediated (at least partially) by ingroup identification and group-based emotions. The identity management strategies are assumed to be effective, that is, they actually change the intergroup relation (e.g., by social competition), change the individual's position in an intergroup relation (e.g., by social mobility), or change the perception of intergroup relation (e.g., by social creativity). This leads to a new appraisal of the intergroup relation that – if relative disadvantage is still perceived – will trigger again certain identity management strategies, and so on. Thus, a clear sequence of processes is expected to determine intergroup behavior and social change.

The hypothesis of sequential processes has been examined in a 4-year longitudinal study with a time lag of 1 year between each measurement (Kessler & Mummendey, 2002). At each measurement point, the results showed basically the same relation between intergroup appraisal, identification and resentment, and intergroup behavior. Moreover, all variables showed substantial stability over time (up to 60% of the variance) with only minor and unsystematic fluctuations at each time point. Finally, the predicted relations between the variables were a result of the stable part of each variable. Taken together, these findings indicate that the sequential ordering of variables in "dependent" and "independent" variables seems arbitrary. Rather, the patterns are more consistent with a bidirectional causality between the variables. Thus, the psychological processes accompanying social change are more complex than a simple linear sequence of processes.

In a recent study concerning Germans' perception of immigrants living in Germany, we found further evidence for the suggested bidirectional causal relations between intergroup appraisals (e.g., perceiving the ingroup as more typical for the whole society than the outgroup), emotional reactions (i.e., resentment and anxiety), prejudice, and social and realistic competition (Kessler et al., 2008a). Finally, we also found evidence for the bidirectional nature of the relation between group-based emotions and identification. According to Gordijn and her colleagues (Gordijn, Wigboldus, & Yzerbyt, 2001; Yzerbyt, Dumont, Wigboldus, & Gordijn, 2003), self-categorization and identification as a group member are important preconditions for the experience of group-based emotions. In addition, more recent studies provided evidence that group-based emotions also influence identification (Kessler & Hollbach, 2005). This finding is consistent with the assumption of a dynamic belief system, which allows for mutual influences between the variables (e.g., Smith, 1982). Such a belief system tends toward consistency. This interpretation fits nicely with alternative dynamics suggested in the research area of emotions. Recent versions of appraisal theories of emotion assume that appraisals, emotion, and the related action tendencies are a dynamical system (Frijda & Zeelenberg, 2001; Lewis, 1996, 2005; Thagard & Nerb, 2002). This dynamic view of emotions suggests that classical appraisal theories conflate two different meanings of appraisal: On the one hand appraisal denotes the triggering events of emotions, and on the other hand appraisal denotes the cognitive content of emotions. The cognitive content of emotions is what is typically examined in studies on the appraisal theories of emotions (Frijda et al., 1989; Roseman et al., 1990), whereas the triggering events are less well understood. The triggering events could be simple events or aspects of an event that stimulate an appraisal and reappraisal process that leads to specific feelings as well as categorizations of experience as a specific emotion. However, the appraisal process itself is influenced by the feelings and the categorization of experience as a distinct emotion. As argued above, this whole process tends toward consistency or emotional "Gestalts" (Thagard & Nerb, 2002). Thus, the development of an emotion consists also in some form of pattern completion in which missing information is added.

This interpretation of intergroup appraisals as a belief system tending toward consistency resonates with intergroup image theory (Alexander, Brewer, & Herrmann, 1999): Intergroup images reflect the structural conditions of intergroup relations, and the emotional (e.g., threat) and behavioral orientations (e.g., attack) of an ingroup toward the outgroup. Moreover, group stereotypes are often not simply lists of attributes, but they reflect the intergroup relations, such as cultural compatibility, goal relations, and status differentials (see Alexander, Brewer, & Livingston, 2005). Image theorists distinguished several generic images of intergroup relations (e.g., enemy, ally, imperialist, dependent, barbarian image). These images are triggered by simple cues and, once triggered, they tend toward consistency and missing information is filled in by the perceivers. According to image theory, the different images are discrete. Thus, it would be interesting to examine whether intergroup perception varies continuously, or whether certain combinations of intergroup appraisals are more stable and therefore more typical.

Indeed, the question must be asked, which variables are the triggers of such a dynamic representation? A very plausible candidate is the perception of negative relative ingroup status because this is likely to assign a clear value differentiation between groups. However, if one perceives an increasing number of people endorsing the possibility of collective action, then this could also trigger the complete representation of being (feeling) collectively disadvantaged. Thus, the triggering event could also be perceived behavior. The current view suggests that various factors may trigger such a belief system. Yet, clearly more research is needed to provide comprehensive answers.

Applying a dynamical model of social change to the context of East Germany means that the feeling of being collectively disadvantaged consists in the evaluation of the relative ingroup status of East Germans toward West Germans, as well as its appraisal as negative and illegitimate. Moreover, this cognitive evaluation is associated with identification as East German and will also elicit emotions such as resentment about the adverse status position of East Germans relative to West Germans and (collective) action tendencies (such as public protest against the West Germans' superiority). Moreover, if one piece of information is not given, we assume that people will fill it in. Thus, the feeling of being disadvantaged as an East German influences and will be influenced by the perceived intergroup situation (e.g., stability and legitimacy of the status relation between East and West Germans), by identification as East German, and by collective action tendencies.

This interpretation of the dynamic within the representation of intergroup relations may also explain how individual representations of intergroup relations can be transformed into socially shared beliefs. The feedback loops within the belief system maintain the representation of disadvantage long enough that by communication the shared attention of people can focus on the same aspects of an event. This will lead to shared interpretations of an intergroup relation triggering similar emotional reactions of group members (Haidt, 2001). According to Klandermans (1996; Simon & Klandermans, 2001; see also Simon, chapter 12 in this volume), such a socially shared belief system of being disadvantaged is part of a collective action frame, which is one of the first steps in the mobilization of people in social movements that aim at social change.

To summarize, the processes accompanying social change show a dynamic that is consistent with a belief system in which each part is reciprocally related to the other parts. Such reciprocal causality has been shown between several variables. We want to emphasize that a sequential modeling of group processes is not an incorrect, but probably an incomplete, description of the ongoing processes in which both causal directions have to be considered. Because of the reciprocal relations of their components, these belief systems do not only reflect social change but also partly develop their own dynamic (e.g., tendency toward consistency). Finally, such belief systems may be an important factor contributing to the development of a shared perception of an intergroup relation (e.g., in order to mobilize group members for collective action).

Conclusions

Our aim in this chapter was to review and examine several aspects of social change, but also to call for a more dynamic understanding of the processes involved. In doing so, our main focus was on collective disadvantage. First, it has been shown that individual and collective disadvantage are different because both refer to different referents (e.g., individual versus group status), and are therefore based on different sets of comparison outcomes. Moreover, individual and collective perceptions of status differentials (e.g., disadvantages) have different consequences. Intergroup behavior in response to collective disadvantage, particularly collective action, is determined by the perception of collective relative deprivation. Collective relative deprivation triggers strong feelings of anger, resentment, or outrage (Smith & Kessler, 2004). These feelings of being disadvantaged are strong determinants of intergroup conflict even when the outgroup is not the direct cause of the perceived disadvantage (Kessler & Mummendey, 2001). Thus, it is not surprising that despite the positive expectation in the beginning, German reunification was also accompanied by negative aspects. However, we believe that as the change in the relation between East Germans and West Germans progresses the conflict between both groups may recede.

Moreover, assessing the dynamic in the representation of inequality, the presented results showed that no clear evidence could be found for a linear sequence of processes. In contrast, the results are more consistent with the assumption of a mutual and reciprocal influence between the variables (Kessler & Mummendey, 2002). This dynamical relation could also be found in the relation between ingroup identification and group-based emotions.

Taken together, these studies reveal insight into two aspects of intergroup behavior. On the one hand, the difference between personal and social identity explains the difference in the determinants and consequences of individual and collective relative deprivation. Moreover, self-categorization determines the subject of perceived deprivation and motivational inclinations to change the status quo. In addition, self-categorization determines who is the target of collective action (i.e., the outgroup) and who may benefit from motivated intergroup behavior (i.e., the ingroup). On the other hand, some motivating factors have been revealed. Group-based emotions, such as anger about being collectively disadvantaged, instigate collective behavior.

Finally, we argued that the assumption of sequential psychological processes should not be maintained. Such a sequence might be appropriate at first glance, because most theories try to explain intergroup behavior. However, despite its practical importance (i.e., behavior as dependent variable), it does not necessarily reveal the underlying psychological processes.

At least the present results indicate that the relations between "evaluation of intergroup relation", "identification", "emotions" and "behavioral preferences" are reciprocal and dynamical. We think that this specific dynamic of processes accompanying social changes leads also to the conclusion that whenever one wants to change such representations, one may have to take into account the self-stabilizing or conservative nature of such a system. However, any intervention may start at various ends by indicating a different view, alternative behavioral options, or variations in the levels of self-categorization in order to produce social change.

Note

1 The lack of clear differentiation between pity and sympathy reflects the fact that most people have difficulties in seeing a clear difference between these two emotion words (in particular with the German language "Mitleid" vs. "Mitgefühl"). However, the distinction becomes intuitively clear when one imagines what one would like another person to feel about oneself: Would you like to be the target of pity ("Mitleid") or sympathy ("Mitgefühl")?

References

Alexander, M. G., Brewer, M. B., & Herrmann, R. K. (1999). Images and affect: A functional analysis of out-group stereotypes. *Journal of Personality and Social Psychology, 77*, 78–93.

Alexander, M. G., Brewer, M. B., & Livingston, R. (2005). Putting stereotype content in context: Image theory and interethnic stereotypes. *Personality and Social Psychology Bulletin, 31*, 781–794.

Arnold, M. B. (1960). *Emotions and personality: Vol. 1. Psychological aspects.* New York: Columbia University Press.

Branscombe, N. R., Schmitt, M. T., & Harvey, R. D. (1999). Perceiving pervasive discrimination among African Americans: Implications for group identification and well-being. *Journal of Personality and Social Psychology, 77*, 135–149.

Brown, R., Gonzalez, R., Zagefka, H., Manzi, J., & Cehajic, S. (2008). Nuestra culpa: Collective guilt and shame as predictors of reparation for historical wrongdoing. *Journal of Personality and Social Psychology, 94*, 75–90.

Cook, T. D., Crosby, F., & Hennigan, K. M. (1977). The construct validity of relative deprivation. In J. Sulls & R. Miller (Eds.), *Social comparison processes: Theoretical and empirical perspectives* (pp. 307–333). Washington, DC: Hemisphere.

Crosby, F. (1976). A model of egoistical relative deprivation. *Psychological Review, 83*, 85–113.

Crosby, F. (1982). *Relative deprivation and working women.* New York: Oxford University Press.

Doosje, B., Branscombe, N. R., Spears, R., & Manstead, A. S. R. (1998). Guilt by association: When one's group has a negative history. *Journal of Personality and Social Psychology, 75*, 872–886.

Festinger, L. (1954). A theory of social comparison processes. *Human Relations, 7*, 117–140.

Folger, R. (1986). A referent cognition theory of relative deprivation. In J. M. Olson,

C. P. Herman, & M. P. Zanna (Eds.), *Relative deprivation and social comparison: The Ontario Symposium* (Vol. 4, pp. 33–55). Hillsdale, NJ: Lawrence Erlbaum Associates, Inc.

Folger, R. (1987). Reformulating the preconditions of resentment: A referent cognition model. In J. C. Masters & W. P. Smith (Eds.), *Social comparison, social justice, and relative deprivation* (pp. 183–215). London: Lawrence Erlbaum Associates Ltd.

Frijda, N. H., Kuipers, P., & ter Schure, L. (1989). Relation between emotions, appraisals and emotional action readiness. *Journal of Personality and Social Psychology, 57*, 212–228.

Frijda, N. H., & Zeelenberg, M. (2001). Appraisal: What is the dependent? In K. R. Scherer, A. Schorr, & T. Johnstone (Eds.), *Appraisal processes in emotion: Theory, methods, research* (pp. 141–157). New York: Oxford University Press.

Gaertner, S. L., Dovidio, J. F., Anastasio, P. A., Bachman, B. A., & Rust, M. C. (1993). The common ingroup identity model: Recategorization and the reduction of ingroup bias. In W. Stroebe & M. Hewstone (Eds.), *European review of social psychology* (Vol. 4, pp. 1–26). London: Wiley.

Gordijn, E. H., Wigboldus, D., & Yzerbyt, V. (2001). Emotional consequences of categorizing victims of negative outgroup behavior as ingroup or outgroup. *Group Processes and Intergroup Relations, 4*, 317–326.

Gurr, T. R. (1970). *Why men rebel*. Princeton, NJ: Princeton University Press.

Haidt, J. (2001). The emotional dog and its rational tail: A social intuitionist approach to moral judgment. *Psychological Review, 108*, 814–834.

Harth, N. S., Kessler, T., & Leach, C. W. (2008). Advantaged groups' emotional reactions to intergroup inequality: The dynamics of pride, guilt, and sympathy. *Personality and Social Psychology Bulletin, 34*, 115–129.

Haslam, S. A., & Reicher, S. (2006). Stressing the group: Social identity and the unfolding dynamics of responses to stress. *Journal of Applied Psychology, 91*, 1037–1052.

Hogg, M. A., & Abrams, D. (1993). Towards a single-process uncertainty-reduction model of social motivation in groups. In M. A. Hogg & D. Abrams (Eds.), *Group motivation. Social psychological perspectives* (pp. 173–190). New York: Harvester Wheatsheaf.

Jetten, J., Branscombe, N. R., Schmitt, M. T., & Spears, R. (2001). Rebels with a cause: Group identification as a response to perceived discrimination from the mainstream. *Personality and Social Psychological Bulletin, 27*, 1204–1213.

Kahneman, D., & Miller, D. T. (1986). Norm theory: Comparing reality to its alternatives. *Psychological Review, 93*, 136–153.

Kessler, T., & Hollbach, S. (2005). Group based emotion as determinants of ingroup identification. *Journal of Experimental Social Psychology, 41*, 677–685.

Kessler, T., & Mummendey, A. (2001). Is there any scapegoat around? Determinants of intergroup conflict at different categorization levels. *Journal of Personality and Social Psychology, 81*, 1090–1102.

Kessler, T., & Mummendey, A. (2002). Sequential or parallel processes? A longitudinal field study concerning determinants of identity management strategies. *Journal of Personality and Social Psychology, 82*, 75–88.

Kessler, T., Mummendey, A., Funke, F., Binder, J., Brown, R., Zagefka, H., et al. (2008a). *We all live in Germany but . . . Ingroup projection, group based emotions and prejudice against immigrants*. Unpublished manuscript, University of Jena, Germany.

Kessler, T., Mummendey, A., & Leisse, U.-K. (2000). The personal–group discrepancy: Is there a common information basis of personal and group judgment? *Journal of Personality and Social Psychology, 79*, 95–109.

Kessler, T., Mummendey, A., & Waldzus, S. (2003). Facets of social identity: Differential preconditions and implications of membership, valence, and commitment. Unpublished manuscript, University of Jena, Germany.

Kessler, T., Noack, P., & Gniewosz, B. (2008b). Common ingroup or common reference frame? An investigation of these two functions of a superordinate category. Unpublished manuscript, University of Exeter.

Klandermans, B. (1996). *The social psychology of protest.* Cambridge, MA: Blackwell Publishers.

Klauer, K. C., & Migulla, G. (1995). Spontanes kontrafaktisches Denken [Spontaneous counterfactual processing]. *Zeitschrift für Sozialpsychologie, 26,* 34–45.

Leach, C. W., Iyer, A., & Pedersen, A. (2007). Angry opposition to government redress: When the structurally advantaged perceive themselves as relatively deprived. *British Journal of Social Psychology, 46,* 191–204.

Leach, C. W., Snider, N., & Iyer, A. (2002). "Poisoning the consciences of the fortunate": The experience of relative advantage and support for social equality. In I. Walker & H.J. Smith (Eds.), *Relative deprivation: Specification, development, and integration* (pp. 136–163). Cambridge: Cambridge University Press.

Lewis, M. D. (1996). Self-organising cognitive appraisals. *Cognition and Emotion, 10,* 1–25.

Lewis, M. D. (2005). Bridging emotion theory and neurobiology through dynamic systems modelling. *Behavioral and Brain Sciences, 28,* 169–245.

Mummendey, A., Kessler, T., Klink, A., & Mielke, R. (1999). Strategies to cope with negative social identity: Predictions by social identity theory and relative deprivation theory. *Journal of Personality and Social Psychology, 76,* 229–245.

Olson, J. M., & Roese, N. J. (2002). Relative deprivation and counterfactual thinking. In I. Walker & H. J. Smith (Eds.), *Relative deprivation. Specification, development, and integration* (pp. 265–286). Cambridge: Cambridge University Press.

Pedersen, W. C., Gonzales, C., & Miller, N. (2000). The moderating effect of trivial triggering provocation on displaced aggression. *Journal of Personality and Social Psychology, 78,* 913–927.

Postmes, T., Young, H., Branscombe, N. R., & Spears, R. (1999). Personal and group motivational determinants of perceived discrimination and privilege discrepancies. *Journal of Personality and Social Psychology, 76,* 320–338.

Reicher, S., & Haslam, S. A. (2006). Rethinking the psychology of tyranny: The BBC prison study. *British Journal of Social Psychology, 45,* 1–40.

Richerson, P., & Boyd, R. (2005). *Not by our genes alone. How culture transformed human evolution.* Chicago: University of Chicago Press.

Roseman, I. J., Spindel, M. S., & Jose, P. E. (1990). Appraisal of emotion-eliciting events: Testing a theory of discrete emotions. *Journal of Personality and Social Psychology, 59,* 899–915.

Runciman, W. G. (1966). Relative deprivation and social justice: A study of attitudes to social inequality in twentieth-century England. Berkeley, CA: University of California Press.

Sartre, J. P. (1964). Skizze einer Theorie der Emotionen [The emotions: A sketch of a theory]. In J. P. Sartre, *Die Transzendenz des Ego, Philosophische Essays 1931–1939.* Hamburg: Rowohlt Verlag. (Original work published 1939.)

Schmitt, M., & Maes, J. (2002). Stereotypic ingroup bias as self-defense against relative deprivation: Evidence from a longitudinal study of the German unification process. *European Journal of Social Psychology, 32*, 309–326.

Simon, B., & Klandermans, B. (2001). Politicized collective identity: A social psychological analysis. *American Psychologist, 56*, 319–331.

Smith, E. R. (1982). Beliefs, attributions, and evaluations: Nonhierarchical models of mediation in social cognition. *Journal of Personality and Social Psychology, 43*, 248–259.

Smith, H. J., Cronin, T., & Kessler, T. (2008). Anger, fear, or sadness: Faculty members' emotional reactions to collective pay disadvantage. *Political Psychology, 29*, 221–246.

Smith, H. J., & Kessler, T. (2004). Group based emotions and intergroup behavior: The case of relative deprivation. In L. Z. Tiedens & C. W. Leach (Eds.), *The social life of emotions* (pp. 292–313). Cambridge: Cambridge University Press.

Smith, H. J., & Ortiz, D. J. (2002). Is it just me? The different consequences of personal and group relative deprivation. In I. Walker & H. J. Smith (Eds.), *Relative deprivation. Specification, development, and integration* (pp. 91–118). Cambridge: Cambridge University Press.

Stouffer, S. A., Suchman, E. A., DeVinney, L. C., Star, S. A. & Williams, R. M. (1949). *The American soldier: Adjustment to army life* (Vol. 1). Princeton, NJ: Princeton University Press.

Tajfel, H. (1972a). Experiments in a vacuum. In J. Israel & H. Tajfel (Eds.), *The context of social psychology* (pp. 69–119). London: Academic Press.

Tajfel, H. (1972b). Introduction. In J. Israel & H. Tajfel (Eds.), *The context of social psychology* (pp. 1–13). London: Academic Press.

Tajfel, H. (1978). Interindividual behaviour and intergroup behaviour. In H. Tajfel (Ed.), *Differentiation between social groups: Studies in the social psychology of intergroup relations* (pp. 27–60). New York: Academic Press.

Tajfel, H., & Turner, J. C. (1979). An integrative theory of intergroup conflict. In W. G. Austin & S. Worchel (Eds.), *The social psychology of intergroup relations* (pp. 33–47). Monterey, CA: Brooks/Cole.

Taylor, S. E. (1998). The social being in social psychology. In D. T. Gilbert, S. T. Fiske, & G. Lindzey (Eds.), *The handbook of social psychology* (4th ed., Vol. 2, pp. 58–95). New York: McGraw-Hill.

Thagard, P., & Nerb, J. (2002). Emotional gestalts: Appraisal, change, and the dynamics of affect. *Personality and Social Psychology Review, 6*, 274–282.

Turner, J. C., & Brown, R. (1978). Social status, cognitive alternatives and intergroup relations. In H. Tajfel (Ed.), *Differentiation between social groups. Studies in the social psychology of intergroup relations* (pp. 201–234). London: Academic Press.

Watkins, E. R. (2008). Constructive and unconstructive repetitive thought. *Psychological Bulletin, 134*, 163–206.

Wright, S. C., Taylor, D. M., & Moghaddam, F. M. (1990). Responding to membership in a disadvantaged group: From acceptance to collective protest. *Journal of Personality and Social Psychology, 58*, 994–1003.

Yzerbyt, V. Y., Dumont, M., Wigboldus, D., & Gordijn, E. (2003). I feel for us: The impact of categorization and identification on emotions and action tendencies. *British Journal of Social Psychology, 42*, 533–549.

14 Cross-group contact effects

Stephen C. Wright
Simon Fraser University

More than 60 years ago, Williams (1947) introduced the *Intergroup Contact Hypothesis*. Several years later, Allport (1954) elaborated this idea in what would become one of the most enduring models in the social psychological study of intergroup relations. The basic premise is quite simple: *Interaction/ contact between members of different groups, under a prescribed set of conditions, can lead to a reduction in prejudice towards the other group.* This hypothesis has inspired hundreds of studies, in dozens of countries, with many different groups. Despite variations in the findings and lively controversies, an extensive meta-analysis (Pettigrew & Tropp, 2006) shows that Allport was, for the most part, correct. Cross-group contact, more often than not, leads to better attitudes towards the outgroup members with whom one interacts, and, importantly, can lead to better general attitudes about the outgroup as a whole. So impressive has been the influence of this hypothesis, that most reviews of the literature (e.g., Brewer & Brown, 1998; Wright & Taylor, 2003) echo James Jones's (1997, p. 324) view that in social psychology, "The principal theoretical, empirical, and applied approach to reducing prejudice is the idea of intergroup contact proposed by G. W. Allport (1954)."

Importantly, Allport's model pointed out that whether contact increases or decreases prejudice depends heavily on how the contact situation is structured. He proposed four essential conditions: (1) members of the two groups must hold equal status during the interaction; (2) they must cooperate (3) to achieve a shared goal; and (4) the interaction should receive support from local authorities and/or norms. For 40 years, most research sought to clarify, elaborate, and test these and other conditions thought to produce optimal contact. In addition, the model influenced several valuable intervention programs (e.g., Aronson, Blaney, Stephan, Sikes, & Snapp's, 1978, influential *Jigsaw Classroom* technique drew directly on Allport's theorizing; see also Jonas, chapter 15 in this volume).

However, this emphasis on optimal conditions produced an ever-growing list. By the mid-1980s both Pettigrew (1986) and Stephan (1987) lamented that the number of necessary contact conditions was so large it threatened to completely undermine the hypothesis. Moreover, the focus on necessary conditions resulted in much less attention on the psychological processes that might explain attitude change during contact. There were lots of data and theorizing about *when* contact would (and would not) reduce prejudice, but less about *why*. This "why"-question has been at the heart of the resurgent interest in contact over the last 15 years.

Optimal cross-group contact: It's all about friends

One solution to the unwieldy list of essential conditions may be to focus on cross-group *friendship*. In an influential review, Pettigrew (1998) described data from a large international survey showing that having cross-group friends predicted lower prejudice, greater support for pro-outgroup policies, and even less prejudice towards other unrelated outgroups. Much smaller effects emerged when someone had outgroup co-workers or neighbors, but not friends. The idea that friendships might be important had been raised by others. Chein, Cook, and Harding (1948) described "friendly feelings" as important 50 years earlier. Amir (1976) described the value of "intimate" contact, Cook (1984) emphasized "acquaintance potential", and Herek and Capitanio (1996) demonstrated the strong positive impact of friendships on heterosexuals' attitudes towards gays and lesbians. However, Pettigrew's integration of friendship with other advances in contact theory was valuable, and subsequent studies continue to demonstrate the particular effectiveness of cross-group friendship (e.g., Brown & Hewstone, 2005; Paolini, Hewstone, Cairns, & Voci, 2004; Turner, Hewstone, & Voci, 2007; Wright, Brody, & Aron, 2005).

My colleagues and I (e.g., Wright et al., 2005) have taken this analysis even further. While Pettigrew concluded that friendship should be added as a fifth essential condition, we propose that none of the many proposed conditions for optimal contact (including Allport's) should be considered *essential*. Rather, all can be seen as *facilitators* of friendship development, and friendship formation provides the unifying framework for organizing these conditions. Rather than debating which are "necessary," all are potential facilitators of feelings of interpersonal closeness, and interpersonal closeness is the primary mechanism that accounts for contact's positive effects.

We sought initial support for this claim by comparing the antecedents of friendships described in the interpersonal relations literature to the list of optimal contact conditions. Although a lengthy one-to-one comparison is not possible here (see Wright et al., 2005), the consistency between the two literatures is glaringly obvious when one compares the framework provided by Bev Fehr (1996) in a review of the known antecedence to friendship, to Pettigrew's (1998) framework for conditions for positive contact. Pettigrew describes *participant characteristics* (individual differences), *situational factors* (elements of the specific interaction situation), and *societal factors* (influences of broader society). Fehr's framework includes *individual factors* (characteristics the individual brings to the interaction), *dyadic factors* (aspects of the relationship and specific interaction), and *environmental factors* (characteristics of the structural environment). These frameworks are almost identical and the specific factors described within each level also show extraordinary overlap. For example, consistent with Allport's claim about the benefits of equal status, discussions of friendship describe the benefit of perceiving the other as a "peer" who holds similar social status. Friendship formation is enhanced when interactions involve cooperation and common goals – two more of Allport's conditions. Similar to Allport's condition of authority and norm support, acceptance by one's peers and family significantly improves the prospects for an interpersonal relationship.

These two reviews emerge from non-overlapping fields within social psychology that have developed entirely independently, and to our knowledge they have never been directly compared. Yet, they show enormous similarity. We see this as evidence that the concept of friendship can provide a unifying framework for understanding many of the conditions previously proposed as necessary for optimal contact.

Why (as opposed to when) does contact improve intergroup attitudes?

Central to the question of *why* cross-group contact influences intergroup attitudes is the issue of generalization. How do experiences with a specific individual alter attitudes towards the larger group to which that individual belongs? In answering this question, some have focused on stereotype disconfirmation (e.g., Desforges et al., 1991). When an outgroup member disconfirms our negative stereotypes, this should undermine these beliefs and improve evaluations of the group. However, contact's impact on stereotypes tends to be relatively small and inconsistent. The larger effects appear on measures of warmth, empathy, respect, and reduced anxiety (e.g., Cook, 1984; Islam & Hewstone, 1993; Paolini et al., 2004; Tropp & Pettigrew, 2005). Cross-group contact seems to involve affect and emotions more than cognitions or thoughts. However, showing that affect is critical leaves unanswered the underlying question – what are the processes that move positive emotions felt for an individual on to the social group to which she/he belongs? My colleagues and I (see Wright, Aron, & Tropp, 2002) believe that Aron and Aron's (1986) *self-expansion model* of interpersonal closeness can provide the basis for a model of this kind of generalization, by exposing more clearly what actually happens when people become friends.

Friendship as including the other in the self

The emotional closeness that defines friendship produces a variety of positive thoughts, feelings, and actions towards the partner. The self-expansion model holds that this increasingly positive orientation towards the other results from the *inclusion of the other in the self*. The general idea is that as people become close, the mental representations of self and other become increasingly overlapped and aspects of the other become part of one's self-concept. As closeness increases, one's personal self is extended to include more and more aspects of one's partner, and the division between self and other becomes increasingly unclear. It is this extension of self that explains the positive orientation towards the other. Positive thoughts and feelings associated with the self are extended to the partner, who is treated increasingly like one treats oneself – feeling pain at their troubles, taking pride in their successes, generously sharing resources, and so on. Thus, friendship can be understood as a process of self-change, whereby the friend becomes part of one's self-concept.

Generalization as including the outgroup in the self

In addition to a precise description of the psychological processes involved in friendship development, this model also provides a basis for understanding generalization of positive attitudes from the outgroup friend to the outgroup as a whole. The logic is this: When one becomes close to an outgroup member, aspects of that person are included in the self. When the friends are reminded that they belong to divergent groups, their partner's group identity becomes salient. Like any other aspect of the partner, this group identity can also be included in the self. Thus, through the close friend, the outgroup itself can be included in the self, and now this *group* is accorded some of the benefits usually granted to the self (e.g., feelings pain at their troubles, taking pride in their successes, generously sharing resources, etc.).

Basic to this *including the outgroup in the self* (IOGS) model is the idea that groups, like individuals, can also be included in the self, and this has now been demonstrated in a number of studies (see Otten, 2002; Tropp & Wright, 2001). There are also several other theoretical perspectives, such as social identity theory (Tajfel & Turner, 1979) and self-categorization theory (Turner, Hogg, Oakes, Reicher, & Wetherell, 1987) that convincingly describe how groups can form integral parts of our self-concept. However, one critical difference between the IOGS model and these approaches is that IOGS allows that outgroups as well as ingroups can become essential to the self. In some instances, inclusion of an outgroup in the self represents psychological preparation for membership in that group. For example, a new friend might give me real entrée to some of her/his groups (e.g., friendship groups, clubs, etc.). In other cases, actually becoming a member of the outgroup may be impossible, or at least very difficult (e.g., racial, ethnic, or occupational groups). In these cases, the connection is entirely psychological. The outgroup's experiences have direct personal meaning, even though I am very aware that I cannot be included in the group.

Most research on cross-group friendships (e.g., Brown & Hewstone, 2005; Paolini et al., 2004; Turner et al., 2007) has measured frequency of contact and/or the number of friends. The IOGS model proposes that, in addition to the quantity of friendly contact, the level of closeness felt for one's friends is critical. The self-change resulting from inclusion will not occur unless a friendship involves feelings of closeness. In support of this, McLaughlin-Volpe, Aron, Wright, and Reis (2007) have shown in three studies involving very different groups that having outgroup friends is associated with positive intergroup attitudes. However, interpersonal closeness (measured by the level of inclusion of the friend in the self) was a much better predictor of positive outgroup attitudes than quantity of contact. In some cases, while high-closeness contact was associated with more positive intergroup attitudes, greater low-closeness contact had no impact or even a *negative* impact on attitudes. Cross-group interactions involving little or no inclusion of the other in the self can be associated with more negative attitudes.

We have also tested our inclusion model in two service-learning programs – where students engage in weekly service at local service agencies (see Brody, Wright, Aron, & McLaughlin-Volpe, 2008). Again, more contact with outgroup members during the program was associated with more positive attitudes toward the outgroup. However, the effect of contact depended on (and was mediated by) the degree to which one specific member of the outgroup was included in the self.

These and other survey studies have supported the basic IOGS model. However, all of these studies involve examining the relationship between variables measured simultaneously and one cannot know conclusively the causal relationship between them. Experimental evidence is needed for us to have real confidence in our causal claims. In a laboratory experiment (Wright et al., 2005), White women were randomly paired with either a cross-group (Asian American or Latina) or a same-group (White) partner. Pairs met four times to engage in a series of friendship-building activities, which successfully produced strong feelings of intimacy in both same-group and cross-group pairs. More importantly, compared to the White/White pairs, White women who made a Latina or Asian American friend reported more positive evaluations and more admiration for the ethnic outgroup, more support for ethnic diversity, and lower endorsement of "anti-minority" policies.[1] Additionally, compared to those with a new White friend, those with a new Latina or Asian friend suggested significantly smaller cuts to the budget of Latino and Asian student associations in a survey that they believed would influence the university administration's budgeting decisions in the coming year. Thus, results from several different indicators supported the claim that making an outgroup friend *caused* improvements in attitudes towards the friend's ethnic group. Finally, for those who made a cross-group friend, scores on several of the attitude measures correlated with the closeness of the friendship. White women who felt closest to their new outgroup friend tended to show the most positive intergroup attitudes.

We have replicated many of these findings in a subsequent experiment using similar procedures and new measures. Most recently, we modified the friendship-making procedures to create an intervention to improve attitudes of community members towards the police force in an American suburb that had experienced police–community strains (Eberhardt, Aron, Davies, Wright, & Bergsieker, 2008). We administered questionnaires at the start and end of four "Citizens' Police Academies" (a 10-week series of meetings organized by the police). At a meeting midway through two of the academies, we implemented our friendship-building intervention with police officer/ community member pairs. The other two academies served as controls and included no friendship-building activities. Comparing measures taken at the beginning of the academies to those taken at the end, as predicted, community members receiving the friendship intervention showed substantially larger increases in admiration for police compared to controls. As importantly, levels of admiration for the police force measured at the end of the academy (4 weeks post-intervention) were predicted by the closeness of the cross-group friendship. Also, how comfortable they felt during the intervention had very little influence on admiration – suggesting that even when making a cross-group friend is uncomfortable, resulting feelings of closeness can still improve attitudes.

The extended intergroup contact effect

There is one obvious shortcoming to suggestions that cross-group friendships are instrumental in positive contact effects. There are many good reasons why most people cannot, or do not, enjoy friendly contact with members of other groups. Thus, the power of cross-group contact to create intergroup tolerance and respect might appear quite limited. However, our focus on friendships also inspired another perspective that provides a partial solution to this concern. *The extended contact hypothesis* (Wright, Aron, McLaughlin, & Ropp, 1997) proposed that simply knowing that an ingroup member has a close relationship with an outgroup member can lead to a more positive attitude toward that outgroup. This means that even a relatively small number of cross-group friendships can have a wider impact on prejudice and can influence intergroup relations on a larger scale.

We introduced this idea with evidence from four studies. Two survey studies demonstrated that greater extended contact predicted more positive interethnic attitudes among White, Latino(a), and African American university students. In an experiment using a "minimal group" procedure, participants placed in groups based on an object-estimation task observed one of three interactions between an ingroup and an outgroup member. The interaction partners were actually actors and pretended to be either close friends, unacquainted strangers, or disliked acquaintances. As predicted, participants who observed the friendly interaction subsequently evaluated the outgroup more positively than those who observed the neutral or hostile interaction. The final study tested experimentally the impact of introducing extended contact into an existing competitive intergroup relationship. Participants were randomly assigned to two groups for a full-day experiment. First, the groups engaged in a series of staged competitions that heightened intergroup tensions and produced negative outgroup evaluations. Next, the intervention involved forming cross-group friendships between two people from each group. Following the intervention, despite continued intergroup competition, participants who had not formed a cross-group friendship themselves but were aware of another's cross-group friendship showed marked improvement in their attitudes towards the outgroup.

Extended contact has subsequently been shown to predict more positive intergroup attitudes among Catholics and Protestants in Northern Ireland (Paolini et al., 2004), among Germans towards "foreigners" and Muslims (Pettigrew, Christ, Wagner, & Stellmacher, 2007), among White and South Asian high school students in Britain (Turner et al., 2007), and among German and Turkish school children (Feddes, Noack, & Rutland, 2008). Intervention studies have shown that extended contact can improve attitudes among children towards immigrants (Liebkind & McAlister, 1999), children with disabilities (Cameron & Rutland; 2006), and ethnic outgroups and refugees (Cameron, Rutland, Brown, & Douch, 2006). This is particularly hopeful, as not everyone need have cross-group friends. A few such relationships may improve the attitudes of many.

Explaining extended contact effects

Initially, we proposed several mechanisms that might account for extended contact effects. One that has received considerable subsequent attention (see Brown & Hewstone, 2005, for a review) involves how observing cross-group friendships can reduce anxiety felt when contemplating and engaging in cross-group interactions. In addition, observing cross-group friendships can lead observers to infer that positive attitudes and supportive action towards the outgroup are normal for their ingroup. Thus, they change their own attitudes and behaviors in order to follow these positive ingroup norms. A recent study on interethnic contact (Wright, Comeau, & Aron, 2007) demonstrated that White and Chinese Canadians who were aware of more friendships between their own group and members of the Indo-Canadian community (Canadians of East Indian descent), believed their ethnic ingroup's norms were more positive towards Indo-Canadians, and this belief in turn predicted more positive attitudes towards Indo-Canadians. Thus, it appears that extended contact shifts an observer's beliefs about what is normal and expected for members of the ingroup, and the observer shifts her/his own beliefs to match these ingroup norms.

Extended contact effects can also be explained with a modification of the IOGS model used to explain direct contact effects. The suggestion is that extended contact sets in motion a "transitive inclusion process" by which observed cross-group friendships provide a conduit that connects the outgroup to the observer's self-concept. The logic is this: First, people spontaneously include ingroup members in the self because of their shared group membership (see Tropp & Wright, 2001). Second, observers spontaneously treat partners in a close relationship as a single cognitive unit in a manner consistent with inclusion of others in the self (Sedikides, Olsen, & Reis, 1993). Thus, when I observe a cross-group friendship, the ingroup member is to some degree part of my self, and the outgroup member is perceived as part of that ingroup member's self. Thus, through the ingroup member, the outgroup member is connected to my self-concept. If the outgroup member is seen to represent the outgroup, my inclusion of that outgroup member in myself allows for the outgroup to be part of myself as well.

This logic is consistent with Heider's (1958) balance theory. If unit relations exist between self and ingroup, between ingroup member and ingroup, between ingroup member and outgroup friend, and between outgroup friend and the outgroup, then balance theory prescribes a unit relationship between the self and the outgroup. The model is also consistent with Andersen and Chen's (2002) idea that we are shaped not only by the characteristics of those with whom we are close, but also by the characteristics of those who are close to those with whom we are close.

Two recent experiments provide experimental tests of all of the proposed links in the transitive inclusion process (Wright, Aron, & Brody, 2008). Together they show that extended contact effects are more pronounced when: (a) the observer is strongly identified with the ingroup (ingroup is included in the self); (b) the ingroup member is seen as prototypical of (or strongly connected to) the ingroup; (c) the ingroup and outgroup members are close friends; and (d) the outgroup member is prototypical of (or strongly connected to) the outgroup.

To summarize, extended contact appears to influence intergroup attitudes by a number of means, including reducing intergroup anxiety, changing beliefs about ingroup norms, and connecting observers to the outgroup so that it can be included in the self. However, while extended contact works, it must also have limitations and boundary conditions. When intergroup attitudes are very negative or when norms against cross-group interactions are explicit, observing a cross-group friendship is just as likely to lead to condemnation of the ingroup member as to improved attitudes towards the outgroup (see Harth, Feddes, Kessler, & White, 2006). Further investigation of these boundary conditions will certainly strengthen our understanding of extended contact.

Categorization and contact effects: Me and you, us and them, or just us?

The focus on cross-group friendships has been a productive new direction for contact research. However, most theorizing about contact over the last 20 years has revolved around three models, all emphasizing the role of categorization. Most early work on contact focused on describing the conditions that lead to successful contact, and lacked clear integration with a more general theory of intergroup relations. However, by the late 1980s Tajfel and

Turner's (1979) social identity theory (SIT) and Turner and colleagues' (1987) self-categorization theory (SCT) had emerged as potent broad models of intergroup relations. These theoretical advances fueled a renaissance in the contact literature and spawned three new models, all focusing on the role of categorization. Surprisingly, however, each made a different recommendation about the level of categorization most likely to lead to positive attitude change during contact.

SIT and SCT describe two basic levels of identity that define a person's self-concept: the personal identity – characteristics that make her/him a unique individual distinct from others; and the collective identity – aspects that connect her/him to others through group memberships. Categorization is the psychological process that determines when one will consider oneself and others in terms of personal versus collective identities. When collective identities are used, categorization also determines which of many possible group memberships becomes the basis for thoughts and actions. Much of the research inspired by SIT and SCT has focused on the potential negative consequences of categorization at the collective level. This strong focus on the negative side of group memberships is clearly a misrepresentation, as collective identities are often very positive influences on human behavior (see Wright & Taylor, 2003). Nonetheless, group-level categorization does provide the basis for group differentiation, stereotyping, ingroup favoritism, and feelings of intergroup anxiety, distrust, and competitiveness (e.g., Insko & Schopler, 1998; Stephan & Stephan, 1985). It can also initiate fears of appearing prejudiced or intolerant (e.g., Shelton, Richeson, & Vorauer, 2006). All of these can reduce the likelihood and undermine the effectiveness of cross-group contact.

From this perspective, Brewer and Miller's (1984) *decategorization model* (DCM) proposes that contact should be structured so that the participants will see each other as unique individuals. That is, attention should be focused on personal, not collective identities. Successful *personalized* contact should lead participants to recognize the greater utility of individuating information, making category information and associated stereotypes and prejudices less useful.

Gaertner and Dovidio's (2000) *common ingroup identity model* (CIIM) proposed a different solution. Recognizing that all group identities are nested in a larger more inclusive categorization (see Turner et al., 1987), the CIIM proposes that cross-group interaction will reduce prejudice when it focuses attention on a larger more inclusive category – a *superordinate identity* – that subsumes both ingroup and outgroup members. Thus, effective contact recategorizes "us and them" into a more inclusive "we." Those who were previously treated as outgroup members are now treated as ingroup members (see Gaertner & Dovidio, 2000, for a review).

The *mutual intergroup differentiation model* (MIDM; Brown & Hewstone, 2005) provides a third perspective. Focusing directly on attitude generalization, this model points out that people must pay at least some attention to group memberships for interactions with an individual to impact on intergroup attitudes. Interactions that are entirely interpersonal may lead to positive feelings towards the other person, but should have no impact on feelings towards the group, because this aspect of identity is never considered. In addition to direct research evidence (see Brown & Hewstone, 2005), this claim is supported by research showing that outgroup members who are recognized as highly representative (rather than unrepresentative) of their group are most effective at altering stereotypes when their actions disconfirm the stereotypes.

When considered individually, each of these models provides a convincing logic. However, considered together, they offer seemingly contradictory prescriptions. DCM calls for a focus on personal identities, MIDM for a focus on collective identities, and CIIM for a focus on a superordinate identity. These discrepancies have been the source of considerable debate.

To make groups salient or not?

It is impossible to provide a detailed critique of each model here, but several points seem critical. First, the basic claim of the MIDM that some degree of group salience is necessary for generalization is highly compelling. An obvious case is when group memberships are invisible (e.g., sexual orientation, political affiliation). If one has positive interactions with someone who does not disclose their membership in this type of outgroup, no matter how much one comes to like and respect them, this will have no influence on attitudes towards the larger group. Only when group membership is disclosed or is exposed by someone/something else can generalization occur. For cross-group contact to improve intergroup attitudes, it needs to be *intergroup* not *interpersonal* contact.

In fact, I have been careful in this chapter to use the term *cross-group contact*, rather than the more common term *intergroup contact*. For contact to be *intergroup*, it should involve people interacting *in terms of* their group memberships (see Tajfel, 1982). Intergroup interactions are guided by knowledge of the norms for intergroup behavior and by one's understanding of the intergroup relationship. Thus, a lot of what has been called "intergroup contact" in the literature has not been *intergroup* at all, and should be properly described as *cross-group* contact – a more general term that does not assume the level of categorization that is guiding interaction.

More generally, models of cross-group contact have often focused only on the negative implications of collective identities. Although some people may believe (particularly those entrenched in the North American ideology of individualism) that it is always better to be treated entirely as an individual, this is simply not true (even in North America). Many of our collective identities are highly meaningful to us. They define who we are. At times, we like, expect, even demand that we are treated on the basis of these group memberships, and we may not easily abandon a meaningful collective identity in favor of being treated solely as a unique individual – decategorization – or in favor of another less important/desirable superordinate category – recategorization (see Hornsey & Hogg, 2000; Simon, Aufderheide, & Kampmeier, 2004). However, MIDM is also not without its challenges. Raising the salience of group memberships, especially when there is a history of intergroup conflict and hostility, has the potential to undermine cross-group interactions. If the shared understanding is that the intergroup relationship is marked by antipathy and hostility, intergroup interactions will be guided by anxiety, suspicion, and anger – obviously not conducive to positive interaction and reduced prejudice. In these cases, ensuring the salience of groups may not be the issue; rather reducing it to a point where non-hostile interactions are possible may be required.

Including the outgroup in the self and the level of categorization

Categorization also has implications for the IOGS model of cross-group friendship. At first glance, it might seem that work on interpersonal closeness is consistent with the idea of decategorization; that friendship development involves interacting at the level of personal identity. Indeed, the IOGS and the DCM approaches share the view that cross-group friends must see each other as unique individuals. However, beyond this these approaches are quite different. The DCM holds that interpersonal interactions undermine the utility of group-level categorization. By focusing on individuating information, people learn that group-level thinking (e.g., stereotypes) is not useful and increasingly abandon the use of categories. In contrast, the IOGS model does not see interpersonal interactions as a means for reducing the utility of group distinctions. Rather, it proposes that it is precisely the continued importance of the other's group membership that allows for the creation of a strong connection between the self and the outgroup. The friend's group membership does not become irrelevant; rather it becomes connected to the self.

Thus, the IOGS model shares with the MIDM the view that group memberships must be recognized. Thus, it also faces the problem that increasing category salience can heighten intergroup differentiation, bias, and anxieties that could undermine friendship formation. However, this model recognizes that, like most relationships, cross-group friendships form over time through repeated interaction. One longitudinal model (Wright, 1995; Wright et al., 2005; see also Pettigrew, 1998) proposes that during initial contact the focus should be on personal identities, thus encouraging interpersonal closeness and reducing difficulties associated with group identities. However, once the outgroup member is to some degree included in the self, the intergroup nature of the friendship should be made salient, making the friend's group membership (the outgroup) available for inclusion in the self. This approach highlights the fact that interactions between the same individuals can change back and forth from interpersonal to intergroup as the contextual salience of different identities shifts (Tajfel, 1982). Even intimate friends can find themselves interacting in terms of their group memberships when situational cues make social identities salient. In fact, the closer the friendship, the greater the variety of situations partners will interact in, and the greater the chance they will be reminded of their group differences. The advantage, however, for friends is that now the outgroup is not a foreign and threatening entity, but rather an important aspect of another person who is already part of the self. Thus, when a period of decategorization leads to friendship, subsequent recognition of group differences can lead to inclusion of the outgroup in the self.

Cross-group contact, category salience, and ingroup projection

A number of other efforts have been made to reconcile and integrate the three dominant categorization approaches (e.g., Brown & Hewstone, 2005; Gaertner & Dovidio, 2000). Recent modifications to the MIDM and CIIM have focused on the possibility that optimal contact involves simultaneous recognition of subgroup memberships and a larger superordinate category. Thus, forming a common ingroup identity need not require entirely forsaking local group identities. Gaertner and Dovidio (2000) describe this as the *dual identity model* and Brown and Hewstone (2005) indicate that subgroup identities should be "sufficiently salient to ensure generalization, but not so salient that it leads to intergroup anxiety, or otherwise exacerbates tensions". Although this may seem a reasonable compromise, support for this approach has been mixed (see Dovidio, Gaertner, Hodson, Houlette, & Johnson, 2005). In addition, Amélie Mummendey and colleagues' (e.g., Mummendey & Wenzel, 1999; Waldzus, Mummendey, & Wenzel, 2005) *ingroup projection model* (IPM) provides a strong theoretical challenge to the dual identity approach, calling into question its theoretical basis and utility as a means of improving intergroup attitudes. Beyond this specific challenge, the IPM also provides a number of other valuable insights that appear to clarify and strengthen the three dominant categorization models of contact.

The IPM takes seriously the idea that all relations between groups must be understood as relations between subgroups within a shared superordinate category (see Turner et al., 1987). It is the superordinate category that provides the context, the standards for comparisons, and the norms for interactions across subgroups. Unlike the CIIM, the IPM does not describe the super-ordinate category primarily as a tool for reducing tensions between subordinate groups. Rather, the IPM holds that when a superordinate category is salient, subgroup members tend to *project* aspects of their subgroup identity onto the prototype of that superordinate category. In other words, we tend to see attributes of our local ingroup as also being attributes of the super-ordinate group. Consequently, members of our subgroup appear to be good representatives – better members – of the superordinate category, while out-group members appear to be poorer representatives. From this perspective, outgroup members are derogated not simply because they are "not us," but because they appear deviant and inferior in terms of the desired character-istics of the superordinate category. They are bad not because they belong to an outgroup, but because they fail to live up to what we see as the standards for the common ingroup.

Although both Brown and Hewstone (2005) and Dovidio and colleagues (Dovidio et al., 2005) have recognized ingroup projection as relevant to their models, the implications of the IPM for contact effects have not been fully explored. For example, the IPM highlights the particularly useful concept of *prototypes*. A prototype contains the attributes that are desirable for mem-bers of a group. It describes the characteristics one should have and the actions one should enact, if one wishes to be a good member of the group. Although other theoretical perspectives recognize that groups have prototypes, the IPM makes it clear that the actual *content* (the specific characteristics) of the prototype can be critical. This point illuminates several interesting and novel perspective on cross-group contact.

The content of a group prototype is to some degree known and shared by all members. However, it is also contested, as subgroups project elements of their local identities onto the superordinate prototype. Although the IPM has primarily described this process in cognitive terms, it also seems reasonable that projection may involve motivational processes as well. That is, not only do members of subordinate groups *tend* to project ingroup characteristics onto the superordinate category, they may also be *motivated* to do so (see Waldzus, Mummendey, Wenzel, & Boettcher, 2004). Thus, if the process is in part motivated, the degree to which cues in the environment have "allowed" or "encouraged" a subgroup to project their characteristics should determine the degree to which they will endorse the superordinate categorization.

One factor determining the degree to which individuals can engage in ingroup projection is the relative status or power of their ingroup vis-à-vis the outgroup. Members of very powerful subgroups may be able to engage in projection to a point where they see near perfect overlap between their subgroup prototype and the superordinate prototype. In contrast, members of small low-status subgroups should have little influence over the content of the superordinate prototype. This inequality in the opportunity for projection between high- versus low-status subgroups may provide an explanation for the often shown differential effectiveness of contact generally, and specifically of recategorization versus a dual identity approach, for majority and minority groups.

Minority groups and recategorization: Insights from IPM

In many cases, minority group members are less interested in interactions that focus on recategorization, and show little improvement in intergroup attitudes in these situations (see Dovidio et al., 2005). The IPM provides a strong potential explanation for this finding. Minority group members can be very aware of the realities of their social world (e.g., Waldzus et al., 2004), thus recognizing the outgroup's greater ability to project traits onto the superordinate prototype. Thus, they would also recognize that endorsing and identifying strongly with the superordinate identity represents de facto assimilation to the majority outgroup. From this perspective, whether subgroup members become aware of, or feel nominally members of, a superordinate category will not determine the effectiveness of recategorization. Rather, it is the degree of perceived overlap between the ingroup prototype and the superordinate category prototype. Majority group members willingly recategorize as members of a superordinate group onto which they can project many of their ingroup traits. Low-status minority group members, who see little opportunity to create overlap between subgroup and superordinate prototypes, approach recategorization with suspicion.

However, the IPM can also provide insights into when recategorization might produce more effective contact for minority group members. The key again is the content of the prototype of the new common ingroup. One possibility would be where the new categorization is not a superordinate group at all, but rather a categorization that is entirely orthogonal (unrelated) to the subgroups. In this case, since the old ingroup/outgroup distinction is simply irrelevant, the content of the old subgroup prototypes is also irrelevant for determining the new common ingroup prototype, and neither group should engage in projection of these old ingroup prototypes. If the new alternative ingroup is positively valued, minority groups should willingly identify with it as a means of enhancing social identity (Hornsey & Hogg, 2000) and should show positive attitudes towards all members of this new ingroup. However, in this case, we face the problem raised earlier by the MIDM. If this new categorization is entirely orthogonal to the old ingroup/outgroup distinction, interactions on the basis of this new categorization will have little or no impact on intergroup attitudes across the old ingroup/outgroup distinction, and there will not be generalization of positive attitudes to the old outgroup as a whole.

However, the IPM might also describe another context that could lead low-status minority group members to willingly endorse and identify with a *true* superordinate categorization. This could occur when they perceive clear opportunities for ingroup projection. For example, information provided directly by an authority or indirectly by situational cues that the minority group will contribute to defining the content of the new common ingroup prototype would allow minority group members to make legitimate claims of prototypicality with this new ingroup. Being able to claim prototypicality makes a group a much more attractive self-definition. Thus, minority group members should engage more vigorously in recategorization if the common ingroup is relatively new, the group prototype is relatively undefined, and it is clear that minority group members will play a critical role in completing the defined tasks of the common ingroup.

This is often the situation in experiments on the CIIM, where the common ingroup is a novel laboratory creation. Often it appears that both subgroups will participate equally in the new group's designated activities. Thus, the ingroup projection process can be readily engaged by members of both groups. Although perhaps more difficult, this same effect might be achieved in "real-world" contexts when, for example, new groups are formed in organizations or school classrooms. Here, members of the low-status minority group could be given clear messages that their subgroup will have equal opportunities to define the new common ingroup's norms and values. They will have equal power to create the prototype for the new department or classroom.

What about when the proposed common ingroup identity is a superordinate group that already exists? Again, the IPM would predict that it is the content of the group prototype that matters. Waldzus, Mummendey, Wenzel, and Weber (2003) showed that a complex representation of the superordinate category, where multiple and different representations are seen to be equally prototypical, leads to more positive intergroup attitudes among subordinate groups. Extending this idea to cross-group contact leads to the prediction that minority group members should be more likely to experience positive contact effects when the shared consensus is that the prototype of the common ingroup is complex. In this situation, minority group members may expect that their local ingroup will be seen as prototypical of the superordinate group and will be valued.

A variation on this idea would hold that rather than being complex, the superordinate prototype could explicitly describe the minority group as a necessary component of the superordinate group. For example, the Canadian national policy of multiculturalism explicitly describes minority cultures as necessary components of the nation's prototype. The presence of cultural minority groups is required *for Canada to be Canada*. The degree to which cultural minorities accept that this is really the consensual definition of Canadian identity should influence their willingness to engage this common ingroup identity as the basis for contact with other cultural groups. Similarly, organizations that describe ethnic diversity as a defining priority (i.e., to describe minority representation is critical to the organization's prototype) should have more success getting minority group members to adopt the organization as a common ingroup identity during cross-ethnic contact. Of course, sustaining positive contact effects will depend on whether daily activities within the organization confirm the stated policy claims.

In short, an IPM's perspective would predict that a common ingroup identity approach should lead to greater engagement in and more positive effects of contact among minority groups when that common identity appears to allow them adequate opportunity for ingroup projection, or where the representation of the common ingroup allows them to make legitimate claims of prototypicality.

Majority groups and recategorization: Insights from IPM

The IPM predicts (e.g., Waldzus et al., 2003) that strong simultaneous identification with both the local ingroup and the superordinate category (the dual identity case) leads to strong tendencies to engage ingroup projection, makes dissimilar outgroups appear more deviant and inferior, and legitimizes their derogation and exclusion. Since high-status majority groups face few constraints that limit ingroup projection, it is not surprising that contact that strengthens a dual identity perspective often does not produce positive attitude change among majority groups (see Dach-Gruschow & Hong, 2006).

Conversely, majority groups tend to show positive effects of contact when the contact engenders full recategorization (see Dovidio et al., 2005). Unlike minority groups, majority group members' powerful position allows for effective ingroup projections, making the superordinate category appear similar to their local ingroup and allowing them to believe they already possess the attributes of *good* members of the superordinate group. Consequently, they welcome the common ingroup representation as this implies that minority group members also endorse this superordinate identity that is comfortable and familiar for them. As long as their ability to engage in ingroup projection is not challenged, the common ingroup provides the basis for treating all members positively.

This analysis based on the IPM is consistent with Dovidio and colleagues' (2005) description of recategorization as "an assimilationist perspective" that asks members of the two groups to become "color-blind." Majority group members often find assimilation and color-blindness appealing, while minority group members often reject them. Assimilation requires that minority group members abandon a cherished social identity (see Hornsey & Hogg, 2000) that can provide the basis for coping with (e.g., Branscombe, Schmitt, & Harvey, 1999) and resisting (see Wright & Lubensky, 2009) the discrimination they face. In addition, a color-blind ideology can lead to continued discrimination, even when majority group members have the most benevolent of intentions (see Schofield, 2006). An IPM approach provides a compelling explanation for why this might be. Imagine, for argument's sake, that majority group members could truly ignore subordinate categories and could interact with outgroup members based only on their "shared humanity." Thus, the treatment of any particular human being is determined by the degree to which they conform to the expectations, norms, and values that are characteristic of the prototype of human beings. However, ingroup projection processes would lead majority group members to perceive the prototypical human to be much more like the prototype of their own ethnic group. So, even a majority group member capable of ignoring an individual's subordinate identities (ethnic group membership) will hold a prototype of the superordinate category (humans) that is biased towards characteristics of his/her own subordinate (ethnic) ingroup. Thus, their expectations, evaluations, and treatment of others will be more appropriate for ethnic ingroup members than ethnic outgroup members.

For example, when White teachers in Canada proclaim to be color-blind, they are likely unaware of the degree to which they have projected the specific characteristics of their White ethnic ingroup onto their prototype of humanity. Thus, even if they could ignore a child's ethnicity (something other psychological research has shown to be very unlikely) and treat them only as "a human being," ingroup projection processes would result in them treating the child more like "a White human being" because their prototype of the category humans contains far more characteristics from the prototype of Whites than the prototype of other ethnic groups. In terms of contact effects, these White teachers' efforts to behave in accordance with their color-blind ideology may lead to genuinely *positive* behaviors towards minority children. These positive actions should generate increasingly positive attitudes towards minority children. However, these interactions are unlikely to lead to recognition of the unique challenges and the continued inequalities minority children face, and (most ironically) they are unlikely to lead the teacher to see the additional burden they themselves add by their implicit expectations that minority children be good *White* children. In short, ingroup projection processes may also help explain evidence that cross-group contact, while inspiring more positive attitudes, fails to inspire advantaged group members to take more meaningful action to reduce social inequalities (see Jackman & Crane, 1986).

In summary, by focusing on the content of the prototype of the common ingroup and how it is derived, in part, by ingroup projection processes, the IPM provides valuable insights into minority/majority differences in endorsement of and positive contact within a common ingroup. It also provides the basis for considering when and, more importantly, *why* it may be possible to increase minority participation in positive cross-group contact within a common ingroup, and to clarify the problems with a dual identity approach for improving majority group attitudes. Thus, there may be other aspects of current theorizing about contact that could benefit from further integration of the IPM perspective.

Promising new directions and conclusions

Although cross-group contact has been the target of more than 60 years of research and theorizing, there remains much more to be understood. In addition to the continued elaboration of the themes described in this chapter, there is a burgeoning new literature examining what actually happens during the specific interactions between members of different groups. Led by researchers like Shelton, Richeson and Vorauer (2006) this work demonstrates that our behavior in cross-group interactions is not only influenced by our attitudes towards the outgroup, but by what we think the other group's attitudes are towards us. In addition, subsequent action is influenced by what comes before in a dynamic interchange between two active agents, each with its own psychological concerns. For example, fear that I might confirm a negative stereotype that I believe others hold about my group can increase concerns about my performance to the point that I fail to act in a fluid effective manner. This leads the other to wonder about my motives and to misrepresent my attitudes. Thus, negative interaction outcomes arise not because I lacked motivation or because I held prejudiced attitudes, but because concerns about the others' expectations produced behavior that was misinterpreted as reflecting negative attitudes. Of course, research and theorizing in this area is even more complex and interesting than this, but suffice to say that this work is certain to elucidate processes that are critical in a world where cross-group interactions are increasingly the norm.

Over the past 60 years, societies have changed! Successful social movements have led to notable reductions in group-based segregation. Dramatic growth in immigration, increasing numbers of refugees, accelerating globalization, and international travel have all produced unprecedented group-based diversity in many societies. Thus, the concerns that initially inspired the contact hypothesis remain as important as ever. However, our societies will continue to evolve and change, and to the degree that the answers we seek are influenced by this changing reality, our theorizing about cross-group contact will also continue to evolve. The focus on friendship in recent years is almost certainly in part the result of the fact that the social forces have made widespread cross-group friendships possible. The focus on societal norms as a mediator of contact effects seems particularly relevant when norms about intergroup relations are being challenged and contested. Extended contact becomes interesting only as the conventions around cross-group friendships change and we are all exposed to more examples of these friendships. The intergroup relationships that seem most relevant depend heavily on local and global changes in "who are the good guys and who are the bad guys." So, like a photographer attempting to capture a moving target, we must continually move and refocus our camera. Yet, the images we produce provide valuable information about the subject we seek to understand.

Note

1 In some cases these effects were stronger, or were only found, when the outgroup friend had a bicultural rather than a monocultural orientation. That is, minority friends who had indicated in a previous unrelated survey that they identified strongly with both mainstream American culture and their ethnic ingroup culture proved to be more effective in improving the intergroup attitudes of White women, than minority friends who had previously indicated that they identified strongly with their ethnic ingroup but not mainstream American culture.

References

Allport, G. W. (1954). *The nature of prejudice*. Menlo Park, CA: Addison-Wesley.
Amir, Y. (1976). The role of intergroup contact in change of prejudice and ethnic

relations. In P. A. Katz (Ed.), *Towards the elimination of racism* (pp. 245–308). Elmsford, NY: Pergamon.

Andersen, S. M., & Chen, S. (2002). The relational self: an interpersonal social-cognitive theory. *Psychological Review, 109*, 619–645.

Aron, A., & Aron, E. N. (1986). *Love as the expansion of self: Understanding attraction and satisfaction*. New York: Hemisphere.

Aronson, E., Blaney, N., Stephan, C., Sikes, J., & Snapp, M. (1978). *The jigsaw classroom*. Beverly Hills, CA: Sage.

Branscombe, N. R., Schmitt, M. T., & Harvey, R. D. (1999). Perceiving pervasive discrimination among African Americans: Implications for group identification and well-being. *Journal of Personality and Social Psychology, 77*, 135–149.

Brewer, M. B., & Brown, R. J. (1998). Intergroup relations. In D. T. Gilbert & S. T. Fiske (Eds.), *The handbook of social psychology* (Vol. 2, 4th ed., pp. 554–594). Boston: McGraw-Hill.

Brewer, M. B., & Miller, M.B. (1984). Beyond the contact hypothesis: Theoretical perspectives on desegregation. In N. Miller & M. B. Brewer (Eds.), *Groups in contact: The psychology of desegregation* (pp. 281–302). Los Angeles: Academic Press.

Brody, S. M., Wright, S. C., Aron, A., & McLaughlin-Volpe, T. (2008). Compassionate love for individuals outside one's social group. In L. Underwood, S. Sprecher, & B. Fehr (Eds.), *The science of compassionate love: Research, theory, and applications* (pp. 283–308). Malden, MA: Wiley-Blackwell.

Brown, R., & Hewstone, M. (2005). An integrative theory of intergroup contact. In M. Zanna (Ed.), *Advances in experimental social psychology* (Vol. 37, pp. 255–343). San Diego, CA: Elsevier Academic Press.

Cameron, L., & Rutland, A. (2006) Extended contact through story reading in school: Reducing children's prejudice toward the disabled. *Journal of Social Issues, 62*, 469–488.

Cameron, L., Rutland, A., Brown, R., & Douch, R. (2006). Changing children's intergroup attitudes toward refugees: Testing different models of extended contact. *Child Development, 77*, 1208–1219.

Chein, I., Cook, S., & Harding, J. (1948). The use of research in social therapy. *Human Relations, 1*, 497–511.

Cook, S. W. (1984). Cooperative interaction in multiethnic contexts. In N. Miller & M. B. Brewer (Eds.), *Groups in contact: The psychology of desegregation* (pp. 155–185). London: Academic Press.

Dach-Gruschow, K., & Hong, Y. (2006). The racial divide in response to the aftermath of Katrina: A boundary condition for common ingroup identity model. *Analyses of Social Issues and Public Policy, 6*, 125–141.

Desforges, D., Lord, C., Ramsey, S., Mason, J., Van Leeuwen, M., West, S., et al. (1991). Effects of structured cooperative contact on changing negative attitudes toward stigmatized social groups. *Journal of Personality and Social Psychology, 60*, 531–544.

Dovidio, J., Gaertner, S., Hodson, G., Houlette, M., & Johnson, K. (2005). Social inclusion and exclusion: Recategorization and the perception of intergroup boundaries. *The social psychology of inclusion and exclusion* (pp. 245–264). New York: Psychology Press.

Eberhardt, J. L., Aron, A., Davies, K., Wright, S. C., & Bergsieker, H. B. (2008). *A social-psychological intervention to improve community relations with police: Initial results*. Unpublished manuscript.

Feddes, A. R., Noack, P., & Rutland, A. (2008) *Group membership matters? Effects of direct and extended cross-ethnic friendship on Turkish (minority) and German (majority) children's intergroup attitudes.* Unpublished manuscript.

Fehr, B. (1996). *Friendship processes.* London: Sage

Gaertner, S. L., & Dovidio, J. F. (2000). *Reducing intergroup bias: The common ingroup identity model.* Ann Arbor, MI: Sheridan Books.

Harth, N. S., Feddes, A. R., Kessler, T., & White, M. (2006, June). Getting to know group members through their friends. Paper presented at SPSSI Conference: Social justice: Research, action and policy, Long Beach, CA.

Heider, F. (1958). *The psychology of interpersonal relations.* New York: Wiley.

Herek, G. M., & Capitanio, J. P. (1996). Some of my best friends: Intergroup contact, concealable stigma, and heterosexuals' attitudes towards gay men and lesbians. *Personality and Social Psychology Bulletin, 22,* 412–424.

Hornsey, M., & Hogg, M. (2000). Intergroup similarity and subgroup relations: Some implications for assimilation. *Personality and Social Psychology Bulletin, 26,* 948–958.

Insko, C. A., & Schopler, J. (1998). Differential distrust of groups and individuals. In C. Sedikides, J. Schopler, & C. A. Insko (Eds.), *Intergroup cognition and intergroup behavior* (pp. 75–107). Hillsdale, NJ: Lawrence Erlbaum Associates, Inc.

Islam, M. R., & Hewstone, M. (1993). Dimensions of contact as predictors of intergroup anxiety, perceived out-group variability, and out-group attitude: An integrative model. *Personality and Social Psychology Bulletin, 19,* 700–710.

Jackman, M., & Crane, M. (1986). "Some of my best friends are Black . . .": Inter-racial friendship and Whites' racial attitudes. *Public Opinion Quarterly, 50,* 459–486.

Jones, J. M. (1997). *Prejudice and racism* (2nd ed.). New York: McGraw-Hill.

Liebkind, K., & McAlister, A. L. (1999). Extended contact through peer modelling to promote tolerance in Finland. *European Journal of Social Psychology, 29,* 765–780.

McLaughlin-Volpe, T., Aron, A., Wright, S. C., & Reis, H. T. (2007). *Intergroup social interactions and intergroup prejudice: Quantity versus quality.* Unpublished manuscript.

Mummendey, A., & Wenzel, M. (1999). Social discrimination and tolerance in inter-group relations: Reactions to intergroup difference. *Personality and Social Psychology Review, 3,* 158–174

Otten, S. (2002). When "I" turns into "we": The self as a determinant of favoritism towards novel ingroups. In J. P. Forgas & K. Williams (Eds.), *The social self: Cognitive, interpersonal and intergroup perspectives.* Philadelphia: Psychology Press.

Paolini, S., Hewstone, M., Cairns, E., & Voci, A. (2004). Effects of direct and indirect cross-group friendships on judgments of Catholic and Protestants in Northern Ireland: The mediating role of an anxiety-reduction mechanism, *Personality and Social Psychology Bulletin, 30,* 770–786.

Pettigrew, T. F. (1986). The intergroup contact hypothesis reconsidered. In M. Hewstone & R. Brown (Eds.), *Contact and conflict in intergroup encounters* (pp. 169–195). New York: Basil Blackwell.

Pettigrew, T. F. (1998). Intergroup contact theory. *Annual Review of Psychology, 49,* 65–85.

Pettigrew, T., Christ, O., Wagner, U., & Stellmacher, J. (2007). Direct and indirect intergroup contact effects on prejudice: A normative interpretation. *International Journal of Intercultural Relations, 31,* 411–425.

Pettigrew, T. F., & Tropp, L. R. (2006). A meta-analytic test of intergroup contact theory. *Journal of Personality and Social Psychology, 90,* 751–783.

Schofield, J. W. (2006). The colorblind perspective in school: Causes and consequences. In J. A. Banks & C. A. McGee Banks (Eds.), *Multicultural education: Issues and perspectives* (6th ed., pp. 271–295). New York: Wiley.

Sedikides, C., Olsen, N., & Reis, H. T. (1993). Relationships as natural categories. *Journal of Personality and Social Psychology, 54,* 13–20.

Shelton, J., Richeson, J., & Vorauer, J. (2006). Threatened identities and interethnic interactions. *European Review of Social Psychology, 17,* 321–358.

Simon, B., Aufderheide, B., & Kampmeier, C. (2004). The social psychology of minority–majority relations. In M. B. Brewer & M. Hewstone (Eds.), *Self and social identity* (pp. 278–297). Malden, MA: Blackwell Publishing.

Stephan, W. G. (1987). The contact hypothesis in intergroup relations. In C. Hendrick (Ed.), *Group processes and intergroup relations. Review of personality and social psychology* (Vol. 9, pp. 13–40). Beverly Hills, CA: Sage.

Stephan, W. G., & Stephan, C. (1985). Intergroup anxiety. *Journal of Social Issues, 41,* 157–176.

Tajfel, H. (1982). *Social identity and intergroup relations,* Cambridge: Cambridge University Press.

Tajfel, H., & Turner, J. C. (1979). An integrative theory of intergroup conflict. In W. G. Austin & S. Worchel (Eds.), *The social psychology of intergroup relations* (pp. 33–47). Monterey, CA: Brooks/Cole.

Tropp, L., & Pettigrew, T. (2005). Differential relationships between intergroup contact and affective and cognitive dimensions of prejudice. *Personality and Social Psychology Bulletin, 31,* 1145–1158.

Tropp, L. R., & Wright, S. C. (2001). Ingroup identification as inclusion of ingroup in the self. *Personality and Social Psychology Bulletin, 27,* 585–600.

Turner, J. C., Hogg, M. A., Oakes, P. J., Reicher, S. D., & Wetherell, M. S. (1987). *Rediscovering the social group: A self-categorization theory.* New York: Blackwell.

Turner, R., Hewstone, M., & Voci, A. (2007). Reducing explicit and implicit outgroup prejudice via direct and extended contact: The mediating role of self-disclosure and intergroup anxiety. *Journal of Personality and Social Psychology, 93,* 369–388.

Waldzus, S., Mummendey, A., & Wenzel, M. (2005). When "different" means "worse": In-group prototypicality in changing intergroup contexts. *Journal of Experimental Social Psychology, 41,* 76–83.

Waldzus, S., Mummendey, A., Wenzel, M., & Boettcher, F. (2004). Of bikers, teachers and Germans: Groups' diverging views about their prototypicality. *British Journal of Social Psychology, 43,* 385–400.

Waldzus, S., Mummendey, A., Wenzel, M., & Weber, U. (2003). Towards tolerance: Representations of superordinate categories and perceived ingroup prototypicality. *Journal of Experimental Social Psychology, 39,* 31–47.

Williams, R. M. Jr (1947). *The reduction of intergroup tensions.* New York: Social Science Research Council.

Wright, S. C. (1995). *The impact of cross-group friendships on intergroup attitudes: An intergroup conflict simulation.* Paper presented at the Society for Experimental Social Psychology, Washington, DC.

Wright, S. C., Aron, A., & Brody, S. M. (2008). Extended contact and including others in the self: Building on the Allport/Pettigrew legacy. In U. Wagner,

L. R. Tropp, & C. Tredoux (Eds.), *Improving intergroup relations: Building on the legacy of Thomas F. Pettigrew*. New York: Wiley.

Wright, S. C., Aron, A., McLaughlin, T., & Ropp, S. A. (1997). The extended contact effect: Knowledge of cross-group friendships and prejudice. *Journal of Personality and Social Psychology, 73*, 73–90.

Wright, S. C., Aron, A., & Tropp, L. R. (2002). Including others (and their groups) in the self: Self-expansion theory and intergroup relations. In J. P. Forgas & K. Williams (Eds.), *The social self: Cognitive, interpersonal and intergroup perspectives*. Philadelphia: Psychology Press.

Wright, S. C., Brody, S. M., & Aron, A. (2005). Intergroup contact: Still our best hope for improving intergroup relations. In C. S. Crandall & M. Schaller (Eds.), *Social psychology of prejudice: Historical and contemporary issues* (pp. 115–142). Seattle, WA: Lewinian Press.

Wright, S. C., Comeau, J., & Aron, A. (2007, July). *Direct and extended contact in a multi-ethnic context*. Annual meeting of the International Society of Political Psychology, Portland, OR.

Wright, S. C., & Lubensky, M. (2009). The struggle for social equality: Collective action versus prejudice reduction. In S. Demoulin, J. P. Leyens, & J. F. Dovidio (Eds.), *Intergroup misunderstandings. Impact of divergent social realities*. New York: Psychology Press.

Wright, S. C., & Taylor, D. M. (2003). The social psychology of cultural diversity: Social stereotyping, prejudice and discrimination. In M. A. Hogg & J. Cooper (Eds.), *Sage handbook of social psychology*. Beverly Hills, CA: Sage.

15 Interventions enhancing intergroup tolerance

Kai J. Jonas
University of Amsterdam

The history of negative intergroup relations and group conflict is long and can fill many books, as is the research on the topic of how to improve intergroup relations (Aboud & Levy, 2000; Stephan, Renfro, & Stephan, 2004b; Stephan & Stephan, 2001; Stephan & Vogt, 2004). This whole volume covers this topic in one way or the other. Looking at the abundance of research on the negative outcomes of intergroup relations, one is tempted to ask whether improvement is possible at all. Interestingly, most of the research addressing this field is preoccupied with the reduction of something negative; that is, discrimination, prejudice, outgroup derogation, or ingroup favoritism. We have pointed to this strikingly one-sided perspective elsewhere (Jonas & Mummendey, 2008), by revealing the potential to generate and maintain something positive in intergroup relations, such as intergroup help or support. In line with Pettigrew (1996) we posit that the reduction or elimination of "negative" intergroup relations is not equal to the establishment of "positive" relations. Similarly, intergroup tolerance, a term often used in juxtaposition to intergroup discrimination, is not dealing with the reduction of negative intergroup relations per se, but instead with the maintenance and the cherishing of the difference. Thus, given the establishment of positive intergroup relations, intergroup tolerance may not be necessary at all. As we reveal later, (intergroup) tolerance is in demand when the other (outgroup) is not evaluated positively or in accordance with one's own standards, but when this deviance is being judged as acceptable and worth being maintained. Therefore treatments to enhance intergroup tolerance must be conceptually different (and must have different goals) than treatments to reduce negative attitudes in intergroup relations, or to enhance positive attitudes in intergroup relations. This chapter seeks to critically review intergroup relations, interventions models, and treatments. To disentangle concepts we seek to establish a conceptualization of intergroup tolerance and a subsequent differentiation of treatment goals. From this we identify a lack of thoroughly developed treatments and, therefore, in the final part of the chapter, we systematize treatment development to close this gap.

What is supposed to be changed or created and when?
Intergroup discrimination or intergroup tolerance

When one asks around in a professional intergroup research environment about "the" intervention program against intergroup discrimination, or to increase intergroup tolerance, one often receives shrugged shoulders or a sermon on relevant models and theories, and only perhaps a name of an intervention (e.g., Blue-Eyes/Brown-Eyes; http://www.janeelliott.com). This response vacuum could be a result of the complexity of the problem. Given high standards for a process analysis and outcome evaluation, it is possible that the field has simply not been able to produce adequate interventions since we can claim to not yet have understood the problem in total. It is astonishing how few well-known specific or universal treatment programs have come out of the impressive research on the contact hypothesis (Pettigrew & Tropp, 2006). Of course, one could argue that it is not necessary to reach a full understanding to design and implement an intervention. This may be true, but there is ample evidence that treatments based on short-sighted theoretical and empirical considerations not only lead to null effects, but even to opposite effects (e.g., boomerang effects of the substance abuse program DARE; Wysong, Aniskiewicz, & Wright, 1994). It could also be because of the foci of our academic careers (Stephan, 2006). With a certain truth to all the reasons given, the field needs to review whether its results should stay in a scientific vacuum or reach applied levels, and subsequently take measures to apply its knowledge. We believe intergroup research has something to offer and needs to anchor itself on the landscape of significant science topics that actually can do good for society. Independent of this general notion, it is relevant to discuss which direction to take in this applied research. Whereas the literature on social discrimination and prejudice is far developed, and processes for interventions are being suggested (Aboud & Levy, 2000; Stephan & Stephan, 2001), the scientific debate on intervention goals and processes is quite underdeveloped.

In many research programs on intergroup discrimination or prejudice the terms "discrimination" and "prejudice" are being used as an antagonist of intergroup tolerance: "we assume that the processes underlying the evaluation of intergroup difference are central for an understanding of social discrimination and, *conversely*, a concept of intergroup tolerance" (Wenzel, Mummendey, Weber, & Waldzus, 2003, p. 461, italics added by this author). The notion of social discrimination and intergroup tolerance as being two ends of one continuum is reflected in its measurement (both concepts in one scale; e.g., Larsen & Long, 1988). This antagonism seems to be empirically backed up by medium strength correlations (Klonis, Plant, & Devine, 2005; Pratto, Sidanius, Stallworth, & Malle, 1994), but we should not consider this case closed. Undoubtedly, social discrimination/prejudice and lack of tolerance share conceptual overlap. But in core aspects they differ, making the assumed antagonism hardly possible (Habermas, 2003). Whereas discrimination and prejudice are well-established social psychological terms, tolerance is not. Discrimination is defined as the perceived negative, illegitim-ate treatment of members of a group, on the basis of them being socially categorized (Mummendey, 1995; Mummendey & Otten, 2001). Thus it is easy to measure discrimination, for example with intergroup treatment measures, or resource allocation paradigms, if the outcomes are perceived as illegitim-ate by one group. Prejudice is defined as the display of negative affect and hostile behavior towards members of a social group – based on derogatory social attitudes or cognitive beliefs (Brown, 1995). Measurement of prejudice can be done by means of scales, for example the modern racism scale (McConahay, 1986). Often lower means on a discrimination/prejudice meas-ure easily get interpreted as more tolerance (Herek, 1987; Wenzel et al., 2003). But is this so? Intergroup tolerance is a term with great appeal, undoubtedly, and it is found in many statements as one of the basic conditions for peaceful living together (Habermas, 2003).

What is tolerance in social psychological terms?

Tolerance needs to be defined first, or at least described, before we can utilize it in our research. Thus we need to derive our working concept from other sub-disciplines of psychology or other sciences, such as philosophy or polit-ical science. Without even going back to the historical treatments on tolerance of ancient Greek philosophers, or later Erasmus of Rotterdam, Montaigne, or Locke, tolerance as a concept is still open for debate in current philosophy (e.g., see Feldmann, Henschel, & Ulrich, 2000; Fernandez, in press; Frost, 2003; Wierlacher, 1996). Keeping our psychological perspective in mind, we seek to define tolerance as an attitude-driven behavior to actively embrace differences on an individual level and also on a collective level, without the intent to eliminate this difference. Tolerance also includes ego-involvement; otherwise it is just indifference or an affirmation of irrelevant issues. To sharpen our definition it is helpful to look at sub-elements of tolerance. Frost (2003) has addressed this functional level and distinguishes six sub-elements within tolerance. The context defining the content to be tolerant about must be clear and defined. It consists at minimum of two actors who hold a norma-tive divergence between them that is covered by an acceptance of the rejected element in the other, all on a voluntary basis. Finally, tolerance contains an attitudinal and a behavioral component. These six elements can be grouped to describe various settings: A permission setting describes a majority allowing a minority to act out their idiosyncrasies. In other words there is a tolerant majority and a minority that profits from this. This setting is often criticized for the mere acquiescence of the other, yet lacking a solution. A coexistence setting pertains to a horizontal array of the actors; here both actors have to be mutually tolerant towards each other. A mutually respecting setting differs from the coexistence on a power dimension. Whereas coexistence can be sim-ply the result of a power equilibrium and the acceptance of the impossibility of each side to win, a setting determined by respect draws on mutually positive acceptance (Bar-Tal, 2004), independent of possible power differences. The settings are helpful to determine what kind of tolerance conflict or pathway of tolerance we deal with, and this has to find a feedback into treatments pertaining to specific contexts. But we still lack an operationalization of tolerance to be able to measure if a treatment has reached its aim or not. Furthermore, on an individual level, the distinctions proposed by Frost are fairly straightforward but, on the group level, being tolerant and still acting in terms of one's ingroup is much more difficult. Ingroup norms can be in the way. It is the task of treatments to differentiate those norms and to make individuals aware of these very different self guides.

The personality psychologist Martin (1964, p. 21) has given the following definition of tolerance:

> Absolute tolerance is a completely neutral attitude toward a group, without any group judgment, favorable or unfavorable. As tolerance increases prejudice decreases, and vice versa, so that absolute tolerance can be expressed as the point on a scale which indicates neither positive nor negative prejudice.

This definition first of all posits that there should be a quadratic link of discrimination (or prejudice) and positive attitudes with tolerance. The definition furthermore is both helpful – it points to groups in particular as targets of tolerance – and problematic on the other hand, because it points to a null effect regarding the measurement. Apart from the measurement problem, which we address subsequently, the tolerance definitions agree on one central aspect: The other is embraced as is, without the tendency to change the other (no imposition of potentially discriminating assimilation requests) or to fully reject the other on the basis of difference. If one formulates a goal for intervention, this goal must entail the potential of a tolerant individual being able to accept others in their diversity, without showing discriminatory tendencies, or assimilation requests. Defined as this, tolerance is still problematic: Tolerance needs to be guarded against its attackers. This might entail intolerant behavior on the side of the actually tolerant people. To reject being able to tolerate is an equation that groups or societies have to compute and reach a consensus on continuously (Frost, 2003). Examples of how hard it is to reach such a consensus can be found all the time in tolerant societies, since tolerance norms are anything but set (for a recent example see the debate around building mosques in inner cities; Giordano, 2007).

Prejudice is easy, but tolerance is difficult to measure

Since we have a grasp of what we need to change with respect to what we want to achieve (what will later be called treatment goals), it is necessary to reflect on how we can measure change or goal attainment. In the political sciences, Finkel, Sigelman, and Humphries (1999) have listed tolerance measures and distinguish general democratic value endorsement and specific topics of political tolerance. As an example of the latter, Marcus, Sullivan, Theiss-Morse, and Stevens (2005) asked participants first to rate political groups and in a second step assessed how much the least-liked group was tolerated. Similarly, in social psychological research approximative questionnaire measures are being used. Brewer and Pierce (2005) use as "tolerance measures" in their study on multiculturalism, an affirmative action endorsement scale, and an affect thermometer for social groups. In another study (Li & Brewer, 2004) attitudes towards diversity in society (e.g., ethnic minorities, homosexuals) were assessed and the data were interpreted as a tolerance measure. Attempts to construct tolerance scales are being undertaken (e.g., for cultural tolerance; Gasser & Tan, 1999), but are usually furnished with a low reception, since the measures do not reach beyond thematically bound attitude assessments within the given research. Taken together, the direct psychological measurement of tolerance is difficult and this has serious effects on prevention or intervention attempts in the field of tolerance. How can we state that a treatment is effective, if we have a hard time measuring its outcome? So far we have argued that the concepts easily used in the context of prevention and intervention in intergroup relations are not as straightforward as we wish. Discrimination can be defined and measured; this cannot be done so easily with tolerance. Clearly these concepts do not define opposite ends of one continuum and it is superficial to call any reduction in discrimination an increase in tolerance.

Finding the appropriate intervention

Given these conceptual intricacies one could end with a formula such as tolerance (in the mutually embracing version) can serve as an abstract goal in general primary prevention treatments, but outcomes must be measured on more concrete sub-goals. A possibility for measuring tolerance could also be to assess the individual's intention to safeguard it, or to measure the ability to accept the other, the unattractive or the different. The researcher or interventionist needs to make a normative decision on these concepts and has to be open about the choice. Examples for those sub-goal choices are justice sensitivity (Jonas, Boos, Backes, Büttner, Ehrental, & Prasse, 2002; using the concept of Schmitt, Gollwitzer, Maes, & Arbach, 2005) or diversity embracement (Tropp & Bianchi, 2006, 2007). But we are aware that those sub-goals are subject to discussion in the eyes of others. These are normative decisions we make, and we cannot make an empirical argument out of it. On the contrary, discrimination reduction can be addressed as a treatment goal, both in prevention and in intervention contexts, and outcomes can be directly measured. An advantage of tolerance goal focus in treatments may be its abstractness, compared to fairly context bound discrimination reduction attempts. It is questionable whether tools to reduce intergroup discrimination lead to generalized effects (or carry over effects) on other categories as well, or if the (positive) effects are limited to the categories used or the specific conflictuous context. Findings are mixed at this point and are most likely highly dependent on the employed treatment. This problem can be circumvented by using a category-independent treatment aiming at intergroup tolerance. If we elaborate this suggested distinction further it points to a question of timing and context as well. The theoretical treatment model we introduce later regards this as a core aspect, but both tolerance models and intergroup relations research hardly address the question: When or in what contexts which of the suggested solutions for intergroup tolerance or against intergroup discrimination (e.g., creating a complex superordinate category in the ingroup projection model; Waldzus & Mummendey, 2004; Wenzel et al., 2003) can serve as an ex post intervention to given acts of discrimination or as an ex ante approach to avoid discriminatory behavior. It is a benefit, for the sake of simplicity, that the intergroup tolerance approach may fall short in contexts of already existing violent conflict between groups, or would be judged as social romanticism of the facilitator of the treatment. We can assume that this only works as an ex ante approach, or in fairly peaceful phases in between outbreaks of conflicts (with narrative data from multiple "peace workshops" pointing in this direction, see for example http://www.heal-reconcile-rwanda.org/). The time has to be right for the respective approach to be a proper fit. In relation to this ex ante and ex post distinction and the decision about the treatment goal of choice, we need to decide on the targeted participant group of the treatment. Ex ante approaches far ahead of any experience of friction or conflict may point to an early onset of treatment in kindergarten and school contexts, but not only. Well-timed booster sessions (i.e., refreshing knowledge) with teenagers and adults may be indicated as well. At the same time, both children and young adults, and adults who actually suffer from discrimination or live in intergroup conflict contexts, may serve as viable subjects of ex post approaches. Experiences of discrimination in the past that are still not fully coped with may open an avenue for tolerance inducing approaches (healing or reconciliation workshops; Staub, Pearlman, Gubin, & Hagengimana, 2005). In this regard, all proposed abstract goals and their underlying intergroup process models – as valid as they are in certain theoretical and laboratory contexts – are in need of validation against the backdrop of "real" conflictuous contexts. Research on intractable conflicts, for example in the Middle East, Sri Lanka, or previously Northern Ireland, has delivered a vast body of analyses and explanations, but also treatments that combine theoretical insight with best practice knowledge. Actually, there is a great dearth with regard to the combination of both aspects. Banks (2006) highlights the need to adapt curricula and treatments to specific characteristics of school contexts, and Dwairy (2004), for example, informs us about majority versus minority membership differences in the context of race relations improvement.

Yet, things become even more complicated. For many dysfunctional behaviors there is a clear solution. Substance abuse can be overcome essentially by not using the substance anymore (for the sake of the comparison we do not elaborate on the complexity of overcoming addictions). An alcoholic has to stop consuming alcohol, but still can drink liquids. A smoker can stop smoking, but still can breathe. But changing dysfunctional behavior becomes more complicated in cases where one simply cannot stop the behavior without dying, becoming disabled, or losing central capacities. In the case of obesity the solution is not to stop eating at all, but to control food intake. Thus, the solution to the dysfunctional behavior in this case is not a complete dissolution, but limited to an attempt at gradual control of the dysfunctional aspects. As an analogy, the same holds for discrimination. We cannot stop it, but we can try to remove certain aspects of it. Discrimination, being based on categorization, is something internally human, given our capacity and need for categorization and thus the simplification of cognitive processes (Macrae, Milne, & Bodenhausen, 1994). Therefore it is not a malign dysfunction of "bad" humans alone, but an essential cognitive function within everyone. This understanding is often counterintuitive or actually outright unbelievable for practitioners or concerned citizens in the context of hate crimes or the derogation of or violence against foreigners. From their perspective individuals showing those discriminating attitudes or behaviors are clearly the bad and ugly, who are maximally different from themselves. They have a hard time accepting that they share commonalities on a psychological level (although their own argument that racism is born in the center of society should allow them to accept that discriminatory behavior is not so far from them, too). Recently, in public discussions of interventions against violence against foreigners, Amélie Mummendey, again to the surprise of many audiences, vigorously argued for the necessity of this function: Legitimate and reasonable use of categorization is necessary and psychologically good, illegitimate use is not. But both rely on the same psychological function. This Janus face of the categorization function allows us to argue against a marginalization of extremists and puts the responsibility on every citizen to ensure intergroup tolerance, and even positive intergroup relations. Otherwise the story would be too simple – the "do-gooders" on the one side, and the ugly, discriminating individuals on the other. The controversial effect of this position is also relevant from a prevention/intervention background. Treatments are usually geared around specific populations that are in danger or at high risk of showing certain unwanted, in this case discriminatory, behavior, or have done so already. Thus, any approach should be based on a risk analysis, and a rough idea of how to reach the population in question with a specific treatment given a predefined goal. But if the capability is present in everyone and a necessary survival tool, an approach geared to any specific group is hard to argue for. In this case, we need to establish additional criteria to determine the target group. Based on the social psychological findings on categorization only a general ex ante approach (to control certain negative aspects of human capacity) would be feasible. On top of this issue the goal of the intervention needs to be determined. It cannot be to stop categorizing altogether, but it could be intergroup tolerance that tells us how to embrace different categories. One could now develop this line of reasoning further and could draw on stereotype activation versus application distinction and apply findings that inhibit the latter or reduce the former.

For the moment the discipline has accumulated a vast body of research on mechanisms to reduce category activation (by means of crossed categorization, Vescio, Judd, & Kwan, 2004), category application (e.g., individual mobility, Verkuyten & Reijerse, 2008;) stereotype activation (e.g., Gilbert & Hixon, 1991; Sassenberg & Moskowitz, 2005), or application (e.g., Devine, 1989; Fein, von Hippel, & Spencer, 1999; Kunda & Sinclair, 1999) but, to a large degree, falls short of integrating them in theoretically derived, evaluated intervention programs. Yet this evidence can provide a rich toolbox for designing interventions or for being cognizant about boundary conditions. In the following, prominent approaches of intergroup relations improvement with a specific focus on intergroup tolerance are placed in this framework. Specifically, benefits and shortcomings of the approaches are discussed, too.

The strengths and weaknesses of intergroup tolerance trainings

As a precedent note to this paragraph, the conceptual purity of the listed approaches is varyied. Quite inevitably, intergroup tolerance trainings almost necessarily include concrete modules that deal with intergroup discrimination as examples of the abstract concept. Thus, some presented treatments may – dependent on weighing in the eye of the beholder – fall more into the category of intergroup discrimination reduction since they work with categories. Still, the goals of the presented approaches pertain more to abstract competencies and attitudes in the sense of tolerance. Of course the presented list is by no means final. In fact we have limited our presentation to approaches or examples that are either well researched, widely used or promising in their conceptualization.

Contact hypothesis

Pettigrew and Tropp (2006) have delivered a comprehensive summary of the effects of the contact hypothesis. Contact in itself is not really a treatment, it is a technique, but it can be part of a treatment that builds on contact and its fostering conditions. Actually, those identified supportive conditions, as mentioned in the meta-analysis, should serve both as framework and content elements for future treatment developments. Contact in general, above and beyond a specific treatment, can be judged as facilitation of a context that fosters the acceptance of specific members of other categories, but also has generalized effects, especially by means of extended contact approaches (Cameron & Rutland, 2006; Cameron, Rutland, & Brown, 2007; Cameron,

Rutland, Brown, & Douch, 2006). Yet it has to be remarked as a limitation for the contact hypothesis in general, that the strongest contact effects "emerge from contact that occurs in recreational and laboratory settings" (Pettigrew & Tropp, 2006, p. 765), and that the extended contact findings in treatment settings (compared to laboratory studies) are obtained only with school children (i.e., generalization for example to adults remains questionable). Still it has to be acknowledged that the contact hypothesis, facilitated in any form whatsoever, serves as the fundamental assumption underlying an almost unmanageable amount of exchange programs, partnership programs, and so on (Nesdale & Todd, 2000). Most likely those programs and their effects could be further improved if the findings of the current meta-analysis were included in a comprehensive treatment model framework to improve the treatment contexts, their implementation, and evaluation.

Diversity trainings

It is quite hard, given the sheer abundance of diversity trainings and their derivatives, to classify this approach conclusively. Theoretically, if one is defining diversity as a state of a social entity that includes members with identifiable differences, diversity does not need groups or categories, since individuals can add to diversity as well. Thus, diversity trainings should fall into the most general form of tolerance goal approaches. On an explicit level, the multitude of trainings share common goals and methods. Embracing the diversity is operationalized either by an intergroup perspective or by a perspective taking approach. Regarding the judgment of effectiveness of diversity trainings, the availability of evaluation data varies tremendously (McCauley, Wright, & Harris, 2000). For some of the trainings designed for high schools, colleges and universities, for example the widespread course offerings such as "Welcoming Diversity" (National Coalition Building Institute, 2007) no systematic evaluation data with promising results are available. Since the year 2000, for others such as the "A World of Difference" (Anti-Defamation League, 2007) program, evaluations have been conducted that show positive effects, but only for high school samples (Anti-Defamation League, 2006). Random control data for other populations, even just university student samples, are still unavailable, but the program is currently administered to those groups. The picture is even sparser for any type of smaller trainings (mostly on an individual university level). Diversity trainings are dealing predominantly with race issues in the US (Peruche & Plant, 2006), and to a lesser degree with other characteristics, such as religion, sexual orientation, and so on. Programs developed before 9/11 are especially prone to a limited approach regarding the new religious foci. Short interventions in the context of strongly belief driven contexts, for example anti-homosexual attitudes, fail to show treatment effects (Cotton-Huston & Waite, 2000). In general, a focus on oppression and on distorted power relations may lead to an increase in awareness, but also to an induction of guilt (Kernahan &

Davis, 2007). Whereas an increase in awareness may be beneficial for developing tolerance behavior in stratified contexts, guilt induction cannot unanimously be judged as positive, because individuals high in guilt can also show defense motivation. As a result, tolerance would decrease. To sum up, diversity trainings are in urgent need of substantial evaluation. Within this endeavor, a conceptual clarification of diversity and tolerance is needed, too.

At the beginning of the chapter we mentioned the "Blue-Eyes/Brown-Eyes" training that is often cited in the context of intergroup discrimination/ tolerance interventions. Our classification as a diversity training may be open to debate. Yet, the objectives of this training are less clear, thus making a subsumption difficult. Above and beyond the unclear goals and processes of this training, which are mainly a result of the lack of openly available documentation, the treatment has to be regarded very critically. First of all, the methods are considered to be ethically questionable (e.g., exposure of participants to threatening contexts without prior consent) and second, the results in the few available evaluations are disappointing (Stewart, LaDuke, Bracht, Sweet, & Gamarel, 2003). In sum, the most well-known treatment is definitely not the most recommendable, given the standards of our discipline.

Coexistence trainings

These treatments rely chiefly on the notion of mutual acceptance (either in power stratified, or equilibrium contexts) that we discussed in the context of tolerance conceptions. Trainings and education models are mostly derived in the environment of intractable conflicts and combine both the practitioner's experiences and the demands of the context, as well as theoretical foundations, such as the contact hypothesis (Ben-Ari, 2004). Furthermore, process models such as the motivation–affect–cognition–behavior–environment model (Desivilya, 2004; MACBE, Pruitt & Olczak, 1995) have been successfully applied and used as both a process model and an intervention theory. Evaluations of these programs are rudimentarily positive for specific contexts (for the Arab–Israeli conflict: Bar-Tal, 2004; Maoz, 2004; Stephan, Hertz-Lazarowitz, Zelniker, & Stephan, 2004a; for the Sri Lankan conflict: Malhotra & Liyanage, 2005). Unfortunately, participant numbers and continuous implementation (thus, evaluation studies available) are yet still too small for conducting meta-analyses. Independent of these limiting factors, the treatments and education programs come very close to the proposed conceptions of intergroup tolerance.

Jigsaw technique

The well-known jigsaw technique (Aronson, 1979; Aronson & Bridgeman, 1979) draws on the particular aspect of interpersonal cooperation to enhance learning that differentiates it from primarily intergroup-based trainings. Evaluation data yield mixed results, but have to be interpreted carefully. Most of the dependent measures have focused on the learning benefit and reveal less promising results. On the contrary, studies investigating the effect on prejudice reduction or intergroup tolerance (Desforges et al., 1991; Walker & Crogan, 1998) paint a more promising picture.

Zivilcourage

Treatments that foster courageous behavior (based on universal human rights) shown in public to the benefit of a threatened third party (Jonas & Brandstätter, 2004) are called *Zivilcourage* trainings in German-speaking contexts, and civil/moral courage (Staub, 2006) trainings or bystander intervention in English-speaking countries. These treatments are designed as a general prevention approach for potential bystanders to increase intervention behavior independent of social categories and personal preferences. Thus, the trainings also foster tolerance towards others, as their (threatened) difference is guarded. To achieve unanimous help and intervention in critical situations, tolerance goals need to be endorsed, otherwise responsibility attributions towards victims come to stand in the way, or intervention category hierarchies can effectively hinder intervention behavior (e.g., more for similar groups). The treatments follow process models of the desired behavior and use an intervention theory geared to these models. Trainings for adults, teenagers, and children are available (Jonas, Boos, & Brandstätter, 2007) that show positive results in evaluations (random control groups, as well as in natural environment, both on attitude, knowledge and behavioral dependent measures and after substantial follow-up assessment). Train-the-trainer trainings are being offered, and manuals have been published (Jonas et al., 2007). In sum, those trainings come close to the demands of our presented intervention models. Shortcomings still are the lack of substantial evaluations with large numbers of participants in different contexts and subsequent meta-analyses.

Taken together, we have focused on interventions to enhance intergroup tolerance. The presented treatments vary in their level of development, implementation and evaluation. Furthermore, differences in quality and theoretical soundness can be diagnosed. In sum, there are shortcomings to overcome. To do so, we now outline elements of a more rigid intervention theory than usually applied in social psychology. Given our summary, this seems necessary to increase the overall quality level of social psychologically rooted intergroup interventions.

In need of an intervention model

In the context of interventions, it is not sufficient just to identify a problem, then come up with a theoretical explanation, significant results and subsequently turn this explanation into some sort of treatment. At first, such a statement may sound trivial – no one would do it like that, one might object – yet many intergroup researchers tend to think along those lines. Of course we do not want to state that theory should not be used to derive interventions, instead we seek to emphasize that solely following theory driven approaches (pertaining to the problem) that are based on experimental data out of our labs is not sufficient. Following such a simplified notion often leads to the omission of process theory and didactic modules of the treatment itself, its specific goal and the associated best practices. Thus, designing, implementing, and evaluating an intervention has to follow a general intervention model in which social psychological theorizing constitutes one element. Before we can determine the optimal type of intervention model, certain terminologies must be defined.

First of all, although not yet distinguished in the title of this chapter, intervention must be conceptually separated from prevention. Furthermore, prevention can be differentiated into three steps: primary, secondary, and tertiary (Gordon, 1987; Kumpfer & Baxley, 1997). This distinction has been introduced in medical sciences first, but has found widespread acceptance from criminology to psychological prevention science. In psychological contexts prevention is usually understood as a treatment to avoid the manifestation of an undesired behavior, or its affective or cognitive precursors. Primary prevention treatment is meant for an application within society in general, irrelevant of specific characteristics (such as social risk factors) of the population. Sometimes this type of prevention is also called universal or general prevention. Secondary prevention is a treatment targeting populations with known risk factors for showing dysfunctional or undesired behavior (or its precursors). This type is also called specific or selective prevention. Finally, tertiary prevention is a treatment designed for populations or groups of individuals who already have shown conspicuous behavior. This type of prevention is also called intervention, since it seeks to revert behavior to "normal" (i.e., predefined standards), or at least to prevent its further spreading. In a nutshell, prevention takes an ex ante position and is about conserving the status quo to avoid negative behavior, whereas intervention is an ex post reaction and deals with changing the status quo back to acceptable behavior. This timeline is relevant in our intergroup context, since we have to deal with the question later of whether a general cognitive ability, such as categorization, can be subject to a prevention approach at all, or whether only malfunctions can be subject to an intervention. Based on this distinction, many sub-typologies of prevention have developed emphasizing particular aspects, such as timing and time-line, or level of treatment. A full review is not possible here, yet we believe that other disciplines have developed prevention strategies further and that prevention work in intergroup relations can benefit greatly from reception of this knowledge. Relevant examples are event-specific prevention (ESP; Neighbors et al., 2007) or the prevention spectrum (Cohen & Swift, 1999) as an approach to enlarge the scope of potential treatment recipients who are targeted (from individual-focus treatment, over community education, provider education, network and coalition fostering, change of organizational practices, to policy and legislation influence).

The question arising is what is the proper treatment in the case of improving intergroup relations, decreasing discrimination or increasing tolerance? Social psychology, in the context of intergroup research, has to derive an answer to this question first and define standards to base its judgment on. Subsequently, the discipline needs to build on existing prevention and intervention frameworks (e.g., Beelmann, 2006; Beelmann & Raabe, 2007; Buunk & Van Vugt, 2008; Stephan, 2006) to develop its own approach. To do so, we integrate all three models into one model that combines the strengths of the separate approaches. The model by Beelmann and Raabe (2007; Beelmann, 2006) is by far the most elaborate and comprehensive; Stephan's (2006) facets (intervention goals, target group analysis, program techniques, psychological process and outcome) are closer to social psychology in their origin and can easily be subsumed in the previous model. The problem–analysis–test–help model (PATH) by Buunk and Van Vugt (2008) shows some overlap with the Beelmann model, yet is less explicit regarding the evaluation demands.

Five central tenets of scientifically funded interventions

Beelmann (2006; and Beelmann & Raabe, 2007) has proposed a general framework specifying conditions for a scientific foundation of treatments. Again, there is substantial overlap with the previously described models, but the criteria pertaining to each tenet are more detailed and thus quite valuable for a substantive contention with intergroup relations treatments.

1   *Empirical legitimacy and normative reasoning are identified as the first tenet for a scientific treatment*
    Buunk and Van Vught (2008) call this the "problem" definition step in their PATH model. In this context questions like "Is there a problem that can be solved by psychological means?" need to be answered, or if there are robust developmental projections possible. On the side of normative reasoning, psychologists need to draw on other sources or disciplines, yet they need to be transparent about their sources of their goals of action.

2   *Developmental foundation*
    This tenet addresses the core question of whether or not change is possible, and how the developmental prognosis can be conceived. This developmental foundation also speaks to the ability of learning processes and information processing. For example, if some populations show limits in their learning potential or their information processing style, this may be because of psycho-social restrictions or self-images that work against an intervention.

3 *Formulation of a program theory*
This step deals with the process analysis of the problem in focus and is equivalent to the "analysis" and parts of the "test" step in PATH. Subsequently psycho-social risk and protection factors need to be defined, as well as developmental trajectories, and if possible, etiological theories of various scopes must be formulated.

4 *Intervention theory*
This central tenet addresses the "how to" of professional treatments and is equivalent to the final "help" step in PATH. For example characteristics such as timing, duration of the treatment, treatment intensity, didactic methodologies, competence and background of facilitators, motivation of clients, and societal background factors need to be reflected. Beelmann and colleagues (2007) state themselves that this aspect is notoriously underdeveloped in prevention/intervention science, but has a tremendous influence on treatment effects. Furthermore, counterintuitive results point to the need to focus on the mentioned aspects (e.g., age effects of early prevention disappear in meta-analyses; Lösel & Beelmann, 2003).

5 *Empirical and practical probation*
As criteria, efficacy and effectiveness evaluations as well as dissemination concerns need to be fulfilled (Flay et al., 2005). For an adequate efficacy judgment not only random (waiting) control group evaluations are necessary, but these need to be replicated by two independent groups of researchers. On the contrary, effectiveness needs to be shown in ecologically valid settings, on top of the efficacy of the treatment. Finally, treatment developers need to be concerned with whom and how the treatment is disseminated (e.g., strategic partners, institutions, etc.).

Taken together, a synthesis of all three models draws a full picture of the standards that intergroup relations treatments face. To anticipate the conclusion, to our knowledge none of the treatments for prevention and intervention offered in this realm fulfills all criteria. Some are stronger on some aspects but fall short on others. Clearly the field has a lot to offer regarding the aspects of problem identification and theoretical as well as process analysis, but this respectable set of knowledge may have been achieved at the cost of adequately turning these findings into prevention/intervention treatment.

Conclusion

The aim of this chapter was threefold. First, we wanted to point at specific problematic issues that are related to intergroup tolerance improvement and discrimination/prejudice reduction. The reduction of discrimination or prejudice does not equal the immediate increase of tolerance. Ideally, besides conceptual considerations, empirical research would disentangle the assumed overlap. Based on such data, the formulation of treatment goals and subsequently their measurement would benefit tremendously. For the moment, we can only warn carefully against oversimplified treatments (with a good selling point to the public, obviously) that may fall short of producing intended effects just because of a poor definition of the core concepts. Second, we wanted to systematize existing approaches and determine their overall quality. Third, we sought to help the introduction of prevention and intervention models into intergroup relations research. Systematic research and theorizing on prevention are fairly new in general and have not yet penetrated far into this sub-discipline of social psychology. These three goals bear the message for the "practitioners" (to follow the distinction by Stephan, 2006) to review their conduct and test assumed "best practice" by means of systematic approaches. "Researchers" should be natural strategic partners in this. For the researchers the message is clear, too. Not every significant finding out of the laboratory can be immediately turned into a successful prevention or intervention tool and doing so is anything but easy. The famous last sentence in our papers or presentations about the applicability of the findings should be more than lip-service. We need alliances of informed and interested members of both categories to bridge the theory-to-practice gap.

The state of the art of intergroup tolerance trainings bears potential, but is at the beginning. Overall, the programs or treatments either lack an embedding into a process model (to psychologically explain the problem, e.g., diversity trainings), or the embedding into an intervention theory (e.g., the contact hypothesis). Treatments fulfilling both of these requirements show deficits on robust evaluation data and on their dissemination, this holds for example for coexistence programs and *Zivilcourage* trainings. In sum, there is much work to be done. From a critical point of view, there is no treatment available that explicitly (in a documented manner) fulfills the suggested criteria. This does not mean that the approaches do not work per se, they may just be in need of robust testing and documentation. As a consequence, the goal of intergroup tolerance is not to be dropped from our agenda. Intergroup prejudice reduction programs (which in general show similar shortcomings to the ones discussed here) are not a full substitution. Their potential for preventive utilization is small; if used in that manner they may actually increase the problem, and their scope is usually bound to very specific dual category contexts. But the discipline is elaborated enough in terms of its theorizing, its research methods and last but not least funding and manpower to take on this demand. Thus, we need to work on the development, implementation, and evaluation of treatments to maintain positive intergroup relations, or to improve negative ones to reach the ideal of a more peaceful world that is usually emphasized in our teaching, writing, and thinking.

References

Aboud, F. E., & Levy, S. R. (2000). Interventions to reduce prejudice and discrimination in children and adolescents. In S. Oskamp (Ed.), *Reducing prejudice and discrimination* (pp. 269–293). Mahwah, NJ: Lawrence Erlbaum Associates, Inc.

Anti-Defamation League (2006). Anti-bias education and peer influence as two strategies to reduce prejudice: An impact evaluation of the Anti-Defamation League peer training program. Available at: http://www.adl.org/education/Yale_Summary.pdf. Retrieved July 5, 2008.

Anti-Defamation League (2007). A World of Difference Institute website: http://www.adl.org/education/edu_awod/default_awod.asp. Retrieved July 5, 2008.

Aronson, E. (1979). *The jigsaw classroom.* Oxford: Sage.

Aronson, E., & Bridgeman, D. (1979). Jigsaw groups and the desegregated classroom: In pursuit of common goals. *Personality and Social Psychology Bulletin, 5,* 438–446.

Banks, J. A. (2006). Improving race relations in schools: From theory and research to practice. *Journal of Social Issues, 62,* 607–614.

Bar-Tal, D. (2004). Nature, rationale and effectiveness of education of coexistence. *Journal of Social Issues, 60,* 253–271.

Beelmann, A. (2006). Wirksamkeit von Präventionsmaßnahmen bei Kindern und Jugendlichen: Ergebnisse und Implikationen der integrativen Erfolgsforschung [Effects of prevention in childhood and adolescence: Results and implications of integrated effectiveness research]. *Zeitschrift für Klinische Psychotherapie und Psychotherapie, 35,* 151–162.

Beelmann, A., & Raabe, T. (2007). *Dissoziales Verhalten von Kindern und Jugendlichen* [Dissocial behavior of children and juveniles]. Göttingen: Hogrefe.

Ben-Ari, R. (2004). Coping with the Jewish–Arab conflict: A comparison among three models. *Journal of Social Issues, 60,* 307–322.

Blue-Eyes/Brown-Eyes (2008). Available at: http://www.janeelliott.com. Retrieved August 19, 2008.

Brewer, M. B., & Pierce, K. P. (2005). Social identity complexity and outgroup tolerance. *Personality and Social Psychology Bulletin, 31,* 428–437.

Brown, R. J. (1995). *Prejudice: It's social psychology.* Oxford: Blackwell.

Buunk, A. P., & Van Vugt, M. (2008). *Applying social psychology: From problems to solutions.* Los Angeles: Sage.

Cameron, L., & Rutland, A. (2006). Extended contact through story reading in school: Reducing children's prejudice toward the disabled. *Journal of Social Issues, 62,* 469–488.

Cameron, L., Rutland, A., & Brown, R. (2007). Promoting children's positive intergroup attitudes toward stigmatized groups: Extended contact and multiple classification skills training. *International Journal of Behavioral Development, 31,* 454–466.

Cameron, L., Rutland, A., Brown, R., & Douch, R. (2006). Changing children's intergroup attitudes toward refugees: Testing different models of extended contact. *Child Development, 77,* 1208–1219.

Cohen, L., & Swift, S. (1999). The spectrum of prevention: Developing a comprehensive approach to injury prevention. *Injury Prevention, 5,* 203–207.

Cotton-Huston, A. L., & Waite, B. M. (2000). Anti-homosexual attitudes in college students: Predictors and classroom interventions. *Journal of Homosexuality, 38,* 117–133.

Desforges, D. M., Lord, C. G., Ramsey, S. L., Mason, J. A., Van Leeuwen, M. D., West, S. C., et al. (1991). Effects of structured cooperative contact on changing negative attitudes towards stigmatized social groups. *Journal of Personality and Social Psychology, 60,* 531–544.

Desivilya, H. S. (2004). Promoting coexistence by means of conflict education: The MACBE model. *Journal of Social Issues, 60,* 339–355.

Devine, P. G. (1989). Stereotypes and prejudice: The automatic and controlled components. *Journal of Personality and Social Psychology, 56,* 5–18.

Dwairy, M. (2004). Culturally sensitive education: Adapting self-oriented assertiveness training to collective minorities. *Journal of Social Issues, 60,* 423–436.

Fein, S., von Hippel, W., Spencer, S. J. (1999). To stereotype or not to stereotype: Motivation and stereotype activation, application, and inhibition. *Psychological Inquiry, 10,* 49–54.

Feldmann, E., Henschel, T. R., & Ulrich, S. (2000). *Toleranz – Grundlage für ein demokratisches Miteinander* [Tolerance – foundation of a democratic together]. Gütersloh: Bertelsmann.

Fernandez, C. (in press). Together but apart, equal but different. On the claims for toleration in multicultural societies. In S. Scuzzarello, C. Kinnvall, & K. Renwick Monroe (Eds.), *On behalf of others: The psychology of care in a global world.* Oxford: Oxford University Press.

Finkel, S. E., Sigelman, L., & Humphries, S. (1999). Democratic values and political tolerance. In J. P. Robinson & P. R. Shaver (Eds.), *Measures of political attitudes* (pp. 203–296). San Diego, CA: Academic Press.

Flay, B. R., Biglan, A., Boruch, R. F., Castro, F. G., Gottfredson, D., Kellam, S., et al. (2005). Standards of evidence: Criteria for efficacy, effectiveness and dissemination. *Prevention Science, 6,* 151–175.

Frost, R. (2003). Toleranz im Konflikt [Tolerance in conflict]. Frankfurt a.M.: Suhrkamp.

Gasser, M. B., & Tan, R. N. (1999). Cultural tolerance: Measurement and latent structure of attitudes toward the cultural practices of others. *Educational and Psychological Measurement, 59,* 111–126.

Gilbert, D. T., & Hixon, J. G. (1991). The trouble of thinking: Activation and application of stereotypic beliefs. *Journal of Personality and Social Psychology, 60,* 509–517.

Giordano, R. (2007). Nein und dreimal nein! [No and thrice no!]. *Frankfurter Allgemeine Zeitung,* available at: http://www.faz.net/s/Rub594835B672714A1DB 1A121534F010EE1/Doc~E87EE751B5D8A4366AC767D05B16CD63E~ATpl~ Ecommon~Scontent.html. Retrieved October 26, 2008.

Gordon, R. S. (1987). An operational classification of disease prevention. In J. A. Steinberg & M. M. Silverman (Eds.), *Preventing mental disorders* (pp. 20–26), Rockville, MD: US Department of Health and Human Services.

Habermas, J. (2003). Intolerance and discrimination. *International Journal of Constitutional Law, 1,* 2–12.

Herek, G. (1987). Religious orientation and prejudice: A comparison of racial and sexual attitudes. *Personality and Social Psychology Bulletin, 13,* 34–44.

Jonas, K. J., Boos, M., Backes, S., Büttner, N. Ehrenthal, J., & Prasse, A. (2002). Göttinger Zivilcourage-Training. *Polizei und Wissenschaft 1/2002,* 72–82.

Jonas, K. J., Boos, M., Brandstätter, V. (2007). *Zivilcourage trainieren: Theorie und Praxis* [Training moral courage: Theory and practice]. Göttingen: Hogrefe.

Jonas, K. J., & Brandstätter, V. (2004). Zivilcourage. Theorien, Befunde und Maßnahmen [Moral courage: Definition, findings, and interventions]. *Zeitschrift für Sozialpsychologie, 35,* 185–200.

Jonas, K. J., & Mummendey, A. (2008). Positive intergroup relations: From reduced outgroup rejection to outgroup support. In U. Wagner, L. Tropp, G. Finchilescu,

& C. Tredoux (Eds.), *Emerging research directions for improving intergroup relations – Building on the legacy of Thomas F. Pettigrew* (pp. 210–224). Malden, MA: Blackwell.

Kernahan, C., & Davis, T (2007). Changing perspective: How learning about racism influences student awareness and emotion. *Teaching of Psychology, 34*, 49–52.

Klonis, S. C., Plant, E. A., & Devine, P. G. (2005). Internal and external motivation to respond without prejudice. *Personality and Social Psychology Bulletin, 31*, 1237–1249.

Kumpfer, K. L., & Baxley, G. B. (1997). *Drug abuse prevention: What works?* Rockville, MD: National Institute on Drug Abuse.

Kunda, Z., & Sinclair, L. (1999). Motivated reasoning with stereotypes: Activation, application, and inhibition. *Psychological Inquiry, 10*, 12–22.

Larsen, K. S., & Long, E. (1988). Attitudes toward sex-roles: Traditional or egalitarian? *Sex Roles, 19*, 1–12.

Li, Q., & Brewer, M. B. (2004). What does it mean to be an American? Patriotism, nationalism, and American identity after 9/11. *Political Psychology, 25*, 727–739.

Lösel, F., & Beelmann, A. (2003). Effects of child skills training in preventing antisocial behavior: A systematic review of randomized evaluations. *Annals of the American Academy of Political and Social Science, 587*, 84–109.

Macrae, C. N., Milne, A. B., & Bodenhausen, G. V. (1994): Stereotypes as energy-saving devices: A peek inside the toolbox. *Journal of Personality and Social Psychology, 66*, 37–47.

Malhotra, D., & Liyanage, S. (2005). Long-term effects of peace workshops in protracted conflicts. *Journal of Conflict Resolution, 49*, 908–924.

Maoz, I. (2004). Coexistence is in the eye of the beholder: Evaluating intergroup encounter interventions between Jews and Arabs in Israel. *Journal of Social Issues, 60*, 437–452.

Marcus, G. E., Sullivan, J. L., Theiss-Morse, E., & Stevens, D. (2005). The emotional foundation of political cognition: The impact of extrinsic anxiety on the formation of political tolerance judgments. *Political Psychology, 26*, 949–963.

Martin, J. G. (1964). *The tolerant personality*. Detroit, MI: Wayne State University Press.

McCauley, C., Wright, M., & Harris, M. E. (2000). Diversity workshops on campus: A survey of current practice at U.S. colleges and universities. *College Student Journal, 34*, 100–114.

McConahay, J. G. (1986). Modern racism, ambivalence, and the modern racism scale. In J. F. Dovidio & S. L. Gaertner (Eds.), *Prejudice, discrimination, and racism* (pp. 91–125). New York: Academic Press.

Mummendey, A. (1995). Positive distinctiveness and social discrimination: An old couple living in divorce. *European Journal of Social Psychology, 25*, 657–670.

Mummendey, A., & Otten, S. (2001). Aversive discrimination. In R. Brown & S. Gaertner (Eds.), *Blackwell handbook of social psychology: Intergroup processes* (pp. 112–132). Malden, MA: Blackwell.

National Coalition Building Institute (2007). Available at: http://www.ncbi.org/home/index.cfm. Retrieved November 29, 2007.

Neighbors, C., Walters, S. T., Lee, C. M., Vader, A. M., Vehige, T., Szigethy, T., et al. (2007). Event-specific prevention: Addressing college student drinking during known windows of risk. *Addictive Behaviors, 32*, 2667–2680.

Nesdale, D., & Todd, P. (2000). Effect of contact on intercultural acceptance: A field study. *International Journal of Intercultural Relations, 24,* 341–360.

Peruche, B. M., & Plant, E. A. (2006). Racial bias in perceptions of athleticism: The role of motivation in the elemination of bias. *Social Cognition, 24,* 438–452.

Pettigrew, T. F. (1996). Generalized intergroup contact effects on prejudice. *Personality and Social Psychology Bulletin, 23,* 173–185.

Pettigrew, T. F., & Tropp, L. R. (2006). A meta-analytic test of intergroup contact theory. *Journal of Personality and Social Psychology, 90,* 751–783.

Pratto, F., Sidanius, J., Stallworth, L. M., & Malle, B. F. (1994). Social dominance orientation: A personality variable predicting social and political attitudes. *Journal of Personality and Social Psychology, 67,* 741–763.

Pruitt, D. G., & Olczak, P. V. (1995). Beyond hope: Approaches to resolving seemingly intractable conflict. In B. B. Bunker & J. Rubin (Eds.), *Conflict cooperation and justice: Essays inspired by the work of Morton Deutsch* (pp. 59–92). San Francisco, CA: Jossey-Bass.

Sassenberg, K., & Moskowitz, G. B. (2005). Don't stereotype, think different! Overcoming automatic stereotype activation by mindset priming. *Journal of Experimental Social Psychology, 41,* 506–514.

Schmitt, M., Gollwitzer, M., Maes, J., & Arbach, D. (2005). Justice sensitivity: Assessment and location in the personality space. *European Journal of Psychological Assessment, 21,* 202–211.

Staub, E. (2006). *A brighter future: Raising caring, non-violent, morally courageous children.* New York: Oxford University Press.

Staub, E., Pearlman, L. A., Gubin, A., & Hegengimana, A. (2005). Healing, reconciliation, forgiving and the prevention of violence after genocide or mass killing: An intervention and its experimental evaluation in Rwanda. *Journal of Social and Clinical Psychology, 24* 297–334.

Stephan, C. W., Hertz-Lazarowitz, R., Zelniker, T., & Stephan, W. G. (2004a). Introduction to improving Arab–Jewish relations in Israel: Theory and practice in coexistence educational programs. *Journal of Social Issues, 60,* 237–252.

Stephan, C. W., Renfro, L., & Stephan, W. G. (2004b). The evaluation of multicultural education programs: Techniques and a meta-analysis. In W. G. Stephan & W. P. Vogt (Eds.), *Education programs for improving intergroup relations: Theory, research and practice* (pp. 227–242). New York: Teachers College Press.

Stephan, W. G. (2006). Bridging the researcher–practitioner divide in intergroup relations. *Journal of Social Issues, 62,* 597–605.

Stephan, W. G., & Stephan, C. W. (2001). *Improving intergroup relations.* Thousand Oaks, CA: Sage.

Stephan, W. G., & Vogt, W. P. (Eds.). (2004). *Education programs for improving intergroup relations: Theory, research and practice.* New York: Teachers College Press.

Stewart, T. L., LaDuke, J. R., Bracht, C., Sweet, B. A. M., & Gamarel, K. E. (2003). Do the "Eyes" have it? A program evaluation of Jane Elliot's "Blue-Eyes/Brown-Eyes" diversity training exercise. *Journal of Applied Social Psychology, 33,* 1898–1921.

Tropp, L. R., & Bianchi, R. A. (2006). Valuing diversity and interest in intergroup contact. *Journal of Social Issues, 62,* 533–552.

Tropp, L. R., & Bianchi, R. A. (2007). Interpreting references to group membership in context: Feelings about intergroup contact depending on who says what to whom. *European Journal of Social Psychology, 37,* 439–451.

Verkuyten, M., & Reijerse, A. (2008). Intergroup structure and identity management among ethnic minority and majority groups: The interactive effects of perceived stability, legitimacy, and permeability. *European Journal of Social Psychology, 38*, 106–127.

Vescio, T. K., Judd, C. M., & Kwan, V. S. Y. (2004). The crossed categorization hypothesis: Evidence of reduction in the strength of categorization, but not intergroup bias. *Journal of Experimental Social Psychology, 40*, 478–496.

Waldzus, S., & Mummendey, A. (2004). Inclusion in a superordinate category, ingroup prototypicality, and attitudes towards outgroups. *Journal of Experimental Social Psychology, 40*, 466–477.

Walker, I., & Crogan, M. (1998). Academic performance, prejudice, and the Jigsaw classroom: New pieces to the puzzle. *Journal of Community and Applied Social Psychology, 8*, 381–393.

Wenzel, M., Mummendey, A., Weber, U., & Waldzus, S. (2003). The ingroup as pars pro toto: Projection from the ingroup onto the inclusive category as a precursor to social discrimination. *Personality and Social Psychology Bulletin, 29*, 461–471.

Wierlacher, A. (1996). Aktive Toleranz [Active tolerance]. In A. Wierlacher (Ed.), *Kulturthema Toleranz. Zur Grundlegung einer interdisziplinären und interkulturellen Toleranzforschung* [Cultural topic tolerance: Regarding the foundation of an interdisciplinary and intercultural tolerance research] (pp. 83–103). München: Iudicium.

Wysong, E., Aniskiewicz, R., & Wright, D. (1994). Truth and DARE: Tracking drug education to graduation as symbolic politics. *Social Problems, 41*, 448–472.

Author index

Subject index